Norman A. McQuown and Sadi Koylan

SPOKEN TURKISH

Book One

Spoken Language Services, Inc.

This is one of a series of self-teaching textbooks in more than thirty languages prepared under the aegis of the American Council of Learned Societies and the Linguistic Society of America. There are four hours of recordings keyed to the printed text.

Spoken Language Services, Inc.
P.O. Box 783
Ithaca, New York 14850

ISBN
0-87950-240-1

Library of Congress Number
74-152747

INTRODUCTION

1. This Course in spoken Turkish is designed as a general introduction to the Turkish language. It contains all the essential grammatical materials for learning to speak everyday Turkish, and its vocabulary, though small, is built around a number of the most useful common situations and current topics. It is based on the principle that you must *hear* a language if you are to understand it when spoken, and that you must practice *speaking* it in order to master its sounds and its forms.

A teacher will often not be available for those for whom this book is written. So the course has been made as nearly self-teaching as possible. This manual covers the course completely and requires the use of no other reference material.

2. The Turkish Language is spoken by about 17 million people distributed between Turkey in Europe and Anatolia or Asia Minor. It is very similar to a number of languages spoken by 15 to 20 millions more in the U. S. S. R. Of these languages, spoken in the Crimea, in the Caucasus, and in the Trans-Caspian areas stretching across Central Asia toward Mongolia, the language spoken in the Soviet Republic of Azerbaijan seems to be most like Turkish.

Variations in language are perfectly natural and are found in every language in the world. So do not be surprised if no two Turks whom you meet seem to talk in exactly the same way. All the people you meet in Turkey will understand the kind of Turkish presented in this manual, and a great many of them, especially in the larger towns and cities and among the fairly well educated will speak it exactly as you find it here. The people in the country areas and even some of the people in the cities, may, however, speak a slightly different kind of Turkish. If the pronunciation you hear is not quite like what is given to you in this manual or what you hear in this course, *imitate the person with whom you are speaking*. Likewise, do not hesitate to use the gestures which you see, for they are part of the language. Imitate them if you can.

3. To Help You in learning to speak Turkish, this course makes use of two tools:

1. a native speaker of the language;
2. this manual.

The two must be used together, as neither is of any use without the other.

This manual has been so organized that it can be used to study by yourself or in a group. If you work in a group, and have no regular teacher, choose one of the group to act as *Group Leader*.

4. A Native Speaker is the only good source of first-hand knowledge of the pronunciation and usage of any language. The method used in this manual requires the presence of a native speaker of Turkish, preferably a person who can be on hand throughout the course, or next best the voice of a native speaker recorded on the phonograph records which are supplied with this manual. The native speaker is referred to as the *Guide*. The Guide's job is to act as a model for you to imitate, and as a check on your pronunciation and usage. It is not his business to be a "teacher" or to "explain" the language to you. *That* is the function of this manual. The Guide should be, if possible, a person who speaks more or less the type of Turkish found in this manual, but he should speak it naturally and without affectation. He should be neither over educated nor too uncultured.

5. This Manual is divided into five major parts, each containing five *learning units* and one unit devoted to *review*. Each unit contains several *sections*, usually the following:

A. Basic Sentences (with Hints on Pronunciation, in Parts I and II, Hints on Spelling, in Part II, and Pronunciation Drill, in Parts III, IV, and V)
B. Word Study and Review of Basic Sentences
C. Review of Basic Sentences (Cont.)
D. Listening In
E. Conversation
F. Conversation (Cont.)

These six sections are followed in each learning unit by a *Finder List* containing all the new words in the particular unit. At the end of the manual are included a summary of all word study material as well as supplementary word lists for Units 13 through 30. All the words in the manual are included in two complete vocabularies, Turkish-English and English-Turkish.

6. The Basic Sentences in each unit are arranged so as to give you a number of new words and a number of new ways of saying things; first broken up into words or short phrases, and then combined in complete sentences.

7. The Aids to Listening which are given in the first twelve units, present a more exact version of the usual Turkish spelling, which is designed to help you in remembering the Turkish words *as they sound*. In this regularized spelling, each Turkish sound is represented by one letter. Every letter always stands for the same sound. It serves as a gradual introduction to the ordinary spelling which has a number of irregularities.

8. **The Hints on Pronunciation** are given you to help you improve your speech in Turkish. No language has sounds exactly like those of any other; and in Turkish you will find some sounds which are quite absent from English, and others which are somewhat but not exactly like English sounds. As you go through the Basic Sentences try to hear and imitate more precisely the sounds described for you in these hints.

9. **Pronunciation Is Important** for a number of reasons: if you expect to be understood when you speak a foreign language, you will have to pronounce it more or less the way the people are used to hearing it. Furthermore, the nearer you get to pronouncing the precise sounds, the easier it will be for your ear to catch the sound as spoken by a native, and the more rapidly you will pick up new words and phrases and make progress in learning the language.

10. **The Native Speaker Is Always Right.** At times this manual or the phonograph records may show one pronunciation and the particular native speaker who acts as your Guide will pronounce something a little different. Always imitate the pronunciation of your Guide rather than that of the phonograph records or of the Turkish spelling.

11. **The Word Study** sections show you certain uses and combinations of words and phrases studied up to that point; you are taught how to take apart the words and phrases which you have heard and how to make new words and phrases on the same model.

12. **The Listening In** section gives you a number of conversations, anecdotes, or stories, which use the vocabulary and constructions you have learned in each unit and in all those preceding. Its purpose is to give you practice in listening to and understanding the foreign language as you might overhear it in normal conversation among Turkish-speaking people, and to furnish you with models for your own conversation practice.

13. **The Conversation Practice** represents the central aim of the course. In order to converse well, you should know everything that you have learned up to that point. When you take part in a conversation, you should do so as easily and naturally as you can. Don't try to bring in new words and phrases that you haven't learned in the material you have been studying; stick to what you have learned and practice it thoroughly.

14. **In Speaking Turkish** you should *not* first figure out what you want to say in English and then translate it into Turkish, word for word. You should apply, instead, the words and expressions you already

know to the given situation. If you cannot immediately rattle off a word or expression to fit a particular situation, go on to another, or ask a question, but under no circumstances attempt to compose long and complicated sentences. As soon as you do, you lapse into English speech habits and stop learning Turkish and Turkish speech habits.

When people speak to you, they will often use words and expressions you do not know. If you can't guess their meaning, try to find out by asking questions in Turkish, or by asking them to repeat slowly, or to explain in simpler terms. If you do this you will constantly learn more and will practice the Turkish you already know in the process.

Your learning of Turkish will not stop, therefore, when you have mastered this material. You will, rather, be able to get around among the people, practice what you know, and steadily pick up more and more words and phrases. Try to learn them as you go. Carry along a notebook to jot down what you want to remember; you can then review this new material from time to time.

You should not wait until you have finished this manual before you start using the language. Start practicing right away. When you have done the first unit, try out the expressions on as many people as possible. When you try out your Turkish, even at this early stage, make it slide off your tongue as smoothly as possible. Be careful not to slip back into a careless English-like pronunciation. Listen closely to what the person says in response, trying to catch as much as you can. The first few times it may be hard to catch even the words you know, but you will improve rapidly if you keep on practicing every chance you get.

CONTENTS

PART ONE

UNIT		Page
1.	GETTING AROUND. Greetings and general phrases. Directions. Comment on the *Aids to Listening*. Asking for things Food Price. Time. Numbers. Leave-taking. Comment on the *Aids to Listening* (*Cont.*) Pronunciation Practices for *a*, *e*, *i*, *o*, *u*.	1
2.	MEETING PEOPLE. Pronunciation Practices for *ı*. Turkish equivalents of English "is". Humming and non-humming sounds. Vowel harmony. "My". "Your". "His, her, its, their". Genitive ("of; -'s"). Possession.	40
3.	WHAT'S YOUR JOB? Pronunciation Practices for *ü*. Review practice for *ı*. Momentary verb ending. Verb roots. Aorist verb ending. Vowel harmony. Turkish equivalents of English "the", "A. an".	76
4.	FAMILY AND FRIENDS. Pronunciation Practices for long vowels *a:* and *o:* and vowel groups. Copula forms ("am", "is", "are"). Zero endings. Personal endings "they", "it, he, she". "I". "You". "We". Copula ("am, is, are") summary. Personal endings with verbs. Summary of personal endings.	107
5.	LET'S TALK ABOUT THE WEATHER. Pronunciation Practices for *ö*. "Our". Vowel Harmony Type I. Plural "more than one" ending. Vowel Harmony Type II. Interrogative (question) ending. "And, too, also" ending.	139
6.	REVIEW.	169

PART TWO

UNIT		Page
7.	Getting a Room. Pronunciation Practices for Turkish "light" *l* (l^y). Hints on Spelling. Syllables. Locative ("at, in, on") ending. Interrogative (question) ending after nouns. "Let's (do it)! "(You) (do it)"! Formal and informal use.	178
8.	Getting Cleaned Up. Pronunciation Practices for Turkish "deep" *l* (*l̇*), and *r*. Hints on Spelling. Turkish equivalents of English "not" (negative ending). Turkish phrase-compounds. Definite objective ending. *-me*, *-ma* action nouns. Infinitives ("to do, etc.").	207
9.	Let's Eat. Pronunciation Practices for Turkish "teeth"-sounds, double consonants, catch in the throat. Vocative ("call")-forms. Future verb ending. Negative future. Interrogative future. Interrogative negative future. Future form used as noun. "With" and "without."	238
10.	Seeing the Sights. Pronunciation Practices for Turkish *p*, *t*, *ç*, k^y, *k* (followed by puff of breath), long vowel *i:*, k^y and g^y. Hints on Spelling: summary of correspondences; defects. Concomitive ("with; and"). Dative ("to, for"). Negative aorist. Interrogative aorist Interrogative negative aorist.	267
11.	Shopping. Pronunciation Practices for Turkish rise and fall of the voice. Hints on Spelling: summary of defects of conventional spelling; remedies in *Standardized Conventional Spelling*. Turkish informal "you" ending. Ablative ("from, out of, than"). Pronouns (summary; irregular genitives and datives). Turkish general personal endings (summary). Turkish aorist copula (summary). Turkish aorist endings (summary). Turkish negative endings (summary).	304
12.	Review.	337

PART ONE UNIT 1

GETTING AROUND

To the Group Leader: Each *unit* of this course is divided into six *sections*. It is suggested that the group spend not less than fifty minutes on each section.

Before you get the group together to work on this first unit, read carefully the following material up to the heading *Useful Words and Phrases* on page 4. When the group meets, read the material aloud to them or have some other member of the group do the reading. The students will follow the reading with their books open. Be sure that your Guide, or the phonograph and records, are ready before the group meets for work on *Section A*. See that the Guide is supplied with a copy of the manual *Kılavuz için talimatname,* which tells him just what he is to do and gives him the Turkish he is to speak to the group. You yourself should consult the English part of the Guide's Manual for further instructions.

You should look through all of the sections of this unit, reading the directions carefully, so that you will have in mind the general plan of the work. Always get clearly in mind the directions for a section before you take that section up in group meeting.

This unit gives you the most immediate and necessary expressions that you will need in meeting people, asking your way, buying things, and counting. The amount of learning and memorizing required for the first unit is considerably greater than that for any later unit. You are given such a large dose at the start because this unit is meant to be a kind of "language first aid" which gives you enough useful expressions to enable you to make ordinary wants known and to carry on a simple conversation in Turkish from the very start.

All but a few of these words and phrases are selected from the phonograph records for the *Turkish Language Guide* (Introductory Series) (TM 30–318). If you have worked with these records, the present unit will serve as a review.

SECTION A—USEFUL WORDS AND PHRASES

In the list of *Useful Words and Phrases* which follows, the English equivalent of these words and phrases is given at the left of the page. Opposite, in the middle column, are the *Aids to Listening* which will help you in getting the sounds. In the third column is the ordinary or *Conventional Turkish Spelling*, to which you are to pay no attention now, but to which you will be able to refer later when you have mastered its irregularities. The *Leader* of the group will first read the *English Equivalent* and pause for the *Guide* to speak the Turkish. Every member of the group then repeats after the Guide. The Guide will then say the Turkish a second time and everybody will repeat after him as before. The Leader will then read the next English Equivalent and the Guide and group will follow the procedure indicated.

If no Guide is available, the *phonograph records* provided for the course should be used. When the group is ready, the Leader will begin playing the appropriate record and the group will repeat right after the Turkish speaker during the silences on the record. The phonograph records can be used with profit even in cases where a Guide is available because they can be heard between meetings of the group, whenever it is convenient to you; they furnish additional practice in hearing Turkish; you may listen only to those portions which you have found difficult; and the records may be played as often as you wish. In case the speaker on the record has a Turkish pronunciation different from that of your Guide, use the records only for listening and understanding and not for imitating.

Whether you are working with a Guide or with the phonograph records, you must repeat each Turkish word and phrase in a loud, clear voice, trying at all times to imitate the pronunciation as closely as you can. Keep constantly in mind the meaning of the Turkish you are about to hear, glancing at the English equivalent whenever you need to remind yourself. When you are hearing the Turkish, keep your eyes on the *Aids to Listening*. But whenever the written form seems to you to differ from the spoken sound, follow the spoken sound always.

In the first five units, do not attempt under any circumstances to pronounce the Turkish before you have heard it. You will only make trouble for yourself if you try to guess the pronunciation by "reading" the *Aids to Listening* and you will get into even more trouble if you try to "read" the ordinary Turkish spelling.

If you are working with a Guide who does not understand English, ask the Leader of your group to demonstrate for you what hand signals to use to let the Guide know when you want him to read more slowly or to repeat.

To the Group Leader: If the Guide does not speak English, he is instructed to follow these hand signals:

1. Index finger raised: BEGIN
2. Hand raised, palm toward the Guide: STOP
3. Palm down, hand moved slowly in semi-circle: SLOWER
4. Beckoning with index finger: REPEAT
5. Hand held palm up and moved quickly up and down. LOUDER

Remember that each phrase you say has a real meaning in Turkish and hence you should always act as though you were really saying something to some-one else. You will learn fastest if, when your book is open, you follow these steps:

1. Keep your eyes on the *Aids to Listening* as you listen to the Turkish being spoken.
2. Repeat immediately what you have heard.
3. Keep in mind the meaning of what you are saying.

Begin the words and phrases as soon as your Guide is ready or when the Leader of your group is ready to play the first phonograph record.

To the Group Leader: Give the members of the group a chance to ask questions about the instructions. Make sure that every-one understands just what he is to do. Then have the students go through the list of *Useful Words and Phrases* once with the books open, repeating in unison after the Guide. Following this first practice, read with the group the *Comment on the Aids to Listening* on page 7. Make sure that everyone understands it.

Now go through the list a second time, just as you did before. And finally, go through it a third time, but let the students take turns repeating individually after the Guide—a sentence to a student. Indicate the order in which the repetitions are to go, who is first, who next, and so on. Continue this individual repetition as long as the 50 minute period permits. Then, just before dismissing the group, read with them the paragraph headed *Check Yourself* on page 8.

Here are some hints that will make the work of the group more effective:

1. Insist that everyone speak up. Don't allow any mumbling! Each member of the group must be able to hear what is being said at all times.
2. Indicate to the Guide that he is to repeat whenever the pronunciation is bad and to keep on repeating until he gets a pronunciation that sounds like Turkish.
3. Urge everyone to mimic to the limit every sound, every inflection, even the mannerisms of the Guide.
4. Keep the work moving. Don't let it drag at any time. See that everyone is listening, not only to the Guide, but to himself and to the others as they repeat after the Guide.
5. Go through all the work yourself. Repeat with the others and take your turn at the individual repetitions.

1. Useful Words and Phrases

Here is a list of useful words and phrases you will need in Turkish. *You should learn these by heart.*

Greetings and General Phrases

ENGLISH EQUIVALENTS	AIDS TO LISTENING	CONVENTIONAL TURKISH SPELLING
Record 1A, beginning.		
[*the*][1] *day*	g^{y}ún.	gün
[*may it be*] *bright*	ày-dín.	aydın
Mr.	báy.	bay
Kaya (*lit.*[2] "*Stone*")	kà-yá!	Kaya
Good morning, Mr. Kaya!	g^{y}ù-n‿áy-dín, bày‿ká-yá!	Gün aydın, bay Kaya!
your evenings	ák-şàm-lá-rı-níz.	akşamlarınız
fortunate	hà-yir-lí.	hayırlı
may [*they*] *be*	òl-sún.	olsun
Mr. Metin (*lit.* "*Strong*")	bày‿mé-tí̇n.	bay Metin
Good evening, Mr. Metin!	ak-şam-la-rı-niz‿há-yır-lí‿ól-sùn, bày‿métí̇n!	Akşamlarınız hayırlı olsun, bay Metin!
I thank [*you*] *!*	te-şék^{y}-k^{y}ú-r‿e-dè-ri̇m!	teşekkür ederim
yours, too!	si̇-zí̇n-dè!	sizin de
Thank you, same to you!	te-şék^{y}-k^{y}ú-r‿e-dè-rí̇m, si̇-zí̇n-dè!	Teşekkür ederim, sizin de!
How are you?	ná-sil-sı-nìz?	Nasılsınız?

[1] Words enclosed in brackets, [ ], are not expressed in the Turkish.
[2] lit. means literal or word for word equivalent.

I ['m] well	i-yí-yìm.	iyiyim
I'm well, thank you!	i-yí-yìm, te-şékʸ-kʸû-r‿e-dè-rím!	İyiyim teşekkür ederim!
you	síz	siz
How are you?	síz ná-sıl-sı-nìz?	Siz nasılsınız?
I, too	bén-dè.	ben de
I ['m] well, too.	bén-dé‿i-yì-yím.	Ben de iyiyim.
Mr. Carr.	bày‿kár.	Bay Kar.
Mrs. Carr.	bá-yán‿kàr.[1]	Bayan Kar.
Excuse [me]!	áf-fe-dèr-si-níz!	Affedersiniz!
Please!	lʸût-fèn!	Lûtfen.
Thank [you]!	te-şékʸ-kʸû-r‿e-dè-rím!	Teşekkür ederim!
any	bír.	bir
thing	şéy.	şey
[it is] not	dè-yílʸ.	değil
You're welcome!	bír‿şèy‿dé-yílʸ!	Bir şey değil!
Yes.	é-vèt.	Evet.
No!	há-yìr!	Hayır!
[Do] you understand?	án-lı-yór-mú-su-nùz?	Anlıyormusunuz?
I understand	án-lí-yo-rùm.	anlıyorum
Yes, I understand.	é-vèt, án-lí-yo-rùm.	Evet, anlıyorum.

[1] *Mrs.* in contrast to Mr. (usually: bá-yàn‿kár)

I [do] not understand.	án-lá-mı-yò-rúm.	anlamıyorum
No, I don't understand.	há-yìr, án-lá-mı-yò-rúm.	Hayır, anlamıyorum.
what?	né?	ne?
you said	dè-di-níz.	dediniz
What did you say?	né‿dé-di-nìz?	Ne dediniz?
slowly	yá-váş‿yá-vàş.	yavaş yavaş
speak!	ko-nú-şú-nùz!	konuşunuz!
Please speak slowly.	(1) lʸǘt-fèn yá-váş‿ya-váş‿ko-nù-şu-núz! (2) [1] lʸǘt-fèn, yá-váş‿ya-váş‿ko-nù-şu-núz!	Lûtfen yavaş yavaş konuşunuz!

Directions

Record 1B, beginning.

here	bú-rá-dà.	burada
[a] restaurant	lʸó-kán-tà.	lokanta
[is] there?	vár-mì?	varmı?
Is there a restaurant here?	bú-ra-da‿lʸo-kán-ta‿vár-mì?	Burada lokanta varmı?
good	ì-yí.	iyi
a	bír.	bir
restaurant	lʸó-kán-tà.	lokanta
there [is]	vár.	var
Yes, there is a good restaurant.	é-vèt, i-yi‿bir‿lʸo-kán-tá‿vàr.	Evet, iyi bir lokanta var.

[1] When two versions are given, the repeated forms on the record are different, and each is presented separately. Otherwise the repeated forms on the record are the same.

this	bú.	bu
where [is it] ?	né-ré-dè?	nerede?
Where is this restaurant?	bú‿l^{y}o-kàn-tá né-ré-dè?	Bu lokanta nerede?
[a] hotel	ò-tél^y.	otel
Is there a hotel here?	bú-ra-da‿o-tél^y‿vár-mì?	Burada otel varmı?
Where is the hotel?	o-tél^y‿né-ré-dè?	Otel nerede?
[the] railroad station	is-tàs-yón.	istasyon
Where's the railroad station?	is-tas-yón‿né-ré-dè?	İstasyon nerede?
[the] toilet	áp-tèst-há:-né.	aptesthane
Where is the toilet?	ap-test-ha:-né‿né-ré-dè?	Aptesthane nerede?
[it's] to [the] right	sà:-dá.	sağda
The restaurant's to the right.	l^{y}ó-kán-tà sà:-dá.	Lokanta sağda.
[It's] to [the] left.	sòl-dá.	Solda.
[It is]n't to [the] right.	sá:-dà‿dé-yil^y.	Sağda değil.
[It's] up ahead.	i-l^{y}èr-dé.	İlerde.
[It's] here.	bú-rá-dà.	Burada.

After you have gone through these *Useful Words and Phrases* once, read the following:

2. Comment on the Aids to Listening

In the *Aids to Listening*, the syllables which you are to speak with more *emphasis* are indicated by the following marks:

(ʹ) is used to show the *strongest syllable* in a word or phrase, that is, in a group of words connected by the curved lines (‿);

(ˋ) is used to show the *next strongest syllable;* and

(ˈ) is used to show other strong syllables.

A hyphen (-) shows the separation of words into *syllables.*

The curved line (‿) connecting words shows the group of words or phrases which are spoken without any pause between them. At an ordinary rate of talking, such a group of words will sound to you as though it were a single word. For example:

yȧ-vȧ́ş‿yȧ-vȧ̀ş 'slowly'

Notice, too, that vowels of adjoining words may be run together. For example:

hȧ-yır-lí‿ȯ́l-sùn 'may [they] be fortunate'

Notice, also, that the last consonant of a preceding word may sound as though it were part of the following word. For example:

gʸü̇-n‿ȧ́y-dín! 'Good morning!'

Now go through the *Useful Words and Phrases* again with your book open, following the same procedure as before. Repeat each word and phrase, immediately after hearing it, in a loud, clear voice. Let yourself go and say the phrases right out.

Go through the *Useful Words and Phrases* once more with your book open, but this time, take turns letting each member of your group repeat individually until everybody has taken part. Keep on the alert. If the Guide asks you to repeat, do so with enthusiasm and try to mimic him as best you can until he is satisfied with your pronunciation. When you have satisfied him, you can be sure that you are speaking understandable Turkish. Continue this individual repetition as long as time permits. If you are using only the phonograph records, your Leader will see to it that you repeat and that everyone gets the most out of this individual performance.

3. Check Yourself

Did you go through the *Useful Words and Phrases* at least twice in unison and at least once more individually?

Did you repeat each word and phrase in a loud, clear voice immediately after hearing it?

Did you follow the pronunciation you heard even when it was different from that shown in your book?

Did you keep in mind the meaning of each word and phrase as you heard and spoke the Turkish?

If you have failed at any point to carry out the instructions, go over the *Useful Words and Phrases* once again as soon as you can, being careful to follow every step in the procedure outlined.

Here are other useful words and phrases which you will want to use immediately if you are in a place where the people speak Turkish. These are being given to you as a "language first aid." *Learn them by heart.*

In working with this material, follow the same procedure that you used with the *Useful Words and Phrases* in Section A. After you have gone through the list once, repeating in unison, read the following *Comment on the Aids to Listening*. Run through the *Pronunciation Practices*. Then go through the list a second and a third time, as in Section A.

1. Useful Words and Phrases (*Cont.*)

Asking for things

Record 1B, after spiral.

hello!	mér-há-bà!	merhaba!
Ahmet!	áh-mèt!	Ahmet
Hello, Ahmet!	mér-há-bà, áh-mèt!	Merhaba, Ahmet!
Hello, Mr. Carr!	mér-há-bà, bày‿kár!	Merhaba, bay Kar!
what is [it]?	né-dìr?	nedir?
What's this?	bú‿né-dìr?	Bu nedir?
in Turkish	túrk^{y}-çé-dè.	türkçede
how	ná-sìl?	nasıl?
[it] is said	dè-nír.	denir
How is this said in Turkish?	türk^{y}-çe-de‿bú‿ná-sil‿dé-nìr?	Türkçede bu nasıl denir?
you wish	(1) àr-zú, e-dí-yór-su-nùz.	arzu ediyorsunuz
	(2) àr-zú e-dí-yór-su-nùz.	
What do you wish?	né‿ár-zù‿e-di-yór-su-nuz?	Ne arzu ediyorsunuz?

cigarette [s]	si-gá-rà.	sigara
I want	is-tí-yo-rùm.	istiyorum
I want cigarettes.	si-gá-rá‿is-ti-yò-rúm.	Sigara istiyorum.
Here you are! (lit. be so kind!)	búy-rùn!	Buyrun!
match [es]	k^{y}ìb-rít.	kibrit
I want matches.	k^{y}ib-rí-t‿is-ti-yò-rúm.	Kibrit istiyorum.

Record 2A, beginning.

your cigarette [s]	si-gá-rá-nìz.	sigaranız
[are] there?	vár-mì?	varmı?
Do you have any cigarettes?	si-gá-ra-nız‿vár-mì?	Sigaranız varmı?
I want a cigarette.	bir‿si-gá-rá‿is-ti-yò-rúm.	Bir sigara istiyorum.
will you give [me]?	ve-rír-mi-si-nìz?	verirmisiniz?
Will you give me a match?	bir‿k^{y}ib-rit‿ve-rír-mi-si-nìz?	Bir kibrit verirmisiniz?

Food

[a] meal	yè-mék^{y}.	yemek
to eat	yè-mék^{y}.	yemek
I want to eat.	yé-mék^{y}‿ye-mé-k^{y}‿is-ti-yò-rúm.	Yemek yemek istiyorum.
bread	èk^{y}-mék^{y}.	ekmek
water	sú.	su
meat	ét.	et
potatoes	pá-tá-tès.	patates

meat and potatoes	ét vé‿pá-tá-tès.	et ve patates
coffee	kàh-vé.	kahve
milk	sǘt.	süt
beer	bí-rà.	bira
wine	ṣà-ráp.	şarap
any	bír.	bir
thing	ṣéy.	şey
to drink	ìç-mékʸ.	içmek
[do] you want?	(1) ís-ti-yór-mú-su-nùz?	istiyormusunuz?
	(2) ís-tí-yór-mú-su-nùz?	
Do you want anything to drink?	bır‿ṣé-y‿iç-mé-kʸ‿ís-ti-yór-mú-su-nùz?	Bir şey içmek istiyormusunuz?
[do] you wish?	ar-zú‿é-di-yór-mú-su-nùz?	arzu ediyormusunuz?
Do you want coffee?	kah-vé‿ar-zú‿é-di-yór-mú-su-nùz?	Kahve arzu ediyormusunuz?
No, thank you!	há-yìr, te-ṣékʸ-kʸǘ-r‿e-dè-rím!	Hayır, teşekkür ederim!
I want milk.	sǘ-t‿ís-ti-yò-rúm.	Süt istiyorum.

Price

how much (money)?[1]	káç‿pá-rà?	kaç para?
you want	ís-tí-yór-su-nùz.	istiyorsunuz
How much do you want?	káç‿pa-rá‿ís-ti-yòr-su-núz?	Kaç para istiyorsunuz?
five	béṣ.	beş
cent[s]	kù-rúṣ.	kuruş
Five cents.	béṣ‿kú-rùṣ.	Beş kuruş.

[1] Words enclosed in parentheses, ( ), are expressed in the Turkish, but are unnecessary in the English equivalents.

how many (pieces)?	káç‿ta:-nè?	kaç tane?
How many do you want?	káç‿ta:-né‿is-ti-yòr-su-núz?	Kaç tane istiyorsunuz?
How much [is] this?	bú‿káç‿pá-rà?	Bu kaç para?
one	bír.	bir
lira	lʸí-rà.	lira
One lira.	bír‿lʸì-rá.	Bir lira.
all of it	hép-sì.	hepsi
how much? (lit. what amount?)	né‿ká-dàr?	ne kadar?
What does the whole thing come to?	hép-si‿né‿ká-dàr?	Hepsi ne kadar?
three	ǘç.	üç
Three liras.	ǘç‿lʸì-rá.	Üç lira.

Record 2B, beginning.

Time

o'clock	sà-át.	saat
how much?	káç.	kaç?
What time [is it], please?	lʸǘt-fèn, sá-át‿kàç?	Lûtfen, saat kaç?
two	ì-kʸí.	iki
[It's] two o'clock.	sá-à-t‿i-kʸí.	Saat iki.
ten	ón.	on
It's ten o'clock.	sá-à-t‿ón.	Saat on.
two (lit. the two)	ì-kʸi-yi.	ikiyi
[it]'s passing	gʸé-çi-yòr.	geçiyor
It's ten past two.	sa-á-t‿i-kʸi-yi‿ón‿gʸé-çi-yòr.	Saat ikiyi on geçiyor.

nine (lit. the nine)	dò-kú-zú.	dokuzu
five	béṣ.	beş
It's five past nine.	sa-ȧt‿do-ku-zú‿béṣ‿g^{y}é-çi-yòr.	Saat dokuzu beş geçiyor.
meal	yè-mék^{y}.	yemek
its time	vàk-tí.	vakti
[it] has come	g^{y}èl^{y}-dí.	geldi
It's time to eat.	(1) yé-mèk^{y}‿vak-ti̍‿g^{y}él^{y}-dı.	Yemek vakti geldi.
	(2) yé-mék^{y}‿vak-ti̍‿g^{y}él^{y}-dì.	
[it is] meal time	yé-mék^{y}‿vák-tì.	yemek vakti
[is]n't [it]?	dé-yíl^{y}-mì?	değilmi?
It's time to eat, isn't it?	yé-mék^{y}‿vák-tì, dé-yíl^{y}-mì?	Yemek vakti, değilmi?
[the] movie	si̍-né-mà.	sinema
at what time?	sá-àt‿káç-tá?	saat kaçta?
[it] starts	báṣ-lí-yòr.	başlıyor
What time does the movie start?	si-né-ma‿sa-ȧt‿káç-tá‿báṣ-lı-yòr?	Sinema saat kaçta başlıyor?
to seven	yè-di̍-yé.	yediye
five	béṣ.	beş
remaining	kà-lá.	kala
The movie starts at five to seven.	(1) si-né-ma‿sa-ȧt‿ye-di-yé‿béṣ‿ka-lá‿báṣ-lı-yòr.	Sinema saat yediye beş kala başlıyor.
	(2) si̍-né-mà sa-ȧt‿ye-di-yé‿béṣ‿ka-lá‿báṣ-lı-yòr.	

this train	bù‿trén.	bu tren
[it] leaves	kàl-kár.	kalkar
What time does this train leave?	bú‿trèn sa-ȧt‿kȧç-tá‿kȧl-kàr?	Bu tren saat kaçta kəlkar?
seven (lit. the seven)	yè-dí-yí.	yediyi
five	béş.	beş
passing	gʸè-çé.	geçe
It leaves at five past seven.	sa-ȧt‿ye-di-yí‿béş‿gʸe-çė‿kȧl-kàr.	Saat yediyi beş geçe kalkar.
eight	sè-kʸíz.	sekiz
at half	bú-çùk-tá.	buçukta
It leaves at half past eight.	sa-ȧt‿sé-kʸíz‿bu-çuk-tȧ‿kȧl-kàr.	Saat sekiz buçukta kalkar.

Record 3A, beginning.

Numbers

one	bír.	bir
two	ì-kʸí.	iki
three	ủç.	üç
four	dőrt.	dört
five	béş.	beş
six	àl-tí.	altı
seven	yè-dí.	yedi
eight	sè-kʸíz.	sekiz
nine	dò-kúz.	dokuz
ten	ón.	on

two	ì-k^{y}í.	iki
two more	ì-k^{y}í‿dá-hà.	iki daha
[they] make four	dőr-dé-dèr.	dört eder
Two and two make four.	i-k^{y}í, ì-k^{y}í‿dá-hà dőr-dé-dèr.	İki, iki daha dört eder.
Four and five are nine.	dőrt, béş‿dá-hà do-kú-zé-dèr.	Dört, beş daha dokuz eder.

Leave-taking

to God	àl-lá-há.	allaha
we have commended [you]	ıs-màr-la-dík.	ısmarladık
Good-bye! (the person leaving)[1]	ál-la-há‿ıs-már-la-dìk!	Allaha ısmarladık!
Good bye! (the person staying)[1] *(lit. [may you go] laughingly)*	g^{y}ü-l^{y}é‿g^{y}ü-l^{y}è!	Güle güle!

After you have gone through these *Useful Words and Phrases* once, read the following:

2. Comment on the Aids to Listening (*Cont.*)

The *pronunciation* of Turkish does not involve any great difficulties. This, of course, does not mean that you can use English sounds in Turkish words and expect to be understood. But you will find that many of the sounds are sufficiently similar to your own so that you will have practically no difficulty with them. However, there are a few Turkish sounds that are different from anything in English. For that reason it is necessary for you to listen carefully and try hard to imitate your Guide. If you do this and follow the *Hints on Pronunciation* which will be given to you from time to time, you will be able to pronounce Turkish so that you can be readily understood.

The written form of the words (in the middle column) serves as an aid to your listening and helps you recall the pronunciation as you have heard it from your Guide. We have therefore tried to make the writing in this middle column correspond as nearly as possible

[1] Additional remarks are also enclosed in parentheses.

to the sound of the language. This regularized spelling will make it easier for you to learn to read the ordinary Turkish spelling, which will be explained in Part II.

We are used to English writing where each vowel-letter can stand for several different sounds, but in Turkish writing, each of the *eight vowel-letters* always stands for the same sound as follows:

LETTER	STANDS FOR	EXAMPLES

These *five* are similar to English vowels:

a	a sound like *a* in *father*	ák-şàm-lár (*evenings*)

PRACTICE 1[1] **Record 3A, after 1st spiral.**

fàt-má.	(*Fatma*)
bá-yàn‿ká-yá.	(*Mrs. Kaya*)
kàl-kár.	(*leaves*)
yá-váş‿yá-vàş.	(*slowly*)

e	a sound like *e* in *pet*	yè-mék^y (*eating*)

PRACTICE 2 **Record 3A, after 2nd spiral.**

né-ré-dè?	(*where?*)
èk^y-mék^y.	(*bread*)
şéy.	(*thing*)
béş.	(*five*)

Hint on Pronunciation: Don't make the mistake of pronouncing *e* with the sound of the *ay* in *day*. If you do so, the Turkish listener, thinking you are saying Turkish *ey*, may not understand your meaning.

[1] *To the Group Leader:* See Unit 2. A. 2. (p. 46) for instructions on how to handle pronunciation practices.

i a sound like *i* in *pit* k^{y}ìb-rít (*match*)

PRACTICE 3 **Record 3A, after 3rd spiral.**

ı-yí-yìm.	(*I'm well*)
sí-zì-n‿ís-mi-níz.	(*your name*)
ì-k^{y}í.	(*two*)
bìr‿k^{y}ib-rít.	(*a match*)

o a sound like *o* in *for* ón (*ten*)

PRACTICE 4 **Record 3A, after 4th spiral.**

yók.	(*there isn't*)
ón.	(*ten*)
sól.	(*left*)
l^{y}ó-kán-tà.	(*restaurant*)

Hint on Pronunciation: Don't pronounce Turkish *o* like the *o* in English *go*, or the Turk, hearing Turkish *o:*, may misunderstand you.

u a sound like *u* in *push* *sú* (*water*)

PRACTICE 5 **Record 3A, after 5th spiral.**

ú-nùt-túm.	(*I've forgotten*)
l^{y}ǘt-fèn.[1]	(*please*)
sú.	(*water*)
kù-rúṣ.	(*cent*)

Hint on Pronunciation: Don't pronounce Turkish *u* like the *u* of English *use*. The sound is not like *yew*, but like *oo* in *took*.

[1] Also pronounced *l^{y}út-fèn*. Here with *ü* instead of *u*.

These *three* are unlike any English vowels:

ı	a sound something like the *u* in *suppose*	àl-tí	(*six*)
ü	a sound like the *i* of *pit*, pronounced with puckered lips	ǘç	(*three*)
ö	a sound like the *e* of *pet*, pronounced with puckered lips	dǿrt	(*four*)

While a group of vowel-letters in English spelling generally has a value altogether different from the value of the vowel-letters separately, a *group of vowel-letters* in Turkish writing has the value of the individual vowel-sounds spoken one after the other with a clear separation:

aa	a group of two sounds, like one Turkish *a* followed by another, each pronounced separately.	sà-át	(*o'clock*)

Turkish has, in addition to its eight simple vowel sounds, drawled or *long vowels:*

a:	a sound like *a* in *father*, but drawn out or drawled	sà:dá	(*on the right*)

The *consonant-letters* are used pretty much as in English, but note the following:

ç	a sound like *ch* in *church*	káç	(*how much*)
kʸ	a sound like *c* in *cute*	kʸìb-rít	(*match*)
gʸ	a sound like *g* in *argue*	gʸǘn	(*day*)
ş	a sound like *sh* in *shin*	béş	(*five*)
h	a sound like *h* in *hand* or *behind*, even at the end of a syllable	kàh-vé	(*coffee*)

y	a sound like *y* in *year*, even in the middle or at the end of a word	há-yìr	(*no*)
l^y	a sound like the *li* of *million*	l^yó-kán-tà	(*restaurant*)

3. Check Yourself

Did you go through the *Useful Words and Phrases* at least twice in unison and at least once more individually?

Did you apply what you learned about the vowel and consonant sounds in *Comment on the Aids to Listening?*

Did you follow the pronunciation you heard even when it was different from that shown in your book?

Did you keep in mind the meaning of each word and phrase as you heard and spoke the Turkish?

If you have failed at any point to carry out the instructions, go over the *Useful Words and Phrases* once again as soon as you can, being careful to follow every step in the procedure outlined.

SECTION C—REVIEW OF USEFUL WORDS AND PHRASES

If your group has time for outside assignments, sections marked *Individual Study* may be done between meetings of the group. Otherwise use them as independent study during a group meeting.

1. Covering the English (Individual Study)

Go back to the *Useful Words and Phrases* in Sections A and B. Cover up the English. Read the Turkish aloud. Keep your voice down if you are working with the rest of the group. Follow the Guide's pronunciation as nearly as you can remember, and test yourself to see if you can recall the meaning of each word and phrase. Check the expressions you are not sure about and after you have gone through the whole list, uncover the English and find their meaning. Repeat this procedure at least three times or until you are satisfied that you know every expression. Then do the following exercise:

2. What Would You Say? (Individual Study)

For each of the following situations, two or more Turkish expressions are given. Read all the expressions aloud and pick out the one you think best fits the situation. For example, you would pick (b) as the right choice for the first situation. After you have made your choice, make sure that you know the meaning of the other expressions offered as possibilities and why they would not fit as well as the one you picked out. At the next meeting of the group, you will compare your choices with those of other members of your group and see how you come out.

1. *You meet Mr. "Stone" one day about six o'clock. You say:*
   a. gʸǜ-n‿áy-dín, bày‿mé-tín!
   b. ak-şam-la-rı-niz‿há-yır-lí‿ól-sùn, bày‿ká-yá!

2. *You offer Mr. "Stone" a cigarette:*
   a. si-gá-ra‿is-ti-yór-mú-su-nùz?
   b. si-gá-rà né-ré-dè?

3. *Mr. "Stone" doesn't want to smoke and says politely:*
   a. i-lʸèr-dé.
   b. há-yìr, te-şékʸ-kʸǘ-r‿e-dè-rim!

4. *Mr. "Stone" looks at his watch and says:*
   a. yé-mékʸ‿vak-ti‿gʸélʸ-dì.
   b. i-kʸí‿i-kʸí‿dá-hà dőr-dé-dèr.

5. *You don't know what time it is, so you ask:*
   a. bú‿né-dìr?
   b. síz né‿is-ti-yòr-su-núz?
   c. sá-àt‿káç?

6. *Mr. "Stone" replies:*
   a. sá-à-t‿ál-tí.
   b. is-tàs-yón bú-rá-dà.

7. *He asks you where to find a restaurant:*
   a. bú-rá-dà né-re-dé‿lʸo-kán-ta‿vàr?
   b. lʸo-kán-ta‿is-ti-yór-mú-su-nùz?

8. *You tell him:*
   a. sá-à-t‿i-kʸí.
   b. i-lʸèr-dé.
   c. bír‿lʸì-rá.

9. *He asks you if you want to eat, saying:*
   a. lʸút-fèn yá-váş‿ya-váş‿ko-nù-şu-núz!
   b. bú‿trèn sa-át‿káç-tá‿kál-kàr?
   c. ye-mékʸ‿ye-mé-kʸ‿is-ti-yór-mú-su-nùz?

10. *You answer, saying yes you do:*
   a. é-vèt. is-tí-yo-rùm.
   b. há-yìr, án-lá-mı-yò-rúm.

11. *You enter the restaurant and greet the waiter:*
   a. is-tàs-yón né-ré-dè?
   b. mér-há-bà, áh-mèt!

12. *He returns the greeting, and when you have chosen a table, asks:*
   a. bú-rá-dà i-yi‿bír‿si-né-ma‿vár-mì?
   b. né‿ár-zù‿e-di-yór-su-nuz?

13. *You turn to Mr. "Stone" and say:*
a. síz búy-rùn!
b. káç‿ta:-né‿is-ti-yòr-su-núz?

14. *Mr. "Stone", turning to the waiter, says:*
a. si-gá-rá‿is-ti-yò-rúm.
b. ét vé‿pa-tá-té-s‿is-ti-yò-rúm.

15. *You then say:*
a. bén-dè.
b. kʸib-ri-t‿ar-zú‿é-di-yór-mú-su-nùz?

16. *Ahmet, the waiter, then asks:*
a. bir‿şé-y‿iç-mé-kʸ‿is-ti-yór-mú-su-nùz?
b. şà-ráp né-ré-dè?

17. *Mr. "Stone" replies:*
a. é-vèt. bí-rà.
b. te-şékʸ-kʸǘ-r‿e-dè-rim!

18. *You then say:*
a. bén káh-vé‿is-ti-yò-rúm.
b. i-yí-yìm, te-şékʸ-kʸǘ-r‿e-dè-rim!

19. *When you have finished eating, you ask for the check, saying:*
a. hép-si‿né‿ká-dàr?
b. tǘrkʸ-çé-dè bú‿ná-sil‿dé-nìr?

20. *Ahmet answers:*
a. án-lı-yór-mú-su-nùz?
b. i-kʸí‿lʸì-rá.

21. *As you leave, you say:*
a. mér-há-bà!
b. ál-la-há‿ıs-már-la-dìk!

22. *Ahmet answers:*
a. sǘ-t‿is-ti-yò-rúm!
b. gʸü-lʸé‿gʸü-lʸè!

Section D—Listening In

1. What Did You Say?

To the Group Leader: Read the English describing the situations in Section C. 2. Skip around the group, calling on different students to speak the Turkish which the situation calls for. Encourage students to give the Turkish, if they can, without reading it from their books. The Guide will correct any student whose pronunciation or use of words is wrong. If there is no Guide, the other members of the group will be prepared to criticize mistakes.

Following this exercise, ask different members of the group to give the meaning in English of the different Turkish expressions listed for each situation.

Go back to the last exercise of the preceding section. The Leader will ask different members of the group the Turkish to be used in each of the situations given. Other members of the group will criticize the choices made if they do not happen to agree with them. The Leader will also ask for the meaning of all of the other expressions. Then go on to the following hearing exercise.

2. Listening In

To the Group Leader: The conversations which appear in this section will be read to the group by the Guide or played on the phonograph records. English equivalents are omitted from the *Listening In* material so that students can get practice in understanding spoken Turkish which uses the vocabulary they know. Meaning, therefore, is to be emphasized.

The first time you go through the conversations, have the Guide repeat a conversation, if necessary, to help clear up meaning, before you go on to the next conversation. If you have no Guide, lift the needle of the phonograph at the end of each conversation and let the students discuss the meaning of any sentences that are not understood.

Go through the conversations a second time without stopping. Pay about equal attention to pronunciation and meaning.

Finally, assign parts and have the students read the conversations. Give everyone a chance. Suggest that the actors actually take the parts, stand up and move around, sit at a table in the restaurant, stand behind the counter in the store, etc. Keep it moving. Get everyone to speak up! Take a part yourself.

Keep your book closed while the Guide reads the following conversations and repeat after him. If you have no Guide, you should use the phonograph records, repeating the Turkish immediately after you hear it. At the end of each conversation take time out to check up on the meaning of what you have heard and said. Ask someone in the group to give you the English equivalent of any expression you do not understand. If necessary, go back to the *Useful Words and Phrases* to find the meaning. Almost all the words and the expressions you have had in *Useful Words and Phrases* occur in the following conversations.

1. *Greetings.*

Record 3A, after 6th spiral.

bày‿ká-yá— gʸǜ-n‿áy-dín, bày‿mé-tín!	Gün aydın, bay Metin!
bày‿mé-tín— gʸǜ-n‿áy-dín, bày‿ká-yá!	Gün aydın, bay Kaya!

bày‿ká-yá—	ná-sil-sı-nìz?	Nasılsınız?
bày‿mė-tín—	i̍-yí-yìm, te-şėk^{y}-k^{y}ű-r‿e-dè-ri̍m! síz ná-sil-sı-nìz?	İyiyim, teşekkür ederim! Siz nasılsınız?
bày‿ká-yá—	bén-dė‿i-yì-yi̍m!	Ben de iyiyim!

2. *Looking for a hotel.*

bày‿kár—	áf-fe-dèr-si-ni̍z!	Affedersiniz!
	bú-ra-da‿o-tėl^{y}‿vár-mì?	Burada otel varmı?
bày‿mė-tín—	é-vèt. i-yi̍‿bi̍-r‿ó-tél^{y}‿vàr.	Evet. İyi bir otel var.
bày‿kár—	bú‿ó-tèl^{y} né-ré-dè?	Bu otel nerede?
bày‿mė-tín—	sà:-dá.	Sağda.
bày‿kár—	te-şėk^{y}-k^{y}ű-r‿e-dè-ri̍m!	Teşekkür ederim!
bày‿mė-tín—	bi̍r‿şèy‿dė-yíl^{y}!	Bir şey değil!

3. *In a restaurant.*

Record 3B, beginning.

bày‿kár—	mér-há-bà, áh-mèt!	Merhaba, Ahmet!
àh-mét—	mér-há-bà, bày‿kár!	Merhaba, bay Kar!
bày‿kár—	ye-mėk^{y}‿vak-ti̍‿dė-yíl^{y}-mì?	Yemek vakti değilmi?
	ye-mėk^{y}‿ye-mė-k^{y}‿i̍s-ti-yò-rúm.	Yemek yemek istiyorum.
àh-mét—	né‿ar-zù‿e-di-yór-su-nuz, bày‿kár?	Ne arzu ediyorsunuz, bay Kar?
bày‿kár—	ét vė‿pa-tá-tė-s‿i̍s-ti-yò-rúm.	Et ve patates istiyorum.
àh-mét—	ek^{y}-mė-k^{y}‿i̍s-ti-yór-mú-su-nùz?	Ekmek istiyormusunuz?
bày‿kár—	é-vèt, l^{y}űt-fèn.	Evet, lûtfen.
àh-mét—	bi̍r‿şė-y‿iç-mė-k^{y}‿i̍s-ti-yór-mú-su-nùz?	Bir şey içmek istiyormusunuz?

bày‿kár—	é-vèt, bí-rà.	Evet, bira.
	hép-si‿né‿ká-dàr¿[1]	Hepsi ne kadar?
àh-mét—	i-kʸí‿lʸì-rá	İki lira.

4. *Going to a movie.*

bày‿kár—	áf-fe-dèr-si-níz! bú-ra-da‿i-yí‿bír‿si-né-ma‿vár-mì?	Affedersiniz! Burada iyi bir sinema varmı?
bày‿mé-tín—	é-vèt. í-lʸer-dé‿bír‿sí-né-má‿vàr.	Evet. İlerde bir sinema var.
bày‿kár—	si-né-ma‿sa-át‿káç-tá‿báş-lı-yòr?	Sinema saat kaçta başlıyor?
bày‿mé-tín—	sá-àt‿yé-di-dé.	Saat yedide.
bày‿kár—	lʸût-fèn, sá-àt‿káç¿[1]	Lûtfen, saat kaç?
bày‿mé-tín—	sá-àt‿béş.	Saat beş.
bày‿kár—	te-şékʸ-kʸû-r‿e-dè-rím!	Teşekkür ederim!
bày‿mé-tín—	bír‿şèy‿dé-yílʸ!	Bir şey değil!

5. *At a store.*

àh-mét—	ak-şam-la-rı-niz‿há-yır-lí‿ól-sùn, bày‿kár!	Akşamlarınız hayırlı olsun, bay Kar!
bày‿kár—	te-şékʸ-kʸû-r‿e-dè-rím, sí-zín-dè!	Teşekkür ederim, sizin de!
àh-mét—	né‿ár-zù‿e-di-yór-su-nuz?	Ne arzu ediyorsunuz?
bày‿kár—	si-gá-rá‿ís-ti-yò-rúm.	Sigara istiyorum.
àh-mét—	búy-rùn!	Buyrun!
bày‿kár—	te-şékʸ-kʸû-r‿e-dè-rím! bú‿né-dìr¿[1]	Teşekkür ederim. Bu nedir?
àh-mét—	kʸìb-rít. kʸib-rí-t‿ar-zú‿é-di-yór-mú-su-nùz?	Kibrit. Kibrit arzu ediyormusunuz?
bày‿kár—	é-vèt. káç‿pá-rà¿	Evet. Kaç para?

[1] A special kind of question. Listen for it and imitate the tone of voice.

àh-mét—	ón‿kú-rùş.	On kuruş.
bày‿kár—	búy-rùn!	Buyrun!
àh-mét—	te-şék^{y}-k^{y}û-r‿e-dè-rím!	Teşekkür ederim!
bày‿kár—	ál-la-há‿ıs-már-la-dìk!	Allaha ısmarladık!
àh-mét—	g^{y}ü-l^{y}é‿g^{y}ü-l^{y}è, bày‿kár!	Güle güle, bay Kar!

6. *Getting ready to leave.*

bày‿kár—	áf-fe-dèr-si-níz, is-tas-yón‿né-ré-dè? sá:-dá-mı-dìr?	Affedersiniz, istasyon nerede? Sağdamıdır?
bày‿mé-tín—	há-yìr. sá:-dà‿dé-yíl^{y}. í-l^{y}èr-dé.	Hayır. Sağda değil. İlerde.
bày‿kár—	bú‿trèn sa-át‿káç-tá‿kál-kàr?	Bu tren saat kaçta kalkar?
bày‿mé-tín—	sa-át‿dör-dü‿ón‿g^{y}é-çè.	Saat dordü on geçe.
bày‿kár—	áf-fe-dèr-si-níz. án-lá-mı-yò-rúm! l^{y}ûtfèn yá-váş‿ya-váş‿ko-nù-şu-núz!	Affedersiniz. Anlamıyorum! Lûtfen yavaş yavaş konuşunuz!
bày‿mé-tín—	bú‿trèn, sa-át‿dör-dü‿ón‿g^{y}é-çè kàl-kár. án-lı-yór-mú-su-nùz?	Bu tren, saat dördü on geçe kalkar. Anlıyormusunuz?
bày‿kár—	é-vèt, án-lí-yo-rùm! te-şék^{y}-k^{y}û-r‿e-dè-rím!	Evet, anlıyorum! Teşekkür ederim!
bày‿mé-tín—	bír‿şèy‿dé-yíl^{y}!	Bir şey değil!

Is there any expression in any of these conversations that you do not understand now? If there is, find the meaning of it or ask other members of your group before you proceed. If no one knows, refer to the *Useful Words and Phrases.*

Go through the conversations once more following the same plan as before. Imitate carefully and be sure to keep in mind the English equivalent of everything you are saying in Turkish.

Finally go through the conversations again but this time take turns. The Leader will assign parts and the exercise is to continue at least until everyone has had a chance to speak one of the parts. Keep this going as long as you have time. When your turn comes, speak clearly and with enthusiasm. Put yourself in the situation and let yourself go. If the Guide asks you to repeat, do so until he is satisfied with your pronunciation.

Section E—Review

1. Covering the Turkish (Individual Study)

Go back to the *Useful Words and Phrases* in Sections A and B. Cover up the Turkish. Read the English silently and test yourself to see if you can speak the Turkish for each word and phrase. Check the expressions you are uncertain about and after you have gone through the whole list, uncover the Turkish and review them. Go through the list once more and continue for at least three times or until you can give the Turkish readily for all the expressions. To make sure of this, pick out expressions at random and see if you can speak out the Turkish quickly. Speak the Turkish aloud and try to imitate your Guide's pronunciation as well as you can remember it. When you have completed this individual study, the group will then proceed to the following exercise.

2. Vocabulary Check-Up

To the Group Leader: Go to the *Useful Words and Phrases* in Sections A and B. Read to the group the English equivalent of the Turkish expressions. Call on different students (not in any fixed order) asking for the correct Turkish for the English.

For instance say to A:

"*tű́rkʸ-çė̀-dè* 'Is there a restaurant here?' *ná-sɨl‿dė-nìr?*"

The students are to respond with their books closed. The Guide will indicate by a negative sign whenever he hears a Turkish expression that is wrong, or, if there is no Guide, the other members of the group will indicate that they do not agree. Immediately ask someone else to give the expression correctly. Any group member who has difficulty in giving the correct Turkish should be told to review the *Useful Words and Phrases* thoroughly before the next meeting of the group. Do not spend any time talking about the *why* of the Turkish; stick to the *how.*

There are two *precautions* which the Leader must observe in all exercises of this sort and in the conversation practice throughout the course. Be sure that everyone understands them. They are as follows:

1. Every Turkish expression must be given smoothly and completely before the student's performance can be considered satisfactory. If there is an error in the first attempt, ask the student to give the expression over again in complete form. If he fumbles badly, turn to someone else.
2. Everyone must speak loud enough, so that all can hear. Every student should be encouraged to call out "Louder, Please!" if he can't hear. Check on this occasionally by pointing to the student who is listening to someone else's Turkish, and ask "What did he say?"

If you do not observe these precautions, much time and effort may be wasted in group meetings.

In order to fix in your mind the expressions you will need in the conversations of the following section, check yourself on your ability to speak the Turkish you have learned. By now you should not have to grope for it. The Leader of the group will ask you to supply in turn the Turkish expressions for the English equivalents which he reads from the *Useful Words and Phrases*. If you have done a thorough job of recalling the Turkish when you are looking only at the English equivalents, as suggested in 1, of this section, you will have no difficulty in responding promptly and smoothly when you hear the English. Your Guide will let you know if your Turkish expressions are not correct. If you have no Guide, the members of the group should be ready to correct faulty expressions.

3. Simple Arithmetic in Turkish

1. Here are the numbers from one to ten. Repeat after your Guide, once with your book open, twice with your book closed.

bír	dőrt	sè-k^{y}íz
ì-k^{y}í	béş	dò-kúz
ǘç	àl-tí	ón
	yè-dí	

2. Here are some sample additions. Repeat after your Guide, as above.

a. i-k^{y}i̍‿i̍-k^{y}í‿dá-hà ká-çé-dèr?	2 + 2 = ?
i-k^{y}i̍‿i̍-k^{y}í‿dá-hà dő r-dé-dèr.	2 + 2 = 4
b. ü̇-ç‿ǘç‿dá-hà ká-çé-dèr?	3 + 3 = ?
ü̇-ç‿ǘç‿dá-hà ál-tì-é-dèr.	3 + 3 = 6
c. bé-ş‿i̍-k^{y}í‿dá-hà ká-çé-dèr?	5 + 2 = ?
bé-ş‿i̍-k^{y}í‿dá-hà ye-dí-é-dèr.	5 + 2 = 7

3. On a sheet of paper, write out the figures for similar problems which do not add up to more than ten. Write, for example, 5 + 3 = 8. The Leader will then ask one of the group to say his problem in Turkish and another to answer it in Turkish. The person answering must not be content to give the sum

but must speak the whole problem. For example, if you have written as your problem the figures 2 + 7 = 9, you say: i-kʸi‿yé-dí‿dá-hà ká-çé-dèr? The one who answers must say: i-kʸi‿yé-dí‿dá-hà do-kú-zé-dèr. Continue this exercise until everyone has had a chance both to ask and to answer.

Section F—Conversation

To the Group Leader: Read once more the precautions under Section E. 2. Then read the following directions with the class. After going through the outlined conversations, encourage the students to strike out for themselves. Spend all the time you can on free conversation practice in an effort to get to the point where students can speak easily and smoothly with a minimum of *ums* and *ers.*

The Leader will assign parts and will ask you to take turns in pairs, carrying on the following conversations. The two persons who are talking together should stand up and act out their parts, speaking as smoothly and naturally as possible. Make it real and get some fun out of it. The Guide will help you if your Turkish is wrong or if your pronunciation is bad. The Leader will prompt you if you are not sure what comes next in your part.

1. Finding a restaurant.

   Mr. Stone approaches Mr. Strong, excuses himself, and asks about a restaurant. Mr. Strong directs Mr. Stone who thanks him. They exchange goodbyes.

2. Eating a meal.

   Mr. and Mrs. Carr enter a restaurant and are greeted by the waiter. He asks what they will have and they order meat and potatoes, bread, drinks and so on. When they have finished they ask for the check, pay and leave.

3. Going to a movie.

   Mr. Carr approaches Mr. Stone and asks about a movie. Mr. Stone gives him directions. Mr. Carr thanks him. At the movie, Mr. Carr asks Ahmet, the ticket-seller, when the movie starts. Ahmet tells him, but Mr. Carr doesn't understand and asks him to repeat. Ahmet repeats slowly. Mr. Carr then asks what the price of admission is, pays, and goes in.

When you can do these conversations rapidly and without hesitation, strike out for yourself and initiate a conversation. Try to use as many as possible of the phrases you have learned in this unit. But do not waste time attempting to say things not found in this unit. Your possibilities are limited here, but as you go on through this manual, they will become ever larger and you soon will be able to talk at length about many different things.

FINDER LIST

This is a complete alphabetical list of all the words and expressions used in this unit. It is for reference only, but you should know all of these before going on to the next unit.

af-fet- . . .	excuse
áf-fe-dèr-si-níz!	Excuse [me]!
àh-mét	Ahmet
áh-mèt!	Ahmet!
àk-şám	evening
ák-şàm-lár	evenings
ák-şám-là-rı-níz	your evenings
ak-şam-la-rı-niz‿há-yır-lí‿ól-sùn!	Good evening! (lit. may your evenings be fortunate!)
àl-láh	God
àl-lá-há	to God
ál-la-há‿ıs-már-la-dìk!	Good-bye! (lit. we have commended [you] to God)
àl-tí	six
ál-tí-é-dèr	make six
an-la- . . .	understand
án-lá-mı-yò-rúm	I [do] not understand
án-lı-yór-mú-su-nùz?	[Do] you understand?
án-lí-yo-rùm	I understand
án-lí-yo-rùm, etc.	see *an-la-* . . .
áp-tèst-há:-né	toilet
áp-tèst-há:-né né-ré-dè?	Where [is the] toilet?

ar-zu‿et- . . .	wish
ar-zú‿é-di-yór-mú-su-nùz?	[Do] you wish?
ár-zú‿e-di-yòr-su-núz	you wish
**ày-dín*	(bright)
gʸù-n‿áy-dín!	Good morning! (lit. let the day be bright!)
baş-la- . . .	start
báş-lí-yòr	[it] starts
sa-át‿káç-tá‿báş-lı-yòr?	At what time does it start?
báy	Mr.
bày‿kár	Mr. Carr
bày‿ká-yá	Mr. Kaya
bày‿mé-tín	Mr. Metin
bà-yán	Mrs.; Miss
bá-yàn‿kár	Mrs. Carr
bá-yán‿kàr	*Mrs.* Carr (in contrast to Mr.)
bá-yàn‿ká-yá	Mrs. Kaya
bén	I
bén-dè	I, too
béş	five
sa-át‿ye-di-yi‿béş‿gʸé-çè.	At five past seven.
sa-át‿do-ku-zú‿béş‿gʸé-çi-yòr.	[It]'s five past nine.
sa-át‿ye-di-yé‿béş‿ká-là.	At five to seven.
béş‿kú-rùş.	Five cents.

* Words marked with the star are not used alone, or in the form starred.

bír	one; a, an; any
bìr‿k^{y}íb-rít	a match
bír‿l^{y}ì-rá	one lira
ì-yí‿bìr‿l^{y}o-kàn-tá	a good restaurant
bìr‿şèy‿dé-yíl^y!	You're welcome! (lit. it isn't anything)
bí-rà	beer
bú	this
bú‿káç‿pá-rà?	How much [is] this?
bú‿l^{y}o-kàn-tá	this restaurant
bú‿né-dìr?	What's this?
bù-çúk	half (after an hour)
sa-át‿sé-k^{y}íz‿bu-çúk-tà.	At half past eight.
bú-rá-dà	here
búy-rùn!	Here you are! (lit. be so kind!)
síz búy-rùn!	You first!
dà-há	more
dőrt béş‿dá-hà	four [and] five (more)
ì-k^{y}í i-k^{y}í‿dá-hà	two [and] two (more)
de- . . .	say
dè-dì-níz	you said
dè-nír	[it] is said
dè-yíl^y	[it is] not
sá:-dà‿dé-yíl^y.	[It is] n't to [the] right.
dé-yíl^y-mì?	[Is it] not?

dò-kúz	nine
do-kú-zė-dèr	makes nine
sa-àt‿**do-ku-zů‿béş**‿g^{y}é-çi-yòr.	[It]'s five past nine.
dő̇r-dė-dèr	see *dő̇rt*
dȍr-dű	see *dő̇rt*
dő̇rt	four
dő̇r-dė-dèr	makes four
sa-ȧt‿dȍr-dü‿ón‿g^{y}ė-**çè**.	At ten past four.
èk^{y}-mék^{y}	bread
et- . . .	do; make
e-di̍-yór-su-nùz	you do, make
ét	meat
é-vèt	yes
fàt-má	Fatma (girl's first name)
g^{y}eç- . . .	pass
g^{y}è-çé	passing
sa-ȧt‿ye-di-yi̍‿béş‿g^{y}é-çè.	At five past seven.
g^{y}é-çi̍-yòr	[it] is passing
sa-ȧt‿do-ku-zů‿béş‿g^{y}é-çi-yòr.	[It]'s five past nine.
sa-ȧ-t‿i-k^{y}i-yi̍‿ón‿g^{y}é-çi-yòr.	[It]'s ten past two.
g^{y}el^{y}- . . .	come
g^{y}èl^{y}-di̍	[it] has come

g^{y}ül^{y}- . . .	laugh
g^{y}ǜ-l^{y}é	laughing
g^{y}ǘ-l^{y}é‿g^{y}ǘ-l^{y}è	Good-bye! (lit. laughingly)
g^{y}ǘn	day
g^{y}ǜ-n‿áy-dín!	Good morning! (lit. may the day be bright!)
há-yìr	no
hà-yir-lí	fortunate
há-yır-lí‿ol-sùn!	May [they] be fortunate!
hép-sì	all
hép-si‿né‿ká-dàr?	How much [does] the whole thing [come to]?
iç- . . .	drink
ìç-mék^{y}	to drink
bír‿şè-y‿íç-mék^{y}	to drink something
ì-k^{y}í	two
sá-à-t‿í-k^{y}í.	[It's] two o'clock.
sa-á-t‿i-k^{y}i-yí‿ón‿g^{y}é-çi-yòr.	[It]'s ten past two.
í-l^{y}èr-dé	up ahead
ì-sím	name
ìs-mí-níz	your name
sí-zì-n‿ís-mi-níz	*your* name
ís-tàs-yón	railroad station
ís-tàs-yón né-ré-dè?	Where [is the] railroad station?

is-te- . . .	want
i̇s-tí-yo-rùm	I want
si-gá-rá‿i̇s-ti-yò-rúm	I want cigarettes
i̇s-ti-yór-mú-su-nùz?	do you want [it]?
i̇s-tí-yór-su-nùz	you want
i̇s-tí-yo-rùm, etc.	see *is-te-* . . .
ì-yí	good; well
i̇-yí‿bir‿lʸo-kàn-tá	a good restaurant
i̇-yí-yìm.	I['m] well.
ıs-mar-la- . . .	commend
i̇s-màr-la-dík	we have commended [you]
ál-la-há‿ıs-már-la-dìk!	Good-bye! (lit. we have commended [you] to God)
káç	how much, how many
sá-àt‿káç? sá-át‿kàç?	What time [is it]?
sá-àt‿káç-tá?	At what time?
káç‿pá-rà?	How much (money)?
káç‿pa-rá‿i̇s-ti-yòr-su-núz?	How much [do] you want?
káç‿tá:-nè?	How many (pieces)?
ká-çé-dèr?	How much [does it] make?
kàç-tá?	at what (amount)?
kà-dár	amount
né‿ká-dàr?	how much? (lit. what amount?)
kàh-vé	coffee
kah-vé‿ar-zú‿é-di-yór-mú-su-nùz?	[Do] you want coffee?

kal- . . .	remain
kà-lá	remaining
sa-át‿ye-di-yé‿béş‿ká-là.	At five to seven.
kalk- . . .	leave
kàl-kár	[it] leaves
sa-át‿káç-tá‿kál-kàr?	At what time does it leave?
kár	(Mr.) Carr
bày‿kár	Mr. Carr
kà-yá	rock; (Mr.) Kaya (lit. "Stone")
bày‿ká-yá	Mr. Kaya
ko-nuş- . . .	speak
ko-nú-şú-nùz!	Speak!
kù-rúş	cent(s)[1]
béş‿kú-rùş	five cents
kʸìb-rít	match(es)[1]
kʸib-rí-t‿is-ti-yò-rúm.	I want matches.
bìr‿kʸib-rít	a match
bir‿kʸib-rit‿ve-rír-mi-si-nìz?	Will you give [me] a match?
lʸí-rà	lira
bír‿lʸì-rá	one lira
úç‿lʸì-rá	three lira

[1] One or a number of them.

l^{y}ó-kán-tà	restaurant
l^{y}ǘt-fèn! (l^{y}út-fèn)[1]	Please!
mér-há-bà!	Hello!
mè-tín	strong; (Mr.) Metin (lit. "Strong")
bày‿mé-tín	Mr. Metin
ná-sìl?	How?
ná-sil‿dé-nìr?	How is [it] said?
ná-sil-sı-nìz?	How [are] you?
né	what
né‿ár-zù‿e-di-yór-su-nuz?	What [do] you wish?
né‿dé-di-nìz?	What did you say?
né-dìr?	What is [it]?
né‿ká-dàr?	How much? (lit. what amount?
né-ré-dè?	Where [is it]?
ìs-tàs-yón né-ré-dè?	Where [is the] railroad station?
ol- . . .	be
òl-sún	may [they] be
há-yır-lí‿ól-sùn!	may [they] be fortunate!
ón	ten
sá-à-t‿ón.	[It's] ten o'clock.
sa-á-t‿i-k^{y}i-yì‿ón‿g^{y}é-çi-yòr.	[It]'s ten past two.
ó-né-dèr	makes ten

[1] Both pronunciations are used.

ò-tél^y	hotel
pà-rá	money
káç‿pá-rà?	How much (money)?
pá-tá-tès	potatoes
sá:	right
sà:-dá	to [the] right
sá:-dá-mı-dìr?	Is [it] to [the] right?
sà-át	time; o'clock
sa-át‿do-ku-zú‿béş‿g^{y}é-çi-yòr.	[It]'s five past nine.
sá-à-t‿i-k^{y}í.	[It's] two o'clock.
sa-á-t‿i-k^{y}i-yi‿ón‿g^{y}é-çi-yòr.	[It]'s ten past two.
sá-àt‿káç? sá-át‿kàç?	What time [is it]?
sá-àt‿káç-tá?	At what time?
sá-à-t‿ón.	[It's] ten o'clock.
sa-át‿sé-k^{y}íz‿bu-çúk-tà.	At half past eight.
sa-át‿ye-di-yi‿béş‿g^{y}é-çè.	At five past seven.
sa-át‿ye-di-yé‿béş‿ká-là.	At five to seven.
sè-k^{y}íz	eight
sa-át‿sé-k^{y}íz‿bu-çúk-tà.	At half past eight.
si-gá-rà	cigarette(s)[1]
si-gá-rá-‿ís-ti-yò-rúm.	I want cigarette[s].
bir‿si-gá-rà	a cigarette
si-gá-rá-nìz	your cigarette[s]
si-gá-ra-nız‿vár-mì?	[Do] you have [any] cigarette[s]?

[1] One or a number of them.

si̍-né-mà	[the] movies
síz	you
sì-zín	yours; your
si̍-zín-dè	yours, too
sól	[the] left
sòl-dá	to [the] left
sú	water
sǘt	milk
sǘ-t‿i̍s-ti-yò-rúm.	I want milk.
şà-ráp	wine
şéy	thing
bìr‿şéy	something, anything
bi̍r‿şèy‿dé-yíl^{y}!	You're welcome! (lit. it isn't anything)
tà:-né	piece
káç‿tá:-nè?	How many (pieces)?
te-şek^{y}-k^{y}ü-r‿et-. . .	thank
te-şék^{y}-k^{y}ǘ-r‿e-dè-rim!	I thank [you]!
trén	train
tǘrk^{y}-çè	Turkish
tǘrk^{y}-çé-dè	in Turkish
tǘrk^{y}-çé-dè bú‿ná-si̍l‿dé-nìr?	How is this said in Turkish?
unut- . . .	forget
ú-nùt-túm	I forgot
ǘç	three

và-kít	time
vàk-tí	its time
yé-mék^y‿vák-tì	[it's] meal time
yé-mék^y‿vak-ti‿g^{y}él^y-di.	[It]'s time to eat.
vár	there [is]
vár-mì?	[Is] there?
vé	and
ét vé‿pá-tá-tès	meat and potatoes
ver- . . .	give
ve-rír-mi-si-nìz?	will you give [me]?
yà-váş	slow
yá-váş‿yá-vàş	slowly
yá-váş‿ya-váş‿ko-nù-şu-núz!	Speak slowly!
yè-dí	seven
sá-àt‿yé-di-dé.	At seven o'clock.
yé-dí-é-dèr	makes seven
yè-di-yé	to seven
sa-át‿ye-di-yé‿béş‿ká-là.	At five to seven.
sa-át‿ye-di-yi‿béş‿g^{y}é-çè.	At five past seven.
ye- . . .	eat
yè-mék^y	to eat; (a) meal; eating
yé-mék^y‿vák-tì	mealtime
yé-mék^y‿vak-ti‿g^{y}él^y-di.	[It]'s time to eat.
yé-mék^y‿yé-mèk^y	to eat (a meal)
yé-mék^y‿ye-mé-k^y‿is-ti-yò-rúm.	I want to eat.
yók	there [is]n't

UNIT 2

MEETING PEOPLE

SECTION A—BASIC SENTENCES

To the Group Leader: Adopt the following steps as standard practice in conducting this course:

1. Before each meeting of the group, be sure to read carefully and get clearly in mind the instructions covering those sections of a unit which you expect to take up in the group meeting.
2. Before each group meeting, see that the Guide is available with his *Kılavuz için talimatname* or that phonograph and records are ready.
3. Have the members of the group read together the instructions that precede each piece of work they are to do before they begin it. Let one member of the group read these instructions aloud while the others follow the reading in their books.
4. Take time, following the reading of all instructions, to make sure that everyone understands exactly what he is to do.

In Section A of Unit 2 follow the same procedure as that outlined for *Useful Words and Phrases* of Section A in Unit 1. Go through the *Basic Sentences* once with everyone repeating in unison after the Guide or phonograph record. Then take up the *Hints on Pronunciation* which follow. Come back to the *Basic Sentences* and go through them once more, with repetitions in unison after the Guide. Pay particular attention to those items of pronunciation you have been working on. Finally, go through the *Basic Sentences* a third time with individual repetition. The Guide will call for as many repetitions as may be necessary to get a pronunciation that sounds to him like Turkish.

Make everyone speak loudly and clearly. Keep the work moving. Don't let it drag.

Begin this section by listening, in the manner already outlined in Section A of the preceding unit, to the *Basic Sentences* which follow. Be sure to keep in mind the meaning of the Turkish by reading silently the English Equivalent. As you listen to the Turkish, keep your eye on the *Aids to Listening*. This will help you imitate accurately the pronunciation you are hearing. Repeat each word and phrase loudly and clearly right after you hear it. As you pronounce the Turkish, do so as though you really meant what you are saying. Do not forget that these words and phrases convey a real meaning and it is up to you to say them as though you were actually using them. Go through the sentences in unison and with your book open.

The *Basic Sentences* are set up as conversations so that you may hear and speak the Turkish as you would hear and speak it if you were talking with Turkish people.

Although numerous characters are introduced in these *Basic Sentences*, it is not important for you to try to keep in mind just who they are or their relationship to one another. You are concerned rather with *what* they say and *how* they say it.

1. Basic Sentences

Mr. Kaya, accompanied by his brother-in-law, Ali, meets Mr. Carr and his friend, Mr. Metin, on the street.

Record 4A, beginning.

ENGLISH EQUIVALENTS	AIDS TO LISTENING	CONVENTIONAL TURKISH SPELLING
	Mr. Kaya	
hello	mér-há-bà!	merhaba
Mr. Carr	bày‿kár.	bay Kar
Hello, Mr. Carr!	mér-há-bà, bày‿kár!	Merhaba, bay Kar!
	Mr. Carr	
Hello, Mr. Kaya how [are] you?	mér-há-bà, bày‿ká-yá, ná-si̍l-sı-nìz?	Merhaba, bay Kaya, nasılsınız?
	Mr. Kaya	
you	síz.	siz
I['m] well, thank you, how [are] you?	i-yí-yìm, te-ṣék^y-k^{y}ǘ-r‿e-dè-ri̍m, síz ná-si̍l-sı-nìz?	İyiyim, teşekkür ederim, siz nasılsınız?

	Mr. Carr	
I['m] well, too.	bén-dè i-yí-yìm.	Ben de iyiyim.
this	bú.	bu
gentleman	zá:t.	zat
is Mr. Metin	báy‿mé-tín-dìr.	bay Metindir.
This gentleman is Mr. Metin.	bú‿zà:t báy‿mé-tin-dir.	Bu zat bay Metindir.
this	bú.	bu
[is] my friend	àr-ka-dá-şím.	arkadaşım
Mr. Metin, this is my friend, Mr. Kaya.	bày‿mé-tín, bú àr-ka-dá-şím, bày‿ká-yá.	Bay Metin, bu arkadaşım, bay Kaya.
	Mr. Metin	
I'm honored!	mü-şér-ré-f‿ól-dùm!	Müşerref oldum!
	Mr. Carr	
Mr. Kaya's	bày‿ká-ya-nín.	bay Kayanın
his wife	kà-rı-sí.	karısı
my wife's	kà-rı-mín.	karımın
[she] is her friend	ár-ka-da-şí-dìr.	arkadaşıdır
Mr. Kaya's wife is my wife's friend.	báy‿ká-ya-nín‿ká-rı-sì ka-rı-mi-n‿ár-ka-da-şí-dìr.	Bay Kayanın karısı karımın arkadaşıdır.
	Mr. Kaya	
this	bú.	bu
my wife's	kà-rı-mín.	karımın
[he] is her brother	kár-de-şí-dìr.	kardeşidir
This is my wife's brother.	bú ka-rı-min‿kár-de-şí-dìr.	Bu karımın kardeşidir.

	Mr. Carr	
I've forgotten	ú-nùt-túm.	unuttum
yours	sì-zín.	sizin
your name	ìs-mi-níz.	isminiz
Excuse me, I've forgotten! What is your name?	áf-fe-dèr-si-níz, ú-nùt-túm! si-zi-n‿is-mi-níz‿nè-dir.	Affedersiniz, unuttum! Sizin isminiz nedir?
	Ali	
mine	bè-ním.	benim
my name	ìs-mím.	ismim
[*is*] *Ali Dag*	á-l^{y}ì‿dá:.	Ali Dağ
My *name is Ali Dag.*	bé-ní-m‿is-mìm á-l^{y}ì‿dá:.	Benim ismim Ali Dağ.
	Mr. Carr	
Record 4B, beginning.		
Thank you!	teşék^y-k^{y}ű-r‿e-dè-rim!	Teşekkür ederim!
Mr. Metin, this is Ali Dag.	bày‿mé-tín, bú á-l^{y}ì‿dá:.	Bay Metin, bu Ali Dağ.
	Ali	
What is your *name, please?*	l^{y}ű́t-fèn, si-zi-n‿is-mi-níz‿nè-dir?	Lûtfen, sizin isminiz nedir?
	Mr. Carr	
My *name's Tom Carr.*	bé-ní-m‿is-mìm tóm‿kár-dìr.	Benim ismim Tom Kardır.
Some weeks later:		
	Ali	
your brothers (*or sisters*)	kár-dèş-l^{y}é-ri-níz.	kardeşleriniz
[*are*] *there* [*any*]?	vár-mì?	varmı?
Have you any brothers or sisters, Mr. Carr?	si-zin‿kar-deş-l^{y}e-ri-niz‿vár-mì, bày‿kár?	Sizin kardeşleriniz varmı, bay Kar?

	Mr. Carr	
a	bi̇́r.	bir
my sister	kíz‿kár-de-şi̇̀m.	kız kardeşim
there [is]	vár.	var
Yes, I have a sister.	**é-vèt**, bi̇r‿kíz‿kar-de-şi̇m‿vàr.	**Evet**, bir kız kardeşim **var.**
	Ali	
your sister's	kíz‿kár-dė-şi-ni-zi̇̀n.	kız kardeşinizin
her name	i̇̀s-mi̇́.	ismi
*What's your sister's **name?***	**kiz**‿kar-de-şi-ni-zi̇-n‿i̇s-mi̇́‿nè-di̇r?	Kız kardeşinizin ismi nedir?
	Mr. Carr	
my sister's	kíz‿kár-dė-şi-mi̇̀n.	kız kardeşimin
her name	i̇̀s-mi̇́.	ismi
[it] is Fatma	fát-má-dìr.	Fatmadır
My sister's name is Fatma.	**kíz**‿kar-de-şi-mi̇-n‿i̇s-mi fát-má-dìr.	Kız kardeşimin ismi Fatmadır.
	Ali	
your sister	kíz‿kár-dė-şi-ni̇̀z.	kız kardeşiniz
is [she] married?	ėv-l^{y}i̇́-mi-di̇̀r?	evlimidir?
Is your sister married?	**kíz**‿kár-dė-şi-ni̇̀z ėv-l^{y}i̇́-mi-di̇̀r?	Kız kardeşiniz evlimidir?
	Mr. Carr	
unfortunately	ma-á-l^{y}ė-sèf.	maalesef
[she] is married	ėv-l^{y}i̇́-di̇̀r.	evlidir
Yes, unfortunately, she is married.	é-vèt, ma-á-l^{y}ė-sèf, ėv-l^{y}i̇́-di̇̀r.	Evet, maalesef, evlidir.

Ali

Mrs. Metin's	bá-yàn‿mé-ti-ni̍n.	bayan Metinin
her sister	kíz‿kár-de-şì.	kız kardeşi
[is] there?	vár-mì?	varmı?
Has Mrs. Metin a sister?	ba-yán‿me-ti-ni̍n‿kiz‿kar-de-şi̍‿vár-mì?	Bayan Metinin kız kardeşi varmı?

Mr. Metin

hers	ò-nún.	onun
her sister	kíz‿kár-de-şì.	kız kardeşi
there isn't	yók-tùr.	yoktur
No, she hasn't any sister.	há-yìr, o-nún‿kiz‿kar-de-şi̍‿yók-tùr.	Hayır, onun kız kardeşi yoktur.

Before you go through the *Basic Sentences* a second time, note the sound values of the following letters:

LETTER	STANDS FOR A SOUND	EXAMPLES	
a	about like *a* in *father*	àr-ká-dáş	(*friend*)
e	about like *e* in *pet*	bén-dè	(*I, too*)
i	about like *i* in *pit*	ìs-mi̍-níz	(*your name*)
o	about like *o* in *for*	yók	(*there [is]n't*)
u	about like *u* in *push*	ú-nùt-túm	(*I've forgotten*)
ı	something like the *u* in *suppose*	ná-sil-sı-nìz	(*how [are] you*)
ü	like the *i* in *pit*, pronounced with puckered lips	mü-şèr-réf	(*honored*)
a:	something like *a* in *father*, drawn out or drawled	dá:	(*mountain*)

k^{y}	like *c* in *cute*
ş	like *sh* in *shin*
y	like *y* in *year*, even in the middle or at the end of a word
l^{y}	something like the *li* in *million*, but run together into a single sound

te-şėk^{y}-k^{y}ú-r‿e-dè-rím	(*thank* [*you*])
kàr-déş	(*brother*)
bày‿kȧ-yá	(*Mr. Kaya*)
ma-á-l^{y}ė-sèf	(*unfortunately*)

Remember that:

A curved line (‿) connecting two words shows that they are pronounced together without any pause or break.

The mark (´) over a vowel indicates that it is pronounced more strongly than any other in the group of words connected by (‿).

The mark (`) over a vowel indicates the next strongest vowel in the group.

The mark (') over a vowel indicates the other fairly strong vowel or vowels in the group. There may be a number of these vowels, but there can be only one vowel with (´) and only one with (`).

Then study the following:

2. Hints on Pronunciation

To the Group Leader: The explanations preceding the *Practices* should be read by the group and discussed before the practice is attempted. Go through each practice as many times as may be necessary to give each member of the group reasonable control of the item of pronunciation that is being taught. Have the group repeat after the Guide, or the phonograph record, first in unison, then individually.

You will find that the practice material[1] is presented in sections on the phonograph record with a narrow space of clear record between each section. This arrangement will make it possible for you to play each section of practice as it is needed.

PRONUNCIATION PRACTICES

Use the same procedure with the following practices that you did with the *Basic Sentences* from which they were selected. Go through them three times, twice with the book open and once with the book closed. Try to

[1]Practices on *a*, *e*, *i*, *o*, *u*, already presented in Unit 1 (first part of Record 3A).

get a clear impression of the sound and try to make your pronunciation as much like that of the Guide or phonograph record as you can.

One of the simple basic vowel-sounds of Turkish which we have met above is unlike any English vowel-sound. If you pronounce *cushion* with puckered lips, and then repeat it with spread lips, pushing the tongue slightly forward, you should get a vowel-sound, between the *c* and *sh*, very much like Turkish *ı*.

Note: This Turkish sound is written with *ı* without a dot over it and is not to be confused with dotted *i*.

Practice pronouncing *cushion* with spread lips, then drop the *-ion* and pronounce *cush-* first with puckered lips and then with spread lips, thus:

PRACTICE 1 **Record 5A, beginning.**

kúş.
kíş.
kúş.
kíş.
kúş.
kíş.
kúş.
kíş. kíş. kíş. kíş.

The first of these is Turkish *kúş* 'bird', and the second is Turkish *kíş* 'winter'.

PRACTICE 2 **Record 5A, after 1st spiral.**

kíz.	(*girl*)
ná-sıl-sı-nìz?	(*how [are] you?*)
kà-rı-sí.	(*his wife*)
há-yìr-lí.	(*fortunate*)

Pay attention to the rhythm and make the sounds no longer and no shorter than you hear the Guide or the record make them. Notice that the vowel sounds are pronounced with clarity even when they are in unaccented syllables.

If you are uncertain about any of the points of pronunciation which have been discussed, ask your Guide to repeat the words and phrases with which you are having trouble, and try to improve your pronunciation. Remember that these notes are only approximate and are at best an imperfect description of the sounds.

When you are satisfied that you can pronounce fairly well all the sounds, go through the *Basic Sentences* once more in unison and with your book open. As you repeat after your Guide, keep your eye on the *Aids to Listening*, and note in particular the examples of the sounds discussed. Do not hesitate to ask your Guide to repeat if you are uncertain about any sound.

Finally go through the *Basic Sentences* again, this time taking turns. Keep your book closed, listen carefully to your Guide, and make sure that your pronunciation satisfied him.

3. Check Yourself

Did you go through the *Basic Sentences* at least twice with your book open and then at least once with your book closed?

Did you repeat each word and phrase immediately after hearing it in a loud, clear voice?

Did you follow the pronunciation you heard even if it seemed different from that shown in your book?

Did you keep in mind the meaning of each word and phrase as you heard and spoke the Turkish?

If your Guide asked you to repeat, did you do so with enthusiasm and as many times as necessary until he was satisfied with what you were saying?

Section B—Word Study and Review of Basic Sentences

1. Word Study (Individual Study)

If your group has time for outside assignments, do the *Word Study* between meetings of the group. Otherwise make it independent study in the group meeting.

In this section we take up some of the words and expressions you have just learned and examine them to see how the language is built. First read the words and expressions in each list and make sure that you understand the meaning of the Turkish. Then read the comment which follows each list. This should make clear to you just how the words function and how they are put together. If there are any points that are not clear to you, make note of them and ask other members of the group about them. Follow the same procedure with each list and each comment.

1. *Turkish equivalents of English "is"*

Observe the following words and phrases:

Column I			*Column II*	
		Group I		
bè-nim	*'mine'*	:	bé-n m-dìr	'[*it*] *is mine*'
èv-lʸí	*'married'*	:	ėv-lʸí-dìr	'[*she*] *is married*'
bày‿mė-tín	*'Mr. Metin'*	:	bȧy‿mė-tín-dir	'[*it*] *is Mr. Metin*'
		Group II		
ét	*'meat'*	:	ét-tìr	'[*it*] *is meat*'
èkʸ-mékʸ	*'bread'*	:	ėkʸ-mékʸ-tìr	'[*it*] *is bread*'
bìr‿kȧr-déṣ	*'a brother'*	:	bi̍r‿kȧr-déṣ-tìr	'[*he*] *is a brother*'

If we compare Column I with Column II, and Group I with Group II, we see that:

1. the part of the words in Column II which means "is" is the *ending -dir*, *-tir*;
2. the form *-dir* is found after words which end in *humming* sounds, like *-m*, *-i*, *-n*;

Note 1: To test whether the final sound of a word "hums" or not, pronounce the word, placing the hands over the ears and drawing out each final sound. If there is a buzzing in the ears, the final sound "hums" and the *-dir* form of the ending is used.

3. the form *-tir* is found after words which end in *non-humming* sounds, like *-t*, *-kʸ*, *-ş*;

Note 2: If, when trying the experiment described above in Note 1, there is no buzzing in the ears, the final sound does not "hum," and the *-tir* form of the ending is used.

4. the *strongest vowel*, marked with ('), is *not* in the ending but in the word before the ending.

Now observe these forms:

	Column I			Column II	
			Group I		
i	kàr-dė-şí	*'his brother'*	:	kȧr-de-şí-dìr	*'[it] is his brother'*
e	né?	*'what?'*	:	né-dìr?	*'what is [it]?'*
e	kàr-déş	*'brother'*	:	kȧr-déş-tìr	*'[it] is [the] brother'*
			Group II		
a	tòm‿kár	*'Tom Carr'*	:	tóm‿kár-dìr	*'[it] is Tom Carr'*
ı	kíş	*'winter'*	:	kíş-tìr	*'[it] is winter'*
a	vár	*'there [is]'*	:	vár-dìr	*'there is'*
			Group III		
o	ón	*'ten'*	:	ón-dùr	*'[it] is ten'*
u	sú	*'water'*	:	sú-dùr	*'[it] is water'*
u	kù-rúş	*'penny'*	:	kụ-rúş-tùr	*'[it] is [the] penny'*

If we compare Column I with Column II, and Groups I, II and III, we see that:

1. the ending meaning "is" does not always have the vowel *i*, as in Group I, but sometimes has *ı*, as in Group II, and sometimes *u*, as in Group III;
2. if the last vowel of the base word is *i* or *e*, as in Group I, the ending has *i*;
3. if the last vowel of the base word is *ı* or *o*, as in Group II, the ending has *ı*;
4. if the last vowel of the base word is *u* or *o*, as in Group III, the ending has *u*.

Note: This pairing-off of vowels between base and ending is called *vowel harmony* and is characteristic of Turkish words.

We see that the idea of '(it, he, she) is' is expressed in Turkish not by a separate word as in English, but by adding one of the *endings -dir, -dır, -dur, -tir, -tır, -tur,* to a word. An English sentence, therefore, such as '[it] is [the] friend' is expressed in Turkish by a single word: *àr-ka-dáş-tìr.*

2. *Turkish equivalents of English "my"*

Observe these forms:

	Column I			*Column II*	
			Group I		
	kà-rí	*'wife'*	:	kà-rím	*'my wife'*
	pà-rá	*'money'*	:	pà-rám	*'my money'*
			Group II		
i	ì-sím	*'name'*	:	is-mím	*'my name'*
e	kàr-déş	*'brother'*	:	kàr-dè-şím	*'my brother'*
ı	kíz	*'daughter'*	:	kì-zím	*'my daughter'*
a	àr-ká-dáş	*'friend'*	:	àr-ka-dà-şím	*'my friend'*
u	kúş	*'bird'*	:	kù-şúm	*'my bird'*
o	ón	*'ten'*	:	ò-núm	*'my ten'*

If we compare Column I with Column II, and Group I with II, we see that:

1. the part of the words in Column II which means 'my' is the ending *-m* after a *vowel* (*ı*, *a*, etc.), as in Group I;
2. it is the ending *vowel plus -m* after a *consonant* (*m*, *ş*, *z*, *n*, etc.), as in Group II;
3. and is *-im*, *-ım*, or *-um* according to the rules of vowel harmony:
   a. *-im* after *i* or *e*;
   b. *-ım* after *ı* or *a*;
   c. *-um* after *u* or *o*;
4. the *strongest vowel*, marked with (´), is that of the ending, *if* the strongest vowel in the base is the *last* one; otherwise the vowel of the ending is *next strongest*, marked with (`), and the strongest vowel remains in the base.

3. *Some Turkish equivalents of English "your"*

Observe the following:

	Column I			*Column II*	
			Group I		
	kà-rí	*'wife'*	:	kà-ri-níz	*'your wife'*
	sı̍-gá-rà	*'cigarette'*	:	si-gá-rá-nìz	*'your cigarette'*
			Group II		
i	k^yìb-rít	*'match'*	:	k^yı̍b-rì-ti-níz	*'your match'*
e	ét	*'meat'*	:	è-tı̍-níz	*'your meat'*
ı	kíş	*'winter'*	:	kì-şi-níz	*'your winter'*
a	àr-ká-dáş	*'friend'*	:	ár-ka-dà-şı-níz	*'your friend'*
u	kúş	*'bird'*	:	kù-şú-núz	*'your bird'*
o	ón	*'ten'*	:	ò-nú-núz	*'your ten, the ten of you'*

If we compare Column I with Column II, and Group I with II, we see that:

1. the part of the words in Column II which means 'your' is *-niz*, *-nız*, *-nuz* after a vowel (*ı*, *a*, etc.) as in Group I;
2. is *-i-niz*, *-ı-nız*, *-u-nuz* after a consonant (*t*, *ş*, *n*, etc.). as in Group II;
3. is -(*i*)-*niz*, -(*ı*)-*nız* or -(*u*)-*nuz* according to the rules of vowel harmony:
   a. -(*i*)-*niz* after *i* or *e*;
   b. -(*ı*)-*nız* after *ı* or *a*;
   c. -(*u*)-*nuz* after *u* or *o*;
4. the *strongest vowel*, marked with (´), is that of the ending, *if* the strongest vowel in the base is the *last* one; otherwise the vowel of the ending is the *next strongest*, marked with (`).

Examples:

àr-ká-d*á*ş : ár-ka-dà-şı-n*í*z

but

sı̍-g*á*-rà : si-g*á*-rá-nìz.

4. *Turkish equivalents of English "his, her, its, their"*

Observe the following:

	Column I			*Column II*	
			Group I		
i	*he-p(i)[1]	*'all'*	:	(*he-pi-si) hép-sì[2]	*'all of it (lit. its all)'*
e	né?	*'what?'*	:	nè-sí?	*'its what?'*
ı	kà-rí	*'wife'*	:	kà-rı-sí	*'his wife'*
a	lʸó-kán-tà	*'restaurant'*	:	lʸo-kán-tá-sì	*'his restaurant'*
			Group II		
i	ì-sím	*'name'*	:	ìs-mí	*'their name'*
e	kàr-déṣ	*'brother'*	:	kàr-dé-ṣi	*'her brother'*
ı	kíz	*'daughter'*	:	kì-zí	*'his daughter'*
a	kà-dár	*'amount'*	:	kà-dá-rí	*'its amount'*
u	kúṣ	*'bird'*	:	kù-ṣú	*'his bird'*
o	ón	*'ten'*	:	ò-nú	*'his ten'*

If we compare Column I with Column II and Groups I and II, we see that:

1. the part of the words in Column II which means 'his, her, its, their' is *-si*, *-sı*, *-su* after vowels (*i*, *e*, *ı*, *a*, etc.), as in Group I;
2. and *-i*, *-ı*, *-u* after consonants (*m*, *ṣ*, *r*, *n*, etc.), as in Group II;
3. is *-(s)i*, *-(s)ı* or *-(s)u* according to the rules of vowel harmony:

   a. -(*s*)*i* after *i* or *e*;

   b. -(*s*)*ı* after *ı* or *a*;

   c. -(*s*)*u* after *u* or *o*;

---

[1]**he-p(i)* 'all' is not used alone, in this form, but is always found either as *hép* 'all', or with one of these 'my, your, his, her, its, their' endings: *hép-sì* 'all of it', *hé-pi-nìz* 'all of you', etc.

[2]*hép-sì* is a shortened form of **he-pi-si.*

4. the *strongest vowel*, marked with (ʹ), is that of the ending, *if* the strongest vowel in the base is the *last* one; otherwise the vowel of the ending is *next strongest*, marked with (ˋ):

Examples:

kàr-déṣ	:	kàr-dé-ṣì
	but	
lʸó-kán-tà	:	lʸo-kán-tá-sì

Since the endings

-(*i*)*m*, -(*ı*)*m*, -(*u*)*m* 'my'

-(*i*)*niz*, -(*ı*)*nız*, -(*u*)*nuz* 'your'

-(*s*)*i*, -(*s*)*ı*, -(*s*)*u* 'his, her, its, their'

indicate the "possessor" of something, and are added to a word which indicates the "thing possessed," we shall call them *possessive* endings.

5. *Turkish equivalents of English "-'s"*

Observe these forms:

	Column I			Column II	
			Group I		
i	kàr-dé-ṣí	*'his brother'*	:	kár-dè-ṣi-nín	*'his brother's'*
ı	kà-rı-sí	*'his wife'*	:	kà-rı-sı-nín	*'his wife's'*
a	bày‿ká-yá	*'Mr. Kaya'*	:	bày‿ká-ya-nín	*'Mr. Kaya's'*
			Group II		
i	kàr-dé-ṣím	*'my brother'*	:	kár-dè-ṣi-mín	*'my brother's'*
e	ò-télʸ	*'hotel'*	:	ò-té-lʸín	*'the hotel's'*
ı	kíz	*'girl'*	:	kì-zín	*'the girl's'*
a	zá:t	*'gentleman'*	:	zà:-tín	*'the gentleman's'*
u	kúṣ	*'bird'*	:	kù-ṣún	*'the bird's'*
o	tóm	*'Tom'*	:	tò-mún	*'Tom's'*

If we compare Column I and Column II, and Group I with Group II, we see that:

1. the part of the words in Column II which means "-'s" is *-nin*, *-nın*, *-nun* after vowels (*i*, *ı*, *a*, etc.), as in Group I;
2. and *-in*, *-ın*, *-un* after consonants (*m*, *l*, *z*, *t*, *ṣ*, etc.), as in Group II;

3. is -(*n*)*in*, -(*n*)*ın* or -(*n*)*un* according to the rules of vowel harmony:
   a. -(*n*)*in* after *i* or *e*;
   b. -(*n*)*ın* after *ı* or *a*;
   c. -(*n*)*un* after *u* or *o*;

4. the *strongest vowel*, marked with (´), is that of the ending, *if* the strongest vowel in the base is the *last* one; otherwise the vowel of the ending is *next strongest*, marked with (`).

We shall call this ending the *genitive* ending.

6. *"Possession" in Turkish*

We have seen the following phrases in the *Basic Sentences* of this unit:

bȧy‿kȧ-ya-nín‿kȧ-rı-sì	*'Mr. Kaya's wife'*
kȧ-rı-mí-n‿ȧr-ka-da-şì	*'my wife's friend'*
kȧ-rı-mín‿kȧr-de-şì	*'my wife's brother'*
kíz‿kar-de-şi-mi-n‿is-mì	*'my sister's name'*
ba-yȧn‿me-ti-nin‿kíz‿kȧr-de-şì	*'Mrs. Metin's sister'*

You will see that in these phrases, the first word (or group of words) (bày‿kȧ-ya-nín, kà-ri-mín) (which indicates the owner or *possessor* of the second word) has the genitive ending -(*n*)*in*, -(*n*)*ın*, -(*n*)*un*, and the second word (kà-ri-sí, àr-ka-dȧ-şí) (which indicates the *thing possessed* by the first) has the "his, her, its, their" possessive ending -(*s*)*i*, -(*s*)*ı*, -(*s*)*u*. So in Turkish you say:

bȧy‿kȧ-ya-nín‿kȧ-ri-sì — '(*Mr. Kaya's his wife*), that is: *Mr. Kaya's wife*'.

2. Covering English and Turkish of Word Study (Individual Study)

Read aloud several times the examples given you in the *Word Study*. Then cover the English and see if you know the meaning of every item. Repeat the operation until you are sure that you know every expression. As a final test, cover the Turkish and see if you can speak out the Turkish expressions by simply looking at the English. Skip about and test yourself thoroughly.

3. Review of Basic Sentences

Review the first half of the *Basic Sentences* with your Guide or the phonograph record. Go through them as many times as you can, taking turns repeating the Turkish individually. Try it with books closed and see how you get along without the help of the *Aids to Listening*. Always keep in mind the meaning of the Turkish you are hearing and speaking. As you go through the *Basic Sentences* be on the lookout for examples of the points in *Word Study* you have just covered.

SECTION C—REVIEW OF BASIC SENTENCES (*Cont.*)

1. Review of Basic Sentences (*Cont.*)

Review the second half of the *Basic Sentences* with your Guide or the phonograph record. For the detailed procedure to be followed read again the instructions for the review of the first half of the *Basic Sentences*.

2. Covering the English of Basic Sentences (Individual Study)

Here is your chance to find out just how well you have learned the meaning of the Turkish expressions you have had up to this point. Go back to the *Basic Sentences* in Section A and cover the English. Read the Turkish aloud and see whether you can supply the English equivalents of the words and phrases. Mark those you are not sure about and after reading the list through, uncover the English and look up their meaning. Cover the English again and repeat the procedure until you can go through the entire list giving all the meanings without difficulty.

3. Word Study Review (Individual Study)

Below is a group of exercises which will drill you on what you have learned in the *Word Study*. Work through each exercise carefully, doing what is asked for and trying to pronounce the words and phrases as you think your Guide would say them. Do not write anything in your book or elsewhere. If you cannot do the exercises rapidly, review again the *Word Study*. Be prepared to give the forms when the Group Leader calls on you for them.

1. Add the proper form of the "*is*" ending to the words in the following list:
   - àh-mét
   - àl-láh
   - àl-tí
   - bú
   - dè-yíl^y
   - k^{y}ìb-rít
   - ná-sìl
   - ṣà-ráp
   - yók
2. Add the proper form of the "*my*" ending to the following words:
   - àl-láh
   - báy
   - bí-rà
   - ét
   - kàh-vé
   - k^{y}ìb-rít
   - pà-rá
3. Add the proper form of the "*your*" ending to the words in 2.
4. Add the proper form of the "*his, her, its, their*" ending to the words in 2.
5. Add the proper form of the *genitive* ending to the words in 2.
6. Combine the forms in the first column with those in the second, adding the proper endings to each:

Example:

kà-rím '*my wife*' : kàr-déṣ '*brother*'
ká-rı-mín‿kár-de-ṣì '*my wife's brother*'

Column I		*Column II*
kár-dè-ṣi-níz	:	kà-rí
tóm	:	sí-gá-rà
bày‿ká-yá	:	pà-rá
à-l^{y}í	:	bí-rà
kíz	:	kàr-déṣ
fàt-má	:	kàh-vé
bá-yàn‿ká-yá	:	ét
àr-ká-dáṣ	:	kíz‿kár-dèṣ
kà-rı-níz	:	kàr-déṣ-l^{y}ér
bú‿l^{y}o-kàn-tá	:	bí-rà

4. What Would You Say? (Individual Study)

For each of the following situations two or more Turkish expressions are given. Read all the expressions aloud and check the one you think best fits each situation. Be sure you know why the other choices are not suitable. At the next meeting of the group you will be asked to say what you have chosen and you will have a chance to test your answers. Do not write anything down.

1. *Mr. "Stone" comes to visit. You say:*
   a. mér-há-bà, bá-yàn‿ká-yá!
   b. mér-há-bà, bày‿ká-yá!

2. *Mr. "Stone" inquires about your health. You answer:*
   a. ná-sıl-sı-nìz?
   b. ì-yí-yìm.

3. *You then ask how Mr. "Stone" is. He answers:*
   a. ná-sıl-sı-nìz?
   b. bén-dè ì-yí-yìm.

4. *You introduce your friend, Mr. "Strong", saying:*
   a. bú bé-nìm‿ki-zím.
   b. bú‿zà:t bày‿mé-tín.
   c. bú tóm‿kár-dìr.

5. *Mr. "Stone" acknowledges the introduction by saying:*
   a. sì-zí-n‿ìs-mi-nìz né-dìr?
   b. mü-şér-ré-f‿ól-dùm.

6. *To your other friends, you say:*
   a. síz ná-sıl-sı-nìz?
   b. bú àr-ka-dá-şím, bày‿ká-yá.
   c. sì-zín‿ká-rı-nìz ná-sìl?

7. *Mentioning Mrs. "Stone" and Mrs. Carr, you say:*
   a. kà-rím bá-yàn‿ká-ya-nín kíz‿kár-de-şì-dìr.
   b. báy‿ká-ya-nín‿ká-rı-sì ka-rı-mi-n‿ár-ka-da-şí-dìr.
   c. bá-yàn‿ká-yá ba-yán‿ka-rin‿ki-zí-dìr.

8. *Mr. "Strong", seeing that you have neglected to mention a third person, who came with Mr. "Stone," in an aside, asks:*
   a. o-nú-n‿ìs-mí‿nè-dìr?
   b. bé-ním‿kár-de-şìm-mì?

9. *You explain how he is related to Mrs. "Stone":*
   a. bú be-nìm‿kár-de-şím-dìr.
   b. ba-yán‿ka-ya-nin‿kár-de-şí-dìr.

10. *Referring to Mr. "Stone's" brother-in-law, you say:*
    a. ìs-mí fàt-má.
    b. é-vèt èv-lʸí.
    c. ìs-mí à-lʸí.

11. *Mrs. "Stone's" brother now asks you what your name is:*
    a. si-zín‿kar-deş-lʸe-ri-níz‿vár-mì?
    b. bú‿né-dìr?
    c. sì-zí-n‿ìs-mi-nìz né-dìr?

12. *You answer:*
    a. bé-ní-m‿ìs-mìm tòm‿kár.
    b. bé-ní-m‿ìs-mìm fàt-má.

13. *Ali then asks:*
a. ka-rı-nı-zin‿kar-deş-lʸe-ri‿vár-mì?
b. si-zin‿kar-deş-lʸe-ri-niz‿vár-mì?

14. *You answer:*
a. há-yìr. kȧr-de-şim‿yók.
b. é-vèt. bir‿kíz‿kar-de-şim‿vàr.

15. *Ali, who is a young bachelor, asks her name. You answer:*
a. ó-nú-n‿is-mì áh-mét-tir.
b. kíz‿kar-de-şi-mi-n‿is-mì fát-má-dìr.

16. *Ali, still curious, asks:*
a. kì-zí ėv-lʸí-mi-dir?
b. bày‿mė-tin ėv-lʸi-mi-dir?
c. kíz‿kȧr-dė-şi-niz ėv-lʸí-mi-dir?

17. *To his disappointment, you answer:*
a. is-mi tóm.
b. bė-ní-m‿is-mim à-lʸí.
c. é-vèt ėv-lʸí-dir.

18. *Ali, discouraged, sees Mrs. "Strong", and then asks:*
a. bȧy‿me-ti-nin‿kar-de-şi‿vár-mì?
b. ba-yȧn‿me-ti-nin‿kiz‿kar-de-şi‿vár-mì?

19. *You end the conversation by saying:*
a. mér-hȧ-bà á-lʸi, ná-sil-sı-nìz?
b. há-yìr, o-nún‿kiz‿kar-de-şi‿yók-tùr.

Section D—Listening In

1. What Did You Say?

To the Group Leader: Read the English describing the situations in *What Would You Say?* of Section C, and call on different students, not in any fixed order, to speak the Turkish which the situation calls for. Encourage the students to give the Turkish, if they can, without reading it from the simplified spelling in their books. Then ask different members of the group to give the meaning in English of the different Turkish expressions listed for each situation.

Go back to the last exercise in the preceding section. The Leader will ask different members of the group to speak the Turkish to be used in each of the situations given. Other members of the group will criticize the choices made if they do not agree with them. The Leader will also ask for the English equivalents of all the other expressions offered as choices, taking turns around the group.

2. Word Study Check-Up

To the Group Leader: As a further check on the students' understanding of the *Word Study*, read the English equivalent of the Turkish expressions given before each comment under *Word Study*. Call on different students, not in any fixed order, to give the correct Turkish for the English. For instance, say to A:

"*tű́rk*ʸ*-çė-dè* 'my brother's wife' *ná-sıl‿dė-nìr?*"

and so on. The Guide will at this point indicate by a negative sign whenever he hears a Turkish expression that is wrong. If there is no Guide, the other members of the group will signal that they do not agree. Immediately ask someone else to give the right answer. Any member of the group who has difficulty in giving the correct Turkish should be told to review the *Word Study* thoroughly before the next meeting of the group. Do not take time in this exercise to talk about the *why*. Stick to the *how*.

As a final exercise, call for the answers to the exercises in *Word Study Review*, in Section C. 3. The Guide will indicate when he hears a wrong Turkish form, and when the correct form has been obtained, he will repeat it for the student until he is satisfied with the student's pronunciation.

The Leader will ask different members of the group to give the correct Turkish for the English equivalents of the expressions you studied in the *Word Study*. If you give the wrong answer, the Guide will let you know by making a negative sign; or, if there is no Guide, the other members of the group will indicate that they think your answer is wrong. The Leader will then immediately call on someone else for the right answer. If you have difficulty in giving the correct Turkish, review the *Word Study* thoroughly.

As a final check the Leader will call for your answers to the exercises in the *Word Study Review* (Sec. C. 3), and the Guide or other members of the group will correct you, if you don't pronounce well.

3. Listening In

To the Group Leader: Re-read the note *To the Group Leader* in Section D. 2 of Unit 1. Follow the same procedure as outlined there. The first time you go through the conversations, check up on the meaning at the end of each conversation. Then go through all of them a second time without stopping. Finally, assign parts and have the students read the conversations. Get them to do a little acting if you can. Encourage them to speak loudly and clearly and to get into the spirit of the situation.

Keep your book closed while the Guide reads the following conversation and repeat after him in unison. If you have no Guide, you should use the phonograph records, repeating the Turkish immediately after you hear it. At the end of each conversation take time out to check up on the meaning of any word or phrase about which you are in doubt. Ask some other member of the group to give you the English equivalent or in case no one knows, go back to the *Basic Sentences* of this unit and make sure that you understand everything before you proceed any further. Go through the conversations a second time, repeating after the Guide individually. Then take parts in the conversations. This exercise contains almost all the new words you have learned in this unit.

1. *A meeting on the street.*

Record 5A, after 2nd spiral.

bày‿mė-tín—	mér-hȧ-bà, bày‿kȧ-yá!	Merhaba, bay Kaya!
bày‿kȧ-yá—	mér-hȧ-bà, bày‿mė-tín!	Merhaba, bay Metin!
bày‿mė-tín—	ná-sil-sı-nìz?	Nasılsınız?
bày‿kȧ-yá—	i-yí-yìm, te-şėk^{y}-k^{y}ű-r‿e-dè-rim!	İyiyim, teşekkür ederim.
	síz‿nà-sil-sı-niz?	Siz nasılsınız?
bày‿mė-tín—	bén-dė‿i-yì-yim.	Ben de iyiyim.

2. *Discussing a friend.*

bày‿mė-tín—	bú‿za:-ti-n‿is-mí‿nè-dir?	Bu zatın ismi nedir?
bày‿kȧ-yá—	àr-ka-dȧ-şím, bày‿kár.	Arkadaşım, bay Kar.
bày‿mė-tín—	bȧy‿kȧ-r‿ėv-l^{y}i-mi-dìr?	Bay Kar evlimidir?
bày‿kȧ-yá—	é-vèt, ėv-l^{y}í-dir.	Evet, evlidir.
bày‿mė-tín—	kar-deş-l^{y}e-ri‿vár-mì?	Kardeşleri varmı?
bày‿kȧ-yá—	é-vèt, bir‿kíz‿kar-de-şi‿vàr.	Evet, bir kız kardeşi var.
bày‿mė-tín—	bú‿kíz‿kar-de-şi-ni-n‿is-mì né-dìr?	Bu kız kardeşinin ismi nedir?
bày‿kȧ-yá—	o-nú-n‿is-mì fȧt-má-dìr.	Onun ismi Fatmadır.
bày‿mė-tín—	fat-mȧ‿ėv-l^{y}í-mi-dìr?	Fatma evlimidir?
bày‿kȧ-yá—	é-vèt, ėv-l^{y}í-dìr.	Evet, evlidir.

3. *Discussing relatives.*

bày‿mé-tín—	bày‿ká-yá, si-zín‿ka-rı-nı-zín‿kar-deş-l^{y}e-rí‿vár-mì?	Bay Kaya, sizin karınızın kardeşleri varmı?
bày‿ká-yá—	é-vèt, bír‿kár-de-şí‿vàr.	Evet, bir kardeşi var.
bày‿mé-tín—	kar-de-şi-ní-n‿is-mí‿nè-dír?	Kardeşinin ismi nedir?
bày‿ká-yá—	ó-nú-n‿ís-mì à-l^{y}í.	Onun ismi Ali.
bày‿mé-tín—	ka-rı-nı-zín‿kar-de-şí‿év-l^{y}í-mi-dìr?	Karınızın kardeşi evlimidir?
bày‿ká-yá—	há-yìr, o-nún‿ka-rı-sí‿yók-tùr.	Hayır, onun karısı yoktur.
bày‿mé-tín—	ba-yán‿ká-yá‿nà-sil?	Bayan Kaya nasıl?
bày‿ká-yá—	ká-rì-m‿í-yí, te-şék^{y}-k^{y}ű-r‿e-dè-rím!	Karım iyi, teşekkür ederim!
bày‿mé-tín—	ál-la-há‿ıs-már-la-dìk!	Allaha ısmarladık!
bày‿ká-yá—	g^{y}ű-l^{y}é‿g^{y}ű-l^{y}è!	Güle güle!

4. *A meeting in front of a restaurant.*

Record 5B, beginning.

bày‿mé-tín—	ak-şam-la-rı-niz‿há-yır-lí‿ól-sùn, bày‿kár!	Akşamlarınız hayırlı olsun, bay Kar!
bày‿kár—	te-şék^{y}-k^{y}ű-r‿e-dè-rím, sí-zín-dè!	Teşekkür ederim, sizin de!
	bú‿ák-şàm ná-síl-sı-nìz?	Bu akşam nasılsınız?
bày‿mé-tín—	te-şék^{y}-k^{y}ű-r‿e-dè-rím!	Teşekkür ederim!
	í-yí-yìm.	İyiyim.
	síz?	Siz?
bày‿kár—	bén-dé‿i-yì-yím.	Ben de iyiyim.
	ye-mék^{y}‿ye-mé-k^{y}‿ís-ti-yór-mú-su-nùz?	Yemek yemek istiyormusunuz?
bày‿mé-tín—	é-vèt, yé-mèk^{y}‿vak-tí‿g^{y}él^{y}-dí.	Evet, yemek vakti geldi.

5. *In the restaurant.*

àh-mét—	báy-làr, né‿ár-zù‿e-di-yór-su-nuz?	Baylar, ne arzu ediyorsunuz?
bày‿kár—	yé-mékʸ‿yé-mèkʸ.	Yemek yemek.
	bén ét vé‿pa-tá-te-s‿ís-ti-yò-rúm.	Ben et ve patates istiyorum.
bày‿mé-tín—	bén-dè, lʸût-fèn.	Ben de, lûtfen.
	bí-ra‿vár-mì?	Bira varmı?
àh-mét—	é-vèt, i-yí‿bí-rá‿vàr.	Evet, iyi bira var.
bày‿mé-tín—	bí-ra‿ís-ti-yór-mú-su-nùz, bày‿kár?	Bira istiyormusunuz, bay Kar?
bày‿kár—	é-vèt. i-kʸí‿bí-rà, lʸût-fèn.	Evet. İki bira, lûtfen.
bày‿mé-tín—	si-gá-ra-dá‿ís-ti-yò-rúm.	Sigara da istiyorum.
bày‿kár—	bír‿kʸib-rít‿ve-rír-mí-si-nìz, áh-mèt?	Bir kibrit verirmisiniz, Ahmet?
àh-mét—	búy-rùn!	Buyrun!
bày‿kár—	te-şékʸ-kʸû-r‿e-dè-rím!	Teşekkür ederim!
bày‿mé-tín—	ál-la-há‿ıs-már-la-dìk, áh-mèt!	Allaha ısmarladık, Ahmet!
àh-mét—	gʸü-lʸé‿gʸülʸè!	Güle güle!

6. *A man's sisters.*

à-lʸí—	bú‿za:-tin‿kar-deş-lʸe-ri‿vár-mì?	Bu zatın kardeşleri varmı?
àh-mét—	é-vèt, vár.	Evet, var.
à-lʸí—	káç‿tá:-nè?	Kaç tane?
àh-mét—	í-kʸí‿tá:-nè.	İki tane.
à-lʸí—	kíz-mì?	Kızmı?
àh-mét—	é-vèt, kíz‿kár-dèş.	Evet, kız kardeş.
à-lʸí—	kiz‿kar-deş-lʸe-rí‿év-lʸi-mi?	Kız kardeşleri evlimi?
àh-mét—	é-vèt, ma-á-lʸé-sèf, ev-lʸí-dír-lʸèr.	Evet, maalesef, evlidirler.

7. *His sister Fatma.*

à-lʸí—	si-zin‿kiz‿kar-de-şi-niz‿vár-mì?	Sizin kız kardeşiniz varmı?
àh-mét—	é-vèt, vár.	Evet, var.
à-lʸí—	kiz‿kar-de-şi-ni-zi-n‿is-mi‿nè?	Kız kardeşinizin ismi ne?
àh-mét—	fàt-má.	Fatma.
à-lʸí—	fat-má‿bú-ra-dà-mi?	Fatma buradamı?
àh-mét—	há-yìr, bù-ra-dá‿dé-yilʸ.	Hayır, burada değil.
	si-né-má-dà.	Sinemada.

Is there any word or phrase in this conversation that you do not understand now? If there is, be sure to find out its meaning by asking members of your group or looking it up in the *Basic Sentences.*

Go through the conversations again following the same plan as before. Imitate carefully and keep in mind the meaning of everything you are saying in Turkish.

Finally go through the conversations a third time. Take turns speaking the parts and continue until everybody has had a chance to speak at least one of the parts. Keep this exercise going as long as you have time. Get the most out of this individual performance and when your turn comes, speak clearly and with feeling. If there is a Guide, he will correct any errors he hears by asking you to repeat. Make every effort to satisfy him with your pronunciation.

SECTION E—CONVERSATION

1. Covering the Turkish of Basic Sentences (Individual Study)

Go back to the *Basic Sentences* of this unit. Cover up the Turkish. Read the English silently and test yourself to see how many words and phrases you can say in Turkish. Check the words you are uncertain about and after you have gone through the whole list, uncover the Turkish and review them. Go through the list once more and continue for at least three times or until you can give the Turkish readily for all the expressions. This test is hard, but if you succeed in saying the Turkish for all the sentences by merely looking at the English, you are doing well. To make sure of this, after you are certain you know the material, pick out expressions at random and see if you can still speak the Turkish quickly. As you practice, you must always speak the Turkish aloud and try to imitate the pronunciation of your Guide as well as you can recall it.

2. Vocabulary Check-Up

To the Group Leader: Go to the *Basic Sentences.* Read to the group the English equivalents of the Turkish expressions. Call on different students, not in any fixed order, asking for the correct Turkish for the English. This check-up is to be conducted in the same way as the *Vocabulary Check-Up* of Section E. 2 of Unit 1. If you have any question about the proper procedure, review the note *To the Group Leader* in that section. Remember not to spend any time talking about the *why* of the Turkish; stick to the *how.*

Before you begin the conversation, check yourself on your ability to speak the Turkish you have learned up to this point. As in the *Vocabulary Check-Up* of Unit 1, the Leader of the Group will ask you to supply in turn the Turkish expressions for the English equivalents which he reads from the *Basic Sentences.* Figure out how to say the Turkish for each English phrase or sentence whether it is your turn to speak or not. Only in this way can you get the most value out of the *Check-Up.* If there is much of the Turkish which you don't know, review the *Basic Sentences* at the first opportunity outside of the group meeting.

3. Conversation

To the Group Leader: This section represents the real purpose of the entire unit. The course is intended to teach you to speak Turkish and to understand it when you hear it spoken. Follow the instructions and give all the time you can to free conversation practice. Any members of the group who have special difficulty recalling the Turkish words and phrases they need to express a meaning should be told to do more work with the *Useful Words and Phrases* and the *Basic Sentences.* They need, in particular, more practice in covering the Turkish and recalling it when they read the English. Practice in getting the meaning of the *Listening In* records will also help. Arrangements should be made for students to play and listen to the records whenever they can between meetings of the group.

Then turn to the outlined conversations which follow. Assign parts and ask the students to act them out. Vary the situations and suggest to the students that they vary the Turkish slightly as they gain confidence in their speaking. Remember to keep the speaking loud enough so that everyone can hear. See that everyone is listening and trying to understand the Turkish that is being spoken.

The Leader will assign parts and will ask you to reproduce the conversational situations which follow. Act your part. Don't be afraid to vary the conversation if you are sure of your Turkish and use the Turkish you have learned in Unit 1 as well as that of Unit 2. Continue this practice until everyone can speak any part of the conversations even though slight changes in the situations are introduced.

1. What's your name?

   Mr. Carr approaches Mr. Stone, excuses himself and tells him his name. Mr. Stone gives his name and asks what he wishes. Mr. Carr asks for directions to the station, train schedule, and so on. Mr. Stone directs him. Mr. Carr says thanks and they take their leave.

2. Family.

   Mr. Strong and Mr. Carr discuss a friend, whether he's married, his brothers and sisters, his wife's brothers and sisters, their names, and so on.

3. Friends and relatives.

   Mr. Strong introduces Mr. Carr to his friend, Ali. Ali explains that Mr. Stone's wife is his sister. Mr. Carr says his wife and Mr. Stone's wife are very good friends. They talk about Mr. Carr's sister. Ali is much interested.

Throw yourself into these conversations. Do the best you can with pronunciation and with the Turkish, but don't worry too much about mistakes. Think more of acting your part and speaking smoothly and as though you mean what you are saying. If there is a Guide, he will help you correct your errors. If you can do this work well, it means that you are actually conversing in Turkish, and that is your chief aim in this course.

SECTION F—CONVERSATION (*Cont.*)

1. Conversation (*Cont.*)

Read again the instructions given in Section F of the preceding unit. Then continue the conversations which you started in Section E of this unit (2). When you feel that you can converse fairly easily, proceed to the following exercise.

2. Questions and Answers

To the Group Leader: Here is a series of questions. When everyone is fairly proficient in the conversations, skip around the group asking these questions, or having the Guide ask them. The answers are always obvious either from the nature of the question or the content of the *Basic Sentences* and *Listening In*. The Guide will accept any answer which is good Turkish and which is possible under the circumstances. If there is no Guide you or other members of the Group may correct the answers given. Encourage each student to ask questions of the Guide, and of the other students.

After finishing the conversation practice, the Leader (or the Guide) will ask you a question from the group which follows. Answer each question to the best of your ability, taking into account what you have learned in this and the previous unit. At the indication of the Leader, ask one of the other students a question, chosen from those which appear below. Feel free to ask the Guide questions at any time. Ask these questions as though you were really interested in the answers. The Guide will correct your mistakes. Repeat as often as he indicates until he is satisfied. If there is no Guide the Leader or other members of your Group will indicate when they disagree.

1. si-zí-n‿is-mi-nìz né-dìr?
2. bú‿zà:-tí-n‿is-mì né-dìr?
3. síz èv-lʸí-mi-si-nìz?
4. si-zin‿kar-deş-lʸe-ri-niz‿vár-mì?
5. si-zín‿kà-rı-nı-zìn is-mí‿nè-dir?
6. si-zin‿kàr-dé-şi-ni-zí-n‿is-mi‿nè-dir?
7. si-zin‿kiz‿kar-de-şi-niz‿vár-mì?
8. kiz‿kar-de-şi-ni-zi-n‿is-mí‿nè-dir?
9. bú si-zi-n‿àr-ka-dá-şı-níz-mì?
10. àr-ka-dàş-là-rı-nı-zí-n‿is-mí‿nè-dir?
11. si-zin‿kar-dèş-lʸé-ri-níz-mì?
12. bú‿bay-la-ri-n‿i-sim-lʸe-rí‿nè-dir?
13. bú‿bày-làr àr-ka-dàş-là-rı-níz-mì?
14. bày‿.......‿kàr-dé-şi-ní-n‿is-mi‿nè-dir?
15. ba-yán‿.......‿kàr-dé-şi-ni-n‿is-mi‿nè-dir?
16. bày‿.......‿kar-deş-lʸe-ri‿vár-mì?
17. ba-yán‿.......‿kiz‿kar-deş-lʸe-ri‿vár-mì?

Take every opportunity between now and the next meeting of the group to try out your Turkish on other members of the group or on native speakers around you. Carry on conversations with them whenever you get a chance. Ask questions. At this stage of the game, don't try to use phrases or sentences which are different from those you have learned thus far in this course.

FINDER LIST

This is a complete alphabetical list of all the words and expressions used in this unit which are in any way new or unusual. From now on we shall not repeat words which have been drilled sufficiently in previous units. This list is for reference only, but you should know all these before going on to the next unit.

àh-mét	Ahmet (boy's name)
áh-mèt!	Ahmet!
àk-şám	evening
bú‿ák-şàm	this evening

à-lʸí	Ali (boy's name)
ȧ-lʸì‿dá:	Ali Dag
ȧ-lʸí-dìr	[it] is Ali
àr-kȧ-dáş	friend
àr-ka-dȧ-şí	her friend
ȧr-ka-da-şí-dìr	[she] is her friend
àr-ka-dȧ-şím	my friend
ȧr-ka-dà-şı-níz	your friend
ȧr-ka-dàş-lár	friends
ȧr-ka-dàş-lȧ-rı-níz	your friends
ȧr-ka-dàş-lȧ-rı-nı-zín	your friends'
ȧr-ka-dáş-lȧ-rı-níz-mì?	[Are they] your friends?
ȧr-ka-dáş-tìr	[it] is [the] friend
báy	Mr.; gentleman
báy-làr!	Gentlemen!
bú‿bȧy-la-rìn	these gentlemen's
bà-yán	Mrs.
bȧ-yàn‿kȧ-yá	Mrs. Kaya
bén	I
bè-ním	*my*, mine
bė-ním-dìr	[it] is mine
bė-ní-m‿is-mìm	*my* name
bír	a, an; one
bir‿kíz‿kar-de-şim‿vàr.	I have a sister (lit. there is a sister of mine).
bir‿kȧr-déş-tìr	[he] is a brother

bí-rà	beer
i-k^{y}i̍‿bí-rà	two beers
bú	this, this one, this person; these
bú‿zà:t	this gentleman
bú-rà-dà	here
bú-ra-dà-mi̍?	[Is she] here?
dá:	mountain; (Mr.) Dag (lit. "Hill")
ȧ-l^{y}ì‿dá:	Ali Dag
dè-yíl^{y}	[she is]n't
èk^{y}-mék^{y}	bread
ėk^{y}-mék^{y}-tìr	[it] is bread
ét	meat
è-ti̍-níz	your meat
ét-tìr	[it] is meat
év	house
èv-l^{y}í	married
ėv-l^{y}í-dìr	[she] is married
ev-l^{y}í-di̍r-l^{y}èr	they are married
ėv-l^{y}í-mi-dìr?	Is [she] married?
ėv-l^{y}í-mi̍-si-nìz?	[Are] you married?
fàt-má	Fatma (girl's name)
fȧt-má-dìr	[it] is Fatma

hép	all (see **he-p(i)*, etc.)
**he-p(i)*	all
hé-pi-nìz	all of you
hé-p(i)-sì	all of it (lit. its "all")
ì-sím	name
i-sìm-lʸér	names
i-sìm-lʸé-rí	their names
ìs-mí	his (her, its, their) name
kíz‿kar-de-şi-ni-zi-n‿is-mi	your sister's name
ìs-mím	my name
ìs-mi-níz	your name
ì-yí	good; well; nice
ì-yí	[She is] well.
kà-dár	amount
kà-dá-rí	its amount
kár	(Mr.) (Mrs.) Carr
bá-yàn‿kár	Mrs. Carr
bá-yàn‿ká-rín	Mrs. Carr's
ba-yán‿ká-rín‿ki-zì	Mrs. Carr's daughter
kàr-déş	brother
kàr-dé-şí	his (her) brother
kár-de-şí-dìr	[he] is her brother, [it] is his brother
kàr-dé-şím	my brother

*Not used alone in this form.

kíz‿kár-de-şìm	my sister
kár-dè-şi-mín	my brother's
kíz‿kár-dé-şi-mìn	my sister's
kár-dé-şi-mín‿ká-rı-sì	my brother's wife
kár-de-şím-mí-dìr?	Is [it] my brother?
kár-dè-şi-nín	his brother's
kár-dèş-l^{y}ér	brothers
kár-dèş-l^{y}e-rí	(his) (her) brothers
kár-dèş-l^{y}é-ri-níz	your brothers (or sisters)
kár-déş-l^{y}é-ri-níz-mì?	[Are they] your brothers?
kár-déş-tìr	[it] is [the] brother
bír‿kár-déş-tìr	[he] is a brother
kà-rí	wife
kà-rím	my wife
kà-ri-mín	my wife's
ká-rı-mín‿ár-ka-da-şì	my wife's friend
ka-rı-mí-n‿ar-ka-da-şí-dìr	[she] is my wife's friend
ka-rı-min‿kár-de-şí-dìr	[he] is my wife's brother
kà-ri-níz	your wife
kà-ri-nı-zín	your wife's
kà-ri-sí	his wife
kà-rı-si-nín	his wife's
kà-yá	rock; (Mr.) Kaya (lit. "Stone")
bày‿ká-ya-nín	Mr. Kaya's
báy‿ká-ya-nín‿**ká-rı-sì**	Mr. Kaya's wife

kíş	winter
kì-şi-níz	your winter
kíş-tìr	[it] is winter
kíz	girl; daughter
kì-zí	his daughter
ki-zí-dìr	[she] is her daughter
kì-zím	my daughter
ki-zím-dìr	[it] is my daughter
kì-zín	the girl's
kíz‿kár-dèş	sister(s)
kíz‿kár-de-şì	her sister
kíz‿kár-de-şìm	my sister
kíz‿kár-dé-şi-mìn	my sister's
kíz‿kár-dé-şi-nìn	his sister's
kíz‿kár-dé-şi-nìz	your sister
kíz‿kár-dé-şi-ni-zìn	your sister's
kíz‿kár-déş-l^{y}e-rì	his sisters
kíz-mì?	[are] they girl[s]?
kù-rúş	cent
kú-rúş-tùr	[it] is [the] penny
kúş	bird
kù-şú	his bird
kù-şúm	my bird
kù-şún	the bird's
kù-şú-núz	your bird

kʸìb-rít	match
kʸib-rì-ti-nzì	your match
lʸò-kán-tà	restaurant
lʸo-kán-tá-sì	his restaurant
ma-á-lʸė-sèf	unfortunately
mè-tín	strong, durable; (Mr.) Metin (lit. "Strong")
báy‿mė-tín-dìr	[he (it)] is Mr. Metin
bá-yàn‿mė-tín	Mrs. Metin
bá-yàn‿mė-ti-nín	Mrs. Metin's
mü-şèr-réf	honored
mü-şér-ré-f‿ól-dùm	I'm honored
ná-sìl	how
ná-sìl?	How [is she]?
né	what
né-dìr?	What is [it]?
nè-sí?	its what (what of its)?
ó	he (she, it, that)
ò-nún	*his* (*her*, *its*)
o-nún‿kíz‿kár-de-şì	a sister of hers
ó-nú-n‿is-mì	*his* name
ol-...	be; become
òl-dúm	I have been (become), I am
mü-şér-ré-f‿ól-dùm	I'm honored

ón	ten
ón-dùr	[it] is ten
ò-nú	his ten
ò-núm	my ten
ò-nu̇-núz	your ten, the ten of you
ò-nún	see *ó*
ò-tél^y	hotel
ò-tė-l^{y}ín	the hotel's
pà-rá	money
pà-rám	my money
si̍-gá-rà	cigarette(s)
si-gá-rȧ-dà	cigarettes, too
si-gá-rȧ-nìz	your cigarette
si-né-mà	movie
si-né-mȧ-dà	at the movies
síz	you
sì-zín	*your*, yours
si̍-zí-n‿i̍s-mi-nìz	*your* name
sú	water
sú-dùr	[it] is water

tóm	Tom
tóm-dùr	[it] is Tom
tò-mún	Tom's
tòm‿kár	Tom Carr
tóm‿kár-dìr	[it] is Tom Carr
u-nut-...	forget
ú-nùt-túm	I've forgotten
vár	there [is], there [are]; have
bi̍r‿kíz‿kar-de-şi̍m‿vàr	I have a sister (lit. there is a sister of mine)
vár-dìr	there is
vár-mì?	[are] there?
kar-deş-l^{y}e-ri-ni̍z‿vár-mì?	Have you any brothers? (lit. are there brothers of yours?)
yók	there [is]n't; hasn't, haven't
yók-tùr	there isn't
o-nún‿kíz‿kar-de-şi̍‿yòk-túr	she hasn't any sister (lit. there isn't any sister of hers)
o-nún‿ka-rı-si‿yók-tùr	he hasn't any wife (lit. there isn't any wife of his)
zá:t	gentleman
bú‿zà:t	this gentleman
bú‿zá:-tìn	this gentleman's

UNIT 3

WHAT'S YOUR JOB?

SECTION A—BASIC SENTENCES

To the Group Leader: Read carefully the note to the Leader preceding Section A of Unit 2. Then go through the *Basic Sentences* once, and take up the *Hints on Pronunciation.* Go through the *Basic Sentences* at least twice more individually, paying especial attention to pronunciation.

Go through the *Basic Sentences,* in unison, in the same way you did for Section A of the preceding unit. Be sure to put plenty of life into your repetition of the sentences. After you have gone through the *Basic Sentences* once in unison and have done the *Hints on Pronunciation*, come back to the *Basic Sentences.* Pay particular attention to the points of pronunciation you have just been working on and go through the sentences at least twice more individually.

1. Basic Sentences

Mr. Akyurek, Mr. Gunduz, Mr. Kurt, and Mr. Akchay apply for jobs in Mr. Carr's office.

ENGLISH EQUIVALENTS	AIDS TO LISTENING	CONVENTIONAL TURKISH SPELLING
	Mr. Carr	
Record 6A, beginning.		
gentlemen	(1) báy-làr! (2) bày-lár.	baylar
Good morning, gentlemen!	gʸù-n‿áy-dín, báy-làr!	Gün aydın, baylar!
	Gentlemen	
Good morning, Mr. Carr!	gʸù-n‿áy-dín, bày‿kár!	Gün aydın, bay Kar!

	Mr. Carr	
What [do] you want?	né‿ár-zù‿e-di-yór-su-nuz?	Ne arzu ediyorsunuz?
	Gentlemen	
work	íş.	iş
we are looking for [it]	a-rí-yó-rùz.	arıyoruz
We're looking for work.	í-ş‿á-rı-yò-rúz.	İş arıyoruz!
	Mr. Carr	
you	síz.	siz
Mr. Akyurek	bá-y‿ák-yü-rèk^{y}.	bay Akyürek
what	né?	ne?
you do	ya-pár-sı-nìz.	yaparsınız
You, Mr. Akyurek, what do you do?	síz, bá-y‿ák-yü-rèk^{y}, né‿ya-pàr-sı-niz?	Siz, bay Akyürek, ne yaparsınız?
	Mr. Akyurek	
secretarial work	k^{y}à:-tip-l^{y}ík^{y}.	kâtiplik
I do	é-dé-rìm.	ederim
I do secretarial work.	k^{y}á:-tip-l^{y}í-k^{y}‿e-dè-rim.	Kâtiplik ederim.
	Mr. Carr	
Mr. Gunduz	bày‿g^{y}ün-dúz.	bay Gündüz
what [do] you do?	né‿ya-pàr-sı-niz?	ne yaparsınız?
You, Mr. Gunduz, what do you do?	síz, bày‿g^{y}ün-dúz, né‿ya-pàr-sı-niz?	Siz, bay Gündüz, ne yaparsınız?
	Mr. Gunduz	
(night-)watchman's work	bèk^{y}-çi-l^{y}ík^{y}.	bekçilik
I do	é-dé-rìm.	ederim
I'm a night-watchman.	bék^{y}-çi-l^{y}í-k^{y}‿e-dè-rim.	Bekçilik ederim.

	Mr. Carr	
Mr. Kurt (*lit.* "*Wolf*")	bày‿kúrt.	bay Kurt
You, Mr. Kurt?	síz, bày‿kúrt?	Siz, bay Kurt?
	Mr. Kurt	
I	bén.	ben
cashier's work	vèz-ne-dár-lík.	veznedarlık
I do	yá-pá-rìm.	yaparım
I'm a cashier.	bén, véz-ne-dár-lík‿ya-pà-rím.	Ben, veznedarlık yaparım.
	Mr. Carr	
and you	vè‿síz.	ve siz
Mr. Akchay	bá-y‿ák-çày.	bay Akçay
And you, Mr. Akchay, what do you do?	vè‿síz, bá-y‿ák-çày, né‿ya-pàr-sı-niz?	Ve siz, bay Akçay, ne yaparsınız?
	Mr. Akchay	

Record 6B, beginning.

janitor's work	ha-dè-mé-l^yík^y.	hademelik
I'm a janitor.	bén ha-dé-mel^{y}í-k^y‿e-dè-rím.	Ben hademelik ederim.
	Mr. Carr	
your jobs	ìş-l^yé-ri-níz.	işleriniz
to your pleasure	hò-şú-nu-zá.	hoşunuza
do [they] go?	(1) g^yí-di-yór-mù?	gidiyormu?
	(2) g^yi-dí-yór-mù?	
Do you like your jobs?	iş-l^ye-ri-níz‿ho-şu-nu-zá‿g^yí-di-yór-mù?	İşleriniz hoşunuza gidiyormu?

Gentlemen

yes	é-vèt.	evet
to our pleasure	hò-şú-mu-zá.	hoşumuza
[they] go	g^{y}i-dí-yòr.	gidiyor
Yes, we do.	é-vèt, ho-şu-mu-zá‿g^{y}i-dí-yòr.	Evet, hoşumuza gidiyor.

Mr. Carr

these gentlemen	bù‿báy-lár.	bu baylar
These gentlemen are Mr. Kaya and Mr. Metin.	bú‿báy-làr, bày‿ká-yá, vé‿bày‿mé-tín.	Bu baylar, bay Kaya, ve bay Metin.
we	bíz.	biz
to you	sì-zé.	size
in our office	o-fì-si-miz-dé.	ofisimizde
work	íş.	iş
to give	vèr-mék^{y}.	vermek
we want	is-tí-yo-rùz.	istiyoruz
We'll give you work in our office.	bíz, si-zé‿o-fi-si-miz-dé‿íş‿ver-mé-k^{y}‿is-ti-yò-rúz.	Biz, size ofisimizde iş vermek istiyoruz.

Gentlemen

very much	çók.	çok
we thank [you]	te-şék^{y}-k^{y}ű-r‿e-dè-riz.	teşekkür ederiz
We thank you very much!	çók‿te-şék^{y}-k^{y}ű-r‿e-dè-riz!	çok teşekkür ederiz!

	Mr. Carr	
now	şím-dì.	şimdi
(to) work	ì-şé.	işe
start!	báş-lá-yı-nìz!	başlayınız!
You're welcome. You may start work now!	bìr‿şèy‿dé-yíl^y. şím-di‿i-şé‿báş-lá-yı-nìz!	Bir şey değil. Şimdi işe başlayınız!

Some time later:

	Mr. Carr	
my	bè-ním.	benim
at my house	è-vím-dé.	evimde
this evening	bú‿ák-şàm.	bu akşam
a gathering	bìr‿tóp-lán-tí.	bir toplantı
there [is]	vár.	var
There's a party this evening at my house.	bé-ní-m‿é-vím-dè bú‿ákşàm bìr‿tóp-lán-tí‿vàr.	Benim evimde bu akşam bir toplantı var.

Record 7A, beginning.

will you come?	g^{y}e-l^{y}ír-mí-si-nìz?	gelirmisiniz?
Will you come, Mr. Metin?	g^{y}e-l^{y}ír-mí-si-nìz, bày‿mé-tín?	Gelirmisiniz, bay Metin?
You, Mr. Kaya?	síz, bày‿ká-yá?	Siz, bay Kaya?
	Gentlemen	
Yes, we'll come!	é-vèt, g^{y}é-l^{y}í-rìz!	Evet, geliriz!
Thanks!	te-şèk^y-k^{y}ür-l^{y}ér!	Teşekkürler!
What time?	sá-àt‿káç-tá?	Saat kaçta?

Mr. Carr

At half past eight.	sa-ȧt‿sé-kʸi̇́z‿bu-çúk-tà.	Saat sekiz buçukta.

Gentlemen

Good-bye!	ȧl-la-há‿ıs-mȧr-la-dìk!	Allaha ısmarladık!

Mr. Carr

Good-bye!	gʸü̇-lʸé‿gʸü̇-lʸè!	Güle güle!

Before you go through the *Basic Sentences* a second time review the sound values of the following letters:

LETTER	STANDS FOR A SOUND	EXAMPLES	
a	about like *a* in *father*	bȧ-y‿ák-çày	(*Mr. Akchay*)
e	about like *e* in *pet*	é-vèt	(*yes*)
i	about like *i* in *pit*	şi̇́m-dì	(*now*)
o	about like *o* in *for*	çók	(*very*)
u	about like *u* in *push*	bù-çúk	(*half*)
ı	something like *u* in *suppose*	ya-pár-si-nìz	(*you do*)
ü	about like *i* in *pit*, pronounced with puckered lips	bày‿gʸün-dü̇́z	(*Mr. Gunduz*)
a:	about like *a* in *father* drawn out or drawled	kʸà:-ti̇́p	(*secretary*)
ç	like *ch* in *church*	çók	(*very*)
kʸ	about like *c* in *cute*	kʸà:-ti̇́p	(*secretary*)
gʸ	about like *g* in *argue*	gʸé-lʸi̇́-rìz	(*we will come*)
h	about like *h* in *hand*	hà-dé-mé	(*janitor*)
y	about like *y* in *year*	bȧ-y‿ák-çày	(*Mr. Akchay*)
lʸ	about like *li* in *million*	dè-yi̇́lʸ	([*it is*] *not*)

Remember:

‿ connects words spoken together without pause or break

ˊ marks strongest vowel

ˋ marks next strongest vowel

ˈ marks other fairly strong vowels

Then study the following:

2. Hints on Pronunciation

To the Group Leader: Follow the same procedure as for the *Hints on Pronunciation* of Unit 2. Have the group read and discuss the explanations, and then go through the *Practices* with the Guide or phonograph record.

One of the simple basic vowel sounds of Turkish which we have met in this unit is unlike any English vowel-sound. If you pronounce *dizzy* with spread lips, as one usually does in English, and then repeat it with puckered lips, you should get a vowel sound, between the *d* and the *z*, very much like Turkish *ü*.

Note: This Turkish sound is written with *ü* with two dots over it, and is not to be confused with *u*, without any dots.

Practice pronouncing *dizzy* with spread lips, then drop the *-zy*, and pronounce *diz-* first with spread lips and then with puckered lips, thus:

PRACTICE 1 **Record 7A, after 1st spiral.**

dı́z.
dǘz.
dı́z.
dǘz.
dı́z.
dǘz.
dı́z.
dǘz. dǘz. dǘz. dǘz.

The first of these is Turkish *dı́z*, 'knee', the second is Turkish *dǘz*, 'straight'. Practice the following:

PRACTICE 2 **Record 7A, after 2nd spiral.**

g^{y}ǘ-l^{y}é‿g^{y}ǘ-l^{y}è!	(*good-bye*)
g^{y}ǘn.	(*day*)
sǘt.	(*milk*)
te-şék^{y}-k^{y}ǘ-r‿e-dè-rím.	(*thank* [*you*])
tǘrk^{y}-çè.	(*Turkish*)
ǘç.	(*three*)
mǘ-şèr-réf.	(*honored*)
bá-y‿ák-yǘ-rèk^{y}.	(*Mr. Akyurek*)
bày‿g^{y}ǘn-dǘz.	(*Mr. Gunduz*)

It is very probable that your Guide, in pronouncing words for you to mimic, will often pronounce them one way when he says them very slowly, and a little differently when he says them quite fast. I on't be disturbed, for that is quite natural. Try to imitate him when he speaks rather fast, rather than when he is "on his good behaviour", because the faster way is the way people usually talk.

Now review Turkish *ı* in the following practice:

PRACTICE 3 **Record 7A, after 3rd spiral.**

àl-t***ı́***.	(*six*)
ày-d***ı́***n.	(*bright*)
báş-lá-y*ı*-n*ı̀*z!	(*start!*)
tòp-lán-t***ı́***.	(*gathering*)
véz-ne-dàr-l***ı́***k.	(*cashier's work*)

Now go through the *Basic Sentences* once more individually, and with your book open. As you repeat after your Guide, keep your eyes on the *Aids to Listening* and note in particular the examples of the sounds discussed. Again do not hesitate to ask your Guide to repeat if you are uncertain about any sound.

Finally, go through the *Basic Sentences* at least once again individually. Keep your book closed, listen carefully to your Guide and make sure that your pronunciation satisfies him.

3. Check Yourself

Did you pronounce *ç* like *ch* in *chin*?
Did you pronounce g^y like *g* in *argue*?
Did you distinguish carefully between *u* spoken with puckered lips, and *ı* spoken with spread lips?

Did you pronounce *ü* with puckered lips, and *i* with spread lips?

Did you note carefully the values of all the other sounds which occur in this unit?

Section B—Word Study and Review of Basic Sentences

1. Word Study (Individual Study)

As in Section B. 1 of Unit 2, read the words and expressions in each list and make sure that you understand the meaning of the Turkish. Then read the comments which follow each list. When you have finished the *Word Study* ask other members of the group about points which are not clear to you.

1. *Turkish equivalents of English "he is doing", etc.*

In the *Basic Sentences* of this and previous units we have seen these forms: *ȧn-lı-yór-mu̇-su-nu̇z?* '[do] you understand?', *ȧn-lí-yo-ru̇m* 'I understand', *ȧn-lá-mı-yò-ru̇m* 'I [do] not understand', *ȧr-zú‿ė-di-yòr-su-nu̇z* 'you want', *g^yė-çi̇́-yòr* '[it] is passing', *bȧş-lí-yòr* '[it] is beginning', *a-rí-yȯ-ru̇z* 'we are looking for [it]', *g^yi-dí-yòr* '[it] is going', *i̇́s-ti̇́-yo-ru̇z* 'we want'. If we tabulate these with others, we get:

	Column I			Column II	
			Group I		
i	g^yit- . . .	'*go*'	:	g^yi̇́-di̇́-yòr	'[*it*] *is going*'
e	ar-zu‿et- . . .	'*wish*'	:	ȧr-zú‿ė-di-yòr-su-nu̇z	'*you wish*'
ı	—	—	:	—	—

a	yap- . . .	*'do'*	:	ya-pí-yò-rùm	*'I am doing'*
u	ko-nuṣ- . . .	*'talk'*	:	kó-nu-ṣú-yò-rùz	*'we are talking'*
o	—	—	:	—	—
			Group II		
e (i)	is-te- . . .	*'want'*	:	is-tí-yór-su-nùz	*'you want'*
ı (a)	a-ra- . . .	*'look for'*	:	a-rí-yò-rùz	*'we are looking for [it]'*
a (a)	baṣ-la- . . .	*'start'*	:	báṣ-lí-yòr	*'[it] is starting'*

If we compare Column I with Column II, and Group I with II, we see that:

1. the part of the forms in Column II which means '[he] is doing', and the like, is the ending *-i-yor*, *-i-yor-su-nuz*, *-ı-yo-rum*, *-u-yo-ruz*, and so on;
2. in Group I, the endings are added directly to the *roots*, listed in Column I;

Note: The part of the forms in Column II which means 'go', 'wish', and so on, is called the *root*, the part from which the rest "grows", or to which we add the endings. Such roots, which we shall mark in our *Finder Lists* and *Vocabularies* with the hyphen and the dots, thus:

yap- . . . 'do, make'

and words made from them by certain endings, and these endings themselves, we shall call *verb roots*, *verbs*, and *verb endings*.

3. in Group II, however, we see that the last vowel of the root (is-te- . . ., a-ra- . . ., baṣ-la- . . .) is lost before the first vowel of these endings (-i-, -ı-, -u-):

baṣ-l(a)- . . . : báṣ-lí-yòr;

4. the endings in Column II:

-i-yor
-i-yor-su-nuz
-ı-yo-rum
-u-yo-ruz
-ı-yo-ruz
-ı-yor

do not all *begin* alike; the initial vowel (-i-, -ı-, -u-) is chosen according to the rules of vowel harmony, *-i-* after *i* or *e*, *-ı-* after *ı* or *a*, *-u-* after *u* or *o*;

5. the endings in Column II do not all *end* alike; we note that the difference is a difference in *person* ("I", "you", "he", "we"), so the last part of these endings (*-su-nuz*, *-um*, *-uz*) is called a *personal* ending;
6. the remaining part of the ending is *-i-yor-*, *-ı-yor-*, *-u-yor-*;
7. the *strongest vowel* (marked ´) is the first vowel of this ending:

Note 1: In the "you" form, however, one frequently hears not only *is-ti-yór-su-nùz*, but also *is-ti-yór-sù-nùz*.

Note 2: Not only in the "you" form, but also in other forms, when they come at the end of a phrase or sentence, the strongest vowel of the form is likewise the *o*, the second vowel of this ending, and it is the second strongest (`) vowel of the phrase:

is-tí-yòr *but* né‿is-ti-yòr?

We note that the forms with this *-i-yor-*, *-ı-yor-*, *-u-yor-* ending are most often equivalent to English forms such as 'we are talking', 'I am doing', and so forth. They refer, therefore, to a temporary or momentary action, so we shall call them *momentary* forms and endings.

2. *Turkish equivalents of English "he does", etc.*

Not all of the verb forms which we have seen thus far have been momentary forms. Among others, we have seen these:

te-şék^y-k^{y}ű-r‿e-dè-rím	*'I thank [you]'*
áf-fe-dèr-si-níz	*'(you will) excuse [me]'*
dè-nír	*'[it] is said'*
ve-rír-mi-si-níz?	*'will you give [me]?'*
kàl-kár	*'[it] leaves'*
dő́r-dé-dèr	*'[it] makes four'*
ya-pár-si-nìz	*'you do'*
yá-pá-rìm	*'I do'*
te-şék^y-k^{y}ű-r‿e-dè-ríz	*'we thank [you]!'*
g^{y}e-l^{y}ír-mi-si-níz?	*'will you come?'*
g^{y}è-l^{y}í-ríz	*'we will come'*

If we tabulate these and others, we get:

	Column I			Column II	
			Group I		
	is-te- . . .	*'want'*	:	ís-tér-si-nìz	*'you want'*
	a-ra- . . .	*'look for'*	:	à-rár	'[*he*] *looks for* [*it*]'
	baş-la- . . .	*'start'*	:	báş-lá-rìz	*'we start'*
			Group II		
e	gʸelʸ- . . .	*'come'*	:	gʸé-lʸí-rìz	*'we will come'*
u	ko-nuş- . . .	*'talk'*	:	kó-nu-şúr-sú-nùz	*'you talk'*
			Group III		
i	gʸit- . . .	*'go'*	:	gʸì-dér	'[*he*] *goes*'
e	et- . . .	*'do'*	:	é-dé-rìm	*'I do'*
a	yap- . . .	*'do'*	:	yá-pá-rìz	*'we do'*

If we compare Column I with Column II, and Group I with II and III, we see that

1. the part of the forms in Column II which means '[he] does', and the like, is the ending *-r-sı-nız*, *-r*, *-rız*, *-i-riz*, *-ur-su-nuz*, *-er*, *-e-rim*, *-a-rız* and so on;
2. if we take off the personal endings (*-si-niz*, *-ız*, *-iz*, *-su-nuz*, *-im*, etc.), we have a number of different endings left (*-r-*, *-r*, *-ir-*, *-ur-*, *-er-*, *-ar-*);
3. the simple *-r-* ending, as in Group I, comes after roots which end in a *vowel* (*is-te- . . .*, *a-ra- . . .*, *baş-la- . . .*);

Note: The *vowels* are *i*, *e*, *ü*, *ö*, *ı*, *a*, *u*, *o* short or long.

4. the *-ir-*, *-ır-*, *-ur-* ending, as in Group II, after *some* of the roots which end in a consonant;

Note: A *consonant* is any sound other than a vowel.

5. the different forms of this *-ir-*, *-ır-*, *-ur-* ending are distributed according to the type of vowel harmony, which we met in Unit 2: *-ir-* after *i* or *e*, *-ır-* after *ı* or *a*, *-ur-* after *u* or *o*;

Note This type of vowel harmony we shall call *Vowel Harmony Type I.*

6. the *-er-*, *-ar-* ending, as in Group III, likewise after *some* of the roots which end in a consonant; this ending follows a different type of vowel harmony:

   -er- after *i*, *e*, *ü*, or *ö*

   -ar- after *ı*, *a*, *u*, or *o*

Note: We shall call this type *Vowel Harmony Type II.*

7. the strongest vowel (marked ´ı) is either that of the ending (-ír-, -íř-, -úr-, -ér-, -ár-), or the one just before the ending (-´-r-) (when the root ends in a vowel):

   yap- . . . yà-pár
   or
   iste- . . . is-tér

8. you have to learn which of the roots ending in a consonant are followed by *-ir-*, *-ır-*, *-ur-* and which are followed by *-er-*, *-ar-*; in the *Finder Lists* of this and following units and in the general vocabularies, we shall indicate with each verb root ending in a consonant, which of the two sets of endings is to be used, thus:

te-şekʸ-kʸü-r‿et- . . . (aor. *-er-*)	'*thank*'
affet- . . . (aor. *-er-*)	'*excuse*'
den- . . . (aor. *-ir-*)	'*be said*'
ver- . . . (aor. *-ir-*)	'*give*'
kalk- . . . (aor. *-ar-*)	'*leave*'

and so on.

We note that the forms with these endings (*-r-*, *-ir-*, *-ır-*, *-ur-*, *-er-*, *-ar-*) are most often equivalent to English forms such as 'we do', 'he does', and so forth. They refer to a general fact, to something true without relation to any particular time. We shall call them *aorist* forms and endings.

3. *Turkish equivalents of English "the"*

In this and the two preceding units we have seen the following:

Column I		*Column II*
	Group I	
gʸűn	:	'[*the*] *day*'
ò-télʸ	:	'[*the*] *hotel*'
is-tàs-yón	:	'[*the*] *railroad station*'
áp-tèst-há:-né	:	'[*the*] *toilet*'
si-né-mà	:	'[*the*] *movie*'

Group II

ì-k^{y}í	:	*'two'*
dò-kúz	:	*'nine'*
yè-dí	:	*'seven'*

Group III

ì-k^{y}i-yí	:	*'two (lit. the two)'*
dò-kú-zú	:	*'nine (lit. the nine)'*
yè-di-yí	:	*'seven (lit. the seven)'*

In Group I, we see that there is nothing in the Turkish in Column I which corresponds to the "the" in the English in Column II.

If we compare Groups II and III, however, we see that the forms in Column I of Group III are longer than the ones in Column I of Group II; those of Group III have endings *-yi*, *-u*, *-yi*. We note that these endings correspond to a "the" in the literal meaning in English. We have met these forms only in phrases such as

sa-à-t‿i-k^{y}i-yi‿ón‿g^{y}é-çi-yòr.

'It's ten past two (lit. the two).'

sa-àt‿do-ku-zù‿béş‿g^{y}é-çi-yòr.

'It's five past nine (lit. the nine)'.

sa-àt‿ye-di-yi‿béş‿g^{y}e-çé‿kàlkàr.

'It leaves at five past seven (lit. the seven)'.

We shall discuss these (ì-k^{y}i-yí, dò-kú-zú, yè-di-yí) and other similar forms later.

With this exception, English "the" is *not expressed* in Turkish.

4. *Turkish equivalents of English "a, an"*

In this and the preceding units we have seen these or similar forms:

Column I		*Column II*
	Group I	
l^{y}ó-kán-tà	:	'[*a*] *restaurant'*
ò-tél^y	:	'[*a*] *hotel'*
si-gá-rà	:	'[*a*] *cigarette'*

Group II

bir‿lʸó-kán-tà	:	*'a restaurant'*
bir‿si-gá-rà	:	*'a cigarette'*
bir‿kár-déṣ	:	*'a brother'*

Group III

bir‿lʸo-kàn-tá	:	*'one restaurant'*
bír‿si-gà-rá	:	*'one cigarette'*
bír‿kár-dèṣ	:	*'one brother'*

If we compare Columns I and II in Group I, we see that there is nothing in the Turkish in Column I which corresponds to the "a" in the English of Column II. Just as with "the", Turkish frequently has no equivalent of English "a, an".

In Group II however, we see that English "a" is equivalent to Turkish *bir* (*bìr*).

In Group III, we see that English "one" is equivalent to Turkish *bír*.

Compare:

bìr‿kár-déṣ 'a brother'
with
bír‿kár-dèṣ 'one brother'

We see that the Turkish equivalent of English "a, an" is *bìr* or *bir* with *next strongest* or *third strongest* vowel, and that the Turkish equivalent of English "one" is *bír* with the strongest vowel.

2. Covering English and Turkish of Word Study (Individual Study)

Before you leave the *Word Study*, cover the English equivalents in each list and make sure that you know the meaning of every Turkish expression. Then cover the Turkish and see if you can say each Turkish expression when you are looking only at the English.

3. Review of Basic Sentences

Review the first half of the *Basic Sentences*. Repeat individually with books closed. Work always to perfect your pronunciation; keep the meaning in mind; and observe examples of the points in *Word Study* you have just covered.

1. Review of Basic Sentences (*Cont.*)

Review the second half of the *Basic Sentences*. Follow the procedure suggested above.

2. Covering the English of Basic Sentences (Individual Study)

Go back to the *Basic Sentences* in Section A, cover the English and test yourself by reading the Turkish, just as you did in Section C of the previous unit. If you are not sure about the meaning of any words or phrases, when you have finished reading the *Basic Sentences* aloud, uncover the English and look up their meaning. Keep this up until you know all the meanings completely.

3. Word Study Review (Individual Study)

Work through the following exercises. Do not write anything down. If you cannot do the work rapidly, review again the *Word Study*. Be prepared to do what is required when the Leader calls on you. Always repeat the entire expression, phrase or sentence as you work.

1. Complete the following sentences by filling in the blanks with the proper forms of the *momentary* endings:
   1. àh-mét   yá-váş‿ya-váş‿ko-núş . . .
   2. şa-rá-p‿i̍-ç . . . -mú-su-nùz?
   3. şi̍m-di‿báş-l(a) . . . ùm.
   4. í-ş‿á-r(a) . . . úz.
   5. bi̍r‿kúrt‿g^{y}é-l^y . . . , dé-yíl^y-mi̍?
2. Complete the following with the proper forms of the *aorist* endings:
   1. o-fi̍-si-mi̍z-dé   i-şé‿sa-át‿káç-tá‿baş-là- . . .iz?
   2. ét‿yé- . . . i̍z, kah-vé‿i̍-ç . . . i̍z.
   3. türk^y-çe‿kó-nuş . . . -mú-su-nùz, bày‿kár?
   4. bày‿g^{y}ün-düz   né‿yá-p . . . ?
   5. o-fi̍-si-ni̍z-dé   káç‿pa-rá‿ve-r . . . -l^{y}èr?

4. What Would You Say? (Individual Study)

In the following exercise you have certain situations presented for which you are to choose the correct expression in Turkish. Read the situation, repeat aloud all of the solutions for each situation, and then indicate for the next class meeting the answer which you consider the most appropriate.

1. *Several men come into your office one morning. You say:*
   a. ak-şam-la-rı-niz‿há-yır-lí‿ól-sùn!
   b. g^{y}ǜ-n‿áy-dín, báy-làr!

2. *You then ask, politely:*
   a. né‿is-ti-yòr-su-núz?
   b. né‿ár-zù‿e-di-yór-su-nuz?

3. *The men answer:*
   a. í-ş‿á-rı-yò-rúz.
   b. káh-vé‿is-ti-yò-rúz.
   c. bir‿şèy‿dé-yil^{y}.

4. *After noting their names, you turn to Mr. Akyurek, and ask:*
   a. si-zin‿kiz‿kar-de-şi-niz‿vár-mì?
   b. né‿ya-pàr-sı-niz?
   c. si-zí-n‿is-mi-niz né-dìr?

5. *Mr. Akyurek answers:*
   a. k^{y}ib-rí-t‿is-ti-yò-rúm.
   b. k^{y}á:-tip-l^{y}í-k^{y}‿e-dè-rim.

6. *You then turn to Mr. Gunduz and ask:*
   a. sü-t‿is-ti-yór-mú-su-nùz?
   b. síz év-l^{y}í-mi-si-nìz?
   c. síz né‿ya-pàr-sı-niz?

7. *Mr. Gunduz replies:*
   a. é-vèt, sǘ-t‿is-ti-yò-rúm.
   b. bék^{y}-çi-l^{y}í-k^{y}‿e-dè-rim.
   c. é-vèt, kı-zi-m‿év-l^{y}í-dìr.

8. *Turning to Mr. Kurt, you say:*
   a. ye-mék^{y}‿ye-mé-k^{y}‿is-ti-yór-mú-su-nùz?
   b. vè‿síz, bày‿kúrt?

9. *Mr. Kurt answers:*
   a. bén, véz-ne-dár-lí-k‿e-dè-rim.
   b. é-vèt, hó-şu-má‿g^{y}i-di-yòr.

10. *Turning to Mr. Akchay, you ask:*
    a. síz, bá-y‿ák-çày, né‿ya-pàr-sı-niz?
    b. né‿á-rı-yòr-su-núz?

11. *Mr. Akchay replies:*
    a. bén, ha-dé-me-l^{y}í-k^{y}‿e-dè-rim.
    b. çók‿te-şék^{y}-k^{y}ǘ-r‿e-dè-rim!

12. *You then ask them:*
    a. si-zi-n‿ar-ka-daş-la-rı-niz‿vár-mì?
    b. bú‿iş-l^{y}é-ri-nìz ho-şu-nu-zá‿g^{y}í-di-yór-mù?

13. *Mr. Gunduz, speaking for them all:*
    a. é-vèt, hó-şu-mu-zá‿g^{y}í-di-yòr.
    b. há-yìr, kiz‿kar-de-şi-miz‿yók-tùr.

14. *Now Mr. Kaya and Mr. Metin come in and you introduce the others to them:*
   a. bú‿bảy-làr bả-y‿ák-çày vẻ‿bày‿gʸün-dűz.
   b. bú‿bảy-làr bày‿kả-yá vẻ‿bày‿mé-tín.

15. *You then explain to the job applicants:*
   a. si-zi-n‿ár-ka-dåş-lá-rı-níz-dìr.
   b. si-zė‿şím-dì o-fi-si-miz-dė‿íş‿ver-mė-kʸ‿is-ti-yò-rúz.

16. *Pleased, they say:*
   a. gʸü-lʸé‿gʸü-lʸè, bày‿kár!
   b. çók‿te-şėkʸ-kʸű-r‿e-dè-riz.

17. *You say politely:*
   a. síz bú-ra-da‿né‿á-rı-yòr-su-núz?
   b. lʸút-fèn, yả-váş‿ya-váş‿ko-nù-şu-núz.
   c. bír‿şèy‿dé-yílʸ!

18. *Bidding them start work right away, you say:*
   a. **bú‿trèn** sa-át‿káç-tá‿kál-kàr?
   b. **şim-di‿båş-lá-yı-nìz!**

19. *When they have gone, you turn to the others and say:*
   a. bé-ní-m‿é-vim-dè bú‿ák-şàm bír‿tóp-lán-tí‿vàr.
   b. si-zín‿kả-rı-lá-rı-nìz ná-sìl?

20. *You ask whether they are coming, and they answer:*
   a. şà-ráp ho-şu-nu-zá‿gʸi-di-yór-mù?
   b. é-vèt, gʸé-lʸi-rìz! te-şékʸ-kʸùr-lʸér!

21. *When they ask what time the party starts, you answer:*
   a. sa-át‿sé-kʸíz‿bu-çúk-tà.
   b. sá-àt‿bír.

22. *They say, as they go out:*
   a. ét vė‿ekʸ-mékʸ‿yė-mèkʸ **çó-k‿i-yì-dír.**
   b. ál-la-há‿ıs-már-la-dìk!

23. *You answer:*
   a. si-né-mà sa-át‿káç-tá‿**báş-lı-yòr?**
   b. gʸü-lʸé‿gʸü-lʸè!

Section D—Listening In

1. What Did You Say?

To the Group Leader: Follow the same procedure as for Section D. 1. of Unit 2. Call on different students (not in any fixed order) to give their answers in Turkish for the exercise *What Would You Say?* in Section C. 4. of this unit. Encourage them to give the answers directly and not from the books, if possible. Then check on the students' knowledge of the meaning in English of the different expressions in Turkish.

Go back to the last exercises in the preceding section. The Leader will call for your answers in Turkish for the exercises. If you can, give the correct answers without reading from the book. Other members of the group will criticize the choice made if they disagree. The Leader will then call for the English equivalents of all the expressions in the exercises.

2. Word Study Check-Up

To the Group Leader: Follow the same procedure as for this part of Section D of Unit 2. Call on various students for the correct Turkish for the English equivalents of the expressions given in the *Word Study*. Make sure that all the students have learned the material thoroughly.

As a final exercise, call for the answers to the exercises in *Word Study Review*, in Section C. 3.

Go back to the *Word Study* in Section B. The Leader will ask different members of the group to give the correct Turkish for the English equivalents of the expressions you went over in the *Word Study*. Be sure you are able to give the correct form without having to read it from the book. If you have any difficulty, review the *Word Study* thoroughly. As a final check the Leader will call for your answers to the exercises in the *Word Study Review* (Sec. C. 3).

3. Listening In

To the Group Leader: Follow the same procedure as for *Listening In* in Section D. 3, of Unit 2. Check up on meaning at the end of each conversation on the first time through; then, after the second time through, assign parts and have the students read the conversations.

Keep your book closed while the Guide reads the following conversations, or while they are played on the phonograph, and repeat the Turkish immediately after hearing it. At the end of each conversation, check up on the meaning of any word or phrase about which you are in doubt, either by asking some other member of the group or by going back to the *Basic Sentences* if no one knows.

Go through the conversations again, with your books open, being sure to imitate carefully and to keep in mind the meaning of everything you are saying. Then take turns speaking the parts. Make the conversations real. Say your part as though you meant it.

1. *Applying for jobs.*

Record 7A, after 4th spiral.

[bày-lár][1]—	g^{y}ù-n‿áy-dín!	Gün aydın!
bày‿kár—	g^{y}ù-n‿áy-dín! né‿ár-zù‿e-di-yór-su-nuz, báy-làr!	Gün aydın! Ne arzu ediyorsunuz, baylar!
bá-y‿ák-yü-rèk^y—	í-ş‿á-rı-yò-rúz, bày‿kár.	İş arıyoruz, bay Kar.
	bé-ní-m‿is-mìm is-ma-i-l^y‿ák-yü-rèk^y.	Benim ismim İsmail Akyürek.
	bén k^{y}á:-tip-l^{y}í-k^y‿e-dè-rim.	Ben kâtiplik ederim.
	si-zin‿k^{y}a:-ti-bi-niz‿vár-mì?	Sizin kâtibiniz varmı?
bày‿kár—	há-yìr, şim-di‿bé-nìm‿k^{y}a:-ti-bim‿yók.	Hayır, şimdi benim kâtibim yok.
bá-y‿ák-yü-rèk^y—	bú àr-ka-dá-şím, bày‿kúrt.	Bu arkadaşım, bay Kurt.
	ó véz-ne-dár-lí-k‿é-dèr.	O veznedarlık eder.
bày‿kúrt—	bén-dé‿i-ş‿á-rı-yò-rúm, bày‿kár.	Ben de iş arıyorum, bay Kar.
	si-zin‿vez-ne-da-rı-niz‿vár-mì?	Sizin veznedarınız varmı?
bày‿kár—	há-yìr, yók.	Hayır, yok.
	si-zi-n‿is-mi-níz‿nè-dir?	Sizin isminiz nedir?
bá-y‿ák-çày—	bé-ní-m‿is-mìm hak-ki‿ák-çày.	Benim ismim Hakkı Akçay.
	bén ha-dé-me-l^{y}í-k^y‿e-dè-rim.	Ben hademelik ederim.
	bir‿ha-de-mé‿is-ti-yór-mú-su-nùz?	Bir hademe istiyormusunuz?
bày‿kár—	é-vèt, há-de-mé-dé‿is-ti-yò-rúm.	Evet, hademe de istiyorum.

2. *They get their jobs.*

Record 7B, beginning.

bày‿kár—	si-zi-n‿is-mi-níz‿nè-dir?	Sizin isminiz nedir?
bày‿g^{y}ün-dúz—	ìs-mím á-l^{y}ì‿g^{y}ün-dúz.	İsmim Ali Gündüz.

[1]Not on record.

bày‿kár—	bày‿g^{y}ün-dǘz, síz‿né‿ya-pàr-sı-nìz?	Bay Gündüz, siz ne yaparsınız?
bày‿g^{y}ün-dǘz—	bén bék^{y}-çi-l^{y}í-k^{y}‿e-dè-rìm.	Ben bekçilik ederim.
bày‿kár—	çó-k‿ì-yì!	Çok iyi!
	be-nìm‿bék^{y}-çím-dé‿yòk.	Benim bekçim de yok.
	bày‿ká-yá, bày‿mé-tín, bú‿báy-làr i-ş‿á-rı-yór-làr.	Bay Kaya, bay Metin, bu baylar is arıyorlar.
	bú‿o-fis-té‿ìş‿vár-mì?	Bu ofiste iş varmı?
bày‿ká-yá—	é-vèt, bày‿kár, ìş‿vár.	Evet, bay Kar, iş var.
bày‿kár—	çó-k‿ì-yì, bìz‿si-zé‿íş‿ver-mé-k^{y}‿is-ti-yò-rúz.	Çok iyi, biz size iş vermek istiyoruz.
bá-y‿ák-yü-rèk^{y}—	çók‿te-şék^{y}-k^{y}ǘ-r‿e-dè-rìz!	Çok teşekkür ederiz!
bày‿kár—	bìr‿şèy‿dé-yil^{y}. şím-di‿i-şé‿báş-lá-yı-nìz!	Bir şey değil. Şimdi işe başlayınız!
bày-lár—	ál-la-há‿ıs-már-la-dìk!	Allaha ısmarladık!
bày‿kár—	g^{y}ü-l^{y}é‿g^{y}ü-l^{y}è!	Güle güle!

3. *Invitations.*

bày‿kár—	e-vim-dé‿bú‿ak-şám‿bìr‿tóp-lán-tí‿vàr.	Evimde bu akşam bir toplantı var.
	bày‿ká-yá, bày‿mé-tín, sìz-de‿g^{y}e-l^{y}ír-mì-si-niz?	Bay Kaya, bay Metin, siz de gelirmisiniz?
bày‿ká-yá—	é-vèt, si-zìn‿top-lan-tı-la-rı-niz‿çók‿hó-şu-má‿g^{y}ì-dèr!	Evet, sizin toplantılarınız çok hoşuma gider!
bày‿mé-tín—	sá-àt‿káç-tá?	Saat kaçta?
bày‿kár—	sa-át‿sé-k^{y}íz‿bu-çúk-tà.	Saat sekiz buçukta.
bày-lár—	ál-la-há‿ıs-már-la-dìk!	Allaha ısmarladık!
bày‿kár—	g^{y}ü-l^{y}é‿g^{y}ü-l^{y}è!	Güle güle.

4. *Fatma is invited to a party.*

à-l^{y}í—	ná-sil-sı-nìz, fát-mà?	Nasılsınız, Fatma?
fàt-má—	çó-k‿ì-yí-yìm.	Çok iyiyim.

à-l^{y}í—	bú‿ak-şám‿bir‿şéy‿yá-pı-yór-mú-su-nùz?	Bu akşam bir şey yapıyormusunuz?
fàt-má—	há-yìr. bi-r‿i-şim‿yók.	Hayır, bir işim yok.
à-l^{y}í—	bú‿ak-şám‿ev-dé‿bir‿tóp-lán-tí‿vàr.	Bu akşam evde bir toplantı var.
	g^{y}e-l^{y}ír-mi-si-nìz?	Gelirmisiniz?
fàt-má—	te-şék^y-k^{y}ű-r‿e-dè-rim. g^{y}é-l^{y}í-rìm.	Teşekkür ederim. Gelirim.
	is-ma-il^y-de‿g^{y}é-l^{y}i-yór-mù?	İsmail de geliyormu?
à-l^{y}í—	é-vèt. g^{y}é-l^{y}í-yòr.	Evet, geliyor.
fàt-má—	bú‿top-lan-ti‿sá-àt‿káç-tá¿	Bu toplantı saat kaçta?
à-l^{y}í—	sa-át‿ón‿bu-çúk-tà.	Saat on buçukta.

5. *At the party.*

hàk-kí—	mér-há-bà, is-má-ìl^y!	Merhaba, İsmail.
ìs-má-íl^y—	mér-há-bà, hák-kì!	Merhaba, Hakkı!
hàk-kí—	top-lan-ti‿ho-şu-nu-zá‿g^{y}i-di-yór-mù?	Toplantı hoşunuza gidiyormu?
ìs-má-íl^y—	é-vèt. çók! kız-lár-dá‿ho-şu-má‿g^{y}i-di-yòr!	Evet. Çok! Kizlar da hoşuma gidiyor!
hàk-kí—	bé-ním-dè! ó‿kiz‿év-l^{y}í-mi?	Benim de! O kız evlimi?
ìs-má-íl^y—	é-vèt, bé-nìm‿ká-rím!	Evet, benim karım!

Section E—Conversation

1. Covering the Turkish of Basic Sentences (Individual Study)

Just as you did in Section E of Unit 2, go back to the *Basic Sentences* of this unit, cover up the Turkish and test yourself to see how many words and phrases you can say in Turkish when you are looking only at the English.

2. Vocabulary Check-Up

To the Group Leader: As in Unit 2, go around the class calling on various students and asking them

"tü̂rkʸ-çè-dè ...... ná-sı̇l‿dė-nı̇̀r?"

for the English equivalents in the *Basic Sentences,* with their books closed. If any student does not answer in a reasonable time, do not allow hemming and hawing; call on another student. Make sure that every student speaks loud enough so that all can hear. Do not allow any mumbling. Any student who cannot give satisfactory answers needs more review of the *Basic Sentences.*

As you did in Unit 2, supply the Turkish expressions for the English equivalents in the *Basic Sentences,* when the Leader calls on you. Give your answers in a clear, loud voice, so that everyone can hear you.

3. Conversation

To the Group Leader: Follow the same procedure as for Section E. 3, of Unit 2. Have the students converse, first following closely the model of the conversations outlined below and then changing the situations slightly.

As you did in the Conversation in Section E. 3, of Unit 2, first go through the conversations outlined below, taking turns. As soon as you can speak the parts smoothly, pass to acting them out in front of the group; keep this up until you can do it easily and smoothly.

You can then change the situations somewhat, and introduce more material from the previous units. Use your imagination in thinking up various combinations of situations. For example, when one person meets another, they can talk about their families, their friends, and their work, and then one can invite the other to go to a restaurant; when they are at the restaurant, one of them can ask the other what he wants, order food, and then pay for it. Or you can have a conversation in which two persons talk about their friends and their friend's work, parents, brothers and sisters, children, and so forth.

1. Applying for a job.
   Mr. Akyurek enters and greets Mr. Carr who asks what he wishes. Mr. Akyurek explains and Mr. Carr asks him what he does. They come to an agreement and Mr. Akyurek gets the job, thanks him, and takes his leave.

2. Invitation to a party.
   Mr. Kaya greets Mr. Carr who returns the greeting and asks how he is. Mr. Kaya answers, thanking him. Mr. Carr explains that he's giving a party and asks Mr. Kaya to come. Mr. Kaya accepts, inquires about the hour, compliments Mr. Carr on his parties, and takes his leave.

3. Meeting on the street.

Mr. Metin meets Mr. Kurt on the street. They exchange greetings, ask about each other's wives, look at their watches, comment on the time, and decide to go to eat. At the restaurant they order a meal, commenting on the wine or the beer, pay the check, and take their leave of each other.

SECTION F—CONVERSATION (*Cont.*)

1. Conversation (*Cont.*)

Continue the conversations started in Section E. If necessary to make the conversations smoother and more successful, review Section E. 1 and 2.

2. Questions and Answers

To the Group Leader: Follow instructions as outlined in Unit 2, Section E. 2. Note that from this unit on most of the questions refer directly to the *Listening In*, or use it as a starting point. It is recommended that you have the class go quickly through the *Listening In* once more before taking up these questions.

Take turns asking and answering the following questions. Ask them of other students and of the Guide. Vary them as far as your vocabulary will permit. Before starting, run quickly through the *Listening In* of this unit once more. You will note that from here on these questions are based directly on or closely related to the *Listening In* of each unit.

1.[1] 1. bá-y‿ák-yǘ-rèk^{y} né‿á-rı-yòr?
2. né‿yá-pàr?
3. bày‿kúrt né‿yá-pàr?
4. báy‿ka-rin‿vez-ne-da-ri‿vár-mì?
5. o-nún‿ha-de-me-si-de‿yók-mù?

2. 6. o-nún‿bek^{y}-çi-si‿vár-mì?
7. o-fis-té‿iş‿vár-mì?

3. 8. báy‿ká-rín‿tóp-lán-tı-la-rì báy‿ka-ya-nin‿ho-şu-ná‿g^{y}i-dér-mì?
9. bú‿tóp-lán-tì sá-àt‿káç-tá?

---

[1]Numbers refer to the conversations of the *Listening In*. Questions 1–5, for example, are based on the material in the first conversation (1. Applying for jobs), 6–7 on the second conversation, and so on.

4. 10. fàt-má bú‿ák-ṣàm bi̍r‿ṣéy‿yá-pı-yór-mù?
11. sí̇z bi̍r‿ṣéy‿yá-pı-yór-mú-su-nùz?
12. á-lʸi-ní̇n‿tóp-lán-tı-sì sá-àt‿káç-tá?
13. si̍z-de‿gʸé-lʸi-yór-mú-su-nùz?

5. 14. is-ma-i-lʸí̇-n‿ár-ka-da-ṣí-dà ó-ra-dà-mi?
15. tòp-lán-tí hak-kı-nin‿ho-ṣu-ná‿gʸi̍-di-yór-mù?
16. ne-lʸér-dé‿ho-ṣu-ná‿gʸi̍-di-yòr?
17. sì-zí̇n?
18. bú-ra-da‿türkʸ-çe‿kó-nu-ṣú-yór-làr-mi?

FINDER LIST

This finder list has all the new words and expressions used in this unit. These as well as those of the previous two units, are words and expressions which by this time you should know quite well.

ák-çày	(Mr.) Akchay (lit. "Whitebrook")
bá-y‿ák-çày	Mr. Akchay
ák-yü̍-rèkʸ	(Mr.) Akyurek (lit. "Whiteheart")
bá-y‿ák-yü̍-rèkʸ	Mr. Akyurek
a-ra- . . .	look for
à-rár	[he] looks for [it]
á-rí-yòr	[he] is looking for [it]
a-rí-yór-làr	they are looking for [it]
á-rı-yór-sú-nùz	you are looking for [it]
a-rí-yó-rùz	we are looking for [it]
á-rí-yòr, etc.	see *a-ra-* . . .
baş-la- . . .	start
báṣ-lá-rìz	we start
báṣ-lá-yı-nìz!	start!
i-ṣé‿báṣ-lá-yı-nìz!	begin work!
báṣ-lí-yo-rùm	I am starting

báy	Mr., gentleman
bá-y‿ák-çày	Mr. Akchay
bá-y‿ák-yü̇-rèk^y	Mr. Akyurek
bày‿g^{y}ün-dǘz	Mr. Gunduz
bày‿kúrt	Mr. Kurt
bày-lár	gentlemen
bèk^y-çí	(night-)watchman
bèk^y-çi̇-l^{y}ík^y	(night-)watchman's work
bék^y-çi-l^{y}í-k^y‿e-dè-rım	I do (night-)watchman's work
bèk^y-çím	my (night-)watchman
bék^y-çím-dè	my (night-)watchman, too
bèk^y-çi̇-sí	his (night-)watchman
bén	I
bè-ním	my
bé-ním-dè	mine, too
bíz	we
çók	very [much]
çó-k‿i̇-yì	very good, very well
çók‿te-şék^y-k^{y}ǘ-r‿e-dè-ríz!	we thank [you] very much!
díz	knee
dǘz	straight
et- . . . (aor. *-er-*)	do
ė-dé-rìm	I do
ė-dé-rìz	we do

év	house
è-vím	my house
ė-vim-dé	at my house
èv-l^{y}í	married
ėv-l^{y}í-mi-si-nìz?	[are] you married?
g^{y}el^y- . . . (aor. *-ir-*)	come
g^{y}ė-l^{y}í-rìz	we'll come
g^{y}e-l^{y}ír-mi-si-nìz?	will you come?
g^{y}ė-l^{y}í-yòr	[he] is coming
g^{y}ė-l^{y}i-yór-mù?	is [he] coming?
g^{y}it- . . . (aor. *-er-*)	go
g^{y}ì-dér	[it] goes (generally)
g^{y}i-dér-mì?	[does it] go?
g^{y}i-dí-yòr	[it] goes (this once)
g^{y}i-dí-yór-mù? (g^{y}i-di-yór-mù?)	[does it] go?
g^{y}ǜn-dǘz	(Mr.) Gunduz (lit. "Day")
bày‿g^{y}ün-dǘz	Mr. Gunduz
hà-dė-mé	janitor
há-de-mé-dè	[a] janitor, too
ha-dè-mė-l^{y}ík^y	janitor's work
ha-dė-me-sí-dè	his janitor, too
hàk-kí	Hakki (boy's name)
hóş	(pleasure)
*hò-şú	his pleasure
*hò-şúm	my pleasure

hò-şú-má	to my pleasure
hó-şu-má‿gʸí-di-yòr	I like [it]
hò-şú-ná	to his pleasure
ho-şu-ná‿gʸi-di-yór-mù?	[does] he like [it]?
*hò-şú-múz	our pleasure
hò-şú-mu-zá	to our pleasure
hó-şu-mu-zá‿gʸi-di-yòr	we like [it]
*hò-şú-núz	your pleasure
hò-şú-nu-zá	to your pleasure
ho-şu-nu-zá‿gʸi-di-yór-mù?	do you like [it]? (lit. does it go to your pleasure?)
iç- . . .	drink
i-çé-rìz	we drink
i-çi-yór-mú-su-nùz?	are you drinking?
*ìs-mà-íl^y^*	Ishmael (boy's name)
is-mà-i-lʸín	Ishmael's
is-te- . . .	want
is-tér-si-nìz	you want
is-ti-yór-mú-su-nùz?	[do] you want?
is-tí-yór-su-nùz (is-ti-yór-sú-nùz)	you want
is-tí-yo-rùz	we want
vér-mé-kʸ‿is-ti-yò-rúz	we want to give
íş	job, work
í-ş‿á-rı-yò-rúz	we are looking for work
iş‿ver-mé-kʸ‿is-ti-yò-rúz	we want to give work

ì-şé	to work
ì-şím	my work
bí-r‿ì-şìm‿yók	I haven't anything to do (lit. a job-of-mine there-isn't)
ìş-l^{y}è-ri-níz	your jobs
kár	(Mr.) Carr
kà-rí	wife
kà-rí-lár	wives
ká-rı-là-rı-níz	your wives
kíz	girl
kìz-lár	girls
kiz-lár-dà	girls, too
kíz‿kàr-dèş	sister
kíz‿kár-dė-şi-mìz	our sister
ko-nuş- . . . (aor. *-ur-*)	talk
kó-nu-şúr-mú-su-nùz?	[do] you speak?
kó-nu-şúr-sú-nùz	you talk
kó-nu-şú-yòr	[he] is talking
kó-nu-şú-yór-làr	they are talking
kó-nu-şú-yór-làr-mı?	are they talking?
kó-nu-şú-yó-rùz	we are talking
kúrt	wolf; (Mr.) Kurt (lit. "Wolf")
bày‿kúrt	Mr. Kurt
bìr‿kúrt	a wolf
k^{y}à:-típ	secretary
k^{y}à:-tì-bí	his secretary

k^{y}à:-ti-bím	my secretary
k^{y}á:-tì-bi-níz	your secretary
k^{y}á:-tìp-l^{y}ík^{y}	secretarial work
k^{y}á:-tip-l^{y}í-k^{y}‿e-dè-rim	I do secretarial work
né	what
nè-l^{y}ér	what (things)
né-l^{y}ér-dè	what (things), too
ó	he, she, it; that
ò-nún	his
ò-fís	office
ó-fì-si-míz	our office
o-fì-sı-miz-dé	in our office
ó-fìs-té	in [the] office
bú‿o-fis-tè	in this office
síz	you
sì-zé	to you
sì-zín?	yours?
şím-dì	now
té-şèk^{y}-k^{y}ǘr	thank(s)
te-şék^{y}-k^{y}ùr-l^{y}ér!	thanks!
te-şek^{y}-k^{y}ü-r‿et- . . . (aor. *-er-*)	thank
te-şék^{y}-k^{y}ǘ-r‿e-dè-riz	we thank [you]
tóp-làn-tí	gathering; "party"
bìr‿tóp-lán-tí	a party

tóp-làn-tı-lár	parties
tóp-làn-tı-la-rí	his parties
tóp-làn-tı-là-rı-níz	your parties
vé	and
vè‿síz	and you
ver- . . . (aor. *-ir-*)	give
vèr-mékʸ	to give
vé-rìr-lʸér	they give (pay)
vèz-nė-dár	cashier
vèz-ne-dá-rí	his cashier
véz-ne-dà-rı-níz	your cashier
véz-ne-dàr-lík	cashier's work
véz-ne-dár-lík‿ya-pà-rím	I do cashier's work
yap- . . . (aor. *-ar-*)	do
yà-pár	[he] does
yá-pá-rìz	we do
ya-pár-sı-nìz	you do
yá-pí-yòr	[he] is doing
yá-pı-yór-mù?	is [she] doing?
yá-pı-yór-mú-su-nùz?	are you doing?
ya-pí-yó-rùm	I am doing
ye- . . .	eat
yé-riz	we eat
yók	there [is]n't
yók-mù?	[is]n't there?

UNIT 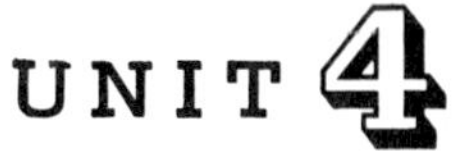

FAMILY AND FRIENDS

SECTION A—BASIC SENTENCES

To the Group Leader: From this point on you will need special instructions only when new sections or procedures are introduced in the learning units. With other sections, simply follow the procedures which have been recommended in the first three units and the instructions provided for the group at the beginning of the sections.

Go through the *Basic Sentences* in unison. Then work on the *Hints on Pronunciation* and after that go through the *Basic Sentences* at least twice more individually.

1. Basic Sentences

Mr. and Mrs. Carr entertain the Kayas, the Metins and their children.

ENGLISH EQUIVALENTS	AIDS TO LISTENING	CONVENTIONAL TURKISH SPELLING
	Mr. Carr	
Record 8A, beginning.		
who all	k^{y}ìm-l^{y}ér?	kimler?
[they] are coming	g^{y}é-l^{y}í-yòr.	geliyor
Who's coming?	k^{y}ím-l^{y}ér‿g^{y}é-l^{y}i-yòr?	Kimler geliyor?
	Mrs. Carr	
[the] Kayas	kà-yá-lár.	Kayalar
[the] Metins	mé-tìn-l^{y}ér.	Metinler
The Kayas [and] the Metins.	kà-yá-lár, mé-tìn-l^{y}ér.	Kayalar, Metinler.

	Mr. Carr	
[the] guests	mi-sà:-fi̍r-l^{y}ér.	misafirler
are [they] coming?	g^{y}e-l^{y}í-yór-mù?	geliyormu?
Are the guests coming?	mi-sa:-fir-l^{y}ér‿g^{y}e-l^{y}í-yór-mù?	Misafirler geliyormu?
	Mrs. Carr	
they are coming	g^{y}e-l^{y}í-yór-làr.	geliyorlar
Yes, they're coming now.	é-vèt, şi̍m-di‿g^{y}e-l^{y}í-yór-làr.	Evet, şimdi geliyorlar.
	Guests	
Good evening!	ak-şam-la-rı-niz‿há-yır-lí‿ól-sùn!	Akşamlarınız hayırlı olsun!
	Mr. and Mrs. Carr	
Come in, please, come in!	búy-rùn, l^{y}ût-fèn, búy-rùn!	Buyrun, lûtfen, buyrun!
	Mrs. Carr	
How are you?	ná-sil-sı-nìz?	Nasılsınız?
	Mrs. Metin	
we [are] well	i̍-yí-yìz.	iyiyiz
We're very well, thank you!	çó-k‿i̍-yí-yìz, te-şék^y-k^{y}ǘ-r‿e-dè-ri̍z!	Çok iyiyiz, teşekkür ederiz!
	Mrs. Kaya	
[are] you well?	i-yí-mi̍-si-nìz?	iyimisiniz?
Are you *well, Mrs. Carr?*	bá-yàn‿kár, si̍z‿i-yí-mi̍-si-nìz?	Bayan Kar, siz iyimisiniz?
	Mrs. Carr	
Yes, I'm well, thank you!	é-vèt, i̍-yí-yìm, te-şék^y-k^{y}ǘ-r‿e-dè-ri̍m!	Evet, iyiyim, teşekkür ederim!

	Mrs. Kaya	
your children	ço-cùk-lá-rı-níz.	çocuklarınız
how [are they]?	ná-sìl?	nasıl?
How are your children?	ço-cúk-lá-rı-níz‿nà-sìl?	Çocuklarınız nasıl?
	Mrs. Carr	
today (lit. this day)	bú‿g^{y}ǜn.	bu gün
they are well	i-yí-dír-l^{y}èr.	iyidirler
Today, they're very well.	bú‿g^{y}ǜn çó-k‿i-yí-dír-l^{y}èr.	Bu gün çok iyidirler.
	Mrs. Metin	
[he is] my son	ò:-lúm.	oğlum
Orhan	òr-hán.	Orhan
This is my son, Orhan.	bú ò:-lúm, òr-hán.	Bu oğlum, Orhan.
	Mrs. Carr	
these	bùn-lár.	bunlar
[are] my daughters	kìz-lá-rím.	kızlarım
Aliye	à-l^{y}í-yé.	Aliye
Shukruye	şǜk^{y}-rü-yé.	Şükrüye
These are my daughters, Aliye and Shukruye.	bùn-lár kìz-lá-rím à-l^{y}í-yé vé‿şǜk^{y}-rü-yé.	Bunlar kızlarım Aliye ve Şükrüye.

Some time later:

Record 8B, beginning.

children	çó-cúk-làr!	çocuklar
in your room	ò-da-niz-dá.	odanızda
amuse yourselves!	éy-l^{y}é-nìn!	eğlenin
Children, you go play in your room!	çó-cúk-làr siz‿ó-da-niz-dá‿ey-l^{y}è-nin!	Çocuklar siz odanızda eğlenin!

Children

all right! (lit. very well!)	pé-kʸ‿i-yì!	pek iyi
mother	án-nè.	anne
All right, mother!	pé-kʸ‿i-yì, án-nè!	Pek iyi, anne!

Mrs. Carr

your son	ò:-lú-núz.	oğlunuz
Muzaffer[1] *(lit. "Victor")*	mú-zàf-fér.	Muzaffer
my daughter	kì-zím.	kızım
Shukruye	şûkʸ-rü-yé.	Şükrüye
with	i-lʸé.	ile
very good	çò-k‿i-yi.	çok iyi
[he] is [a] friend	ár-ka-dáş-tìr.	arkadaştır
Mrs. Kaya[2]*, your son, Muzaffer*[1]*, is a very good friend of my daughter, Shukruye.*	(1) bá-yàn‿ka-yá, ò:-lú-núz, mú-zàf-fér, kı-zim‿şükʸ-rü-yé-m‿i-lʸè çó-k‿i-yi‿ár-ka-dáş-tìr. (2) bá-yàn‿ká-yá, ò:-lú-núz, mú-zàf-fér, kı-zim‿şükʸ-rü-yé‿i-lʸè çó-k‿i-yi‿ár-ka-dáş-tìr.	Bayan Kaya, oğlunuz, Muzaffer, kızım Şükrüye ile çok iyi arkadaştır.

Mrs. Kaya

right	dò:-rú.	doğru
Yes, quite right!	é-vèt, çók‿dó:-rù!	Evet, çok doğru.

[1]Record has "Victor".
[2]Record has "Stone".

	Mrs. Carr	
they	òn-lár.	onlar
to the movies	si-né-má-yà.	sinemaya
always	dá-ı̍-mà.	daima
together	bé-rà:-bér.	beraber
they go	g^{y}ı̍-dèr-l^{y}ér.	giderler
They always go to the movies together.	on-lár‿si-né-má-yà dá-i-ma‿be-rá:-bér‿g^{y}i-dér-l^{y}èr.	Onlar sinemaya daima beraber giderler.
Later:		
what [is] it	né‿ò?	ne o?
are you going	g^{y}ı̍-di-yór-mú-su-nùz?	gidiyormusunuz?
What's this, are you going?	né‿ò g^{y}ı̍-di-yór-mú-su-nùz?	Ne o gidiyormusunuz?
	Mr. Metin	
late	g^{y}éç.	geç
we've stayed	kàl-dík.	kaldık
Yes, we've stayed very late.	é-vèt, çók‿g^{y}éç‿kál-dìk.	Evet, çok geç kaldık.
	Mrs. Kaya	
every	hér.	her
morning	sà-báh.	sabah
early	èr-k^{y}én.	erken
they get up	kàl-kár-lár.	kalkarlar
The children get up early every morning.	çó-cùk-lár, hér‿sá-bàh ér-k^{y}én‿kál-kár-làr.	Çocuklar, her sabah erken kalkarlar.

	Guests	
God	àl-láh.	Allah
rest	rá-hàt-lík.	rahatlık
may [he] give [you]!	vèr-sín!	versin
Good night!	al-láh‿ra-hát-lík‿vérsìn!	Allah rahatlık versin!

Record 9A, beginning.

	Mr. Carr	
Good night to you! (lit. to you, too)	si̍-zé-dè!	Size de!

	Guests	
very much	çók.	çok
we have amused ourselves	èy-lʸén-dík̍ʸ.	eğlendik
We've had a very nice time!	çó-k‿éy-lʸén-dìkʸ!	Çok eğlendik!

Before you go through the *Basic Sentences* a second time, *note* the sound values of the following letters:

LETTER	STANDS FOR A SOUND	EXAMPLES	
c	like *g* in *gem* Note: Be careful to pronounce this Turkish letter like English *g* as in *gem* or *gin*, not like English *c*.	çò-cúk	(*child*)
o:	drawled or long like *ou* in *soul*	dò:-rú	(*right*)

Review the sound values of these letters:

ç	like *ch* in *chin*	çò-cúk	(*child*)
gʸ	like *g* in *argue*	gʸéç	(*late*)

h	like *h* in *head, behead,* even when at the end of a word or syllable	sà-báh	(*morning*)
ü	like *i* as in *pit,* with puckered lips	şǜkʸ-rǘ-yé	(*Shukruye*)
a:	about like *a* in *father,* but drawn out or drawled	mi̍-sà:-fír	(*guest*)

Remember:

a	about as in *father*	àl-láh	(*God*)
e	about as in *pet*	èr-kʸén	(*early*)
i	about as in *pit*	şím-dì	(*now*)
o	about as in *for*	òr-hán	(*Orhan*)
u	about as in *put*	búy-rùn!	(*come in!*)
ı	somewhat like *u* in *suppose*	kì-zím	(*my daughter*)
ş	like *sh* in *shin*	şǜkʸ-rǘ-yé	(*Shukruye*)
y	like *y* in *year* even in the middle or at the end of a word	búy-rùn!	(*come in!*)
kʸ	like *c* in *cute*	èr-kʸén	(*early*)
lʸ	like *li* in *million*	à-lʸi̍-yé	(*Aliye*)
‿	connects words spoken together without pause or break		
ˊ	marks strongest vowel		
ˋ	marks next strongest vowel		
ˈ	marks other fairly strong vowels		

Now Study the following:

2. Hints on Pronunciation

Two of the vowel sounds which we have met in this unit are not quite like similar sounds in English. One of them, the *a:*, we have met before in Units 1, 2, and 3. The other, the *o:*, we have met for the first time in Unit 4. In Units 1 and 3, we described *a:* as being *drawled* or *long*, something like the *a* in *father*. Here we have described *o:* as being *drawled* or *long*, something like the *ou* in *soul*. Turkish vowels are divided into two groups, *short* (like i, e, ı, a, o, u) and *long* (like *a:*, *o:*). The *short vowels* are pronounced quite short. They are "clipped" and are never drawn out. The *long vowels*, on the other hand, are drawn out, or drawled. One must be very careful to pronounce both *short* and *long* vowels clearly, or many confusions may result.

Note: *Long vowels* will always be clearly marked with *:* after the vowel: long *a* = *a:*, long *o* = *o:*.

Practice the following words with *a:*:

PRACTICE 1 **Record 9A, after 1st spiral.**

ȧp-tèst-h*ȧ:*-né	(*toilet*)
s*à:*-dá	(*at [the] right*)
t*à:*-né	(*piece*)
z*á:*-t	(*gentleman*)
kʸ*à:*-tip	(*secretary*)
bė-r*à:*-bér	(*together*)
mi-s*à:*-fír	(*guest*)

and with *o:*:

PRACTICE 2 **Record 9A, after 2nd spiral.**

ȯ:-lúm.	(*my son*)
ȯ:-lú-núz.	(*your son*)
d*ȯ:*-rú.	(*right*)

Note: You must be careful to distinguish clearly between long vowels, such as *a:*, and groups of two distinct vowels, such as *aa*. Compare the following:

PRACTICE 3 **Record 9A, after 3rd spiral.**

sà-á-ti.		(*his watch*)
	with	
zà:-tí.		(*her gentleman*)
sà-á-tí.		
zà:-tí.		

Now go through the *Basic Sentences* once more individually, with your book open, and once with your book closed.

3. Check Yourself

Are you taking every opportunity to practice your Turkish by talking with other members of the group or with Turkish speaking people whom you may meet?

SECTION B—WORD STUDY AND REVIEW OF BASIC SENTENCES

1. Word Study (Individual Study)

Work through the following as recommended in the previous units.

1. *The Turkish equivalents of "am", "is", "are"; personal endings "they", "it, he, she"*

a. We have seen numbers of forms such as *né-dìr*? 'what is [it]?', *yók-tùr* 'there isn't', *èv-lʸí-dìr* '[she] is married', and so on, and we have already identified the *-dir*, *-dır*, *-dur*, *-tir*, *-tır*, *-tur* ending. In the forms we mention above, the ending means "is". Observe, however, the following:

	Column I			Column II	
			Group I		
	à-l^{y} -yé	*'Aliye'*	:	á-l^{y}i-yé-dìr	'[*it*] *is Aliye*'
	yók	*'not'*	:	yók-tùr	*'there isn't* [*any*]'
	ì-yí	*'well'*	:	i̍-yí-dìr	'[*he*] *is well*'
	èv-l^{y}í	*'married'*	:	év-l^{y}í-dìr	'[*she*] *is married*'
	çò-cùk-lár	'[*the*] *boys*'	:	ço-cúk-lár-dìr	'[*it*] *is* [*the*] *boys*'
	ì-yi̍-l^{y}ér	'[*the*] *good ones*'	:	i̍-yi-l^{y}ér-dìr	'[*it*] *is* [*the*] *good ones*'
			Group II		
i	ì-yí	*'well'*	:	i-yí-di̍r-l^{y}èr	*'they are well'*
u	çò-cúk	*'child'*	:	ço-cúk-túr-làr	*'they are (just) children'*
i	èv-l^{y}í	*'married'*	:	ev-l^{y}í-di̍r-l^{y}èr	*'they are married'*

If we compare Group I with Group II, we see that:

1. the *-dir*, *-dır*, *-dur*, *-tir*, *-tır*, *-tur* ending does not necessarily mean only 'is', as in Group I, but may also mean 'are', as in Group II;
2. in addition to the "is, are" ending in Group II, we have an ending *-l^{y}er*, *-lar*, which means 'they';
3. the *-l^{y}er*, *-lar* "they" ending follows Vowel Harmony Type II, as did the *-er-*, *-ar-* aorist ending which we studied in Unit 3; that is, *-l^{y}er* is found after vowels *i*, *e*, *ü*, *ö* and *-lar* after vowels *ı*, *a*, *u*, *o*;
4. although 'they' in Group II is expressed by the ending *-l^{y}er*, *-lar*, 'it (he, she)' in Group I is not expressed by any similar ending. In other words, 'it (he, she)' is expressed by the absence of an ending, by nothing, or by "*zero*".

Note: *Zero-endings* will play a very important part in the make-up of Turkish as they do in many languages.

This particular *zero* (*i-yi-dir-*0* '*he* is well') is a personal ending and means 'it (he, she)'.

Now observe the following:

1. ço-cúk-lár-dìr	'[*they*] *are* [*the*] *children*'
2. ì-yi̍-l^{y}ér	'*they* [*are*] *well*'
3. ì-yi̍-l^{y}ér	'[*it*] [*is*] [*the*] *good ones*'

We see that in 1, when the word, to which the *-dir -l^{y}er*, *-dır-lar*, etc. "they are" ending is added, already has an ending *-l^{y}er*, *-lar* ("more than one"), one usually omits the *-l^{y}er*, *-lar* "they" ending, that is, *not*

*ço-cuk-lar-dır-lar   but *rather*   *ço-cuk-lar-dır-0

as above in 1.

Note: This kind of omission is common in Turkish. If an element has already been expressed *once* in a word or phrase or sentence, one avoids repeating it.

Here, therefore, in the presence of the first *-l^{y}er*, *-lar* "more than one" ending, the second *-l^{y}er*, *-lar* "they" ending, does not appear, or is "*zero*".

In 2, we notice another omission. Instead of *i-yí-di̍r-l^{y}èr*, we have *ì-yi̍-l^{y}ér*. Here the "is, are" ending is not used, or is "*zero*".

In 3, instead of *i̍-yi-l^{y}ér-dìr*, we have just *ì-yi-l^{y}ér*, as above in 2. Here, the "is, are" ending is likewise "*zero*".

Note: Because the two forms *i-yí(-dir)-l^{y}èr* 'they (are) well', and *i̍-yi-l^{y}ér(-dìr)* '[it] (is) [the] good ones' frequently fall together (ì-yi̍-l^{y}ér), they are also frequently interchanged, so that the second form (i̍-yi-l^{y}ér-dìr) may also mean 'they are well'. Observe:

either de-yíl^y-di̍r-l^{y}èr }
or de-yi̍l^y-l^{y}ér-dìr } '*they are not*'

b. We have seen a number of forms such as *vár* 'there [is]', *ná-sìl*? 'how [are] [they]?', *èv-l^{y}í-mì*? 'is [she] married?', *ì-yí* '[she] [is] well'. Observe the following:

	Column I			*Column II*
		Group I		
vár	'*there* [*is*]'	:	vár-dìr	'*there is*'
ėv-l^{y}í-mì?	'[*is*] [*she*] *married?*'	:	ėv-l^{y}í-mi-dìr?	'*is* [*she*] *married?*'
ì-yí	'[*she*] [*is*] *well*'	:	i̍-yí-dìr	'[*she*] *is well*'
ò:-lúm	'[*he*] [*is*] *my son*'	:	ȯ:-lúm-dùr	'[*he*] *is my son*'
bày‿mė-tín	'[*it*] [*is*] *Mr. Metin*'	:	bȧy‿mė-tín-dìr	'[*it*] *is Mr. Metin*'
		Group II		
èv-l^{y}ı-l^{y}ér	'*they* [*are*] *married*'	:	ev-l^{y}í-dír-l^{y}èr	'*they are married*'
ì-yi̍-l^{y}ér	'*they* [*are*] *well*'	:	i̍-yi-l^{y}ér-dìr	'*they are well*'
		Group III		
ná-sìl?	'*how* [*are*] [*they*]?'	:	ná-sil-dır-làr?	'*how are they?*'
ėv-l^{y}í-mì?	'[*are*] [*they*] *married?*'	:	ėv-l^{y}í-mi-di̍r-l^{y}èr?	'*are they married?*'

If we compare Column I with Column II and Groups I, II, and III, we see that:

1. in Column II, we have the *-dir*, *-dır*, etc. "is, are" ending with all the forms;
2. in Column I, however, this "is, are" ending is not *-dir*, *-dır*, etc., but is absent, or is "*zero*";

Note: The forms in Column I are most common. The too frequent use of the *-dir*, *-dır*, etc. ending is considered affected. However, the *-dir*, *-dır*, etc. ending has a number of special connotations (additional meanings) in special combinations which we shall see later.

3. in Group I, the "*zero*" ending means 'is', in Group II, 'are';
4. in Group III, not only the ending "are" is "*zero*", but also the ending "they".

c. Finally, observe:

	Column I			*Column II*
i̍-yí-yìm	'*I* [*am*] *well*'	:	i-yí-yi̍m-dìr	'*I am well*'
çó-cú-ùm	'*I* [*am*] [*a*] *child*'	:	çocú-úm-dùr	'*I am* [*a*] *child*'

We see that:

1. the forms in Column II, have the *-dir*, *-dır*, etc. ending;
2. here this ending means "am";
3. the forms in Column I, do not have this ending, but have "zero" instead.

So, to *summarize*, we have seen that not only "is", but also "are" and "am", may be expressed in two ways;

1. most often, by *-0*;
2. occasionally by the ending *-dir*, *-dır*, *-dur*, *-tir*, *-tır*, *-tur*.

We have also seen that the personal ending 'it (he, she)', used with either form of the "is, are, am" ending, is always *-0*.

We have likewise seen that the personal ending "they", used with either form of the "is, are, am" ending, is

1. most often *-l^{y}er*, *-lar*;
2. occasionally *-0*.

Since the words which have the "is, are, am" endings (*-dir*, *-dır*, etc.) (*-0*) are frequently used to tie one part of a sentence to another:

bén ço-cú-úm-dùr *I am [a] child'*

we shall call the endings and the forms which have them *copula* forms and endings.

2. *The Turkish personal ending "I"*

We have seen the form *i̇-yí-yìm* 'I [am] well'. Tabulating this with other similar forms, we get:

	Column I			Column II	
			Group I		
i	ì-yí	*'well'*	:	i̇-yí-yìm	*'I [am] well'*
i	èv-l^{y}í	*'married'*	:	év-l^{y}i-yìm	*'I [am] married'*
			Group II		
ı	kíz	*'girl'*	:	kí-zìm	*'I [am] [a] girl'*
a	àr-kà-dáş	*'friend'*	:	ár-ka-dá-şìm	*'I [am] [a] friend'*
u	çò-cúk	*'child'*	:	çó-cú-ùm	*'I [am] [a] child'*

If we compare Column I with Column II, and Group I with II, we see that:

1. it is the *first* part of the forms in Column II, the part which we see in Column I, which means 'well', 'girl', and so on.

Note 1: This part may be called the *base*. In the list above, *ì-yí*, *èv-lʸí*, *kíz*, *àr-kà-dáş*, *çò-cúk* are bases. Such bases and all words derived from them by various endings, and these endings themselves, we shall call *noun bases*, *nouns*, and *noun endings*.

Note 2: These particular personal endings are used here with the *copula*, which is the only *verb form* which may be added to a noun base, as an ending.

2. the *second* part of the forms in Column II, is the part which means "I";
3. this part which means "I" has different forms; it follows the type of vowel harmony which we have seen in the *momentary* ending *-i-yor*, *-ı-yor*, *-u-yor*, that is Vowel Harmony Type I, *i* after *i* or *e*, *ı* after *ı* or *a*, *u* after *u* or *o*;
4. the ending "I" is *-yim*, *-yım*, *-yum* after vowels as in Group I;
5. the ending is *-im*, *-ım*, *-um* after *consonants* as in Group II;
6. the *strongest vowel* is *not* in the ending, but in the base before it.

3. *The Turkish personal ending "you"*

We have seen the forms *ná-sil-sı-nìz*? 'how [are] you?', *èv-lʸí-mi-si-nìz?* '[are] you married?'. Tabulating these with others we get:

	Column I			Column II	
i	ì-yí	*'well'*	:	i-yí-si-nìz	*'you [are] well'*
i	ėv-lʸí-mì?	'( ) *married?'*	:	ėv-lʸí-mi-si-nìz?	*'[are] [you] married?'*
ı	ná-sìl?	*'how?'*	:	ná-sil-sı-nìz?	*'how [are] you?'*
a	àr-kà-dáş	*'friend'*	:	ár-ka-dáş-si-nìz	*'you [are] (the) friend(s)'*
u	çò-cúk	*'child'*	:	ço-cúk-sú-nùz	*'you [are] (the) child(ren)'*

If we compare Column I with Column II, we see that:

1. the personal ending which means 'you' follows Vowel Harmony Type I, *i* after *i* or *e*, *ı* after *ı* or *a*, and *u* after *u* or *o*;
2. the ending is *-si-niz*, *-sı-nız*, *-su-nuz*;
3. the *strongest vowel* is *not* in the ending, but in the base before it.

4. *The Turkish personal ending "we"*

We have seen the form *i̍-yí-yìz* 'we [are] well'. Tabulating this with others, we get:

	Column I			*Column II*	
			Group I		
i	ì-yí	*'well'*	:	i̍-yí-yìz	*'we [are] well'*
ı	èv-l^{y}ı́	*'married'*	:	ė̍v-l^{y}ı́-yı̀z	*'we [are] married'*
			Group II		
e	kàr-déş	*'brother(s)'*	:	kȧr-dé-şi̍z	*'we [are] brother[s]'*
a	àr-kȧ-dáş	*'friend(s)'*	:	ȧr-ka-dá-şı̀z	*'we [are] friend[s]'*
u	çò-cúk	*'child(ren)'*	:	çó-cú-ùz	*'we [are] child[ren]'*

If we compare Columns I and II, and Group I with Group II, we see that:

1. the personal ending which means "we" follows Vowel Harmony Type I, *i* after *i* or *e*, *ı* after *ı* or *a*, *u* after *u* or *o*;
2. the ending "we" is *-yiz*, *-yız*, *-yuz* after a *vowel* as in Group I;
3. the ending is *-iz*, *-ız*, *-uz* after a *consonant* as in Group II;
4. the *strongest vowel* is not in the ending, but in the base before it.

5. *Turkish equivalents of 'am', 'is', 'are' (summary)*

Group I (base ending in a vowel)

i-yí-yi̍m(-dìr)	*'I (am) well'*
i̍-yí(-dìr)	*'[he] (is) well'*
i̍-yi-l^{y}ér(-dìr)	*'[it] (is) [the] good ones'*
i-yí-yi̍z(-dìr)	*'we (are) well'*
i-yí-si̍-nìz(-di̍r)	*'you (are) well'*
i-yí(-di̍r)(-l^{y}èr)	*'(they) (are) well'*

Group II (base ending in a consonant)

ȧr-ka-dá-şim(-dìr)	*'I (am) [the] friend'*
ár-ka-dáş(-tìr)	*'[he] (is) [the] friend'*
ár-ka-dȧş-lár(-dìr)	*'[it] (is) [the] friends'*
ár-ka-dá-şiz(-dìr)	*'we (are) friend[s]'*
ár-ka-dáş-si-nìz(-dir)	*'you (are) friend[s]'*
ár-ka-dáş(-tir)(-làr)	*'(they) (are) friend[s]'*

Note 1: The endings in parentheses may often be omitted. Some occur occasionally, others very rarely.

Note 2: The strongest vowel in these forms with the *copula* ending, is in neither the personal ending nor in the copula ending, but always in the base before both of them.

6. *Turkish personal endings with verbs*; *summary of personal endings*

Thus far we have mentioned the personal endings only as used with the various forms of the copula ending, and the combination as used with *noun bases*. The personal endings, however, are far more often used with *verbs*. We list a few such verb forms among those we have seen:

	Column I			*Column II*	
			Group I		
e	e-der- . . .	*'doing'*	:	ė-dé-rìm	*'I do'*
a	ya-par- . . .	*'doing'*	:	yȧ-pá-rìm	*'I do'*
o	an-lı-yor- . . .	*'understanding'*	:	ȧn-lí-yo-rùm	*'I understand'*
o	baş-lı-yor- . . .	*'starting'*	:	bȧş-lí-yo-rùm	*'I am starting'*
			Group II		
	g^{y}i-di-yor- . . .	*'going'*	:	g^{y}i̍-dí-yòr	*'[he] is going'*
	g^{y}e-l^{y}i-yor- . . .	*'coming'*	:	g^{y}é-l^{y}í-yòr	*'[he] is coming'*
	a-rar- . . .	*'looking for'*	:	à-rár	*'[he] looks for [it]'*
	de-nir- . . .	*'being said'*	:	dè-nír	*'[it] is said'*

Group III

i	g^{y}e-l^{y}ir- . . .	*'coming'*	:	g^{y}ė-l^{y}í rì̇z	*'we come'*
e	i-çer- . . .	*'drinking'*	:	i̇-çé-rì̇z	*'we drink'*
a	baş-lar- . . .	*'starting'*	:	báş-lá-rìz	*'we start'*
u	ko-nu-şu-yor- . . .	*'talking'*	:	kó-nu-şú-yó-rùz	*'we are talking'*

Group IV

i	ve-rir- . . .	*'giving'*	:	ve-rír-si̇-nì̇z	*'you give'*
e	is-ter- . . .	*'wanting'*	:	is-tér-si̇-nì̇z	*'you want'*
a	ya-par- . . .	*'doing'*	:	ya-pár-si-nìz	*'you do'*
u	ko-nu-şur- . . .	*'talking'*	:	kó-nu-şúr-sú-nùz	*'you talk'*
o	a-rı-yor- . . .	*'looking for'*	:	a-rí-yór-su-nùz	*'you are looking for [it]'*

Group V (a)

i	ve-rir- . . .	*'giving'*	:	vė-rì̇r-l^{y}ér	*'they give'*
o	ko-nu-şu-yor- . . .	*'talking'*	:	kó-nu-şú-yór-làr	*'they are talking'*

Group V (b)

iş-l^{y}e-ri-ni̇z‿ho-şu-nu-zá‿g^{y}i̇-di-yór-mù? *'do you like your jobs (lit. do they go to your pleasure)?'*

kız-lár-dá‿ho-şu-má‿g^{y}i̇-di-yòr. *'I like the girls, too (lit. they go to my pleasure)'*

g^{y}i-di-yor- . . .	*'going'*	:	g^{y}i̇-dí-yòr	*'[they] go'*

Summarizing:

I	-(y)im, -(y)ım, -(y)um	*'I'*
II	-0	*'he (she, it)'*
III	-(y)iz, -(y)ız, -(y)uz	*'we'*
IV	-si-niz, -sı-nız, -su-nuz	*'you'*
V(a)	-l^{y}er, -lar	*'they'*
V(b)	-0	*'they'*

Note: Here we see that likewise with the momentary and aorist verb endings, the personal endings usually do *not* have the *strongest vowel*; with the aorist ending, however, the *-lʸer*, *-lar* "they" personal ending *does* have the strongest vowel (vė-rı̀r-lʸér) and even with the momentary ending, the vowel of the "they" ending is next strongest (kȯ-nu-şú-yȯr-lȁr).

2. Covering English and Turkish of Word Study (Individual Study)

Review this *Word Study* by reading aloud all of the Turkish expressions. Then cover the English and make sure that you know the meaning of every item. Finally, cover the Turkish and see if you can say each Turkish expression when you are looking only at the English.

3. Review of Basic Sentences

With Guide or records, review the first half of the *Basic Sentences* for better pronunciation, meaning and examples of points in the *Word Study*.

SECTION C—REVIEW OF BASIC SENTENCES (*Cont.*)

1. Review of Basic Sentences (*Cont.*)

Review the second half of the *Basic Sentences*.

2. Covering the English of Basic Sentences (Individual Study)

Go back to the *Basic Sentences* in Section A, and read them aloud covering up the English. Note any words or phrases you are not sure about, and, when you have finished reading the *Basic Sentences*, uncover the English and look up the meaning of what you did not get. Keep this up until you know all the meanings completely.

3. Word Study Review (Individual Study)

Work through the following exercises. Do not write anything down. If you cannot do the work rapidly, review again the *Word Study*. Be prepared to do what is required when the Leader calls on you. Always repeat the entire expression, phrase or sentence as you work.

1. Give the *English equivalents* of the forms in italics in the following sentences:

   1. kà-yá-lár şi̍m-di‿*ná-sìl? i-yí-dír-lʸèr.*
   2. báy‿ká-ya-ní-n‿ó:-lù ba-yán‿me-ti-ni̍n‿ki-zí‿i̍-lʸè *èv-lʸí-mì?*
   3. bú‿ák-şàm *né-re-dé-lʸèr?*
   4. fat-má‿şi̍m-di‿*év-lʸí.*
   5. bú‿sá-bàh *ná-sil-sı-nìz? i̍-yí-yìm.*
   6. òn-lár şi̍m-di‿çó-k‿i-yi̍‿*ár-ka-dàş-tìr.*
   7. mú-zàf-fér kʸi̍-mí-n‿*ó:-lù?*
   8. bú‿gʸûn ka-rı-niz‿*ná-sìl? i̍-yí-dìr.*

2. Add the proper forms of the "*I*" *personal ending* to the following words:

   a. bèkʸ-çí
   dè-yílʸ
   hà-dé-mé
   kʸà:-típ (kʸa:-ti-b-)
   kʸím
   mi̍-sà:-fír
   vèz-né-dár
   yà-váş

   b. gʸi-de(-)r-. . .
   baş-la(-)r-. . .
   ko-nu-şu(-)r-. . .
   ya-pı-yo(-)r-. . .
   an-la-mı-yo(-)r-. . .

3. Add the proper forms of the "*you*" *personal ending* to the words in 2.

4. Add the proper forms of the "*we*" *personal ending* to the words in 2.

4. What Would You Say? (Individual Study)

Read aloud each of the following and then pick out the expression you think most suitable:

1. *The guests arrive and greet their hosts. They say:*
   a. kʸib-ri̍-t‿i̍s-ti-yór-mú-su-nùz?
   b. ak-şam-la-rı-niz‿há-yır-lí‿ól-sùn!
   c. si̍-né-mà né-ré-dè?

2. *The hosts return your greeting, and then say:*
   a. búy-rùn, lʸút-fèn, búy-rùn.
   b. há-yìr, şi̍m-di‿ev-dé‿dé-yílʸ-dìr.

3. *Mrs. Carr then asks about Mrs. Kaya's health, saying:*

a. kì-zi-níz ná-sìl?
b. bú-rá-dà sú‿ná-sìl?
c. bá-yàn‿ká-yá, ná-sil-sı-nìz?

4. *Mrs. Kaya replies:*

a. bé-ni̍-m‿ó:-lùm çó-k‿i̍-yi̍.
b. çó-k‿i-yi̍-yi̍m, te-şék^y-k^{y}ú-r‿e-dè-ri̍m.

5. *Mrs. Kaya then asks Mrs. Carr:*

a. vè‿si̍z, bá-yàn‿kár, i-yi̍-mi̍-si-ni̍z?
b. si-zi̍-n‿o:-lu-núz‿vár-mì?

6. *Mrs. Carr replies that she is well, and Mrs. Kaya then asks about her children:*

a. kar-de-şi-ni̍z‿ná-sìl?
b. ço-cùk-lá-rı-níz ná-sìl?

7. *In answer, Mrs. Carr says:*

a. kíz‿kár-de-şi̍m şi̍m-di‿çó-k‿i̍-yi̍.
b. çó-k‿i̍-yi̍.
c. bú‿g^{y}ǜn çó-k‿i-yi̍-dir-l^{y}ér.

8. *Then Mrs. Metin introduces her son, saying:*

a. bú si̍-zi̍-n‿ó:-lu-nùz!
b. bú ò:-lúm. i̍s-mi̍ òr-hán.

9. *Mrs. Kaya asks Mrs. Carr what her two daughters' names are. She replies:*

a. bú mú-zàf-fér vè‿bú òr-hán.
b. bú à-l^{y}i̍-yé, vè‿bú şǜk^y-rǘ-yé.

10. *Mrs. Carr tells the children to go to their room and amuse themselves there. She says:*

a. si-né-ma-yá‿g^{y}i̍-di̍n!
b. çó-cúk-làr si̍z ó-da-niz-dá‿éy-l^{y}è-ni̍n!

11. *The children answer:*

a. há-yìr, án-nè!
b. pé-k^y‿i̍-yi̍, án-nè!

12. *Mrs. Carr tells Mrs. Kaya about her daughter's friendship with Mrs. Kaya's son. Mrs. Carr says:*

a. si-zi̍-n‿ar-ka-daş-la-rı-niz‿vár-mì?
b. si̍-zi̍-n‿ó:-lu-nùz mú-zàf-fér, be-ni̍m‿şük^y-rü-yé-m‿i̍-l^{y}è çó-k‿i-yi̍‿ár-ka-dàş-tir.

13. *Mrs. Kaya agrees with her saying:*

a. há-yìr, dé-yi̍l^y-di̍r!
b. é-vèt, çók‿dó:-rù!

14. *Mrs. Carr remarks that her daughter is always going to the movies with Muzaffer Kaya. She says:*

a. si-né-má-yà dá-i-ma‿be-rá:-bér‿g^{y}i-dér-l^{y}èr.
b. şǜk^y-rü-yé á-l^{y}i̍‿i̍-l^{y}è i-yi̍‿ár-ka-dáş-tìr.

15. *Later, as they prepare to leave, Mrs. Carr, surprised, says:*

a. né‿ò g^{y}i-di-yór-mú-su-nùz?

b. kah-vé‿is-ti-yór-mú-su-nùz?

16. *Mrs. Kaya explains why they have to go early:*

a. si-né-ma-yá‿g^{y}it-mé-k^{y}‿is-ti-yò-rúz.

b. çó-cùk-lár, hér‿sá-bàh ér-k^{y}én‿kál-kár-làr.

17. *Mr. and Mrs. Carr exclaim, as their guests leave:*

a. g^{y}ù-n‿áy-dín!

b. al-láh‿ra-hát-lík‿vér-sìn!

18. *They return the good-bye, saying:*

a. çó-k‿i-yì!

b. si-zé-dè, báy vé‿bá-yàn‿kár!

19. *As the guests go out, they call back:*

a. tóp-làn-tí ná-sìl?

b. çó-k‿éy-l^{y}én-dìk^{y}! çók‿te-şék^{y}-k^{y}û-r‿e-dè-riz.

SECTION D—LISTENING IN

1. What Did You Say?

Give your answers in Turkish for the last exercise in the preceding section, when the Leader calls for them. Do it without reading from the book, if possible. Other members of the group will criticize your choice if they disagree with it. Then give the English equivalents of all the expressions in the exercise.

2. Word Study Check-Up

Give the correct Turkish for each English expression in the *Word Study*, without having to read it from the book. If you cannot do this easily, it means you need to put in more work on the *Word Study*. The Group Leader will give the English and call on different members of the group for the Turkish. As a final check the Leader will call for your answers to the exercises in the *Word Study Review* (Sec. C. 3).

3. Listening In

With your book closed, listen to the following conversations as read by the Guide or phonograph record. Repeat the Turkish immediately after hearing it. After the first repetition of each conversation, check up on the meaning of anything you do not understand, by asking someone else or by going back to the *Basic Sentences* if no one knows.

Go through the conversations again with books open, following the same plan as before, imitating carefully and keeping in mind the meaning of everything you say. Finally, take parts and carry on the conversation.

1. *In the office.*

Record 9A, after 4th spiral.

bày‿kár—	gʸù-n‿áy-dín, bá-y‿ák-yü-rèkʸ!	Gün aydın, bay Akyürek!
bá-y‿ák-yü-rèkʸ—	gʸù-n‿áy-dín, bày‿kár!	Gün aydın, bay Kar!
	bú‿gʸün‿ná-sil-sı-nìz?	Bu gün nasılsınız?
bày‿kár—	i-yí-yìm.	İyiyim.
	síz?	Siz?
bá-y‿ák-yü-rèkʸ—	bén-dé‿i-yì-yim.	Ben de iyiyim.
	bú‿ák-şàm biz-dé‿bir‿tóp-lán-tí‿vàr.	Bu akşam bizde bir toplantı var.
	síz vé‿bá-yàn‿kár gʸe-lʸír-mi-si-nìz?	Siz ve bayan Kar gelirmisiniz?
bày‿kár—	é-vèt. te-şékʸ-kʸú-r‿e-dè-riz!	Evet. Teşekkür ederiz!

2. *The guests arrive.*

bày‿ká-yá—	ak-şam-la-rı-niz‿há-yır-lí‿ól-sùn!	Akşamlarınız hayırlı olsun!
bày‿kár—	te-şékʸ-kʸú-r‿e-dè-rim, si-zín-dè!	Teşekkür ederim, sizin de!
	búy-rùn, lʸût-fèn, búy-rùn!	Buyrun, lûtfen, buyrun!
bá-yàn‿kár—	ná-sil-sı-nìz, bá-yàn‿mé-tín?	Nasılsınız, bayan Metin?
bá-yàn‿mé-tín—	çó-k‿i-yì-yim, te-şékʸ-kʸú-r‿e-dè-rim!	Çok iyiyim, teşekkür ederim!
bá-yàn‿ká-yá—	ço-cuk-la-rı-niz‿ná-sìl, bá-yàn‿kár?	Çocuklarınız nasıl, bayan Kar?
bá-yàn‿kár—	bú‿gʸün ço-cùk-lá-rím çó-k‿i-yí-dir-lʸèr.	Bu gün çocuklarım çok iyidirler.
bá-yàn‿mé-tín—	bú ò:-lúm òr-hán.	Bu oğlum Orhan.
bá-yàn‿ká-yá—	bùn-lár be-nim‿ço-cùk-lá-rím, lʸèy-lʸá: vé‿mú-zàf-fér.	Bunlar benim çocuklarım, Leylâ, ve Muzaffer.
bá-yàn‿kár—	be-ni-m‿i-kʸì‿ki-zím‿vàr.	Benim iki kızım var.
	bú à-lʸi-yé vè‿bú şùkʸ-rü-yé.	Bu Aliye ve bu Şükrüye.

	çó-cúk-làr!	Çocuklar!
	ò-da-niz-dá‿ey-l^{y}è-nín!	Odanızda eğlenin!
bá-yàn‿mé-tín—	bíz‿bú-ra-da‿kó-nuş-má-k‿ís-ti-yò-rúz.	Biz burada konuşmak istiyoruz.
çó-cùk-lár—	pé-k^{y}‿í-yì, án-nè!	Pek iyi, anne!
bá-yàn‿kár—	mú-zàf-fér kı-zim‿şük^{y}-rü-yé‿í-l^{y}è çó-k‿i-yí‿ár-ka-dáş-tìr.	Muzaffer kızım Şükrüye ile çok iyi arkadaştır.
bá-yàn‿ká-yá—	çók‿dó:-rù!	Çok doğru!
	on-lár‿si-né-má-yà dá-i-ma‿be-rà:-bér‿g^{y}i-dér-l^{y}èr.	Onlar sinemaya daima beraber giderler.

3. *Time to go.*

Record 9B, beginning.

bá-yàn‿kár—	né‿ò g^{y}í-di-yór-mú-su-nùz?	Ne o gidiyormusunuz?
bày‿mé-tín—	é-vèt. çók‿g^{y}éç‿kál-dìk.	Evet. Çok geç kaldık.
bày‿ká-yá—	bíz‿hér‿sá-bàh ér-k^{y}én‿kál-kà-riz.	Biz her sabah erken kalkarız.
mi-sà:-fír-l^{y}ér—	ál-la-há‿ıs-már-la-dìk!	Allaha ısmarladık!
	al-láh‿ra-hát-lík‿vér-sìn!	Allah rahatlık versin!
bày‿kár—	g^{y}ü-l^{y}é‿g^{y}ü-l^{y}è!	Güle güle!
	sí-zé-dè!	Size de!

4. *The old gang.*

òr-hán—	mér-há-bà, á-l^{y}ì!	Merhaba, Ali!
à-l^{y}í—	mér-há-bà, ór-hàn. fat-má‿ná-sìl?	Merhaba, Orhan. Fatma nasıl?
òr-hán—	ì-yí. şim-di‿èv-l^{y}í.	İyi. Şimdi evli.
à-l^{y}í—	hák-kí‿i-l^{y}è-mí?	Hakkı ilemi?
òr-hán—	é-vèt. hák-kí‿í-l^{y}è.	Evet. Hakkı ile.
à-l^{y}í—	ço-cuk-la-ri‿vár-mì?	Çocukları varmı?

òr-hán—	há-yìr, yók.	Hayır, yok.
à-l^{y}í—	á-l^{y}i-yé‿nè-re-dé?	Aliye nerede?
òr-hán—	bù-ra-dá‿dé-yíl^y, si-né-má-dà.	Burada değil, sinemada.
	kíz‿kár-de-şí-m‿i-l^{y}é‿be-rá:-bèr!	Kız kardeşim ile beraber!
à-l^{y}í—	şim-di‿ye-mék^y‿ye-mé-k^y‿ís-ti-yór-mú-su-nùz?	Şimdi yemek yemek istiyormusunuz?
òr-hán—	síz?	Siz?
à-l^{y}í—	é-vèt. ís-tí-yo-rùm.	Evet. İstiyorum.
òr-hán—	ó‿l^{y}o-kàn-tá í-yí-mì?	O lokanta iyimi?
à-l^{y}í—	é-vèt. e-tí‿çó-k‿í-yì.	Evet. Eti çok iyi.

5. *Wine, women and movies.*

mú-zàf-fér—	şa-ráp‿ho-şu-nu-zá‿g^{y}í-di-yór-mù?	Şarap hoşunuza gidiyormu?
ìs-má-íl^y—	é-vèt. çók!	Evet. Çok.
mú-zàf-fér—	fat-ma-nin-da‿hó-şu-ná‿g^{y}í-di-yòr.	Fatmanın da hoşuna gidiyor.
ìs-má-íl^y—	şá-ráp-mì? or-há-n‿i-l^{y}é‿íç-mék^y-mì?	Şarapmı? Orhan ile içmekmi?
mú-zàf-fér—	í-k^{y}i-sí-dè.	İkisi de.
	si-né-ma-ya‿g^{y}it-mék^y-té‿hó-şu-nà‿g^{y}i-di-yór.	Sinemaya gitmek de hoşuna gidiyor.
ìs-má-íl^y—	bú‿ák-şàm si-né-ma-yá‿g^{y}í-di-yò-rúz.	Bu akşam sinemaya gidiyoruz.
mú-zàf-fér—	k^{y}ím-l^{y}ér‿g^{y}í-di-yòr?	Kimler gidiyor?
[ìs-má-íl^y][1]—	bíz. fát-mà‿i-l^{y}é‿bén.	Biz. Fatma ile ben.
	be-ra:-bér‿g^{y}e-l^{y}ír-mí-si-nìz?	Beraber gelirmisiniz?
mú-zàf-fér—	é-vèt. g^{y}é-l^{y}í-rìz.	Evet. Geliriz.
	sá-àt‿se-k^{y}íz-dé l^{y}éy-l^{y}à:‿i-l^{y}é‿bén sí-zé‿g^{y}é-l^{y}i-yò-rúz.	Saat sekizde Leylâ ile ben size geliyoruz.
ìs-má-íl^y—	pé-k^y‿í-yì! sè-k^{y}íz-dé!	Pek iyi! Sekizde!

[1]Not on the record.

Section E—Conversation

1. Covering the Turkish of Basic Sentences (Individual Study)

Cover the Turkish of the *Basic Sentences* and practice saying the Turkish equivalents of the English expressions.

2. Vocabulary Check-Up

As in previous units, the Group Leader will call on various members of the group to give the Turkish expressions which correspond to the English in the *Basic Sentences*.

3. Conversation

Work through the following outlined conversations, taking parts. Act them out in front of the group; keep this up until you can do them easily and smoothly. When the outlined conversations go well, then change the situations somewhat. You now have more material which you can work into additional conversations. Invent topics as you did for the previous units.

1. Guests at a party.

   The Kayas and the Metins arrive and exchange greetings with their hosts, the Carrs. They inquire about the health of each other's children. They send the children off to amuse themselves elsewhere. They talk, drink beer, wine, etc. The ladies discuss their children. The men smoke. Later they break up, making their excuses.

2. Meeting in front of the movies.

   Mr. Gunduz meets Mr. and Mrs. Metin who invite him to accompany them to the movies. He accepts and they talk about the hour, and whether the movie is good or not. After the movie, they take their leave of each other.

Section F—Conversation (*Cont.*)

1. Conversation (*Cont.*)

Continue the conversations started in Section E, with a review of parts 1 and 2 of the section if necessary.

2. Questions and Answers

First run through the *Listening In* once more. Then answer the following questions when the Guide asks you, or take turns asking them of others and answering them.

1. 1. bày‿kár bú‿g^{y}ǜn ná-sìl?
2. báy vé‿bá-yàn‿kár top-lan-tı-yá‿g^{y}e-l^{y}í-yór-làr-mí?
3. bày‿kár né‿dí-yòr?

2. 4. bá-yàn‿mé-tín ná-sìl?
5. báy‿ká-rín‿ço-cúk-la-rì bú‿g^{y}ǜn i-yí-mi-dír-l^{y}èr?
6. bá-yàn‿ká-rín káç‿kı-zi‿vàr?
7. i-sím-l^{y}e-rí‿nè?
8. bày-lár né‿yap-má-k‿ís-ti-yór-làr?
9. k^{y}ím‿şük^y-rü-yé‿i-l^{y}é‿çó-k‿i-yí‿ár-ka-dàş-tir?
10. né-re-yé‿dá-i-ma‿be-ra:-bér‿g^{y}i-dér-l^{y}èr?

3. 11. k^{y}ìm-l^{y}ér hér‿sa-bá-h‿ér-k^{y}én‿kál-kár-làr?

4. 12. fàt-má á-l^{y}í‿i-l^{y}é-mi‿év-l^{y}ì?
13. on-la-rín‿ço-cuk-la-rí‿vár-mì?
14. k^{y}ím‿si-nè-ma-dá?
15. k^{y}í-mín‿kiz‿kar-de-şí‿i-l^{y}é‿be-rá:-bèr?
16. a-l^{y}í‿şím-di‿ye-mék^y‿ye-mé-k^y‿ís-ti-yór-mù?
17. l^{y}o-kán-ta-nın‿né-sí‿çó-k‿í-yì?

5. 18. is-ma-i-l^{y}ín‿ho-şu-ná‿né‿g^{y}í-di-yòr?
19. fát-ma-nìn-dá‿né?
20. bú‿ák-şàm fát-mà‿i-l^{y}é‿is-ma-íl^y né-re-yé‿g^{y}í-di-yór-làr?
21. l^{y}éy-l^{y}à:‿i-l^{y}é‿mu-záf-fér ón-lá-r‿i-l^{y}é‿be-rá:-bèr g^{y}it-mé-k^y‿is-tí-yór-làr-mí?
22. sá-àt‿káç-tá?

FINDER LIST

àl-láh	God
al-làh‿ra-hát-lík‿vér-sìn!	Good night! (lit. may God give rest!)
à-l^{y}í-yé	Aliye (girl's name)
án-nè	mother
bé-rà:-bér	together

bíz	we; us
bìz-dé	at our house (lit. at us)
bú	this
bú‿g^{y}ǜn	today (lit. this day)
bùn-lár	these (people)
búy-rùn!	come in!
çò-cúk	child; boy
çó-cùk-lár	(the) children
çó-cúk-làr!	children!
ço-cùk-lá-rí	her (their) children
ço-cùk-lá-rı-níz	your children
dá-i̍-mà	always
de- . . .	say
dì-yór	[he] says (lit. is saying)
dè-yíl^{y}	not
dé-yil^{y}-dìr	[he] is not
de-yi̍l^{y}-l^{y}ér-dir	they are not
dò:-rú	right
çók‿dó:-rù!	quite right!
èr-k^{y}én	early
év	house; home
èv-dé	at home

ey-l^{y}en- . . . (aor. *-ir-*)	enjoy oneself, amuse oneself
èy-l^{y}én-díк^y!	we've amused ourselves
ėy-l^{y}é-nìn!	amuse yourself!
g^{y}éç	late
g^{y}el^y- . . . (aor. *-ir-*)	come
g^{y}e-l^{y}ír-mı̍-si-nìz?	will you come?
g^{y}ė-l^{y}í-yòr	[they] are coming
g^{y}e-l^{y}í-yór-làr	they are coming
g^{y}e-l^{y}í-yór-làr-mi?	are they coming?
g^{y}e-l^{y}í-yór-mù?	are [they] coming?
g^{y}it- . . . (aor. *-er-*)	go
g^{y}ı̍-dèr-l^{y}ér	they go
g^{y}í-dìn!	go!
g^{y}ı̍-di-yór-mú-su-nùz?	are you going?
g^{y}ìt-ték^y	to go
g^{y}ı̍t-mék^y-tè	to go, too
g^{y}ǘn	day
bú‿g^{y}ǜn	today (lit. this day)
hér	every
hér‿sá-bàh	every morning
ì-k^{y}í	two
ì-k^{y}ı̍-sí	the two of them (lit. their two)
ı̍-k^{y}i-sí-ḍè	both (of them)

ì-l^{y}é	with
á-l^{y}í‿i̍-l^{y}è	with Ali
á-l^{y}í‿i-l^{y}è-mi̍?	with Ali?
hák-kí‿i̍-l^{y}è	with Hakki
hák-kí‿i-l^{y}è-mi̍?	with Hakki?
şǘk^y-rü-yé-m‿i̍-l^{y}è	with my Shukruye
ì-yí	good; well
i̍-yí-dìr	[he] is good
i̍-yí-di̍r-l^{y}èr	they are well
i-yí-mi-di̍r-l^{y}èr?	are they well?
ì-yi̍-l^{y}ér	good ones
i̍-yi-l^{y}ér-dìr	[it]'s [the] good ones
i-yí-mi̍-si-nìz?	[are] you well?
i̍-yí-yìm	I['m] well
i̍-yí-yìz	we [are] well
kal- . . . (aor. *-ır-*)	stay, remain
kàl-dík	we've stayed
kalk- . . . (aor. *-ar-*)	get up; leave
kál-ká-rìz	we get up
kàl-kár-lár	they get up
kàr-déş	brother
kár-dé-şìz	we [are] brother[s]

kíz	daughter; girl
kì-zìm	I [am] [a] girl
kí-zìm-dìr	I am [a] girl
kìz-lár	daughters
kìz-là-rím	my daughters
ko-nuş- . . . (aor. *-ur-*)	talk
kò-nùş-mák	to talk
k^{y}ím	who
k^{y}ìm-l^{y}ér	who all (more than one)
k^{y}ì-mín	whose
l^{y}èy-l^{y}á:	Leylâ (girl's name)
mi-sà:-fír	guest
mi-sà:-fír-l^{y}ér	guests
mù-zàf-fér	Muzaffer (boy's name) (lit. "Victor")
ná-sìl	how?
ná-sìl?	how [are] [they]?
né	what
né‿ò	what! what's this?
né‿ò g^{y}í-di-yór-mú-su-nùz	What's this, are you going?
né-rè-dè?	where?
né-re-dé-l^{y}èr?	where [are] they?
né-rè-yè?	where (lit. whither)?

ó	he (she, it)
òn-lár	they
òn-lá-rín	of them, their
ò-dá	room
ò-dá-níz	your room
ó-da-nìz-dá	in your room
òr-hán	Orhan (boy's name)
ò-úl	son
ò:-lúm	my son
ó:-lúm-dùr	[it]'s my son
ò:-lú-núz	your son
ò:-lúm, etc.	see *ò-úl*
pék^{y}	very
pé-k^{y}‿ì-yì	all right! (lit. very well)
rá-hàt-lík	rest
al-láh‿ra-hát-lík‿vér-sìn!	Good night! (lit. may God give rest!)
sà-át	hour; o'clock; watch; clock
sà-á-tí	his watch
sà-báh	morning
sì-né-mà	movie(s)
si-né-má-dà	in the movies
sì-né-má-yà	to the movies

síz	you
sì-zé	to you; to your house
sí-zé-dè	to you, too
şùk^{y}-rǘ-yé	Shukruye (girl's name)
şùk^{y}-rǘ-yém	my Shukruye
tòp-làn-tí	party
tóp-làn-tı-yá	to [the] party
ver- . . . (aor. *-ir-*)	give
vèr-sín!	may [he] give!
yap- . . . (aor. *-ar-*)	do
yàp-mák	to do
zá:t	gentleman
zà:-tí	her gentleman

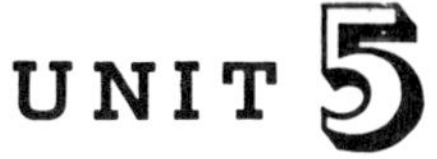

UNIT 5

LET'S TALK ABOUT THE WEATHER

SECTION A—BASIC SENTENCES

Go once through the *Basic Sentences* in unison, then do the *Hints on Pronunciation*, and then go twice more through the *Basic Sentences* individually.

1. Basic Sentences

Mr. Kaya and Mr. Carr get in out of the rain.

ENGLISH EQUIVALENTS	AIDS TO LISTENING	CONVENTIONAL TURKISH SPELLING
Record 10A, beginning.		
	Mr. Carr	
Good morning, Mr. Kaya! How are you today?	g^yù-n‿áy-dín, bày‿ká-yá! bú‿g^yùn ná-sil-sı-nìz?	Gün aydın, bay Kaya! Bu gün nasılsınız?
	Mr. Kaya	
Good morning, Mr. Carr! I'm very well.	g^yù-n‿áy-dín, bày‿kár! çó-k‿i-yi-yìm.	Gün aydın, bay Kar! Çok iyiyim.
	Mr. Carr	
weather	hà-vá.	hava
Do you like this weather?	bú‿há-và ho-şu-nu-zá‿g^yi-di-yór-mù?	Bu hava hoşunuza gidiyormu?
	Mr. Kaya	
Yes, I like it very much!	é-vèt, çók‿hó-şu-má‿g^yi-di-yòr!	Evet, çok hoşuma gidiyor!

	Mr. Carr	
[the] sun	g^{y}ü̂-néş.	güneş
beautifully	g^{y}ü̂-zél^{y}.	güzel
[it] is shining	pár-lí-yòr.	parlıyor
The sun's shining nicely, isn't it?	g^{y}ü-néş‿g^{y}ü-zél^{y}‿pár-lı-yòr, dė-yil^{y}-mì?	Güneş güzel parlıyor, değilmi?
	Mr. Kaya	
cool	sè-rín.	serin
breeze	rü̂z-g^{y}ár.	rüzgâr
[it] is blowing	ė-sí-yòr.	esiyor
Yes. And there's a cool breeze blowing.	é-vèt. se-rín‿bir‿rüz-g^{y}ár-dá‿é-si-yòr.	Evet. Serin bir rüzgâr da esiyor.
	Mr. Carr	
[the] birds	kùş-lár.	kuşlar
in [the] trees	a-àç-lár-dá.	ağaçlarda
they are singing	ö-tü̂-yór-làr.	ötüyorlar
The birds are singing in the trees.	kuş-lár‿a-aç-lar-dá‿ö-tü̂-yór-làr.	Kuşlar ağaçlarda ötüyorlar.
	Mr. Kaya	
but	fá-kàt.	fakat
further	dà-há.	daha
on (lit. yonder)	ö̂-té-dé.	ötede
what [is] there?	né‿vàr?	ne var?
But what's that over there?	fá-kàt da-há‿ö-te-dé‿né‿vàr?	Fakat daha ötede ne var?
	Mr. Carr	
Where?	né-rė-dè?	Nerede?

Mr. Kaya

on [the] horizon	ú-fùk-tá.	ufukta
you see [it[1]]	g^{y}ö-rû-yór-su-nùz.	görüyorsunuz
On the horizon. You see it, don't you?	ú-fùk-tá. g^{y}ö-rû-yór-su-nùz, dé-yíl^{y}-mì?	Ufukta. Görüyorsunuz, değilmi?

Mr. Carr

there	ó-rá-dà.	orada
black	kà-rá.	kara
clouds	bú-lùt-lár.	bulutlar
[they] are gathering	tóp-la-ní-yòr.	toplanıyor
Black clouds are gathering there.	ó-ra-da‿ka-rá‿bu-lút-!ár‿tóp-lá-nı-yòr.	Orada kara bulutlar toplanıyor.

Record 10B, beginning.

lightning	şim-şék^{y}‿pa-ril-tı-la-rì.	şimşek parıltıları
thunder	şim-şék^{y}‿sés-l^{y}e-rì.	şimşek sesleri
[they] are approaching	yák-la-şí-yòr.	yaklaşıyor
The thunder and lightning are getting nearer.	şim-şék^{y}‿pa-ril-tı-la-rì vé‿şim-şék^{y}‿sés-l^{y}e-rì yák-la-şí-yòr.	Şimşek parıltıları ve şimşek sesleri yaklaşıyor.

Mr. Kaya

heaven	g^{y}ők^{y}.	gök
its face	yû-zû.	yüzü
[it] is getting dark	ká-ra-rí-yòr.	kararıyor
The sky is getting dark.	g^{y}ők^{y}‿yü-zû ká-ra-rí-yòr.	Gök yüzü kararıyor.

[1]Not on record.

	Mr. Carr	
come on!	háy-dì!	haydi
let's run!	kò-şá-lím!	koşalım
Come on, let's run!	háy-dì, kò-şá-lím!	Haydi, koşalım!
	Mr. Kaya	
rain	yà:-múr.	yağmur
to fall	yà:-má-á.	yağmağa
[it] is starting	báş-lí-yòr.	başlıyor
Yes, it's starting to rain.	é-vèt, ya:-múr‿yá:-ma-á‿báş-lı-yòr.	Evet, yağmur yağmağa başlıyor.
	Mr. Carr	
we're getting wet	ı̀s-la-ní-yó-rùz.	ıslanıyoruz.
on [the] corner	k^{y}ö̀-şé-dé.	köşede
shelter	sì-i-nák.	sığınak
We're getting wet!	ı̀s-la-ní-yó-rùz!	Islanıyoruz!
There's a shelter on the corner.	k^{y}ö-şe-dé‿bi̍r‿si-ı-nák‿vàr.	Köşede bir sığınak var.
	Mr. Kaya	
there (lit. thither)	ó-rá-yà.	oraya
Let's run there!	ó-ra-yá‿kó-şa-lìm!	Oraya koşalım!
	Mr. Carr	
[it] is stopping	di̍-ni̍-yòr.	diniyor
Now the rain is stopping.	şi̍m-di‿ya:-múr‿di̍-ni̍-yòr.	Şimdi yağmur diniyor.

Mr. Kaya

your right	hàk-kı-níz.	hakkınız
there [is]	vár.	var
[they] are passing	gʸé-çi-yòr.	geçiyor
[it] is coming out	gʸö-zü-kʸű-yòr.	gözüküyor
You're right, the clouds are passing, the sun is coming out.	hák-kı-níz‿vàr, bu-lut-lár‿gʸé-çi-yòr, gʸü-néş‿gʸö-zü-kʸű-yòr.	Hakkınız var, bulutlar geçiyor, güneş gözüküyor.

Mr. Carr

again	tékʸ-ràr.	tekrar
Now the weather is nice again!	şim-di‿ha-vá‿tékʸ-rár‿gʸü-zèlʸ!	Şimdi hava tekrar güzel!

Mr. Kaya

Good-bye!	ál-la-há‿ıs-már-la-dìk!	Allaha ısmarladık!

Mr. Carr

Good-bye!	gʸü-lʸé‿gʸü-lʸè!	Güle güle!

Before you go through the *Basic Sentences* a second time, *review* the sound values of these letters:

LETTER	STANDS FOR A SOUND	EXAMPLES	
c	like g in *gem* or *gin*	çò-cúk	(*child*)
o:	drawled or long like *ou* in *soul*	dò:-rú	(*right*)

Remember:

a	about as in *father*	hà-vá	(*weather*)
e	about as in *pet*	é-vèt	(*yes*)
i	about as in *pit*	i-yi-yìm	(*I['m] well*)
o	about as in *for*	çók	(*very much*)

u	about as in *put*
ı	somewhat like *u* in *suppose*
ü	like *i* in *pit*, with puckered lips
ö	like *e* in *pet*, with puckered lips
a:	drawled like *a* in *father*
ç	like *ch* in *chin*
kʸ	like *c* in *cute*
gʸ	like *g* in *argue*
ş	like *sh* in *shin*
h	like *h* in *head*
y	like *y* in *year* even in the middle of a word
lʸ	like *li* in *million*
‿	connects words spoken together without pause or break
´	marks strongest vowel
`	marks next strongest vowel
'	marks other fairly strong vowels

kúş	(*bird*)
sì-i-nák	(*shelter*)
gʸù-zélʸ	(*beautiful*)
kʸò-şé	(*corner*)
yà:-múr	(*rain*)
gʸé-çi-yòr	([*it*] *is passing*)
tékʸ-ràr	(*again*)
rùz-gʸár	(*breeze*)
gʸù-néş	(*sun*)
hàk-ki-níz	(*your right*)
yák-la-şí-yòr	([*it*] *is approaching*)
gʸù-zélʸ	(*beautiful*)

Then study the following:

2. Hints on Pronunciation

One of the simple basic vowel sounds of Turkish which we have met in this lesson is unlike any English vowel sound. If you pronounce "en" (the name of the letter *n*) several times with spread lips, as one usually does in English, and then repeat it with puckered lips, you get a vowel sound, before the *n*, very much like Turkish *ö*.

Note: This Turkish sound is written with *ö* with two dots over it, and is not to be confused with *o*, without any dots.

Practice pronouncing "en" (the letter *n*) first with spread lips, and then with puckered lips, thus:

PRACTICE 1 **Record 11A, beginning.**

én.
ő́n.
én.
ő́n.
én.
ő́n.
én.
ő́n. ő́n. ő́n. ő́n.

The first of these is Turkish *én* 'most', the second is Turkish *ő́n* 'front'.

PRACTICE 2 **Record 11A, after 1st spiral.**

dő́rt.	*(four)*
ȍ-tǘ-yòr.	*([it] sings)*
gʸȍ-rǘ-yòr.	*([it] sees)*
ȍ̀-tė-dé.	*(over there)*
gʸő́kʸ.	*(heaven)*
kʸȍ̀-şé.	*(corner)*
gʸȍ-zü-kʸǘ-yòr.	*([it] is coming out)*

Now go twice through the *Basic Sentences* individually, once with book open, and once with book closed.

Section B—Word Study and Review of Basic Sentences

1. Word Study (Individual Study)

1. *The Turkish equivalents of English "our"*

We have seen forms such as *hò-şu-mu̇-zá* 'to our pleasure', *o-fì-si-miz* 'our office'. Tabulating these and similar forms we get:

	Column I			*Column II*	
			Group I		
i	à-l^{y}í	*'Ali'*	:	à-l^{y}i-míz	*'our Ali'*
e	án-nè	*'mother'*	:	án-né-mìz	*'our mother'*
ü	....	....	:	....	....
ö	....	....	:	....	....
ı	kà-rí	*'wife'*	:	kà-ri-míz	*'our wife'*
a	pà-rá	*'money'*	:	pà-rá-míz	*'our money'*
u	....	....	:	....	....
o	....	....	:	....	....
			Group II		
i	k^{y}ìb-rít	*'match'*	:	k^{y}ib-rì-ti-míz	*'our match'*
e	kàr-déṣ	*'brother'*	:	kár-dè-ṣi-míz	*'our brother'*
ü	g^{y}ǘn	*'day'*	:	g^{y}ǜ-nü-mǘz	*'our day'*
ö	dő́rt	*'four'*	:	dö̀r-dü-mǘz	*'the four of us (lit. our four)'*
ı	kíz	*'daughter'*	:	kì-zi-míz	*'our daughter'*
a	àr-ká-dáṣ	*'friend'*	:	ár-ka-dà-ṣı-míz	*'our friend'*
u	ù-fúk	*'horizon'*	:	ùf-kú-múz	*'our horizon'*
o	ón	*'ten'*	:	ò-nú-múz	*'the ten of us'*

If we compare Column I with Column II, and Group I with Group II above, we see that:

1. the Turkish *possessive* ending 'our' has a number of different forms;
2. the ending is *-miz*, *-müz*, *-mız*, *-muz* after a *vowel*, as in Group I;
3. it is *-i-miz*, *-ü-müz*, *-ı-mız*, *-u-muz* after a consonant, as in Group II;

4. the (second) vowel of this ending is the *strongest vowel* of the forms in Column II, when it is the *last* vowel of the forms in Column I, which is strongest (kàr-déṣ : kár-dè-ṣi-mìz); but if any other vowel of the forms in Column I is strongest, then the ending vowel is second strongest (án-nè : án-né-mìz);

5. here we see what we have called *Vowel Harmony Type I* (see Unit 3 B. 1. 2) in its complete form, with its *four* possible correspondence types; in the following table, we summarize the possibilities of this type of vowel harmony:

Turkish Vowel Harmony Type I

i	ü	ı	u	base final-syllable vowels
e	ö	a	o	
i	ü	ı	u	ending vowel

A base, whose final syllable contains the vowel *i* or *e*, is followed by the vowel *i* in those endings which follow Vowel Harmony Type I.

A base, whose final syllable contains the vowel *ü* or *ö*, is followed by the vowel *ü* in such endings.

A base, whose final syllable contains the vowel *ı* or *a*, is followed by the vowel *ı* in such endings.

A base, whose final syllable contains the vowel *u* or *o*, is followed by the vowel *u* in such endings.

Here is a list of the endings, which we have studied up to now, which follow Vowel Harmony Type I:

Unit 2

-dir, -dür, -dır, -dur	(after "humming" sounds)	*'is, are, am'*
-tir, -tür, -tır, -tur	(after other sounds)	
-m	(after vowel)	*'my'*
-im, -üm, -ım, -um	(after consonant)	
-niz, -nüz, -nız, -nuz	(after vowel)	*'your'*
-i-niz, -ü-nüz, -ı-nız, -u-nuz	(after consonant)	
-si, -sü, -sı, -su	(after vowel)	*'his, her, its, their'*
-i, -ü, -ı, -u	(after consonant)	

-nin, -nün, -nın, -nun	(after vowel)	(*possessor*)
-in, -ün, -ın, -un	(after consonant)	
	Unit 3	
-i-yor, -ü-yor, -ı-yor, -u-yor		(*momentary*)
-ir, -ür, -ır, -ur	(only after consonant)	(*aorist*)
	Unit 4	
-yim, -yüm, -yım, -yum	(after vowel)	'*I*'
-im, -üm, -ım, -um	(after consonant)	
-si-niz, -sü-nüz, -sı-nız, -su-nuz		'*you*'
-yiz, -yüz, -yız, -yuz	(after vowel)	'*we*'
-iz, -üz, -ız, -uz	(after consonant)	
	Unit 5	
-miz, -müz, -mız, muz	(after vowel)	'*our*'
-i-miz, -ü-müz, -ı-mız, -u-muz	(after consonant)	

We shall also study in the present unit (see below) this ending:

-mi?, -mü?, -mı?, -mu? (*interrogative*)

2. Turkish noun ending "more than one"

We have already seen many forms such as *bày-lár*, 'gentlemen', *çò-cùk-lár* 'children', *kùş-lár* 'birds', *ìş-lʸér* 'jobs', and so on. If we tabulate similar forms, we get:

	Column I			*Column II*	
			Group I		
i	íş	'*job*'	:	ìş-lʸér	'*jobs*'
e	án-nè	'*mother*'	:	án-né-lʸèr	'*mothers*'
ü	gʸǘn	'*day*'	:	gʸǜn-lʸér	'*days*'
ö	gʸő̈kʸ	'*sky*'	:	gʸö̀kʸ-lʸér	'*skies*'

Group II

ı	pá-rìl-tí	*'flash'*	:	pá-rìl-tı-lár	*'flashes'*
a	rǜz-g^{y}ár	*'breeze'*	:	rǘz-g^{y}àr-lár	*'breezes'*
u	bù-lút	*'cloud'*	:	bú-lùt-lár	*'clouds'*
o	ó	*'he'*	:	òn-lár	*'they'*

If we compare Column I with II, and Groups I and II, we see that:

1. the ending which means 'more than one' has two forms (*-l^{y}er*, *-lar*);
2. the vowel of the ending of the forms in Column II is *strongest* when it is the last vowel of the base (Column I) which is strongest (bù-l*ú*t : bú-lùt-l*á*r); otherwise, the ending-vowel is *second strongest* (án-nè : án-né-l^{y}èr);
3. this "more than one" ending we shall call the *noun plural* ending or simply the *plural* ending;
4. this *-l^{y}er*, *-lar* noun plural ending does not follow *Vowel Harmony Type I*, which we summarized above; it follows what we have called *Vowel Harmony Type II* (see Unit 3. B. 1. 2), which we shall summarize in the following table:

Turkish Vowel Harmony Type II

i ü / e ö	ı u / a o	base final-syllable vowels
e	a	ending vowel

A base, whose final syllable contains the vowel *i*, *e*, *ü*, or *ö*, is followed by the vowel *e* in those endings which follow Vowel Harmony Type II.

A base, whose final syllable contains the vowel *ı*, *a*, *u*, or *o*, is followed by the vowel *a* in such endings.

Here are the endings which we have studied up to now, which follow Vowel Harmony Type II:

Unit 3

-er, -ar	(only after consonant)	(*aorist*)

Unit 4

-l^{y}er, -lar		*'they'*

-l^{y}er, -lar (*noun plural*)

We shall also study in the present unit (see below) this ending:

-de, -da	(after "humming" sounds)	*'and, too, also'*
-te, -ta	(after other sounds)	

3. *Turkish question forms*

We have seen a number of forms such as *ȧn-lı-yór-mú-su-nùz?* 'do you understand?', *vár-mì?* '[is] there?', *ve-rír-mi-si-nìz?* 'will you give?', etc. If we tabulate a number of them, we get:

	Column I			*Column II*	
			Group I		
i	ì-yí	*'good'*	:	i-yí-mì?	*'[is] it good?'*
e	ȧ-l^{y}í‿i-l^{y}è	*'with Ali'*	:	ȧ-l^{y}í‿i-l^{y}è-mi?	*'([is] [it]) with Ali?'*
ı	kíz	*'daughter(s)'*	:	kíz-mì?	*'([are] [they]) daughters?'*
a	şà-ráp	*'wine'*	:	şá-ráp-mì?	*'([is] [it]) wine?'*
o	yók	*'there [is]n't'*	:	yók-mù?	*'[is]n't there?'*
a	sȧ:-dá-dìr	*'[it] is to [the] right'*	:	sa:-dá-mi-dìr?	*'is [it] to [the] right?'*
i	i-yí-dir-l^{y}èr	*'they are well'*	:	i-yí-mi-dir-l^{y}èr?	*'are they well?'*
i	i-yí-si-nìz	*'you [are] well'*	:	i-yí-mi-si-nìz?	*'[are] you well?'*
i	kȧr-de-şím-dìr	*'[it] is my brother'*	:	kȧr-de-şím-mi-dìr?	*'is [it] my brother?'*
i	ėv-l^{y}í-dìr	*'[she] is married'*	:	ėv-l^{y}í-mi-dìr?	*'is [she] married?'*
			Group II		
i	ve-rír-si-nìz	*'you give'*	:	ve-rír-mi-si-nìz?	*'will you give?'*
e	g^{y}ì-dér	*'[it] goes'*	:	g^{y}i-dér-mì?	*'does [it] go?'*
a	kȯ-nu-şú-yȯr-làr	*'they are talking'*	:	kȯ-nu-şú-yȯr-làr-mi?	*'are they talking?'*

o	gʸe-lʸí-yór-su-nùz	*'you are coming'*	:	gʸé-lʸi-yór-mú-su-nùz?	*'are you coming?'*
o	yá-pí-yòr	*'[she] is doing'*	:	yá-pı-yór-mù?	*'is [she] doing?'*
o	ís-tí-yo-rùm	*'I want'*	:	ís-ti-yór-mú-yùm?	*'[do] I want?'*
a	yá-pá-rìz	*'we do'*	:	ya-pár-mi-yìz?	*'[do] we do?'*
ü	gʸö̀-rû̀r	*'he sees'*	:	gʸö́-rû́r-mù?	*'[does] he see?'*

If we compare Column I with Column II, we see that:

1. the forms in Column II all contain the ending *-mi, -mü, -mı, -mu;*
2. this ending follows Vowel Harmony Type I;
3. the forms in Group I are *nouns* with the *copula* ending; we see that the *-mi, -mü, -mı, -mu* ending comes
   a. before the personal endings (*-si-niz);*
   b. before the copula ending (*-0; -dir, -dır,* etc.)
4. the forms in Group II are *verbs* with various *personal* endings*;* we see that the *-mi, -mü, -mı, -mu* ending comes before all personal endings except the "they" ending:
   a. before *-yum* 'I', *-0* 'he', *-yız* 'we', *-si-niz* 'you';
   b. after *-lar;*
5. the *strongest vowel* is always before the *-mi, -mü, -mı, -mu* ending, never on it; we note that only in the momentary forms (yá-pí-yòr : yá-pı-yór-mù?) is there any change in the position of the strongest vowel, to bring it up to the syllable just before the ending; in the "they" form, however, *kó-nu-şú-yór-làr-mi?*, there is no change in the distribution of *strongest* and next strongest vowels, so that it is the next strongest vowel of the "they" ending that comes just before the *-mi, -mü*, etc.

   However, when the "they" form comes at the end of a sentence, the *strongest vowel* frequently shifts to the *-yor-:*

   ó-ra-ya‿gʸit-mé-kʸ‿ís-ti-yór-làr-mi? 'do they want to go there?'

The difference in meaning between Column I and Column II is the difference between a *statement* and a *question.* So we shall call the forms in Column II *question* or *interrogative* forms, and this ending (*-mi, -mü, -mı, -mu*) the *interrogative* ending.

4. *Turkish equivalents of English 'and, too, also'*

We have seen a number of forms like *sí-zín-dè* 'yours, too', *síz-dè* 'you also', *í-kʸi-sí-dè* 'both of them', *bír‿rüz-gʸár-dà* 'and a wind'. If we tabulate them with others, we get:

	Column I			Column II	
			Group I		
i	sì-zi̇n	*'yours'*	:	si̇-zi̇n-dè	*'yours, too'*
e	bén	*'I'*	:	bén-dè	*'I, too'*
ü	gʸǘn	'[*the*] *day*'	:	gʸǘn-dè	'[*the*] *day, too*'
ı	fàt-mȧ-nín	*'Fatma's'*	:	fȧt-ma-nín-dà	*'Fatma's, too'*
a	kìz-lár	'[*the*] *girls*'	:	kiz-lár-dà	'[*the*] *girls, too*'
u	ò:-lúm	*'my son'*	:	ȯ:-lúm-dà	*'my son, too'*
o	ón	*'ten'*	:	ón-dà	*'ten, too'*
			Group II		
i	bi̇̀r‿kʸib-ri̇́t	*'a match'*	:	bi̇̀r‿kʸi̇b-rít-tè	*'a match, too'*
e	gʸi̇̀t-mékʸ	*'to go'*	:	gʸi̇t-mékʸ-tè	*'to go, too'*
ü	sǘt	*'milk'*	:	sǘt-tè	*'milk, too'*
ö	gʸő̈kʸ	*'heaven'*	:	gʸő̈k-tè	*'heaven, too'*
ı	kíş	*'winter'*	:	kíş-tà	*'winter, too'*
a	àr-kȧ-dáş	'[*the*] *friend*'	:	ȧr-ka-dáş-tà	'[*the*] *friend, too*'
u	kúş	'[*the*] *bird*'	:	kúş-tà	'[*the*] *bird, too*'

If we compare Columns I and II, Groups I and II, we see that:

1. the ending which means 'and, too, also' follows Vowel Harmony Type II;
2. the ending is *-de, -da* after bases which end in "humming" sounds, such as *-n, -r, -m;*
3. the ending is *-te, -ta* after bases which end in "non-humming" sounds, such as *-t, -k*ʸ, *-ş;*

Note: Compare the distribution of the forms of the copula ending (*-dir, -dür*, etc.) which we have seen in Units 2 and 4.

4. the *strongest vowel* is always in the base, never in the ending.

2. Covering English and Turkish of Word Study (Individual Study)

Check yourself on your knowledge of the *Word Study* by covering first the English, then the Turkish, and making sure you know everything thoroughly.

3. Review of Basic Sentences

With the Guide or records, review the first half of the *Basic Sentences* as in previous units.

SECTION C—REVIEW OF BASIC SENTENCES (*Cont.*)

1. Review of Basic Sentences (*Cont.*)

Review the second half of the *Basic Sentences*.

2. Covering the English of Basic Sentences (Individual Study)

Go through the *Basic Sentences* covering up the English and reading aloud the Turkish. Check up on anything you do not know, until you are sure of everything.

3. Word Study Review (Individual Study)

Work through the following exercises. Do not write anything down. If you cannot do the work rapidly, review again the *Word Study*. Be prepared to do what is required when the Leader calls on you. Always repeat the entire expression, phrase or sentence as you work.

1. Add the proper forms of the Turkish possessive ending "*our*" to the following words:

àl-tí
bí-rà
çó-cùk-lár
év
*he-p(i)
ís-tàs-yón
íş
kàh-vé
kúş
lʸó-kán-tà
mi-sà:-fír-lʸér
sǘt
trén

2. Add the proper forms of the *noun plural* ending to the following words:

àk-ṣám
àr-ká-dáṣ
ì-sím
ís-tàs-yón
kàr-déṣ
kúrt
lʸó-kán-tà
ò-télʸ
ò-úl
ṣéy

3. Change the following statements into *questions:*

1. hér‿kìz gʸù-zélʸ.
2. tǘrkʸ-çe‿kó-nu-ṣúr-sú-nùz.
3. ṣa-ráp‿hó-ṣu-ná‿gʸì-dèr.
4. ì-yí-yìz.
5. gʸö-rǘr-sǘ-nǜz.
6. bék-çi-lʸìk‿ya-pár-làr.
7. bír‿ṣé-y‿án-lá-mı-yò-rúm.
8. dé-yìlʸ-lʸér.
9. o-nún‿ço-cúk-la-rí‿vàr.
10. i-lʸér-dé-dìr.

4. Add the proper form of the "*and, too, also*" ending to the following words:

bíz
bú-rá-dà
bú‿sá-bàh
bú‿zà:t
çò-cúk
ís-ma-í-lʸ‿í-lʸè
ó
òn-lár
pá-tá-tès
tó-mún‿ká-rı-sì

4. What Would You Say? (Individual Study)

Read aloud each of the following and then pick out the expression you think most suitable:

1. *Mr. Carr meets Mr. Kaya one morning on the street. He says:*

a. al-láh‿ra-hát-lík‿vér-sìn!
b. gʸù-n‿áy-dín, bày‿ká-yá! ná-sil-sı-nìz?

2. *Mr. Kaya answers:*

a. gʸù-n‿áy-dín! çó-k‿ì-yí-yìm, te-ṣékʸ-kʸǘ-r‿e-dè-rím.
b. sí-zín-dè! ì-yí-yìm.

3. *Mr. Carr asks him how he likes the weather, saying:*
   a. ó‿g^{y}ü-zél^y‿kiz‿ho-ṣu-nu-zá‿g^{y}i̍-di-yór-mù?
   b. ya:-múr‿ho-ṣu-nu-zá‿g^{y}i̍-dı-yór-mù?
   c. bú‿ha-vá‿ho-ṣu-nu-zá‿g^{y}i̍-di-yór-mù?

4. *Mr. Kaya answers:*
   a. é-vèt! ṣi̍m-di‿çó-k‿i̍-yì!
   b. é-vèt! çók‿hó-ṣu·má‿g^{y}i̍-di-yòr!

5. *Mr. Carr looks at the sky, and remarks:*
   a. g^{y}ü-néṣ‿çók‿g^{y}ű-zél^y‿pár-lı-yòr, dé-yíl^y-mi̍?
   b. si-né-ma-ya‿g^{y}i-dér-mi̍-si-ni̍z?

6. *Mr. Kaya agrees with him, and adds:*
   a. há-yìr, g^{y}ű-zèl^y‿de-yi̍l^y-l^{y}ér!
   b. é-vèt. se-ri̍n‿bi̍r‿rüz-g^{y}ár-dá‿é-si-yòr.

7. *To Mr. Carr's ears comes another sign of spring weather, and he says:*
   a. kìz-lár   l^{y}o-kán-tá-dà   kó-nu-ṣú-yór-làr!
   b. kùṣ-lár   a-áç-làr-dá   ö-tű-yór-làr.

8. *Mr. Kaya, however, has caught signs of a change in the weather, and as he looks into the distance, he says:*
   a. fá-kàt   dá-há‿ö-te-dè, né‿vàr?
   b. k^{y}ȍ-ṣé-dé né‿vàr?

9. *Mr. Carr looks, too, and asks:*
   a. u-fuk-tá‿bi̍r‿ṣéy‿vár-mì?
   b. ȍ-fi-si̍m-dé   i̍ṣ‿vár-mì?

10. *Mr. Kaya answers Mr. Carr's question:*
   a. ó-rá-dà   trén‿g^{y}i̍-di-yòr.
   b. u-fuk-tá‿ka-rá‿bu-lút-lár‿tóp-lá-nı-yòr.

11. *Mr. Carr sees other signs, and remarks:*
   a. ṣi̍m-ṣék^y‿pa-ril-tı-la-rì   vé‿ṣim-ṣék^y‿sés-l^{y}e-ri̍ yák-la-ṣí-yòr.
   b. g^{y}ő́k^y‿yű-zȕ   çók‿g^{y}ü-zèl^y.

12. *Mr. Kaya, as it gets darker, adds:*
   a. é-vèt, çók‿g^{y}ü-zél^y‿pár-lı-yòr!
   b. g^{y}ő́k^y‿yű-zȕ   ká-ra-rí-yòr.

13. *Mr. Carr, as the first drops fall, cries:*
   a. yá-váṣ‿ya-váṣ‿g^{y}i̍-de-l^{y}i̍m!
   b. háy-di̍   kò-ṣá-lím!

14. *Mr. Kaya, as more drops fall, says:*
   a. çó-k‿éy-l^{y}e-ni-yò-rúz!
   b. é-vèt. yá:-múr‿ya:-ma-á‿báṣ-lı-yòr.

15. *It begins to come down hard, and Mr. Carr says:*
   a. bú‿há-và   çók‿g^{y}ü-zèl^y!
   b. is-la-ní-yo-rùz!

16. *Mr. Carr, after looking around, points ahead, and says:*
   a. be-ni̍-m‿é-vi̍m   ó-rá-dà.
   b. k^{y}ö-ṣe-dé‿bi̍r‿si-ı-nák‿vàr.

17. *Mr. Kaya looks, too, and then suggests:*

a. ó-ra-yá‿kó-şa-lìm!

b. is-là-na-lím!

18. *They take refuge there, and after a while, Mr. Carr looks out, and says:*

a. yà:-múr hó-şu-má‿gʸi-dèr.

b. şím-dì, ya:-múr‿dí-ní-yòr.

19. *Mr. Kaya agrees with him, looks about and notices other signs of the end of the shower:*

a. bú-lùt-lár çók‿ká-rà!

b. hák-kı-níz‿vàr, bu-lút-lár‿gʸé-çi-yòr, gʸü-néş‿gʸö-zü-kʸü-yòr.

20. *Mr. Carr, seeing that the weather has cleared up, says:*

a. yá:-múr‿ya:-ma-á‿báş-lı-yòr.

b. hà-vá tékʸ-rár‿gʸü-zèlʸ!

21. *Mr. Kaya goes his way, saying:*

a. mér-há-bà, ná-sil-sı-nìz?

b. ak-şam-la-rı-niz‿há-yır-lí‿ól-sùn!

c. ál-la-há‿ıs-már-la-dìk!

22. *Mr. Carr replies, as he goes off:*

a. gʸü-lʸé‿gʸü-lʸè.

b. hák-kı-níz‿vàr!

Section D—Listening In

1. What Did You Say?

Give your answers in Turkish for each of the exercises in the preceding section, when the Leader calls for them. Then, as the Leader calls for them, give the English equivalents of all the expressions in the exercise.

2. Word Study Check-Up

As you have done in the previous units, go back to the *Word Study* and give the correct Turkish for each English expression, without having to read it from the book. The Leader or one of the members of the group should read the English. As a final check the Leader will call for your answers to the exercises in the *Word Study Review* (Sec. C. 3).

3. Listening In

With your book closed, listen to the following conversations as read by the Guide or phonograph record. Repeat the Turkish immediately after hearing it. After the first repetition of each conversation, check up on the meaning of anything you do not understand, by asking someone else or by going back to the *Basic Sentences* if no one knows. Repeat again if necessary, then take parts and carry on the conversation.

1. *A shower in May.*

Record 11A, after 2nd spiral.

bày‿kár—	g^{y}ù-n‿áy-dín, bày‿ká-yá!	Gün aydın, bay Kaya!
	ná-sil-sı-nìz?	Nasılsınız?
bày‿ká-yá—	g^{y}ù-n‿áy-dín, bày‿kár!	Gün aydın, bay Kar!
	çó-k‿i-yí-yìm, te-şék^{y}-k^{y}ű-r‿e-dè-rim!	Çok iyiyim, teşekkür ederim!
bày‿kár—	bú‿ha-vá‿ho-şu-nu-zá‿g^{y}i-di-yór-mù?	Bu hava hoşunuza gidiyormu?
bày‿ká-yá—	é-vèt! çók‿hó-şu-má‿g^{y}i-di-yòr!	Evet! Çok hoşuma gidiyor!
bày‿kár—	g^{y}ù-néş bú‿g^{y}ùn çók‿g^{y}ü-zèl^{y}, dé-yíl^{y}-mì?	Güneş bu gün çok güzel, değilmi?
bày‿ká-yá—	é-vèt, çók‿g^{y}ü-zél^{y}‿pár-lı-yòr.	Evet, çok güzel parlıyor.
bày‿kár—	bú‿rüz-g^{y}àr ho-şu-nu-zá‿g^{y}i-di-yór-mù?	Bu rüzgâr hoşunuza gidiyormu?
bày‿ká-yá—	é-vèt, çók‿se-rin‿bir‿rüz-g^{y}ár-dá‿é-si-yòr.	Evet, çok serin bir rüzgâr da esiyor.
bày‿kár—	a-aç-lar-dá‿né‿vàr?	Ağaçlarda ne var?
bày‿ká-yá—	a-aç-lar-dá‿kuş-lár‿ö-tű-yór-làr.	Ağaçlarda kuşlar ötüyorlar.
bày‿kár—	fá-kàt, dá-há‿ö-te-dè, né‿vàr?	Fakat, daha ötede, ne var?
bày‿ká-yá—	u-fuk-tá‿ka-rá‿bu-lút-lár‿tóp-lá-nı-yòr.	Ufukta kara bulutlar toplanıyor.
bày‿kár—	şim-şék^{y}‿pa-ril-tı-la-rí‿g^{y}ö-zü-k^{y}ü-yòr.	Şimşek parıltıları gözüküyor.
bày‿ká-yá—	şim-şék^{y}‿sés-l^{y}e-rí-dé‿yák-lá-şı-yòr.	Şimşek sesleri de yaklaşıyor.
bày‿kár—	g^{y}ők^{y}‿yü-zù ká-ra-rí-yòr.	Gök yüzü kararıyor.
bày‿ká-yá—	háy-dì! kò-şá-lím!	Haydi! Koşalım!
bày‿kár—	is-la-ní-yó-rùz!	Islanıyoruz!
bày‿ká-yá—	k^{y}ö-şe-dé‿bir‿si-ı-nák‿vàr.	Köşede bir sığınak var.
bày‿kár—	ó-ra-yá‿kó-şa-lìm!	Oraya koşalım!
bày‿ká-yá—	bú-ra-da‿çó-k‿i-yí-yìz!	Burada çok iyiyiz!
bày‿kár—	é-vèt, fá-kàt, şim-di‿ya:-múr‿di-ní-yòr.	Evet, fakat, şimdi yağmur diniyor.

bày‿ká-yá—	hák-kı-níz‿vàr! bu-lut-lá.‿rüz-gʸâ-r‿i-lʸé‿gʸé-çí-yòr.	Hakkınız var! Bulutlar rüzgâr ile geçiyor.
bày‿kár—	şím-di‿ha-vá‿tékʸ-rár‿gʸü-zèlʸ.	Şimdi hava tekrar güzel.

2. *In the shelter.*

Record 11B, beginning.

à-lʸí—	mér-há-bà, mú-záf-fèr! há-và‿gʸü-zélʸ, dé-yílʸ-mì?	Merhaba, Muzaffer! Hava güzel, değilmi?
mú-zàf-fér—	mér-há-bà, á-lʸì! há-yìr! gʸü-zèlʸ‿dé-yílʸ!	Merhaba, Ali! Hayır! Güzel değil!
à-lʸí—	fá-kàt, u-fuk-tá‿şim-şékʸ‿pa-ril-tı-la-ri‿gʸü-zélʸ‿pár-lı-yòr! dé-yílʸ-mì?	Fakat, ufukta şimşek parıltıları güzel parlıyor! Değilmi?
mú-zàf-fér—	é-vèt, gʸü-zélʸ‿pár-lı-yòr, fá-kàt, ya:-múr‿gʸü-zèlʸ‿dé-yílʸ!	Evet, güzel parlıyor, fakat, yağmur güzel değil!
à-lʸí—	be-ním‿yá:-múr-dá‿ho-şu-mà‿gʸi-di-yór.	Benim yağmur da hoşuma gidiyor.
mú-zàf-fér—	ó á-lʸi-yé-mì?	O Aliyemi?
à-lʸí—	é-vèt, à-lʸí-yé.	Evet, Aliye.
	mér-há-bà, á-lʸí-yè!	Merhaba, Aliye!
à-lʸí-yé—	mér-há-bà! şím-di‿ya:-múr‿ya-váş‿ya-váş‿dí-ní-yòr.	Merhaba! Şimdi yağmur yavaş yavaş diniyor.
à-lʸí—	mú-záf-fèr! kʸím‿gʸé-li-yòr¿	Muzaffer! Kim geliyor?
mú-zàf-fér—	né-ré-dè?	Nerede?
à-lʸí—	kʸò-şé-dé. lʸéy-lʸá:-mì?	Köşede. Leylâmı?
mú-zàf-fér—	é-vèt, lʸèy-lʸá:!	Evet, Leylâ!
	bú‿gʸùn çók‿gʸü-zélʸ‿gʸö-zü-kʸü-yòr.	Bu gün çok güzel gözüküyor.
à-lʸí-yé—	mér-há-bà, lʸéy-lʸà:!	Merhaba. Leylâ!

mú-zàf-fér—	çó-cúk-làr! kʸö-şe-dé‿bír‿si-né-má‿vàr. i-yí-mì?	Çocuklar! Köşede bir sinema var. İyimi?
à-lʸi-yé—	é-vèt, çó-k‿i-yì.	Evet, çok iyi.
	şím-di‿çók‿gʸü-zélʸ‿bír‿fí-lʸím‿vàr.	Şimdi çok güzel bir filim var.
lʸèy-lʸá:—	ó-ra-ya‿gʸit-mé-kʸ‿is-ti-yór-mú-su-nùz?	Oraya gitmek istiyormusunuz?
mú-zàf-fér—	é-vèt! gʸì-dé-lʸím!	Evet! Gidelim!
à-lʸí—	háy-dì!	Haydi!

3. *On a corner.*

bìr‿zá:t—	áf-fe-dèr-si-niz, is-tas-yón‿né-ré-dè?	Affedersiniz, istasyon nerede?
bá-y‿ák-yü-rèkʸ—	is-tas-yón‿dá-há‿ö-te-dè, kʸö-şé-dé.	İstasyon daha ötede, köşede.
zá:t—	çók‿te-şékʸ-kʸű-r‿e-dè-rím! trén‿sa-át‿káç-tá‿kál-kı-yòr?	Çok teşekkür ederim! Tren saat kaçta kalkıyor?
bá-y‿ák-yü-rèkʸ—	sa-á-t‿o-nú‿dó-kúz‿gʸe-çé‿kál-kı-yòr.	Saat onu dokuz geçe kalkıyor.
zá:t—	te-şèkʸ-kʸür-lʸér!	Teşekkürler!
bá-y‿ák-yü-rèkʸ—	bír‿şèy‿dé-yílʸ!	Bir şey değil!

4. *The evening out.*

hàk-kí—	né‿is-ti-yòr-su-núz, çó-cúk-làr!	Ne istiyorsunuz, çocuklar!
à-lʸí—	bíz si-né-ma-yá‿gʸí-di-yò-rúz.	Biz sinemaya gidiyoruz.
	si-z‿ó-ra-ya‿gʸit-mé-kʸ‿is-ti-yór-mú-su-nùz?	Siz oraya gitmek istiyormusunuz?
hàk-kí—	é-vèt. háy-di‿gʸì-dé-lʸím!	Evet. Haydi gidelim!
à-lʸí—	án-ne-niz‿be-ra:-bér‿gʸel-mé-kʸ‿is-tér-mì?	Anneniz beraber gelmek istermi?
hàk-kí—	há-yìr. o-nú-n‿ev-dé‿i-şí‿vàr.	Hayır. Onun evde işi var.
	bi-zé‿bú‿ak-şám‿mi-sá:-fír-lʸér‿gʸé-lʸi-yòr.	Bize bu akşam misafirler geliyor.

à-l^{y}i̍—	k^{y}i̍m-l^{y}ér‿g^{y}é-l^{y}i-yòr?	Kimler geliyor?
hàk-kí—	án-ne-mi-n‿ár-ka-dáş-la-rí‿g^{y}é-l^{y}i-yòr.	Annemin arkadaşları geliyor.
à-l^{y}i̍—	g^{y}ü-zél^y‿kız-làr-mi?	Güzel kızlarmı?
hàk-kí—	há-yìr, g^{y}ü-zèl^y‿de-yi̍l^y-l^{y}ér.	Hayır, güzel değiller.
	èv-l^{y}i̍-l^{y}ér.	Evliler.
à-l^{y}i̍—	si̍-z‿ev-dé‿kal-má-k‿i̍s-ti-yór-mú-su-nùz?	Siz evde kalmak istiyormusunuz?
hàk-kí—	há-yìr!	Hayır!

5. *The boys drink.*

şûk^y-rü-yé—	a-l^{y}i̍‿dá-i-ma‿g^{y}éç‿g^{y}é-l^{y}ìr.	Ali daima geç gelir.
l^{y}èy-l^{y}á:—	şi̍m-di‿né-ré-dè?	Şimdi nerede?
şûk^y-rü-yé—	l^{y}o-kán-tá-dà.	Lokantada.
	ó-ra-da‿bi̍-rá‿i̍-çèr.	Orada bira içer.
l^{y}èy-l^{y}á:—	bi̍-ra‿o-nún‿çòk‿ho-şu-ná‿g^{y}i̍-dér, dé-yi̍l^y-mì?	Bira onun çok hoşuna gider, değilmi?
şûk^y-rü-yé—	é-vèt, çók.	Evet, çok.
	hak-kí-dá‿çó-k‿i̍-çèr.	Hakkı da çok içer.
l^{y}èy-l^{y}á:—	hák-kı-níz‿vàr!	Hakkınız var!
	fá-kàt, o-nún‿ho-şu-ná‿şá-ráp‿g^{y}i̍-dèr.	Fakat, onun hoşuna şarap gider.
şûk^y-rü-yé—	bi̍-rà, şa-ráp‿çó-k‿i̍-yì, fá-kàt, ma-á-l^{y}é-sèf, bi̍-z‿év-dé‿ká-lı-yò-rúz!	Bira, şarap çok iyi, fakat, maalesef, biz evde kalıyoruz!

Section E—Conversation

1. Covering the Turkish in Basic Sentences (Individual Study)

Cover the Turkish of the *Basic Sentences* and practice saying the Turkish equivalents of the English expressions.

2. Vocabulary Check-Up

Give the Turkish expressions for the English equivalents in the *Basic Sentences* as the Leader calls for them.

3. Conversation

As you have done in the *Conversation* in the previous units, begin to converse by following the models outlined below fairly closely; then change the situations somewhat. By now you have a fair amount of material that you can bring into your conversations. Invent new combinations of subject matter.

Work through these situations, saying in Turkish whatever fits the situation, taking parts as you have done in previous units.

1. A spring shower.

   Mr. Carr meets Mr. Kaya on the street. They exchange greetings and begin to talk about the weather, the air, the sky, the birds, etc. As they talk it begins to cloud up. They talk about the clouds, the breeze, the thunder and lightning, and so on. Mr. Carr sees a shelter, points it out and they run there. They follow the progress of the shower and when it is over, they break up and each goes his way.

2. In a store.

   Mr. Kaya enters a store and is greeted by Ahmet, the clerk. He asks for cigarettes. Ahmet gives them to him. He asks the price, pays and leaves.

3 In the office.

   Osman (òs-mán) comes in and says good morning to his father Mr. Akyurek, who returns the greeting. Mr. Akyurek introduces Osman to his friend Mr. Metin. Mr. Metin wonders whether Osman isn't a friend of his daughter Ayesha (ày-ṣé). Osman says that he is, and Mr. Akyurek adds that they always go to the movies together. Osman takes his leave.

Section F—Conversation (*Cont.*)

1. Conversation (*Cont.*)

Continue the conversations started in Section E with a review of parts 1 and 2 of the section if necessary.

2. Questions and Answers

First run through the *Listening In* once more. Then answer the following questions when the Guide asks you, or take turns asking them of others and answering them:

1. 1. bú‿gʸǜn ha-vá‿ná-sìl?
2. báy‿ka-ya-nin‿ho-şu-ná‿gʸi-di-yór-mù?
3. gʸü-néş‿ná-sil‿pár-lı-yòr?
4. rüz-gʸár-da‿ná-sìl?
5. a-aç-lar-dá‿kuş-lár‿né‿yá-pı-yór-làr?
6. bú-lùt-lár né-re-dė‿tóp-lá-nı-yòr?
7. né-lʸér‿gʸö-zü-kʸü-yòr?
8. gʸők ʸ‿yü-zǜ şim-di‿gʸü-zélʸ-mì?
9. ya:-mur-dá‿is-la-ní-yór-làr-mi?
10. né-re-yė‿kó-şu-yór-làr?
11. ó-ra-da‿ná-sıl-dir-làr?
12. şim-di‿ya:-múr‿né‿yá-pı-yòr?
13. bú-lùt-lár né‿i-lʸė‿gʸé-çi-yòr?
14. ha-vá‿tėkʸ-rar‿ná-sìl?

2. 15. ú-fùk-tá şim-şékʸ‿pa-ril-tı-la-rì ná-sil‿pár-lı-yòr?
16. a-lʸi-nin‿né-dė‿hó-şu-nà‿gʸi-di-yór?
17. kʸím‿gʸé-lʸi-yòr?
18. a-lʸi-yė‿né‿di-yòr?
19. şim-di‿kʸím-dė‿gʸé-lʸi-yòr?
20. ná-sil‿gʸö-zü-kʸü-yòr?
21. kʸö-şe-dė‿né‿vàr?
22. i-yí-mì?
23. ó-ra-da‿şim-di‿né‿vàr?
24. ó-ra-ya‿gʸit-mėkʸ‿is-ti-yór-làr-mi?

3. 25. bá-y‿ák-yü-re-yin‿tré-nì sa-át‿káç-tá‿kál-kı-yòr?

4. 26. kʸím-lʸér‿si-nė-ma-ya‿gʸit-mė-kʸ‿is-ti-yór-làr?
27. hák-kı-ní-n‿àn-ne-si be-ra:-bér‿gʸel-mė-kʸ‿is-tér-mì?
28. o-nú-n‿ev-dė‿ne-sí‿vàr?
29. kʸi-mi-n‿ar-ka-daş-la-ri‿gʸé-lʸi-yòr?
30. òn-lár gʸü-zélʸ‿kız-làr-mi?
31. hàk-kí ón-lá-r‿i-lʸė‿be-rá:-bèr ev-dė‿kal-má-k‿is-ti-yór-mù?

5. 32. kʸím‿dá-i-ma‿gʸéç‿gʸé-lʸir?
33. a-lʸi‿şim-di‿né-ré dè?
34. ó-ra-da‿né‿yá-pı-yòr?
35. né‿o-nún‿çók‿hó-şu-nà‿gʸi-dér?
36. kʸím-dė‿çó-k‿i-çèr?
37. o-nún‿ho-şu-ná‿né‿gʸi-dèr?
38. kìz-lár né-re-dė‿ká-lı-yór-làr?

FINDER LIST

à-áç	tree
á-àç-lár	trees
a-áç-làr-dá	in [the] trees
à-l^{y}í	Ali
à-l^{y}i-míz	our Ali
án-nè	mother
án-nė-mìz	our mother
àr-kȧ-dáş	friend
ár-ka-dà-şı-míz	our friend
ár-ka-dáş-tà	[the] friend, too
ày-şé	Ayesha (girl's name)
bù-lút	cloud
bú-lùt-lár	clouds
dà-há	more; further
dá-há‿ö-te-dè	over there (lit. further on)
dè-yíl^{y}	not
dé-yíl^{y}-mì?	[is] [it] not?
din- . . . (aor. *-er-*)	stop
di-ní-yòr	[it] is stopping
dör-dü-műz, etc.	see *dőrt*
dőrt	four
dör-dü-műz	the four of us (lit. our four)

ėn — most

es- . . . (aor. *-er-*) — blow (the wind)
ė-sí-yòr — [it] is blowing

fá-kàt — but

fì-l^{y}ím — film, moving picture

g^{y}eç- . . . (aor. *-er-*) — pass
g^{y}ė-çí-yòr — [they] are passing

g^{y}it- . . . (aor. *-er-*) — go
g^{y}ì-dė-l^{y}ím! — let's go!

g^{y}ö́k^{y} — heaven; sky
g^{y}ö́k^{y}‿yü̇-zǜ — the sky (lit. heaven face)
g^{y}ö̀k^{y}-l^{y}ér — heavens; skies

g^{y}ör- . . . (aor. *-ür-*) — see
g^{y}ö-rǘ-yór-su-nùz — you (are) see(ing)
g^{y}ö̀-rǘr — [he] sees
g^{y}ö̇-rǘr-mù? — does [he] see?

g^{y}ö-zük^{y}- . . . (aor. *-ür-*) — come out, appear
g^{y}ö̇-zü-k^{y}ǘ-yòr — [it] is coming out

g^{y}ǘn — day
g^{y}ǜ-nü̇-mǘz — our day
g^{y}ǜn-l^{y}ér — days
g^{y}ǘn-dè — [the] day, too

g^{y}ǜ-néş	sun
g^{y}ǜ-zél^{y}	beautiful(ly), nice(ly)
hák	right
hàk-ki-níz	your right
hák-kı-níz‿vàr	you're right (lit. there is your right)
hà-vá	weather; air
háy-dì!	come on!
íş	job
ìş-l^{y}ér	jobs
ıs-lan- . . . (aor. *-ır-*)	get wet
is-la-ní-yo-rùz	we're getting wet
is-là-na-lím!	let's get wet!
kà-rá	black
ka-rar- . . . (aor. *-ır-*)	darken, get dark
ká-ra-rí-yòr	[it] is getting dark
kàr-déş	brother
kár-dè-şi-míz	our brother
kà-rí	wife
kà-ri-míz	our wife
kíz	daughter
kì-zi-míz	our daughter

koş- . . . (aor. *-ar-*)	run
kò-şà-lím!	let's run!
kúş	bird
kùş-lár	birds
kúş-tà	[the] bird, too
kʸìb-rìt	match
kʸìb-rì-ti-miz	our match
bìr‿kʸìb-rìt-tè	a match, too
kʸò-şé	corner
kʸò-şė-dé	on [the] corner
né	what
né‿vàr?	What [is] there?
né-rė-yè?	where? (lit. whither?)
ó	he (she, it, that)
òn-lár	they
ón	ten
ón-dà	ten, too
ò-nú-múz	the ten of us
ó-rà-dà	there
ó-rà-yà	there (lit. thither)
òs-mán	Osman (boy's name)
ṓn	front

öt- . . . (aor. *-er-*)	sing (birds)
ö-tǘ-yór-làr	they are singing
ȍ-té	yonder, other side
ȍ-té-dé	on; beyond, on the other side
dá-há‿ő-te-dè	over there (lit. further on)
pà-rá	money
pà-rá-míz	our money
pá-rìl-tí	flash
pa-rìl-ti-lár	flashes
pa-rìl-ti-la-rí	its flashes
şi̍m-şékʸ‿pa-ril-tı-la-rì	lightning
par-la- . . .	shine
pár-lí-yòr	[it] is shining
rǜz-gʸár	breeze
rǘz-gʸàr-lár	breezes
se-ri̍n‿bi̍r‿rǘz-gʸár-dà	and a cool breeze
sè-ri̍n	cool
sés	noise; voice
sès-lʸér	noises
sès-lʸé-ri̍	its noises
şi̍m-şékʸ‿sés-lʸe-rì	thunder
sì-i-nák	shelter
şà-ráp	wine
şá-ráp-mì?	([is] [it]) wine?

şìm-şék^{y}	thunder and lightning
şi̍m-şék^{y}‿pa-ril-tı-la-rì	lightning
şi̍m-şék^{y}‿sés-l^{y}e-rì	thunder
ték^{y}-ràr	again
top-lan- . . . (aor. *-ır-*)	gather
tȯp-la-ní-yȯr	[they] are gathering
ù-fúk	horizon
u̇-fùk-tá	on [the] horizon
ùf-ku̇-múz	our horizon
ya:- . . . (aor. *-ar-*)	fall (rain, snow, etc.)
yà:-mȧ-á	to fall
ya:-múr‿yȧ:-ma-á‿báş-lı-yȯr	[it]'s beginning to rain
yak-laş- . . . (aor. *-ır-*)	approach
yȧk-la-şí-yȯr	[they] are approaching
yà:-múr	rain
ya:-múr‿yȧ:-ma-á‿báş-lı-yȯr	[it]'s starting to rain
yap- . . . (aor. *-ar-*)	do
né‿yȧ-pa-lìm?	what are we to do?
yű̇z	face
yȕ-zű	it's face
g^{y}ő̇k^{y}‿yü̇-zȕ	the sky (lit. heaven's face)

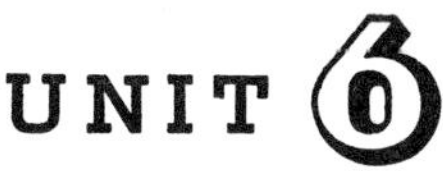

REVIEW

To the Group Leader: This unit is intended to furnish the group with a review of the work done to date: understanding of the stock of words, and of the ways of using them covered in the *Word Study*. Pronunciation should be noticed whenever the students are talking. Either the Guide or, if there is no Guide, the Leader and other students should correct faulty pronunciation.

This unit contains a number of tests which will help you make sure that you have thoroughly covered the work of the first five units of the course. They will show you what you need to restudy or review.

Section A—Word Study Review

To the Group Leader: Section A is a *Word Study* review in which are provided sets of exercises drilling on everything covered in the *Word Study* sections of Units 2 through 5. Follow the instructions carefully. These exercises may be prepared outside class hours, or individually in class. Nothing is to be written in the books. When the material has been thoroughly studied, skip around the class asking individuals to do what is required in the particular exercise.

In this section a number of drill exercises are given to test whether you have learned the uses of words and endings outlined in Units 2 through 5. Work through these exercises carefully. Follow the instructions exactly reading the completed forms and sentences aloud. Do not write anything in your books, but be prepared to give the completed forms and sentences, when the Leader calls on you.

I. *Answer in Turkish* (Ex.: dört‿dőrt‿dá-hà sé-kʸí-zé-dèr.):

1. bi-r‿i-kʸí‿dá-hà ká-çé-dèr?
2. i-kʸi‿űç‿dá-hà ká-çé-dèr?
3. üç‿dőrt‿dá-hà ká-çé-dèr?
4. dört‿béş‿dá-hà ká-çé-dèr?
5. bé-ş‿űç‿dá-hà ká-çé-dèr?

6. al-ti‿bır‿dá-hà ká-çé-dèr?
7. se-kʸíz‿bír‿dá-hà ká-çé-dèr?
8. do-kúz‿bír‿dá-hà ká-çé-dèr?
9. i-kʸí‿dőrt‿dá-hà ká-çé-dèr?
10. üç‿béş‿dá-hà ká-çé-dèr?

II. *Fill in the blanks with the proper forms of the copula endings:*

-dir, -dür, -dır, -dur
-tir, -tür, -tır, -tur *'is, are'*

1. bú‿kʸíb-rìt bé-ním‐‐ˋ‐.
2. bú ká-rím‐‐ˋ‐.
3. bú şa-ráp-mi-dìr sú-mú‐‐ˋ‐?
4. bú dőr-dü-mü-zűn‐‐ˋ‐.
5. ís-tàs-yón né-re-dè‐‐ˈ‐?
6. bùn-lár çó-k‿i-yí‿ár-ka-dàş‐‐ˈ‐.
7. bú çók‿ká-ra‿bír‿bu-lùt‐‐ˈ‐.
8. bùn-lár kʸíb-rít‐‐ˋ‐.
9. bú‿bú-lùt çók‿ká-rá‐‐ˋ‐.
10. çók-mú-dùr? é-vèt! çók‐‐ˋ‐.
11. bú çók‿gʸü-zélʸ‿bí-r‿ét‐‐ˋ‐.
12. káç-tìr? dőrt‐‐ˋ‐.

III. *Fill in the blanks with the proper forms of the possessive endings:*

-(i)m, -(ü)m, -(ı)m, -(u)m *'my'*
-(i)-miz, -(ü)-müz, -(ı)mız, -(u)-muz *'our'*
-(i)-niz, -(ü)-nüz, -(ı)-nız, -(u)-nuz *'your'*

1. bé-ním‿ki-zˋ‐ çók‿gʸü-zélʸ-dìr.
2. sí-zín‿ço-cúk-la-r‐‐‐ˋ‐ çó-k‿i-yí-dír-lʸèr.
3. bú‿gʸü-zélʸ‿kìz çók‿hó-ş‐‐‐á‿gʸí-di-yòr!
4. bíz év-lʸí-yìz. ço-cúk-la-r‐‐‐ˊ‐‿vàr.
5. sí-zí-n‿é-v‐‐‐ˋ‐ ná-sil-dìr?
6. kà-rí‐‐ˊ‐ şím-di‿ná-sìl?
7. bè-ním káç‿ta:-né‿é-vˋ‐‿vàr?

IV. *Fill in the blanks with the proper forms of the possessive and possessor endings.*

-(s)i, -(s)ü, -(s)ı, -(s)u *'his, her, its, their'*
-(n)in, -(n)ün, -(n)ın, -(n)un *possessor* (-'s, -s')

1. báy‿ká-ya‐‐ˊ‐‿ká-rı‐‐ˋ
be-ním‿kíz‿kár-de-şìm-dír.
2. ó:-lu-mˊ‐‐‿ís-mˋ mu-záf-fér-dìr.
3. bú‿kʸíb-rìt kʸí-mˊ‐‐dìr? bé-ním-dìr.
4. ó bá-y‿ak-yü-re-yˈ‐‿né‐‐ˊ‐dìr?
ó o‐‐ˈ‐‐‿ó:-lˊ‐dùr.
5. òn-lá-rˊ‐ káç‿pa-ra‐‐ˈ‿vàr? í-kʸí‿ku-ru-şˈ‿vàr.
6. on-la-rˈ‐‿ki-z‐‐‐ˊ‐‐‿is-mˋ lʸéy-lʸá:-dìr.
7. kar-de-şi-mˈ‐‿ká-rı‐‐‐‐‐ˊ‐‐‿is-mˋ şükʸ-rü-yé-dìr.
8. bú kʸí-mˊ‐‐dìr? kár-de-şi-mˊ‐‐dìr.

9. bȧy‿kȧ-r–́–‿ço-cúk-la-r–̂ çȯk‿gʸü-zélʸ-dı̀r.

10. o––́––‿én‿gʸü-zélʸ‿kı-z–̂ bú-dùr.

V. *Fill in the blanks with the correct forms of the personal endings:*

-(y)im, -(y)üm, -(y)ım, -(y)um — *'I'*
-0 ("zero") — *'he, she, it'*
-(y)iz, -(y)üz, -(y)ız, -(y)uz — *'we'*
-si-niz, -sü-nüz, sı-nız, -su-nuz — *'you'*
-lʸer, -lar — *'they'*

1. bíz çó-k‿i-yi‿ár-ka-dà-ş–́–!
2. bá-y‿ák-yü-rèkʸ kʸá:-tip-lʸíkʸ‿yá-pàr____.
3. kùş-lár a-aç-lar-dȧ‿ö-tú-yȯr––̂–.
4. ço-cuk-la-rı-niz‿ná-sìl? çó-k‿i-yì-dir––́–.
5. siz‿ná-sil––––––̂–? çó-k‿i-yì––́–, te-şékʸ-kʸú-r‿e-dè-r–́–.
6. síz bú-ra-da‿né‿yá-pı-yòr––––––́–?
7. kʸí-m‿ò? bé-n–̂–!

VI. *Fill in the blanks with the correct form of the verb in parentheses with the momentary or the aorist endings, as the case may be:*

-r — *aorist*
-er, -ar — *aorist*
-ir, -ür, -ır, -ur — *aorist*
-i-yor-, -ü-yor-, -ı-yor-, -u-yor- — *momentary*

1. si-né-mà hé-r‿ák-şàm sa-ȧt‿káç-tȧ‿____ (baş-la- . . .)?
2. síz dá-i-mà yá-váş‿ya-váş‿____ (ko-nuş- . . .).
3. bíz hér‿gʸùn ó-ra-yȧ‿____ (gʸit- . . .).
4. şím-dì síz né‿____ (yap- . . .)?
5. gʸü-zélʸ‿bír‿kùş bú‿sá-bàh ____ (öt- . . .)
6. çó-cùk-lár hér‿sá-bàh çó-k‿er-kʸén____ (kalk- . . .).
7. gʸü-zélʸ‿kiz-làr hó-şu-nu-zá‿____ (gʸit- . . .).
8. ká-rá‿bu-lút-làr u-fuk-tá‿____ (top-lan- . . .).
9. bú‿ák-şàm çók‿se-rín‿bír‿rüz-gʸá-r‿. . . . (es- . . .).
10. túrkʸ-çé‿ko-núş-màk şím-di‿ho-şu-nu-zá‿____-mù? (gʸit- . . .).

VII. *Fill in the blanks with the correct forms of the interrogative ending:*

-mi, -mü, -mı, -mu

1. bú i-yí––́–dìr?
2. vár-mì? yók––̂?
3. ki-zı-nı-zín––́–dìr?
4. káç? i-kʸí-mì? dórt––̂?

VIII. *Fill in the blanks with the correct forms of the endings 'and, too, also':*

-de, da
-te, -ta

1. bén---.
2. ó---.
3. bú-ra-dà---.
4. ár-ka-dáş---.
5. bir‿kʸib-rit---.
6. báy‿kúrt---.

Section B—Conversation

To the Group Leader: Assign parts and have the students work through the outlined conversations. When everyone has had a chance to take part, encourage the students to branch out and start conversations on related topics.

Here are a number of outlined conversations. Take parts and work through them. When you can do these well, go on to freer discussion of similar things, using as much of the content of previous lessons as possible. Ask questions in Turkish and answer them.

1. Student meets teacher.

The student, Mr. Jones, meets his teacher, Mr. Carr, on the street, and says good morning (in Turkish). Mr. Carr returns the greeting. They ask about each other's health, talk about the weather. Mr. Carr points out that a shower is coming up. Mr. Jones looks blank and starts to talk English. Mr. Carr asks him to talk Turkish and Mr. Jones tries asking Mr. Carr to please speak slowly. Mr. Carr repeats his remarks on the rain. Mr. Jones now understands and suggests that they run to a shelter.

2. Father and son in a restaurant.

Mr. Akyurek and his son, Osman, enter a restaurant and take a table. The waiter, Ahmet, greets them and takes their order. They order, discuss the drink, ask for cigarettes and matches, ask for the check, pay and leave.

3. Osman and Ayesha in a movie.

Osman asks Ayesha if she likes the film. She says she does. They see Ali and Aliye, go over to them, greet them, talk about the movie, make plans for afterward. They go to a restaurant and order beer.

4. Looking for a job.

Mr. Kurt enters the building, asks the janitor where to find Mr. Carr's office. The janitor tells him and he thanks him. He enters the office, and asks the secretary whether Mr. Carr is in. She says he is and sends Mr. Kurt in. He and Mr. Carr exchange greetings. Mr. Kurt explains his business. Mr. Carr says he needs a cashier (or secretary, etc.) and asks him to begin work. Mr. Kurt thanks him and takes his leave.

5. A party.

Mr. and Mrs. Carr's guests arrive with their children. They exchange greetings. The Carrs ask their guests in. They inquire about each other's health, that of the children. They send the children off. The women discuss the children and their friendships. The men smoke and drink (beer or wine). The women have coffee. They discuss their likes and dislikes in matters of drinks. They discuss Ali who hasn't yet arrived and his whereabouts. When Ali arrives they send him off to find the other children. Later they talk about the late hour, and making their excuses, they break up.

SECTION C—LISTENING IN (QUESTIONS)

To the Group Leader: Following are sets of questions on short conversations which are to be read by the Guide or the phonograph records. Have the Guide read (or play on the record) each conversation through twice. Then have the students read and answer the questions listed below for the particular conversation. Insist on complete answers. You will find the correct answers in the Guide's Manual.

Listen to the Guide or to the phonograph record as each one of the conversations is read. It will be repeated twice, so listen carefully the second time for anything you didn't catch the first time through. Then be prepared to answer in Turkish, on the particular conversation, the questions listed below. If you cannot do this without hesitation you need to review the previous *Listening In's*.

1. *Mr. Kaya and Mr. Metin go to a restaurant.*

Record 12A, beginning.

1. bày‿ká-yá ná-sìl?
2. báy‿ká-ya-nín‿ká-rı-sì vé‿ço-cùk-lá-rí ná-sıl-dir-làr?
3. bày‿mé-tin né‿yap-má-k‿is-ti-yòr?
4. né-re-dé‿i-yi‿bir‿lʸo-kàn-tá‿vár?
5. né-re-yé‿gʸi-de-lʸìm?

6. ná-sil‿g^{y}i-de-l^{y}ìm?
7. bày‿ká-yá vé‿bày‿mé-tín né‿yé-me-k^y‿is-ti-yór-làr?
8. bày‿mé-tín né‿iç-mé-k^y‿is-ti-yòr?
9. k^{y}ím‿bi-ra‿iç-mé-k^y‿is-ti-yòr?

2. *Going to visit a friend.*

Record 12A, after 1st spiral.

1. ó-tèl^y-dé k^{y}i-mí-n‿ar-ka-da-ṣi‿vàr?
2. hak-kı-ni-n‿ár-ka-dá-ṣı-ní-n‿is-mì né-dìr?
3. bá-y‿ák-yü-rèk^y né‿iṣ‿yá-pàr?
4. hák-kı-ní-n‿ó-fi-sin-dè-mi?
5. hàk-kí ó-ra-da‿çók‿kal-má-k‿is-ti-yór-mù?

3. *Going to a movie.*

Record 12A, after 2nd spiral.

1. bú‿ák-ṣàm né-re-yé‿g^{y}i-di-yór-làr?
2. k^{y}i-mí-n‿i-l^{y}è?
3. k^{y}i-mín‿kiz‿kar-de-ṣi-ní-n‿is-mì l^{y}éy-l^{y}á:-dìr?
4. l^{y}ey-l^{y}á:‿g^{y}ü-zél^y-mı?
5. ná-sil-dìr?

4. *Going to a party.*

Record 12A, after 3rd spiral.

1. bú‿ák-ṣàm né‿vàr?
2. k^{y}ím‿g^{y}é-l^{y}i-yòr?
3. kàç-tá?

5. *Guests.*

Record 12A, after 4th spiral.

1. k^{y}im-l^{y}ér‿g^{y}é-l^{y}i-yòr?
2. né‿vakit‿g^{y}é-l^{y}i-yór-làr?
3. bày‿ká-yá ná-sìl?
4. bá-y‿ká-ya-ní-n‿ár-ka-dá-ṣì né‿va-kit‿g^{y}é-l^{y}i-yòr?
5. bày‿ká-yá né‿iç-mé-k^y‿is-ti-yòr?

6. *Getting up early.*

Record 12B, beginning.

1. à-lʸí ó‿sá-bàh né‿yap-má-k‿is-ti-yòr?
2. kʸí-mín‿ka-rı-si‿gʸé-lʸi-yòr?
3. sá-àt‿káç-tá?
4. şím-dì sá-àt‿káç?
5. né‿yá-pa-lìm?
6. né‿vàr?
7. né‿yá-ı-yòr?
8. şím-di‿né‿yá-pàr?
9. né í-lʸèr-dé?
10. né‿gʸé-lʸi-yòr?
11. áh-me-dín‿ká-rı-sì ó-ra-dà-mi?

7. *The family goes out.*

Record 12B, after 1st spiral.

1. çó-cùk-lár né‿va-kít‿gʸí-di-yór-làr?
2. kʸím-dé‿gʸí-di-yòr?
3. os-mán‿gʸit-mé-kʸ‿ís-ti-yór-mù?
4. o-nún‿né-sí‿vàr?
5. òn-lár né‿i-lʸé‿gʸí-di-yór-làr?

8. *Hakki gets a job.*

Record 12B, after 2nd spiral.

1. hak-ki‿né‿á-rı-yòr?
2. o-nú-n‿ís-mí‿nè?
3. né‿yá-pàr?
4. báy‿me-ti-nín‿véz-ne-da-ri‿vár-mì?
5. hak-ki‿şím-di‿baş-la-má-k‿ís-tér-mi?
6. ó‿o-fis-tè hér‿gʸǜn í-ş‿er-kʸén-mi‿báş-làr?
7. kàç-tá?

9. *Tom Carr leaves town.*

Record 12B, after 3rd spiral.

1. tóm tǘrkʸ-çe‿án-lı-yór-mù?
2. ah-mét‿şím-di‿ná-sil‿kó-nu-şu-yòr?
3. is-tas-yón‿né-ré-dè?
4. sa-át‿káç-tá‿trèn‿vár?
5. tóm şím-di‿án-lı-yór-mù?

10. *At the station.*

Record 12B, after 4th spiral.

1. şi̍m-di‿sá-át‿kàç?
2. né-re-dé‿bi̍r‿l^{y}o-kàn-ta‿vár?
3. l^{y}o-kán-tá-dà   tóm‿né‿i̍s-ti-yòr?
4. ó‿sa-át-tè   ye-mék^y‿ve-rí-yór-làr-mi̍?
5. sa-át‿káç-tá‿báş-lı-yór-làr?

SECTION D—TRUE-FALSE

Record 13A and 13B.

To the Group Leader: Section D is a true-false quiz which is to be read to the group by the Guide or the phonograph records. Each student is to write the numbers from 1 to 40 on a sheet of paper. After hearing each statement in Turkish, the students are to mark T opposite the number of that statement if they consider it a true statement, and F if they consider it false. If the students understand the Turkish they will have no difficulty in deciding whether or not the statements are true or false.

Use the first item in the quiz as a practice item. When you are ready to start, announce "Statement 1," and give the signal to the Guide to begin, or put on the phonograph record. The Guide or the record will then read the Turkish statement:

"bú‿báy-làr   bá-yàn‿mé-tín   vé‿ba-yán‿ká-yá-dìr,"

and will repeat the statement once more. Explain to the group that, since the meaning of this statement is:

"These gentlemen are Mrs. Metin and Mrs. Kaya,"

they should write F after the figure 1 on their papers. Then announce "Statement 2" and continue with the Guide or phonograph record. Each statement in Turkish is to be presented twice. When working with a Guide, continue to call the number of each statement throughout the quiz so that the students will have no trouble keeping the proper place. Take the quiz with the rest of the group.

In the back of the Guide's manual you will find a list giving the correct answers (T or F) for the Turkish items, together with the English translations. After the quiz is over, read to the group the correct answers, T or F for each item. The students are to check their papers. Find the average number of correct answers per student for your group and include your own answers. Any student who gets less than the average number of answers or less than 80% (whichever is higher) correct, needs more thorough study and review of the preceding units.

Use the rest of the period to repeat the Turkish expressions for which students had the wrong answer and read the English equivalents of these statements if they wish to have them. Be sure that the students understand the meaning of all the items which they got wrong; those are the items on which their vocabulary is weak and needs further study.

Section D is a true-false quiz. After you have marked the numbers 1 to 40 on a sheet of paper, your Leader will have the Guide read, or will play the phonograph records containing a number of statements in Turkish. As you hear each sentence, decide whether the statement it makes is true or false. Decide whether the statement is *usually* true or *usually* false. Do not go into particular cases. If you think the statement is true, mark *T* opposite the number corresponding to the number of the sentence that has just been spoken. If you think it is false, mark *F* opposite the number. The first item will be a practice item and will show you just how you are to proceed with the rest of the sentences.

After you have done this work, the Leader will go through your answers with you as a group, and will tell you which statements are true and which are false. Score your paper, counting one for each correct answer. The Leader will figure out the average score for your group. If your score falls below the average of the group as a whole, you need more study and review of the previous units.

Use the rest of the period to go over the sentences again with your Guide or records. For each item on which you are wrong, be sure that you understand why you are wrong, and what the true meaning of the item is.

If you come out well on this quiz, that indicates that you have a pretty good understanding of the word stock you have covered to date.

PART TWO — UNIT 7

GETTING A ROOM

From this unit on, you will find certain comments on the *Conventional Turkish Spelling* in the *Hints on Spelling.*

You will notice also that from this unit on, in the *Aids to Listening*, the hyphens are no longer used to divide words into syllables.

SECTION A—BASIC SENTENCES

Go once through the *Basic Sentences* in unison, concentrating on the *Aids to Listening*, then do the *Hints on Pronunciation;* go once through the *Basic Sentences* individually, and then read the *Hints on Spelling.* The last time through individually, notice also the *Conventional Turkish Spelling.*

1. Basic Sentences

Tom Carr finds a hotel and takes a room.

ENGLISH EQUIVALENTS	AIDS TO LISTENING	CONVENTIONAL TURKISH SPELLING
	Tom Carr	
Record 14A, beginning.		
in this town	bù‿şehırdé.	bu şehirde
Is there a good hotel in this town?	bú‿şehi̍rdè iyi̍‿bi̍r‿otél^{y}‿vármì?	Bu şehirde iyi bir otel varmı?
	Mr. Metin	
[*a*] *little*	áz.	az
Yes, there is. It's up ahead a little.	évèt, vár. àz‿il^{y}érdé.	Evet, var. Az ilerde.

	Tom Carr	
hotel-keeper	ótèlʸcí.	otelci
are you [he]?	sízmi̍sinìz?	sizmisiniz?
Are you the manager?	otelʸci̍‿sízmi̍sinìz?	Otelci sizmisiniz?
	Manager	
I am	bénìm.	benim
Yes, I am.	évèt, bénìm.	Evet, benim.
pleasantly	hóş.	hoş
you've come	gʸèlʸdi̍níz.	geldiniz
Welcome!	hóş‿gʸélʸdinìz!	Hoş geldiniz!
	Tom Carr	
pleasant	hóş.	hoş
we've found [it]	bùldúk.	bulduk
Thank you!	hóş‿búldùk!	Hoş bulduk.
	Manager	
a room?	bi̍r‿ódámì?	bir odamı?
Do you want a room?	bi̍r‿odámi‿árzù‿ediyórsunuz?	Bir odamı arzu ediyorsunuz?
	Tom Carr	
(for) myself	bèním.	benim
and for my wife	vé‿kárím‿i̍çìn.	ve karım için
Yes, I want a room for myself and my wife.	évèt, bèním vé‿kárím‿i-çìn bi̍r‿ódá‿i̍stiyòrúm.	Evet, benim ve karım için bir oda istiyorum.

English	Pronunciation	Turkish
she	ó.	o
later	sónrà.	sonra
[she] will come	g^{y}èl^{y}écék^y.	gelecek
She'll be here later.	ó‿sónrá‿g^{y}él^{y}ecèk^y.	O sonra gelecek.
	Manager	
of [the] hotel	ótèl^{y}ín.	otelin
on its second floor	ik^{y}ínci‿kátındà.	ikinci katında
We have a very nice room on the second floor of the hotel.	otel^{y}ín‿ik^{y}ínci‿kátındà çók‿g^{y}üzél^y‿bír‿ódamíz‿vàr.	Otelin ikinci katında çok güzel bir odamız var.
	Tom Carr	

Record 14B, beginning.

English	Pronunciation	Turkish
its (daily) rate	g^{y}ùndél^{y}iyí.	gündeliği
How much is it a day?	g^{y}ündel^{y}iyí‿káç‿párà?	Gündeliği kaç para?
	Manager	
just	yálnìz.	yalnız
Just three lira.	yálnız‿űç‿l^{y}ìrá.	Yalnız üç lira.
in (lit. with) [the] elevator	asánsőrl^{y}è.	asansörle
let's go up!	çìkálím!	çıkalım!
Let's go up in the elevator, please!	búyrùn asánsőrl^{y}é‿çikalìm!	Buyrun asansörle çıkalım!
Do you like it?	hoşunuzá‿g^{y}ídiyórmù?	Hoşunuza gidiyormu?
	Tom Carr	
Yes, it's very nice!	évèt, çók‿g^{y}üzèl^y!	Evet, çok güzel!

	Manager	
at [the] hotel?	otél^{y}démì?	oteldemi?
you will eat	yémék^{y}‿yiyecèk^{y}siniz.	yemek yiyeceksiniz
Will you eat at the hotel?	otel^{y}démi‿yemék^{y}‿yiyecèk^{y}siniz?	Oteldemi yemek yiyeceksiniz?
We have a good restaurant.	iyi‿bir‿l^{y}okántamiz‿vàr.	İyi bir lokantamız var.
	Tom Carr	
first (lit. still before) (that)	dàhá‿évvèl^{y}.	daha evvel
to wash (oneself)	yikànmák.	yıkanmak
[and] to shave	tráş‿ólmàk.	traş olmak
Yes, but I want to wash and shave first.	évèt, fákàt dàhá‿evvél^{y}‿yıkánmàk, tráş‿olmák‿istiyòrúm.	Evet, fakat daha evvel yıkanmak, traş olmak istiyorum.
	Manager	
sir	éféndìm.	efendim
Very well, sir!	pék^{y}‿iyì, éféndìm!	Pek iyi, efendim!
dinner (lit. the evening meal)	ákşám‿yémeyì.	akşam yemeği
and (lit. with)	ìl^{y}é.	ile
[it] is between (lit. on its interval)	árasindádìr.	arasındadır
Dinner is between six and nine o'clock.	ákşám‿yémeyi saát‿alti‿il^{y}é‿dókúz‿árasindàdir.	Akşam yemeği saat altı ile dokuz arasındadır.
else (lit. other)	bàşká.	başka
Do you want anything else?	başká‿bir‿şéy‿istiyórmúsunùz?	Başka bir şey istiyormusunuz?

Tom Carr

towel	hàvlú.	havlu
Yes, a towel.	évèt, bìr‿hávlú.	Evet, bir havlu.

Manager

[*the*] *servant*	hìzmétçí.	hizmetçi
[*she*] *probably forgot* [*it*]	únùtmúş.	unutmuş
Sorry! The servant probably forgot it.	áffedèrsiníz! hìzmétçì‿unútmúş.	Affedersiniz! Hizmetçi unutmuş.

Before you go through the *Basic Sentences* a second time, read the following:

2. Hints on Pronunciation

We have seen many instances of the sound which we have represented with the letter l^y, and we have described this sound as similar to the *li* of million. This description is, of course, only approximate. Turkish l^y is much lighter and more liquid sounding than English *l*. In English *l* the tongue is hollowed out like the bowl of a spoon, and the tip of the tongue is up. In Turkish l^y the tongue is arched like the back of a spoon, and the tip of the tongue is down behind the lower teeth. If we compare English *el* (the name of the letter *l*) with Turkish *é*l^y (el) 'hand,' we can hear the difference quite clearly:

PRACTICE 1 **Record 15A, beginning.**

(ENGLISH)	*(TURKISH)*
"el"	él^y
"el"	él^y
"el"	él^y

Listen carefully to the guide or the phonograph record for this difference and try to imitate it. Then practice the following words which contain l^y:

PRACTICE 2 **Record 15A, after 1st spiral.**

gʸùzélʸ.	güzel	(*beautiful*)
òtélʸ.	otel	(*hotel*)
dáhá‿évvèlʸ.	daha evvel	(*first*)
dèyílʸ.	değil	([*it is*] *not*)
ìsmáílʸ.	İsmail	(*Ishmael*)

PRACTICE 3 **Record 15A, after 2nd spiral.**

gʸèlʸír.	gelir	(*comes*)
ìlʸé.	ile	(*with*)
gʸùndélʸíkʸ.	gündelik	(*daily rate*)
gʸǘlʸé‿gʸǘlʸè.	güle güle	(*good-bye*)
maálʸésèf.	maalesef	(*unfortunately*)
àlʸí.	Ali	(*Ali*)
èvlʸí.	evli	(*married*)
éylʸénìn.	eğlenin	(*enjoy yourself*)

PRACTICE 4 **Record 15A, after 3rd spiral.**

lʸèylʸá:.	Leylâ	(*Leyla*)
lʸírà.	lira	(*lira*)
lʸókántà.	lokanta	(*restaurant*)
lʸû́tfèn.	lûtfen	(*please*)

Before you go through the *Basic Sentences* a third time, read the following:

3. Hints on Spelling

From this unit on, we shall comment on the third column of *Conventional Turkish Spelling*, that is, the usual Turkish spelling which you will find in newspapers and magazines, in books and on signs. You will not find many differences between the regularized spelling (*Aids to Listening*) in Column II and the *Conventional Turkish Spelling* in Column III. We note below the differences found in this unit:

AIDS TO LISTENING		CONVENTIONAL SPELLING
l^y	:	**l**
l^{y}i	:	li
l^{y}e	:	le
lyü	:	lü
l^{y}a:	:	lâ
l^{y}o	:	lo
l^{y}u	:	lû
il^y	:	il
el^y	:	el
ül^y	:	ül

Examples:

l^{y}írà	:	lira
g^{y}èl^{y}écék^y	:	gelecek
g^{y}ǘl^{y}ünǜz!	:	gülünüz!
l^{y}èyl^{y}á:	:	Leylâ
l^{y}ókántà	:	lokanta
l^{y}útfèn	:	lûtfen
dèyíl^y	:	değil
òtél^y	:	otel
g^{y}ül^y- . . .	:	gül- . . .

AIDS TO LISTENING		CONVENTIONAL SPELLING
k^y	:	**k**
k^{y}i	:	ki
k^{y}ü	:	kü
k^{y}ö	:	kö
ek^y	:	ek
ürk^y	:	ürk
ök^y	:	ök

Examples:

i̇k^{y}ìncí	:	ikinci
g^{y}özük^{y}ǘyòr	:	gözüküyor
k^{y}ȍşé	:	köşe
pék^y	:	pek
tǘrk^{y}çè	:	türkçe
g^{y}ö́k^y	:	gök

g^y	:	**g**
g^{y}i	:	gi
g^{y}e	:	ge
g^{y}ü	:	gü
g^{y}ö	:	gö
g^{y}a	:	gâ

Examples:

g^{y}i̇díyòr	:	gidiyor
g^{y}éç		geç
g^{y}ǘl^{y}ünǜz!	:	gülünüz!

g^{y}ö̇zük^{y}ǘyòr : gözüküyor
rǜzg^{y}ár : rüzgâr

: (length) : zero

a: : a

Example:
bérà:bér : beraber

: (length) : ğ

a: : ağ

Example:
sá: : sağ

zero : ğ

zero : ğ

We shall continue to note these differences in the next few units, until we have examples of all of them. We have seen above that k^y frequently corresponds to simple *k* in the conventional spelling, l^y to simple *l*, and so on. We shall summarize all these correspondences in Unit 10 and give the rules for them. In Unit 11 we shall point out the defects of the *Conventional Spelling* and shall present our *Standardized Conventional Spelling* in which we remedy these defects. Then from Unit 13 on we shall use only this standardized spelling.

Examples:
yàár : yağar
çócúùm : çocuğum

y : ğ

ey : eğ

Example:
éyl^{y}énìn : eğlenin

iyi : iği

Example:
g^{y}ǜndéliyi : gündeliği

eyi : eği

Example:
dèyíl^y : değil

In the *Aids to Listening* of this unit, we no longer use the hyphen to divide words into *syllables*. By now the simple rules for dividing words into syllables should be apparent. They apply not only to the pronunciation of spoken words, but also to the breaking of words at the end of the line in the *Conventional Turkish Spelling*. Only *one* consonant goes with the following vowel. The others, one or more, remain with the preceding vowel.

Examples:
türk-çe, lût-fen, pa-ra

Section B—Word Study and Review of Basic Sentences

1. Word Study (Individual Study)

1. Turkish equivalents of English "at, in, on"

In this and previous units we have seen forms like *búràdà* (burada) 'here', *sà:dá* (sağda) 'on the right', *kàçtá* (kaçta) 'at what time?'. Tabulating similar forms, we get:

		Column I				Column II	
				Group I			
i	bíz	biz	*'we'*	.	bìzdé	bizde	*'at our house (lit. at us)'*
e	év	ev	*'house'*	:	èvdé	evde	*'at home'*
ü	sǘt	süt	*'milk'*	:	sǜtté	sütte	*'in [the] milk'*
ö	gʸǿkʸ	gök	*'heaven'*	:	gʸờkʸté	gökte	*'in [the] heaven(s)'*
				Group II			
ı	tòplánt	toplantı	*'gathering'*	:	tóplàntıdá	toplantıda	*'at [the] gathering'*
a	òdá	oda	*'room'*	:	òdádá	odada	*'in [the] room'*
u	ùfúk	ufuk	*'horizon'*	:	úfùktá	ufukta	*'on [the] horizon'*
o	sól	sol	*'left'*	:	sòldá	solda	*'on [the] left'*

If we compare the forms in Column I with those in Column II, and the Column II forms in Group I with those in Group II, we see that:

1. the part of the forms in Column II which means 'at, in, on' is the ending *-de*, *-da*, *-te*, *-ta;* this ending follows Vowel Harmony Type II;
2. the forms *-de*, *-da* are used after humming sounds such as *z*, *v*, *i*, *a*, *l;*
3. *-te*, *-ta* is used after other sounds ("non-humming") such as *t*, *kʸ*, *k;*
4. we notice also that the *strongest vowel* in a word with this ending is the vowel of the ending itself, if the strongest vowel in the base (Column I) is the last one (tòplánt*í* : tóplántıd*á*); otherwise the vowel of the ending is next strongest (t*ǘ*rkçè : tǘrkçéd*è*).

Note: This is sometimes the only difference in form between bases with this ending and those with the ending which means 'and, too, also', when the strong vowel is the strongest vowel in the base before the ending. Compare:

bízdè bizde 'we too' : bìzdé bizde 'at our house'.

Here are other forms with this ending which we have met in Units **1-7**:

búrádà	burada	***'here'***
nérédè?	nerede?	***'where?'***
sà:dá	sağda	***'on [the] right'***

sòldá	solda	*'on [the] left'*
ilʸèrdé (ilʸèridé)	ilerde (ileride)	*'on ahead, up ahead'*
tǘrkʸçédè	türkçede	*'in Turkish'*
kàçtá?	kaçta?	*'at what time?'*
búçùktá	buçukta	*'at the half (hour)'*
yèdidé	yedide	*'at seven (o'clock)'*
ofisìmizdé	ofisimizde	*'in our office'*
évìmdé	evimde	*'at my house'*
ófìsté	ofiste	*'in [the] office'*
ódanìzdá	odanızda	*'in your room'*
aáçlàrdá	ağaçlarda	*'in [the] trees'*
ȍtédé	ötede	*'on [the] other side'*
órádà	orada	*'there'*
kʸȍşédé	köşede	*'on [the] corner'*
ófisìmdé	ofisimde	*'in my office'*
ótèlʸdé	otelde	*'in [the] hotel'*

If we cut off this ending, we find that some of the forms already have certain endings, such as the "my", "our", "your" (possessive) endings or the "more than one" (plural) ending. If we cut off these, we find the following bases without difficulty: *sá:*, *sól*, *tǘrkʸçè*, *káç*, *bùçúk*, *yèdí*, *ȍfís*, *év*, *òdá*, *àáç*, *ȍté*, *kʸȍşé*, *òtélʸ*.

From *ilʸèrdé*, we get **ilʸer*, which does not exist in this form, but *ilʸéri* is a Turkish word meaning 'ahead, forward'. The full form, therefore, is *ilʸèridé*, of which *ilʸèrdé* is a *shortened form*. We shall meet these shortened forms from time to time.

búràdà, *nérèdè*, *óràdà* exist only in forms with some ending or other, there being no **bura*,[1] **nere*, **ora* alone. The meaning of these *non-existent bases*, however, is clear: 'this place', 'what place', 'that place', and we have seen the first parts alone: *bú* 'this', *né* 'what', *ó* 'that'. If we cut these off, we have only non-existent **ra*, **re* left, which seem to mean 'place'.

In this unit we have seen forms with a slightly *different form of the ending* discussed above. Observe:

[1] Starred (*) forms do not occur in ordinary speech.

	Column I				Column II	
kàtí	katı	*'its floor (storey)'*	:	kȧtìndá	katında	*'on its floor'*
àrásí	arası	*'its interval'*	:	àrasindá	arasında	*'between (lit. on its interval)'*

Other such forms are:

yȕzű	yüzü	*'its face'*	:	yüzȕndé	yüzünde	*'on its face'*
k^{y}ȍşési	köşesi	*'his corner'*	:	k^{y}ȍşesindé	köşesinde	*'in his corner'*
ȍdalárí	odaları	*'their rooms'*	:	ȯdalàrindá	odalarında	*'in their rooms'*

Comparing Column I with II:

1. we note the *longer forms* of the locating ending: *-nde, -nda;*
2. these forms likewise follow Vowel Harmony Type II;
3. they are found after the possessive ending -(*s*)*i*, -(*s*)*ü*, -(*s*)*ı*, -(*s*)*u* 'his, her, its, their'.

This ending which means 'at, in, on' indicates the location, so we shall call it the *locative* ending.

2. Turkish interrogative ending -mi, -mü, -mı, -mu, after nouns

In Unit 5. B. 1. 3, we saw the interrogative ending as used with certain verb forms, such as *istiyórmúsunùz* (istiyormusunuz?) 'do you want?', and with the forms with the copula ending 'is, are, am', such as *ėvl^{y}imidȉr* (evlimidir?) 'is she married?'. Here we see it as used with *noun* forms. Observe:

bȉr‿ȯdá	bir oda	*'a room'*	:	bi̇r‿ȯdámì?	bir odamı?	*'a room?'*
ȯtèl^{y}dé	otelde	*'in [the] hotel'*	:	otėl^{y}démȉ?	oteldemi?	*'in [the] hotel?'*

Whereas in the verb forms, such as *i̇stiyórmúsunùz*, and the forms with the 'is, are, am' copula ending, such as *ėvl^{y}i̇midȉr*, the interrogative ending frequently came before a part of the complete form, in the *noun* forms, given above, the *-mi, -mü, -mı, -mu* always comes *after* the complete form of the noun (base plus ending), at the very end.

The *strongest vowel* in these forms, too, is always *before* the *interrogative* ending, never on it.

3. *Turkish equivalents of English 'let's (do it)!'*

In previous units we have seen forms like *kòşàlím!* (koşalım!) 'let's run!', *g^{y}ìdèl^{y}ím!* (gidelim!) 'let's go!'. Tabulating these and similar forms we get:

	Column I				Column II		
				Group I			
i	g^{y}it- . . .	git- . . .	*'go'*	:	g^{y}ìdèl^{y}ím!	gidelim!	*'let's go!'*
e	ver- . . .	ver- . . .	*'give'*	:	vèrèl^{y}ím!	verelim!	*'let's give!'*
ü	g^{y}ül^y- . . .	gül- . . .	*'laugh'*	:	g^{y}ǜl^{y}èl^{y}ím!	gülelim!	*'let's laugh!'*
ö	g^{y}ör- . . .	gör- . . .	*'see'*	:	g^{y}ö̀rèl^{y}ím!	görelim!	*'let's see [it]!'*
				Group II			
ı	çık- . . .	çık- . . .	*'go up'*	:	çìkàlím!	çıkalım!	*'let's go up!'*
a	yap- . . .	yap- . . .	*'do'*	:	yàpàlím!	yapalım!	*'let's do [it]!'*
u	konuş- . . .	konuş- . . .	*'talk'*	:	kònùşalím!	konuşalım!	*'let's talk!'*
o	koş- . . .	koş- . . .	*'run'*	:	kòşàlím!	koşalım!	*'let's run!'*
				Group III			
e (i)	ye- . . .	ye- . . .	*'eat'*	:	yìyèl^{y}ím!	yiyelim!	*'let's eat!'*
a (ı)	başla- . . .	başla- . . .	*'begin'*	:	bàşlıyàlím!	başlıyalım!	*'let's begin!'*

If we compare the verb roots in Column I with the full verb forms in Column II, Group I with Group II, and Groups I and II with III, we note that:

1. the ending which means 'let's . . . . .' is *-el^{y}im*, *-alım* after a *consonant:*
2. it is *-yel^{y}im*, *yalım* after a vowel;
3. its first vowel follows Vowel Harmony Type II, and its second vowel follows Vowel Harmony Type I;
4. the *strongest vowel* is the second vowel of the ending, the last vowel of the form, when this is the only ending.

In Group III, we also note that the verb roots *ye- . . .*, *başla- . . .* have changed to *yi- . . .*, *başlı- . . .*, or rather that *e* has changed to *i*, and *a* to *ı*, before the *-y-* of this particular ending. This change is quite common and we shall note other examples of it as we meet them.

The English equivalent is not always 'let's . . . . .'. Note:

né‿yápalìm? Ne yapalım? *'What are we to do? What shall we do?'*

4. *Some Turkish equivalents of English* '(*you*) (*do it*)!'

In previous units, we have seen forms like *ėylʸénìn!* (eğlenin!) 'amuse yourselves!', *gʸídìn!* (gidin!) 'go!'. Tabulating similar forms, we get:

	Column I				Column II		
				Group I			
i	gʸit- . . .	git- . . .	*'go'*	: gʸídinìz!	gidiniz!	*'go!'*
e	gʸelʸ- . . .	gel- . . .	*'come'*	: gʸélʸinìz!	geliniz!	*'come!'*
ü	gʸülʸ- . . .	gül- . . .	*'laugh'*	: gʸúlʸünûz!	gülünüz!	*'laugh!'*
ö	öt- . . .	öt- . . .	*'sing (birds)'*	: ő̈tünûz!	ötünüz!	*'sing!'*
ı	çık- . . .	çık- . . .	*'go up'*	: çíkinìz!	çıkınız!	*'go up!'*
a	yap- . . .	yap- . . .	*'do'*	: yápinìz!	yapınız!	*'do [it]!'*
u	konuş- . . .	konuş- . . .	*'talk'*	: konúşúnùz!	konuşunuz!	*'talk!'*
o	koş- . . .	koş- . . .	*'run'*	: kóşúnùz!	koşunuz!	*'run!'*
				Group II			
	ye- . . .	ye- . . .	*'eat'*	: yíyinìz!	yiyiniz!	*'eat!'*
	başla- . . .	başla- . . .	*'begin'*	: báşláyınìz!	başlayınız!	*'begin!'*
				Group III			
	gʸit- . . .	git- . . .	*'go'*	: gʸídìn!	gidin!	*'go!'*
	ye- . . .	ye- . . .	*'eat'*	: yíyìn!	yiyin!	*'eat!'*
	eylʸen- . . .	eğlen- . . .	*'amuse oneself'*	: ėylʸénìn!	eğlenin!	*'amuse yourself!'*
	buyur- . . .	buyur- . . .	*'be so kind'*	: *búyúrùn![1] (shortened form: *búyrùn*)	buyurun! (buyrun!)	*'be so kind!'*

[1]Not used in this full form in ordinary conversation.

If we compare, in Group I, the verb roots in Column I with the full form in Column II, we see that:

1. the ending which means '(you) (do it)!' is *-iniz, -ünüz, -ınız, -unuz;*
2. that is, it follows Vowel Harmony Type I.

If we compare Group I with Group II, we see that:

1. the ending is *-iniz, -ünüz, -ınız, -unuz* only after a consonant;
2. it is *-yiniz, -yünüz, -yınız, -yunuz* after a root which ends in a *vowel*.

This form is used when speaking *formally* either to *one* or to *more than one* person.

In Group III, we see a *shorter form* of this same ending, -(*y*)*in*, -(*y*)*ün*, and so on.

This shorter form may be used when speaking formally to *only one* person. It is always used when speaking *informally* to *more than one* person. Later on we shall learn the form for speaking informally to only one person.

We also note that the *strongest vowel* of the forms is the *last one of the root*, the one just before the ending.

The forms *yíyìniz, yíyìn* are irregular in that they have changed the root *ye-* . . . to *yi-* . . ., or rather the *e* to *i* before the following *y*.

2. Covering English and Turkish of Word Study (Individual Study)

Check yourself on your knowledge of the *Word Study* by covering, first the English, then the Turkish, and making sure you know everything thoroughly.

3. Review of Basic Sentences

With the Guide or records, review the first half of the *Basic Sentences* as in previous units.

SECTION C—REVIEW OF BASIC SENTENCES (*Cont.*)

1. Review of Basic Sentences (*Cont.*)

Review the second half of the *Basic Sentences*.

2. Covering the English of Basic Sentences (Individual Study)

Go through the *Basic Sentences* covering up the English and reading aloud the Turkish. Check up on anything you do not know, until you are sure of everything.

3. **Word Study Review** (Individual Study)

Work through the following exercises. Do not write anything down. If you cannot do the work rapidly, review again the *Word Study*. Be prepared to do what is required when the Leader calls on you. Always repeat the entire expression, phrase or sentence as you work.

1. Add the corresponding forms of the *locative* ending to the following nouns:

àácí (ağacı)
bír (bir)
dá: (dağ)
dòkúz (dokuz)
fìlʸím (filim)
kàyálár (kayalar)
sìınáí (sığınağı)
ǘç (üç)

2. Add the corresponding forms of the *interrogative* ending to the following nouns:

béndè (bende)
èvimizdé (evimizde)
gʸǘzèlʸlʸér (güzeller)
ílʸèrdé (ilerde)
bày‿káyanín (bay Kayanın)
óráyà (oraya)
sáàt‿dokúzdá (saat dokuzda)

3. Give the corresponding "*let's* (*do it*)!" forms of the following verbs:

ara- . . .	(ara- . . .)
de- . . .	(de- . . .)
eylʸen- . . .	(eğlen- . . .)
gʸeç- . . .	(geç- . . .)
gʸelʸ- . . .	(gel- . . .)
iç- . . .	(iç . . .)
kal- . . .	(kal- . . .)
kalk- . . .	(kalk- . . .)
ol- . . .	(ol- . . .)
unut- . . .	(unut- . . .)
yıkan- . . .	(yıkan- . . .)

4. Give the corresponding "(*you*) (*do it*)!" forms of the verbs in 3 above.

4. **What Would You Say?** (Individual Study)

Read aloud each of the following and then pick out the expression you think most suitable:

1. *Tom Carr, approaching a native of the town, asks whether there's a good hotel in town:*

a. çócúùm! konúşúnùz!	Çocuğum! Konuşunuz!
b. bú‿şehirdè iyi‿bir‿otél^{y}‿vármì?	Bu şehirde iyi bir otel varmı?

2. *Mr. Metin, the native, says there is a good hotel and directs Tom to it:*

a. évèt. vár. àz‿il^{y}érdé.	Evet. Var. Az ilerde.
b. ófisìmizdé né‿yápalìm?	Ofisimizde ne yapalım?

3. *Entering the hotel, Tom sees a man and asks:*

a. síz k^{y}ímsinìz?	Siz kimsiniz?
b. ótèl^{y}cí sízmisinìz?	Otelci sizmisiniz?

4. *The man says he is and then says politely:*

a. háyìr! bén hádeméyìm!	Hayır! Ben hademeyim!
b. évèt. bénìm. hóş‿g^{y}él^{y}dinìz!	Evet. Benim. Hoş geldiniz!

5. *Tom answers politely in return:*

a. hóş‿búldùk!	Hoş bulduk!
b. bú‿şehrin‿sinèmasındá g^{y}üzél^{y}‿bir‿fil^{y}im‿vármì?	Bu şehrin sinemasında güzel bir filim varmı?

6. *The hotel-keeper then inquires:*

a. otel^{y}imizin‿l^{y}okántasındà yemék^{y}‿yemék^{y}‿istiyórmúsunùz?	Otelimizin lokantasında yemek yemek istiyormusunuz?
b. bir‿odámi‿arzú‿édiyòrsunúz?	Bir odamı arzu ediyorsunuz?

7. *Tom answers:*

a. évèt, bènim vé‿kárím‿için bir‿ódá‿istiyòrúm.	Evet, benim ve karım için bir oda istiyorum.
b. bú‿şehrin‿otél^{y}l^{y}erindè iyi‿şaráp‿vármì?	Bu şehrin otellerinde iyi şarap varmı?

8. *The hotel-keeper suggests a room:*

a. háyìr, maál^{y}ésèf yóktùr, fákàt çók‿iyi‿biramiz‿vàr.	Hayır, maalesef yoktur, fakat çok iyi biramız var.
b. ik^{y}inci‿káttà g^{y}üzél^y‿bir‿ódamíz‿vàr.	İkinci katta güzel bir odamız var.

9. *Tom then wants to know what the rates are:*

a. bú‿otél^{y}dè g^{y}üzél^y‿hizmetçi‿kızlari‿vármì?	Bu otelde güzel hizmetçi kızları varmı?
b. g^{y}ǜndél^{y}iyi káç‿pàrà?	Gündeliği kaç para?

10. *The hotel-keeper then proposes that they take a look:*

a. g^{y}üzél^y‿yüzl^{y}èr hóşumá‿g^{y}idiyòr!	Güzel yüzler hoşuma gidiyor!
b. asánsőrl^{y}é‿çikalìm!	Asansörle çıkalım!

11. *After Tom has taken a look, he says:*

a. háyìr, maál^{y}ésèf g^{y}üzèl^y‿deyil^{y}l^{y}ér.	Hayır, maalesef güzel değiller.
b. çók‿hóşumá‿g^{y}idiyòr.	Çok hoşuma gidiyor.

12. *The hotel-keeper then inquires about food:*

a. otél^{y}démì yémék^y‿yiyecèk^{y}siniz?	Oteldemi yemek yiyeceksiniz?
b. kùşlár né‿yérl^{y}èr?	Kuşlar ne yerler?

13. *Tom is not quite ready to eat, so he says:*

a. dáhá‿évvèl^y sinémayá‿g^{y}itmék^y‿istiyòrúm.	Daha evvel sinemaya gitmek istiyorum.
b. évèt, fákàt dáhá‿évvèl^y yikànmák, tráş‿olmák‿istiyòrúm.	Evet, fakat daha evvel yıkanmak, traş olmak istiyorum.

14. *The hotel-keeper tells him about the dinner hour:*

a. hér‿g^{y}ǜn saát‿üç‿il^{y}é‿dőrt‿árasındà yá:múr‿yáàr.	Her gün saat üç ile dört arasında yağmur yağar.

b. ȧkşám‿yémeyi saát‿alti‿ilʸė‿dókúz‿ára-sindȧdir. — Akşam yemeği saat altı ile dokuz arasındadır.

15. *As Tom goes to clean up, he misses something, and asks:*

a. bú‿otėlʸdè iyi‿şaráp‿vármì? — Bu otelde iyi şarap varmı?

b. lʸútfèn, bir‿havlú‿verirmisiniz? — Lûtfen, bir havlu verirmisiniz?

16. *The hotel-keeper explains its absence:*

a. áffedèrsiniz! hizmétçi‿unútmùş. — Affedersiniz! Hizmetçi unutmuş.

b. áffedèrsiniz! únùttúm! — Affedersiniz! Unuttum!

Section D—Listening In

1. What Did You Say?

Give your answers in Turkish for each of the exercises in the preceding sections, when the Leader calls for them. Then, as the Leader calls for them, give the English equivalents of all the expressions in the exercise.

2. Word Study Check-Up

As you have done in the previous units, go back to the *Word Study* and give the correct Turkish for each English expression, without having to read it from the book. The Leader or one of the members of the group should read the English. As a final check the Leader will call for your answers to the exercises in the *Word Study Review* (Sec. C.3).

3. Listening In

With your book closed, listen to the following conversations as read by the Guide or phonograph record. Repeat the Turkish immediately after hearing it. After the first repetition of each conversation, check up on the meaning of anything you do not understand, by asking someone else or by going back to the *Basic Sentences* if no one knows. Repeat again if necessary, then take parts and carry on the conversation.

1. *Asking for a hotel.*

Record 15A, after 4th spiral.

òsmán— şehrinizdé‿iyi‿bir‿otėlʸ‿vármì? — Şehrinizde iyi bir otel varmı?

àlʸí—	évèt. çók‿gʸüzélʸ‿bir‿ótélʸ‿vàr.	Evet. Çok güzel bir otel var.
òsmán—	nérédè?	Nerede?
àlʸí—	àz‿ilʸérdé.	Az ilerde.
òsmán—	háydi‿óraýá‿gʸìdelʸìm!	Haydi oraya gidelim!

2. *Downstairs in the hotel.*

ótèlʸcí—	hóş‿gʸélʸdinìz!	Hoş geldiniz!
òsmán—	hóş‿búldùk!	Hoş bulduk!
	bir‿ódá‿ìstiyòrúm.	Bir oda istiyorum.
ótèlʸcí—	ìkʸiniz‿içìnmì?	İkiniz içinmi?
òsmán—	háyìr. yálnız‿bénìm‿içìn.	Hayır. Yalnız benim için.
ótèlʸcí—	otelʸimizìn‿ikʸìncí‿kátındà gʸüzélʸ‿bır‿ódamíz‿vàr.	Otelimizin ikinci katında güzel bir odamız var.

3. *Looking at a room.*

ótèlʸcí—	búyrùn asánsőrlʸé‿çikalìm!	Buyrun asansörle çıkalım!
òsmán—	áffedèrsinìz, únùttúm. odá‿káç‿párà?	Affedersiniz, unuttum. Oda kaç para?
ótèlʸcí—	gʸündèlʸiyí ìkʸí‿lʸìrá.	Gündeliği iki lira.
òsmán—	çók‿ìyì!	Çok iyi!
ótèlʸcí—	bú‿ódà hoşunuzá‿gʸìdiyórmù?	Bu oda hoşunuza gidiyormu?
òsmán—	évèt. çók‿gʸüzèlʸ!	Evet. Çok güzel!
ótèlʸcí—	otelʸdémí‿yemékʸ‿yemékʸ‿ìstiyòrsunúz?	Oteldemi yemek yemek istiyorsunuz?
òsmán—	évèt. búrádà.	Evet. Burada.

4. *Asking about the service.*

Record 15B, beginning.

ótèlʸcí—	ákşám‿yémeyì saát‿altí‿ilʸé‿dókúz‿árasindàdir.	Akşam yemeği saat altı ile dokuz arasındadır.

òsmán—	şimdi‿saàt‿káç?	Şimdi saat kaç?
ótèl^{y}ci—	áltí‿búçùk.	Altı buçuk.
	şimdimi‿yemék^y‿yemék^y‿istiyòrsunúz?	Şimdimi yemek yemek istiyorsunuz?
òsmán—	háyìr. sónrà.	Hayır. Sonra.
	dáhá‿evvél^y‿yıkánmàk, tráş‿olmák‿istiyòrúm.	Daha evvel yıkanmak, traş olmak istiyorum.
	havlú‿nérédè?	Havlu nerede?
ótèl^{y}ci—	yókmù? áffedèrsiniz.	Yokmu? Affedersiniz.
	hizmetçi‿unútmúş.	Hizmetçi unutmuş.
	başká‿bir‿şéy‿istiyórmúsunùz?	Başka bir şey istiyormusunuz?
òsmán—	évèt. bú‿ákşàm ánkará‿tréni saát‿káçtá‿g^{y}él^{y}ecèk^y?	Evet. Bu akşam Ankara treni saat kaçta gelecek?
ótèl^{y}ci—	saát‿dókúz‿buçúktà.	Saat dokuz buçukta.

5. *In the hotel restaurant.*

òsmán—	ya:múr‿yá:maá‿báşlıyòr!	Yağmur yağmağa başlıyor!
	né‿yápalìm?	Ne yapalım?
	èrk^{y}én, fákàt şimdi‿l^{y}okántayá‿g^{y}idel^{y}ìm, yémék^y‿yiyel^{y}ìm!	Erken, fakat şimdi lokantaya gidelim, yemek yiyelim!
	bera: bér‿g^{y}el^{y}írmisiniz?	Beraber gelirmisiniz?
àl^{y}í—	çók‿teşék^{y}k^{y}úr‿edèrim, g^{y}él^{y}irìm.	Çok teşekkür ederim, gelirim.
	şimdi‿yémék^y‿yémèk^y dáhá‿iyì!	Şimdi yemek yemek daha iyi!
òsmán—	bú‿l^{y}okàntá çók‿hóşumá‿g^{y}idiyòr.	Bu lokanta çok hoşuma gidiyor.
	yemeyi‿çók‿g^{y}üzèl^y.	Yemeği çok güzel.
àl^{y}í—	şarabídá‿iyì.	Şarabı da iyi.

6. *Killing time.*

àl^{y}í—	ṣi̍mdi‿ya:múr‿di̍níyòr.	Şimdi yağmur diniyor.
òsmán—	sáàt‿káç?	Saat kaç?
àl^{y}í—	yédí‿búçùk.	Yedi buçuk.
òsmán—	çók‿g^{y}èç‿déyíl^{y}.	Çok geç değil.
	kàrím saát‿dokúz‿buçúk‿trénı́‿il^{y}é‿g^{y}él^{y}ecèk^{y}.	Karım saat dokuz buçuk treni ile gelecek.
	dáhá‿évvèl^{y} bi̍r‿ṣéy‿yápalìm!	Daha evvel bir şey yapalım!
àl^{y}í—	istásyón‿k^{y}öṣesi̍ndè bi̍r‿sinémá‿vàr.	İstasyon köşesinde bir sinema var.
	bén óraya‿g^{y}i̍tmék^{y}‿i̍stiyòrúm.	Ben oraya gitmek istiyorum.
	sízdé‿g^{y}èl^{y}ini̍z!	Sizde geliniz!
òsmán—	pék^{y}‿i̍yì! g^{y}ìdél^{y}ím!	Pek iyi! Gidelim!

7. *In the movie.*

òsmán—	bú‿fi̍l^{y}ìm hoṣunuzá‿g^{y}i̍diyórmù?	Bu filim hoşunuza gidiyormu?
àl^{y}í—	évèt, çók! çók‿éyl^{y}eníyórùm!	Evet, çok! Çok eğleniyorum!
òsmán—	béndè.	Bende.
àl^{y}í—	sigáranız‿vármì?	Sigaranız varmı?
òsmán—	búyrùn!	Buyrun!

8. *On the street.*

àl^{y}í—	ṣi̍mdi‿havá‿dáhà‿sérín,[1] déyíl^{y}mì?	Şimdi hava daha serin, değilmi?
òsmán—	évèt. ṣi̍mdi‿sáàt‿káç?	Evet. Şimdi saat kaç?
àl^{y}í—	saát‿dokuzú‿ón‿g^{y}éçiyòr.	Saat dokuzu on geçiyor.
òsmán—	trén‿ṣi̍mdi‿g^{y}él^{y}íyòr.	Tren şimdi geliyor.
àl^{y}í—	g^{y}él^{y}iyórmù? erk^{y}én‿déyíl^{y}mì?	Geliyormu? Erken değilmi?

[1]should be: dáhá‿sérìn '*cooler*'; dáhà‿sérín '*still cool*'

SECTION E—CONVERSATION

1. Covering the Turkish in Basic Sentences (Individual Study)

Cover the Turkish of the *Basic Sentences* and practice saying the Turkish equivalents of the English expressions.

2. Vocabulary Check-Up

Give the Turkish expressions for the English equivalents in the *Basic Sentences* as the Leader calls for them.

3. Conversation

As you have done in the *Conversation* in the previous units, begin to converse by following the models outlined below fairly closely; then change the situations somewhat. Invent new combinations of subject matter.

1. Getting a room.

   Tom Carr excuses himself and asks for a hotel. Ahmet replies and gives directions. Tom doesn't understand right away and asks Ahmet to repeat (*tekʸrár‿edérmisiniz?*) (tekrar edermisiniz?) and to speak slowly. Ahmet repeats and explains about the food and drink of the hotel. Tom thanks him and they say good-bye.

2. At the hotel.

   Tom enters, looks about, sees a man, and asks for the hotel-keeper. The man says he is the manager and asks what Tom wants. Tom explains the kind of room he wants, they go up and look at it; he asks about the restaurant, meal hours, and so on. He goes to clean up, notices there is no towel and asks for one. The hotel-keeper apologizes and blames it on the servant girl.

3. Conversation in the cocktail lounge.

   Tom comes in, sees another man there, introduces himself. The man gives his name in turn. Tom offers him a cigarette. They order drinks and talk about the beer and wine there. They talk about the weather, rain, sunshine, etc. Tom's friend observes that there's sunshine every morning. Tom is pleased and explains that he likes to get up early. Tom's friend says so do his children. Tom is surprised that his friend is married and has children. They go on talking about the children.

4. They leave.

Tom explains to his friend that he has to meet his wife. They talk about the time, the train schedule, etc. Tom invites his friend to come with him. They call for the check, pay and leave.

5. On the street.

As Tom and his friend walk along, they talk about the weather, the rain, etc. As they come to the station, Tom hears the train. They hurry.

6. His wife arrives.

Tom introduces his wife. As they leave the station, it begins to rain again. They take shelter, talk about the rain. They wonder what to do for the evening and decide on a movie.

Section F—Conversation (*Cont.*)

1. Conversation (*Cont.*)

Continue the conversations started in Section E with a review of parts 1 and 2 of the section if necessary.

2. Questions and Answers

First run through the *Listening In* once more. Then answer the following questions when the Guide asks you, or take turns asking them of others and answering them:

1.	1. k^{y}imin‿şéhrindè iyi‿bir‿ótél^{y}‿vàr?	Kimin şehrinde iyi bir otel var?
	2. bú‿ótèl^{y} násìl?	Bu otel nasıl?
	3. nérédè?	Nerede?
	4. néreyé‿g^{y}idel^{y}ìm?	Nereye gidelim?
2.	5. ótèl^{y}cí né‿diyòr?	Otelci ne diyor?
	6. òsmán né‿istiyòr?	Osman ne istiyor?
	7. bú‿ódà k^{y}imín‿içìn?	Bu oda kimin için?

3.	8. né‿il^{y}é‿çikalìm?	Ne ile çıkalım?
	9. g^{y}ündel^{y}iyi̍‿káç‿pàrà?	Gündeliği kaç para?
	10. òdá osmanin‿hoşuná‿g^{y}i̍diyórmù?	Oda Osmanın hoşuna gidiyormu?
	11. òsmán néredé‿yemék^y‿yemék^y‿i̍stiyòr?	Osman nerede yemek yemek istiyor?
4.	12. ákşám‿yémeyì né‿vákìt?	Akşam yemeği ne vakit?
	13. òsmán dáhá‿évvèl^y né‿yapmák‿i̍stiyòr?	Osman daha evvel ne yapmak istiyor?
	14. ósmanín‿ódasindà né‿yòk?	Osmanın odasında ne yok?
	15. ánkará‿tréni̍ saát‿káçtá‿g^{y}él^{y}ecèk^y?	Ankara treni saat kaçta gelecek?
5.	16. şímdì néreyé‿g^{y}i̍diyórlàr?	Şimdi nereye gidiyorlar?
	17. àhmét k^{y}i̍mín‿i̍l^{y}è yémék^y‿yemék^y‿i̍stiyòr?	Ahmet kimin ile yemek yemek istiyor?
	18. l^{y}ókántà hoşlarıná‿g^{y}i̍diyórmù?	Lokanta hoşlarına gidiyormu?
	19. ó‿l^{y}okántanın‿yémeyì násìl?	O lokantanın yemeği nasıl?
6.	20. şímdì né‿di̍niyòr?	Şimdi ne diniyor?
	21. şi̍mdi‿sáàt‿káç?	Şimdi saat kaç?
	22. g^{y}éçmì?	Geçmi?
	23. ósmanín‿kárısì saát‿káç‿treni̍‿il^{y}é‿g^{y}él^{y}ecèk^y?	Osmanın karısı saat kaç treni ile gelecek?
	24. néredé‿bir‿sinèmá‿vár?	Nerede bir sinema var?
	25. k^{y}ím‿óraya‿g^{y}itmék^y‿i̍stiyòr?	Kim oraya gitmek istiyor?
	26. k^{y}ímdé‿g^{y}él^{y}iyòr?	Kimde geliyor?
7.	27. fìl^{y}ím al^{y}ini̍n‿hoşuná‿g^{y}i̍diyórmù?	Filim Alinin hoşuna gidiyormu?
	28. ósmaníndámì?	Osmanındamı?
	29. osmanin‿sigárası‿vármì?	Osmanın sigarası varmı?
8.	30. şi̍mdi‿havá‿násìl?	Şimdi hava nasıl?
	31. trén váktíndémì erk^{y}énmi̍‿g^{y}él^{y}iyòr?	Tren vaktindemi, erkenmi geliyor?

FINDER LIST

We include here, for the first time, in parentheses after each entry, the ordinary or conventional spelling. We shall carry this through Unit 11.

àkşám (akşam)	evening
ákşám‿yémeyì (akşam yemeği)	dinner (lit. evening meal)
ánkàrà (Ankara)	Ankara, Angora (capital of Turkey)
ánkará‿trénì (Ankara treni)	the Ankara train (train from Ankara)
**ara*	interval
àrásí (arası)	its interval
àrasındá (arasında)	between (lit. on its interval)
àsànsőr (asansör)	elevator
asánsőrl^{y}è (asansörle)	in (lit. with) [the] elevator
áz (az)	[a] little
àz‿il^{y}érdé (az ilerde)	up ahead a little
bàşká (başka)	else (lit. other)
báşká‿bir‿şèy	(something) (anything) else
başla- . . . (başla- . . .)	start, begin, commence
bàşlıyálím! (başlıyalım!)	let's begin!
báşláyınìz! (başlayınız!)	begin!
bén (ben)	I
bénìm (benim)	I am
bèním (benim)	my, mine; (for) me
béním‿içìn (benim için)	for me

bíz (biz)	we
bìzdé (bizde)	at our house (lit. at us)
bùçúk (buçuk)	half (hour)
saát‿dókúz‿buçúk‿trénì (saat dokuz buçuk treni)	the nine thirty (half past nine) train
bul- . . . (bul- . . .) (aor. *-ur-*)	find
bùldúk (bulduk)	we've found [it]
**bura*	this place
búrádà (burada)	in this place, here
buyur- . . . (buyur-) (aor. *-ur-*)	be so kind
búyrùn! (buyrun!)	please
*búyúrùn! (buyurun!)	see *búyrùn* (buyrun)
çık- . . . (çık- . . .) (aor. *-ar-*)	go up
çòcúk (çocuk)	child; boy
çócúùm! (çocuğum!)	my child!
dàhá (daha)	more; still
dáhá‿évvèl^{y} (daha evvel)	still before, first, before(hand)
èféndìm (efendim)	sir
èvvél^{y} (evvel)	before
dáhá‿évvèl^{y} (daha evvel)	first, before(hand)
él^{y} (el)	hand

g^{y}el^y- . . . (gel- . . .) (aor. *-ir-*)	come
g^{y}èl^{y}diníz (geldiniz)	you've come
g^{y}èl^{y}écék^y (gelecek)	[she] will come
g^{y}ǘn (gün)	day
g^{y}ǜndé (günde)	per (lit. at the) day
g^{y}ǜndél^{y}ík^y (gündelik)	daily rate
g^{y}ǜndél^{y}iyí (gündeliği)	its (daily) rate
g^{y}ündèl^{y}iyí (gündeliği)	see *g^{y}ǜndél^{y}iyí* (gündeliği)
hàvlú (havlu)	towel
hizmètçí (hizmetçi)	servant; maid
hóş (hoş)	pleasure; pleasing; pleasant(ly)
hóş‿g^{y}él^{y}dinìz! (hoş geldiniz!)	welcome! (lit. you came pleasantly)
hóş‿búldùk! (hoş bulduk!)	thank you! (lit. we've found it pleasant)
ìçín (için)	for
bénim‿içìn (benim için)	for me
içínmì? (içinmi?)	[is it] for?
ìk^{y}í (iki)	two
ìk^{y}iníz (ikiniz)	the two of you
ik^{y}ìncí (ikinci)	second
ìl^{y}é (ile)	and (lit. with)
ìl^{y}érí (ileri)	forward
il^{y}èrdé (ilerde)	up ahead
il^{y}èridé (ileride)	see *il^{y}èrdé* (ilerde)

ìyí (iyi)	good
dȧhá‿i̇yì (daha iyi)	better
kát (kat)	floor, storey
kàtí (katı)	its floor
kȧtìndá (katında)	on its floor
kʸím (kim)	who
kʸìmín (kimin)	whose; (for) (with) whom
kʸi̇mín‿i̇çìn (kimin için)	for whom
kʸimín‿i̇lʸè (kimin ile)	with whom
**nere*	what place
nérėdè (nerede)	in what place, where
ó (o)	she (he, it)
òdá (oda)	room
bi̇r‿ódámì (bir odamı?)	a room?
**ora*	that place
órȧdà (orada)	in that place; there
òtélʸ (otel)	hotel
ȯtèlʸcí (otelci)	hotel-keeper, manager
otėlʸdémì? (oteldemi?)	at [the] hotel?
sónrà (sonra)	later
şàráp (şarap)	wine
şàrábí (şarabı)	its wine

şèhír (şehir)	town; city
şèhrí (şehri)	his town
şèhrín (şehrin)	of the town
şèhriníz (şehriniz)	your town
tek^{y}rar‿et- . . . (tekrar et- . . .) (aor. *-er-*)	repeat
tek^{y}rár‿edérmisiniz? (tekrar edermisiniz?)	will you repeat?
traş‿ol- . . . (traş ol- . . .) (aor. *-ur-*)	shave (oneself)
tráş‿ólmàk (traş olmak)	to shave (oneself)
unut- . . . (unut- . . .) (aor. *-ur-*)	forget
únùtmúş (unutmuş)	[she] (probably) forgot [it]
únùttúm (unuttum)	I forgot [it]
vàkít (vakit)	time
vàktíndé (vaktinde)	on time (lit. in its time)
yálnìz (yalnız)	just, only
ya:- . . . (yağ- . . .) (aor. *-ar-*)	fall (rain, snow, and so forth)
yá:múr‿yáàr (yağmur yağar)	it rains
ye- . . . (ye- . . .)	eat
yèmék^{y} (yemek)	food; a meal
yèméyí (yemeği)	its food, its meal
yiyecék^{y}siniz (yiyeceksiniz)	you will eat
yìyél^{y}ím (yiyelim!)	let's eat!
yíyìn! (yiyin!)	eat!
yíyinìz! (yiyiniz!)	eat!
yıkan- . . . (yıkan- . . .) (aor. *-ır-*)	wash (oneself)
yıkànmák (yıkanmak)	to wash (oneself)

UNIT 8

GETTING CLEANED UP

SECTION A—BASIC SENTENCES

Go through the *Basic Sentences* in unison, concentrating on the *Aids to Listening*, then do the *Hints on Pronunciation;* go once through the *Basic Sentences* individually, and then read the *Hints on Spelling*. The last time through individually, notice also the *Conventional Spelling*.

1. Basic Sentences

Tom Carr washes up assisted by his friend, Ahmet.

ENGLISH EQUIVALENTS	AIDS TO LISTENING	CONVENTIONAL TURKISH SPELLING
	Tom Carr	
Record 16A, beginning.		
hot	sìcák.	sıcak
the water	sùyú.	suyu
will you draw [it]?	ákıtírmisınìz?	akıtırmısınız?
Will you draw the hot water, please, Ahmet?	l^{y}ûtfèn, sıcák‿suyú‿ákıtírmisınìz, áhmèt?	Lûtfen, sıcak suyu akıtırmısınız, Ahmet?
	Ahmet	
[a] bath	bányò.	banyo
to take	ạlmák.	almak
do you want?	istiyórmúsụnùz?	istiyormusunuz?
Do you want to take a bath?	bányo‿almák‿istiyórmúsunùz?	Banyo almak istiyormusunuz?

Tom Carr

I do not want [to]	istémiyòrúm.	istemiyorum
No, I don't.	háyìr, istémiyòrúm.	Hayır, istemiyorum.
my face	yùzümű.	yüzümü
to wash	yìkámák.	yıkamak
my teeth	dişlʸèrimi.	dişlerimi
to[1] brush	òvmák.	ovmak
I just want to wash my face and brush my teeth.	yálnız‿yüzümű‿yikamàk, dişlʸerimi‿óvmák‿istiyòrúm.	Yalnız yüzümü yıkamak, dişlerimi ovmak istiyorum.

Ahmet

here is	ìşté.	işte
your soap	sabùnúnúz.	sabununuz
Here's your soap.	iştè‿sabúnunúz.	İşte sabununuz.
your tooth brush	diş‿firçanìz.	diş fırçanız
Where's your tooth brush?	diş‿firçanìz nérédè?	Diş fırçanız nerede?

Tom Carr

my tooth brush	diş‿firçàm.	diş fırçam
small	kʸùçűkʸ.	küçük
of my bag	çántámìn.	çantamın
[it is] on [the] inside	içindé.	içinde
My tooth brush is in my small bag.	diş‿firçàm kʸüçükʸ‿cántamìn‿içindè.	Diş fırçam küçük çantamın içinde.

[1]Not on record.

	Ahmet	
your shaving	tráş‿ólmanìz.	traş olmanız
[is it] necessary?	l^{y}á:zímmì?	lâzımmı?
Do you have to shave?	tráş‿olmaniz‿l^{y}á:zímmì?	Traş olmanız lâzımmı?
	Tom Carr	
Yes, unfortunately.	évèt, maál^{y}ésèf.	Evet, maalesef.

Record 16B, beginning.

my shaving brush	tráş‿firçàm.	traş fırçam
my razor	ústúràm.	usturam
of the clothes brush	él^{y}bi:sé‿firçasınìn.	elbise fırçasının
[it is] at its side	yánìndá.	yanında
My shaving brush, my soap and my razor are beside the clothes brush.	tráş‿firçàm, sàbúnúm, vé‿ústúràm él^{y}bi:sè‿fırçasınin‿yánìndá.	Traş fırçam, sabunum, ve usturam elbise fırçasının yanında.
	Ahmet	
Here they are.	ìşté.	İşte.
your shaving mirror	tráş‿áynanìz.	traş aynanız
And here's your shaving mirror.	vé‿işté‿tráş‿áynanìz.	Ve işte traş aynanız.
	Tom Carr	
the bottle of eau de Cologne	kolónyá‿şişesinì.	kolonya şişesini
will you bring [it]?	g^{y}étirírmìsinìz?	getirirmisiniz?
Will you bring the bottle of eau de Cologne?	kolónya‿şişesinì‿g^{y}étirírmìsinìz?	Kolonya şişesini getirirmisiniz?

my hair(s)	sàçlárımí.	saçlarımı
my combing	tàrámám.	taramam
[it is] necessary	lʸà:zím.	lâzım
I have to comb my hair.	saçlarımi‿táramám‿lʸá:zìm.	Saçlarımı taramam **lâzım.**
[the] comb	tàrák.	tarak
Where's the comb?	tarák‿nérédè?	Tarak nerede?
	Ahmet	
of [the] table	másánìn.	masanın
[it] is on its top	üzéri̍ndédìr.	üzerindedir
It's on the table.	másanın‿üzéri̍ndédìr.	Masanın üzerin**dedir.**
	Tom Carr	
it	ònú.	onu
I do not see [it] (lit. am not seeing [it])	gʸő́rmüyòrúm.	görmüyorum
I don't see it.	onú‿gʸő́rmüyòrúm.	Onu görmüyorum.
	Ahmet	
perhaps	gá:lʸi̍bà.	galiba
of [the] towel	hàvlúnún.	havlunun
at its under side	àltíndá.	altında
Perhaps it's under the towel.	gá:lʸi̍bà hávlunún‿áltindà.	Galiba havlunun altın**da.**
	Tom Carr	
I can't find [it].	bulámıyòrúm.	Bulamıyorum.
	Ahmet	
Here it is.	ìşté.	İşte.

	Tom Carr	
servant's work	hìzmètçil^{y}ík^y.	hizmetçilik
you do	yapíyórsunùz.	yapıyorsunuz.
Thanks! You make a good servant, Ahmet!	teşèk^{y}k^{y}ürl^{y}ér! çók‿i-yi‿hìzmétçil^{y}ík^y‿yápı-yòrsunúz, áhmèt!	Teşekkürler! Çok iyi hizmetçilik yapıyorsunuz, Ahmet!

Before you go through the *Basic Sentences* a second time, read the following:

2. Hints on Pronunciation

There are, as we have noted, two *l* sounds in Turkish, the one which we have written *l*^{y}, and which we discussed in the previous unit, and the other which we have written, as in English, with plain *l*. This "plain *l*" is fairly similar to English *l*. But it is deeper and more hollow-sounding. If we pronounce a strong "w" and then slide right into the "plain *l*" sound, we will get something close to this deep Turkish *l*. Here are some examples:

PRACTICE 1 **Record 17A, beginning.**

ò*l*sún.	olsun	(*may* [*they*] *be*)
násì*l*.	nasıl	(*how*)
só*l*dádìr.	soldadır	([*it*]'*s to* [*the*] *left*)
kà*l*kár.	kalkar	([*it*] *leaves*)
à*l*tí.	altı	(*six*)
À*ll*áh.	Allah	(*God*)
òú*l*.	oğul	(*son*)
bù*l*dúk.	bulduk	(*we've found* [*it*])
yá*l*nìz.	yalnız	(*just, only*)

PRACTICE 2 **Record 17A, after 1st spiral.**

háyìr*lí*.	hayırlı	(*fortunate*)
àn*l*ámıyòrúm.	anlamıyorum	(*I [do] not understand*)
kà*l*á.	kala	(*remaining*)
òn*l*ár.	onlar	(*they*)
véznedàr*l*ík.	veznedarlık	(*cashier*)
ò:*l*úm.	oğlum	(*my son*)
bù*l*út.	bulut	(*cloud*)
hàv*l*ú.	havlu	(*towel*)
ko*l*ónyá‿şişesı	kolonya şişesi	(*eau de Cologne bottle*)

We have had many instances of Turkish *r*. Turkish *r* is not quite like English *r*. English *r* is weak and relaxed. Turkish *r*, however, is stronger and tenser and the tip of the tongue is up behind the upper teeth. Between two vowels it sounds very much like American *-tt-* in words such as *better*, *butter*, *Betty*, and so on. At the beginning of a word (*ráhàtlík*), or of a syllable after a consonant (*kʸìbrít*), or at the end of a syllable (*kàrdéş*), it is a bit weaker, and at the end of a word (*vár*), it may lose some of its humming sound and shade off toward English *sh*. When doubled (*müşèrréf*) it is quite strong, trilled as opera singers sometimes pronounce *r*'s. Here are some examples:

PRACTICE 3 **Record 17A, after 2nd spiral.**

*r*áhàtlík.	rahatlık	(*rest*)
kʸìb*r*ít.	kibrit	(*match*)
són*r*à.	sonra	(*later*)
t*r*én.	tren	(*train*)
bú*r*ádà.	burada	(*here*)
sigá*r*à.	sigara	(*cigarette*)

dò:*r*ú.	doğru	(*right*)
kà*r*í.	karı	(*wife*)

PRACTICE 4 **Record 17A, after 3rd spiral.**

mé*r*hábà.	merhaba	(*hello*)
kà*r*déş.	kardeş	(*brother*)
bí*r*.	bir	(*one*)
vá*r*.	var	(*there* [*is*])
müşè*rr*éf.	müşerref	(*honored*)

Before you go through the *Basic Sentences* a third time, read the following:

3. Hints on Spelling

Note the following differences between the *Aids to Listening* and the *Conventional Spelling*.

AIDS TO LISTENING		CONVENTIONAL SPELLING
k^y	:	**k**
ük^y	:	ük
Example:		
k^yùçúk^y	:	küçük
(length)	:	**ğ**
o:	:	oğ
Examples:		
ò:lúm	:	oğlum
dò:rú	:	doğru
(zero)	:	**ğ**
Examples:		
òúl	:	oğul
tàráí	:	tarağı

We have noted here only such cases as did not happen to occur in the previous unit.

AIDS TO LISTENING		CONVENTIONAL SPELLING
(length)	:	**zero**
i:	:	i
Example:		
él^{y}bì:sé	:	elbise

Section B—Word Study and Review of Basic Sentences

1. **Word Study** (Individual Study)

1. *Turkish equivalents of English "not"*

We have already seen these forms:

anlámıyòrúm	anlamıyorum	*'I [do] not understand (lit. am not understanding)'*
i̇stémiyòrúm	istemiyorum	*'I [do] not want [to]'*
gʸő́rmüyòrúm	görmüyorum	*'I [do] not see (lit. am not seeing)'*

Now observe the following similar forms:

Column I

·çi̇ni̇̀z!	içiniz!	*'drink!'*
gʸélʸi̇niz̀!	geliniz!	*'come!'*
kóşúnùz!	koşunuz!	*'run!'*
bàşláyınìz!	başlayınız!	*'start!'*
yi̇̀yélʸi̇́m!	yiyelim!	*'let's eat!'*
bàşlıyálím!	başlıyalım!	*'let's begin!'*
kónùşalím!	konuşalım!	*'let's talk!'*
i̇çiyórsúnùz	içiyorsunuz	*'you are drinking'*
i̇sti̇yòr	istiyor	*'[he] wants'*
gʸülʸű́yórùz	gülüyoruz	*'we are laughing'*

Column II

Group I

:	i̇́çméyini̇̀z!	içmeyiniz!	*'[do]n't drink!'*
:	gʸélʸméyinìz!	gelmeyiniz!	*'[do]n't come!'*
:	kóşmáyınìz!	koşmayınız!	*'[do]n't run!'*
:	bàşlámayınìz!	başlamayınız!	*'[do]n't start!'*

Group II

:	yémi̇yelʸi̇̀m!	yemiyelim!	*'let's not eat!'*
:	bàşlámıyálìm!	başlamıyalım!	*'let's not begin!'*
:	konúşmıyálìm!	konuşmıyalım!	*'let's not talk!'*

Group III

:	i̇́çmiyòrsunúz	içmiyorsunuz	*'you are not drinking'*
:	i̇stémiyòr	istemiyor	*'[he] [does]n't want'*
:	gʸű́lʸmüyòrúz	gülmüyoruz	*'we are not laughing'*

gʸörúüyórlàr	görüyorlar	*'they are seeing'*	:	gʸǿrmüyórlàr	görmüyorlar	*'they [do]n't see (lit. they are not seeing)'*
çıkíyórùm	çıkıyorum	*'I am going up'*	:	çíkmıyòrúm	çıkmıyorum	*'I am not going up'*

If we compare the forms in Column I with those in Column II of all three groups, we see that the ending which means "not" is *-m(e)-*, or *-m(a)-*, that is,

1. it follows Vowel Harmony Type II;
2. before the *y* of the endings in the forms in Group II the *a* has changed to *ı*, and the *e* to *i;*
3. it loses its vowel *e* or *a* before the momentary ending, *-iyor-*, *-üyor-*, and so forth, just as a verb root ending in a vowel loses the vowel before the momentary ending (Unit 3. B. 1. 1.);
4. the *strongest vowel* is the one *immediately before the ending;*
5. the 'do [it]!' ending and the 'let's . . .' ending in Groups I and II have the form which follows a vowel, the one beginning in *-y-*.

We shall call this ending which means "not," the *negative* ending, and we see it here as used with momentary, 'let's . . .', and 'do [it]!' verb forms.

2. *Turkish equivalents of English "hyphen-words" such as "meal-time", and so on*

In Units 1 to 8, we have met the following:

yémékʸ‿vákti̇̀	yemek vakti	*'meal time'*
gʸǿkʸ‿yüzǜ	gök yüzü	*'sky (lit. heaven face)'*
şi̇mşékʸ‿pariltılarì	şimşek parıltıları	*'lightning (lit. lightning flashes)'*
şi̇mşékʸ‿séslʸerì	şimşek sesleri	*'thunder (lit. thunder sounds)'*
ȧkşám‿yémeyì	akşam yemeği	*'dinner (lit. evening meal)'*
i̇stásyón‿kʸöşesì	istasyon köşesi	*'station corner'*
ánkȧrȧ‿tréni̇̀	Ankara treni	'[*the*] *Ankara train*'
díş‿firçasì	diş fırçası	*'tooth brush'*
tráş‿áynasì	traş aynası	*'shaving mirror'*
kolónyȧ‿şi̇şesì	kolonya şişesi	'[*the*] *eau de Cologne bottle*'

If we examine these forms we see that they consist of two words; the first one answers the question "what" (Turkish *né*) and has no ending; the second is the thing talked about in such questions as "what bottle," "what brush," "what meal," and so forth, and has the *possessed form ending* -(*s*)*i*, -(*s*)*ü*, and so on, which here always means 'its,' although the 'its' is not necessary in English.

We note also that in these phrases the *strongest vowel* is found in the first word and the next strongest in the second.

Although forms like *dı́ş‿fı̇rçası̀* (*diş fırçası*), as we have given them here, mean no more than '[the] tooth brush', without specifying the owner, they may also mean 'his (her, its, their) tooth brush', with the owner indicated. When one says 'my' or 'our' or 'your', therefore, these endings are substituted for the -*s*(*i*), -(*s*)*ü*, -(*s*)*ı*, -(*s*)*u* ending, and we get:

dı́ş‿firçàm (diş fırçam) *'my tooth brush'*
ákşám‿yeméyimı̀z (akşam yemeğimiz) *'our dinner'*
tráş‿áynanı̀z (traş aynanız) *'your shaving mirror'*

We see from these examples, that the basic form of these phrase-compounds is really just one noun followed by another, both endingless, the first having the strongest vowel, and the second the next strongest vowel. We have met one such "simple" phrase-compound: *kíz‿kàrdèş* (kız kardeș) 'sister'.

These Turkish phrases are like English "hyphen-words", or "compound-words". In Turkish the sign of the compound is the ending -(*s*)*i*, -(*s*)*ü*, and so on, attached to the second word. In English we often put a hyphen between the two words. We shall call such Turkish word groups *phrase-compounds*.

3. *Turkish equivalents of English "him, her, it, them", "the", and similar forms:*

In this unit we have seen the form *ònú* (onu):

onú‿gʸö́rmüyòrúm. Onu görmüyorum. *'I do not see* it.'

If we were talking about several things we would say:

onları́‿gʸö́rmüyòrúm. Onları görmüyorum. *'I do not see* them.'

Now if we specified these *definite objects* about which we are talking, we should say, for example:

sǜtǘ vé‿suyú‿gʸö́rmüyòrúm. Sütü ve suyu görmüyorum. *'I do not see* the *milk and* the *water.'*

Now compare these other sentences with similar forms:

sıcák‿suyú‿ákıtírmisınìz? Sıcak suyu akıtırmısınız?	'*Will you draw* the *hot water?*'
kolónya‿şişesi*ni*‿gʸétirírmisinìz? Kolonya şişesini getirirmisiniz?	'*Will you bring* the *eau de Cologne bottle?*'

The definite objects thus far specified are 'it, them, *the* water, *the* milk, *the* hot water, *the* eau de Cologne bottle'. We notice that Turkish considers 'it, them,' and the equivalents of the English forms with 'the' as all equally *definite.*

Now note the following:

yüzüm*ǘ*‿yíkamàk, dişlerim*i*‿óvmák‿istiyòrúm. Yüzümu yıkamak, dişlerimi ovmak istiyorum.	'*I want to wash my face* (*and*) *brush my teeth.*'
saçlarım*i*‿táramám‿lʸá:zìm. Saçlarımı taramam lâzım.	'*I have to comb my hair.*'

Turkish also considers the forms with the 'my, his, her, its, their, our, your' (possessive) endings as *definite* forms.

Note also the following:

saát‿ikʸiy*i*‿ón‿gʸéçiyòr. Saat ikiyi on geçiyor.	'*It's ten past* (*lit. passing*) *two.*'
saát‿ediy*i*‿béş‿gʸéçè. Saat yediyi beş geçe.	'*At five past* (*lit. passing*) *seven.*'
saát‿dörd*ǘ*‿ón‿gʸeçè. Saat dördü on geçe.	'*At ten past* (*lit. passing*) *four.*'
saát‿on*ú*‿dókúz‿gʸéçè. Saat onu dokuz geçe.	'*At nine past* (*lit. passing*) *ten.*'

The hour of the day is also considered as a *definite* form. We have seen that these *definite objects,* to which we can refer in English directly with *the* . . ., or indirectly with *him*, *her*, *it*, or *them*, have a characteristic ending which we have italicized above. We may now summarize the forms with this ending:

Group I

	Column I				Column II		
i	dìşlʸérím	dişlerim	'*my teeth*'	:	dişlʸèrimí	dişlerimi	'*my teeth*'
e	bén	ben	'*I*'	:	bèní	beni	'*me*'

ü	yǜzǘm	yüzüm	*'my face'*	:	yǜzü̍mǘ	yüzümü	*'my face'*
ö	dö́rt	dört	*'four'*	:	dö̀rdǘ	dördü	*'four'*
ı	sàçlárím	saçlarım	*'my hair(s)'*	:	sáçlàrımí	saçlarımı	*'my hair(s)'*
a	ònlár	onlar	*'they'*	:	ònlárí	onları	*'them'*
u	dòkúz	dokuz	*'nine'*	:	dòkúzú	dokuzu	*'nine'*
o	ó(n)	o	*'he, she, it'*	:	ònú	onu	*'him, her, it'*
also:							
ü	sǘt	süt	*'milk'*	:	sǜtǘ	sütü	'the *milk*'
o	ón	on	*'ten'*	:	ònú	onu	*'ten'*

Group II

i	ìkʸí	iki	*'two'*	:	ìkʸi̍yí	ikiyi	*'two'*
e	şìşé	şişe	*'bottle'*	:	şìşéyí	şişeyi	'the *bottle*'
u	sú	su	*'water'*	:	sùyú	suyu	'the *water*'
i	yèdí	yedi	*'seven'*	:	yèdi̍yí	yediyi	*'seven'*

Group III

i	kolónyá‿şi̍şesì kolonya şişesi	*'eau de Cologne bottle'*	: :	kolónyá‿şi̍şesinì kolonya şişesini	'the *eau de Cologne bottle*'
also:					
ü	gʸö́kʸ‿yü̍zǜ gök yüzü	*'sky'*	: :	gʸö́kʸ‿yüzünǜ gök yüzünü	'the *sky*'
ı	dí̍ş‿fırçasì diş fırçası	*'tooth brush'*	: :	dí̍ş‿fırçasınì diş fırçasını	'the *tooth brush*'

We have already met all except the last two of these forms in the sentence examples above.

Note that the base of *ònú* 'him, her, it', is really **on*, which does not exist in this form as an independent word. The existing form is *ó* 'he, she, it, that'. The form *on also appears in *ònlár* 'they', *ònún* 'his, her, its'.

Likewise, the form *bùnú* 'this', has a non-existent base **bun*, which we find here, and in *bùnlár*, *bùnún*. The form *bú* is the existing base form.

If we compare Column I with Column II, in Group I, we see that the ending follows Vowel Harmony Type I: *i*, *-ü*, *-ı*, *-u*.

If we compare Group I with Group II, we see that only after a *consonant* is this the ending. After a *vowel*, the ending is *-yi*, *-yü*, *-yı*, *-yu*.

If we then compare Group III with Groups I and II, we see that after the ending -(*s*)*i*, -(*s*)*ü*, (*s*)*ı*, -(*s*)*u*, his, her, its, their', the ending is *-ni*, *-nü*, *-nı*, *-nu*.

If we compare the English equivalents of Column I with those of Column II, we note that the difference expressed by this Turkish ending is usually not expressed in English.

We do, however, notice the difference between 'I' and 'me', 'they' and 'them', 'he, she, it', and 'him, her, them', or between 'milk', in general, and 'the milk', specifically.

In Turkish, all words which can be used in the positions, in the sentences above, there occupied by the forms *ònú*, *ònlàrí*, *sütǘ*, *dişlʸèrimi*, *dördǘ*, and so on (whose English equivalents are 'it', 'them', '*the* milk', 'my teeth', 'four', and so forth), are considered to be definite objects, and always have the ending -(*y*)*i*, -(*y*)*ü*, -(*y*)*ı*, -(*y*)*u* or *-ni*, *-nü*, *-nı*, *-nu*, described above, and we shall call this ending, therefore, the *definite objective ending*.

4. *Turkish equivalents of English words such as "doing, running, talking"*

In this unit we have seen the following:

tráş‿ólmanìz lʸâ:zímmì? — '*Do you have to shave?* (*lit. Is your shaving necessary?*)'
Traş olmanız lâzımmı?

saçlarımi‿tàramám‿lʸà:zìm. — '*I have to comb my hair* (*lit. my combing my hair is necessary*).'
Saçlarımı taramam lâzım.

Other similar sentences are:

şarabi‿içmém‿lʸà:zìm. — '*I have to drink the wine* (*lit. my drinking the wine is necessary*).'
Şarabı içmem lâzım.

gʸülʸmemiz‿lʸà:zìm. — '*We have to laugh* (*lit. our laughing is necessary*).'
Gülmemiz lâzım.

tarai‿bùlmasí‿lʸà:zìm. — '*He has to find the comb* (*lit. his finding the comb is necessary*).'
Tarağı bulması lâzım.

Summarizing the above forms, such as "shaving", "combing", and so on, and adding a few more to complete the picture, we find:

	Column I				*Column II*		
				Group I			
i	iç- . . .	iç- . . .	*'drink'*	:	ìçmé	içme	*'drinking'*
e	ye- . . .	ye- . . .	*'eat'*	:	yèmé	yeme	*'eating'*
ü	g^yül^y- . . .	gül- . . .	*'laugh'*	:	g^yǜl^{y}mé	gülme	*'laughing'*
ö	g^yör- . . .	gör- . . .	*'see'*	:	g^yö̀rmé	görme	*'seeing'*
				Group II			
ı	çık- . . .	çık- . . .	*'go up'*	:	çı̀kmá	çıkma	*'going up'*
a	tara- . . .	tara- . . .	*'comb'*	:	tàrámá	tarama	*'combing'*
u	bul- . . .	bul- . . .	*'find'*	:	bùlmá	bulma	*'finding'*
o	traş‿ol- . . .	traş‿ol- . . .	*'shave'*	:	tráş‿ólmà	traş‿olma	*'shaving'*

If we compare Column I with Column II, and Group I with Group II, we find that the Turkish ending, which has as an English equivalent forms in "-ing", is *-me*, *-ma*, that is,

1. it follows Vowel Harmony Type II;
2. when this ending is the only one, the *strongest vowel* is the *vowel of the ending* itself.

This ending may be added to any *verb root*, and the resulting form is a *noun* to which one may add the 'my, his, her, its, our, your, their' (*possessive*) endings, as in the sentences above, or any of the other endings which one may add to nouns. Note, also, that these *-me*, *-ma*, nouns may be preceded by other nouns with the definite objective ending, just as the corresponding verb may be so preceded.

The resulting forms name the activity expressed by the verb roots, and so we shall call them action nouns, or more specifically *-me*, *-ma action nouns*.

We have seen these *-me*, *-ma* action nouns used above with the possessive endings in a construction with *l^{y}à:zím* (lâzım), to express the idea 'have to do something'. We shall see that they may also be used in other ways.

5. *Turkish equivalents of English forms "to do, to see, to come" and so forth*

yemék^y‿yemék^y‿istiyórmúsunùz?
Yemek yemek istiyormusunuz?
'Do you want to eat (lit. to eat a meal)?'

bir‿şéy‿içmék^y‿istiyórmúsunùz?
Bir şey içmek istiyormusunuz?
'Do you want anything to drink (lit. to drink a thing)?'

sizé‿iş‿vermék^y‿istiyòrúz.
Size iş vermek istiyoruz.
'We want to give you work.'

sinémayá‿g^{y}itmék^y‿istiyòrúz.
Sinemaya gitmek istiyoruz.
'We want to go to the movies.'

konúşmák‿istiyòrúz.
Konuşmak istiyoruz.
'We want to talk.'

yikànmák, tráş‿olmák‿istiyòrúm.
Yıkanmak, traş olmak istiyorum.
'I want to wash (myself) (and) to shave.'

bányo‿almák‿istiyórmúsunùz?
Banyo almak istiyormusunuz?
'Do you want to take a bath?'

yálnız‿yüzümű‿yikamàk, dişl^{y}érimí‿ov-mák‿istiyòrúm.
Yalnız yüzümü yıkamak, dişlerimi ovmak istiyorum.
'I just want to wash my face (and) brush my teeth.'

Summarizing the above forms, such as "to eat', "to drink", "to give", and so forth, and adding a few more to round out the picture, we have:

	Column I				*Column II*		
				Group I			
i	iç- . . .	iç- . . .	*'drink'*	:	içmék^y	içmek	*'to drink'*
e	ye- . . .	ye- . . .	*'eat'*	:	yèmék^y	yemek	*'to eat'*

ü	g^{y}ül^{y}- . . .	gül- . . .	*'laugh'*	:	g^{y}ǜl^{y}mék^{y}	gülmek	*'to laugh'*
ö	g^{y}ör- . . .	gör- . . .	*'see'*	:	g^{y}ö̀rmék^{y}	görmek	*'to see'*
			Group II				
ı	çık- . . .	çık- . . .	*'go up'*	:	çı̀kmák	çıkmak	*'to go up'*
a	al- . . .	al- . . .	*'take'*	:	àlmák	almak	*'to take'*
u	konuş- . . .	konuş- . . .	*'talk'*	:	kónùşmák	konuşmak	*'to talk'*
o	ov- . . .	ov- . . .	*'brush'*	:	òvmák	ovmak	*'to brush'*

If we compare Column I with Column II, and Group I with Group II, we see that:

1. the ending equivalent to English "to" in forms such as "to do", "to see", and so on, is Turkish *-mek*^{y}, *-mak;*
2. this ending follows Vowel Harmony Type II;
3. the *strongest vowel* is the *vowel of the ending* itself, when this is the only ending added to the verb root.

Since forms such as *ìçmék*^{y} (içmek), *àlmák* (almak) and so forth, do not define or limit the verb root by a personal ending such as 'I, 'we', 'you', and so on, or by endings such as the momentary or the aorist, we shall call them not-limited or *infinitive* forms.

We have seen these infinitive forms used above before forms derived from the verb root *iste- . . .* 'want'. We shall later see infinitives used in other ways. They act much more like *nouns* than verbs, as we shall see. We have already seen one infinitive used exactly like a noun in a Turkish phrase-compound; the infinitive *yèmék*^{y} (yemek) 'to eat' also means '[a] meal' and we see it used just like a noun in *yèmék*^{y}*‿vàktì* (yemek vakti) 'meal-time'.

2. Covering English and Turkish of Word Study (Individual Study)

Check yourself on your knowledge of the *Word Study* by covering first the English, then the Turkish, and making sure you know everything thoroughly.

3. Review of Basic Sentences

With the Guide or records, review the first half of the *Basic Sentences* as in previous units.

1. Review of Basic Sentences (*Cont.*)

Review the second half of the *Basic Sentences.*

2. Covering the English of Basic Sentences (Individual Study)

Go through the *Basic Sentences* covering up the English and reading aloud the Turkish. Check up on anything you do not know, until you are sure of everything.

3. Word Study Review (Individual Study)

Work through the following exercises. Do not write anything down. If you cannot do the work rapidly, review again the *Word Study.* Be prepared to do what is required when the Leader calls on you. Always repeat the entire expression, phrase or sentence as you work.

1. Change the verb forms in the following sentences from positive to *negative:*

1. gʸüzélʸ‿bir‿filʸím‿árıyálìm. Güzel bir filim arıyalım.
2. "èvdè‿yók" déyiniz! "Evde yok" deyiniz!
3. bizím‿tóplántımizdà èylʸeníyórlàr. Bizim toplantımızda eğleniyorlar.
4. èrkʸén‿kálkalìm! Erken kalkalım!
5. yüzünüzü‿yıkáyinìz! Yüzünüzü yıkayınız!

2. Combine the nouns in Column I with those in Column II to form *phrase-compounds:*

Column I		*Column II*	
bányò	banyo	fìrçá	fırça
yǘz	yüz	hàvlú	havlu
şàráp	şarap	şişé	şişe
sáç	saç	fìrçá	fırça
òtélʸ	otel	òdá	oda
çòcúk	çocuk	yǘz	yüz

kíz	kız	sés	ses
kúş	kuş	ét	et
kíş	kış	gʸűn	gün
kíz	kız	ìsím (ism-)	isim (ism-)
àkşám	akşam	èlʸbi:sé	elbise

3. Add the various *possessive* endings to the first and the last of the phrase-compounds in 2.

4. Add the corresponding forms of the *definite objective* ending to the nouns in parentheses in the following sentences:

1. (gʸők ʸ‿yüzű)‿gʸörüyórmúsunùz? (Gök yüzü) görüyormusunuz?
2. (diş‿fırçàm)‿gʸétirirmisinìz? (Diş fırçam) getirirmisiniz?
3. (bùnlár)‿ànlámıyòrúm. (Bunlar) anlamıyorum.
4. bú‿(sűt)‿içérmisinìz? Bu (süt) içermisiniz?
5. saát‿(beş)‿ón‿gʸeçé‿gʸélʸecèkʸ. Saat (beş) on geçe gelecek.

5. Complete the following sentences with the proper forms of the *-me, -ma action nouns*, based on the verb roots in parentheses:

1. ónlár‿ilʸè bènim yávás‿yaváş‿(konuş- . . .)‿lʸá:zìm. Onlar ile benim yavaş yavaş (konuş- . . .) lâzım.
2. hér‿gʸűn onún‿érkʸén‿(kalk- . . .)‿lʸá:zìm. Her gün onun erken (kalk- . . .) lâzım.
3. yüzümüzű‿(yıka- . . .)‿lʸá:zìm. Yüzümüzü (yıka- . . .) lâzım.
4. sáàt‿birdé sizin‿yémékʸ‿(ye- . . .)‿lʸá:zìm. Saat birde sizin yemek (ye- . . .) lâzım.

6. Complete the following sentences with the prope[r] forms of the *infinitives*, based on the verb roots i[n] parentheses:

1. şimdi‿işé‿(başla- . . .)‿istiyórmúsunùz? Şimdi işe (başla- . . .) istiyormusunuz?
2. sıcák‿suyú‿(akıt- . . .)‿istérmisinìz? Sıcak suyu (akıt- . . .) istermisiniz?
3. áhmét‿ilʸè toplantıyá‿(gʸit- . . .)‿istémiyòrúm. Ahmet ile toplantıya (git- . . .) istemiyorum.
4. yüzümű‿(yıka- . . .) (tráşta‿ol- . . .)‿istiyòrúm. Yüzümü (yıka- . . .) (traş da ol- . . .) istiyorum.

4. What Would You Say? (Individual Study)

Read aloud each of the following and then pick out the expression you think most suitable:

1. *Tom Carr, speaking to his friend, says:*

a. lʸútfèn, sıcák‿suyú‿ákıtírmísınìz? — Lûtfen, sıcak suyu akıtırmısınız?

b. lʸútfèn, parayi‿ákítınìz! — Lûtfen, parayı akıtınız!

2. *Ahmet, the friend, asks him:*

a. elʸlʸerinizi‿yıkamák‿istiyórmúsunùz? — Ellerinizi yıkamak istiyormusunuz?

b. bányo‿almák‿istiyórmúsunùz? — Banyo almak istiyormusunuz?

3. *Tom explains why he wants the hot water:*

a. yálnız‿yüzümû‿yıkamák‿istiyòrúm. — Yalnız yüzümü yıkamak istiyorum.

b. élʸbi:semi‿yıkamák‿istiyòrúm. — Elbisemi yıkamak istiyorum.

4. *Tom adds that he wants to brush his teeth:*

a. dişlʸérimi‿ovmák‿istiyòrúm. — Dişlerimi ovmak istiyorum.

b. diş‿fırçami‿yikamák‿istiyòrúm. — Diş fırçamı yıkamak istiyorum.

5. *Ahmet finds the soap, but can't locate the tooth brush:*

a. iştè‿sabúnunúz. diş‿firçanìz nérédè? — İşte sabununuz. Diş fırçanız nerede?

b. iştè‿sabúnunúz. élʸbi:sé‿firçanìz nérédè? — İşte sabununuz. Elbise fırçanız nerede?

6. *Tom tells him where to find it:*

a. másanin‿altındàdir. — Masanın altındadır.

b. kʸüçükʸ‿çántamin‿içindèdir. — Küçük çantamın içindedir.

7. *Ahmet asks Tom if he has to shave:*

a. dişlʸerinizi‿ovmák‿lʸá:zímmì? — Dişlerinizi ovmak lâzımmı?

b. tráş‿olmaniz‿lʸá:zímmì? — Traş olmanız lâzımmı?

8. *Tom says he does, and tells Ahmet where to find his shaving stuff:*

a. háyìr. ónú‿yápmàm l^{y}á:zìm‿déyil^{y}.
b. évèt, maál^{y}ésèf. tráş‿fırçàm, sàbúnúm vé‿ústúràm él^{y}bi:sé‿fırçasının‿yanındàdır.

Hayır. Onu yapmam lâzım değil.
Evet, maalesef. Traş fırçam, sabunum ve usturam elbise fırçasının yanındadır.

9. *Ahmet finds them and says:*

a. néredél^{y}èr? onları‿bulámıyòrúm.
b. ìşté.

Neredeler? Onları bulamıyorum.
İşte.

10. *Tom then asks for his after-shaving lotion:*

a. şáráp‿şişésinì g^{y}étíriniz, áhmèt!
b. kolónyá‿şişésinì g^{y}étirírmisiníz?

Şarap şişesini getiriniz, Ahmet!
Kolonya şişesini getirirmisiniz?

11. *Ahmet brings it and Tom says:*

a. saçlarımı‿táramám‿l^{y}á:zìm. tàrák néredè?
b. onú‿içméyìn, áhmèt!

Şaçlarımı taramam lâzım. Tarak nerede?
Onu içmeyin, Ahmet!

12. *Ahmet, a little weary, says:*

a. táràınız, másanın‿üzérindè.
b. onú‿aríyórùm!

Tarağınız, masanın üzerinde.
Onu arıyorum!

13. *Tom, looking around, still doesn't locate it:*

a. gá:l^{y}ibà, ódà çántamın‿içindè.
b. onú‿g^{y}ő́rmüyòrúm!

Galiba o da çantamın içinde.
Onu görmüyorum!

14. *Ahmet, disgusted, says:*

a. él^{y}inizdédìr.
b. hávlunuzún‿altındàdır.

Elinizdedir!
Havlunuzun altındadır.

Section D—Listening In

1. What Did You Say?

Give your answers in Turkish for each of the exercises in the preceding section, when the Leader calls for them. Then, as the Leader calls for them, give the English equivalents of all the expressions in the exercise.

2. Word Study Check-Up

As you have done in the previous units, go back to the *Word Study* and give the correct Turkish for each English expression, without having to read it from the book. The Leader or one of the members of the group should read the English. As a final check the Leader will call for your answers to the exercises in the *Word Study Review* (Sec. C. 3).

3. Listening In

With your book closed, listen to the following conversations as read by the Guide or phonograph record. Repeat the Turkish immediately after hearing it. After the first repetition of each conversation, check up on the meaning of anything you do not understand, by asking someone else or by going back to the *Basic Sentences* if no one knows. Repeat again if necessary, then take parts and carry on the conversation.

1. *Going out.*

Record 17A, after 4th spiral.

àhmét—	bú‿ákşàm néreyé‿gʸídiyòrsunúz?	Bu akşam nereye gidiyorsunuz?
òsmán—	bír‿tóplántıyá‿gʸídiyòrúm.	Bir toplantıya gidiyorum.
àhmét—	kʸímín‿tóplántısì?	Kimin toplantısı?
òsmán—	báy‿káyanín‿tóplántısì.	Bay Kayanın toplantısı.
àhmét—	saát‿káçtá‿gʸitmeníz‿lʸá:zìm?	Saat kaçta gitmeniz lâzım?
òsmán—	bír‿sáát‿sònrá. sèkʸízdé.	Bir saat sonra. Sekizde.
àhmét—	kʸímín‿ilʸé‿gʸídiyòrsunúz?	Kimin ile gidiyorsunuz?
òsmán—	bír‿árkadáşím‿ílʸè.	Bir arkadaşım ile.
	fákàt, dáhá‿évvèlʸ yémékʸ‿yemékʸ‿ístiyòrúm.	Fakat, daha evvel yemek yemek istiyorum.
àhmét—	ótelʸín‿lʸokàntasındámı?	Otelin lokantasındamı?
òsmán—	évèt. búrádà.	Evet. Burada.

2. *Eating.*

òsmán—	şimdi‿yemékʸ‿yèmékʸ‿lʸá:zìm.	Şimdi yemek yemek lâzım.
	lʸûtfèn, yemeyimi‿gʸetíriǹiz!	Lûtfen, yemeğimi getiriniz!
àhmét—	yemékʸ‿ilʸè bir‿şéy‿içmékʸ‿istiyórmúsunùz?	Yemek ile bir şey içmek istiyormusunuz?
òsmán—	évèt. bir‿şişé‿şáráp‿gʸetiriniz!	Evet, bir şişe şarap getiriniz!
àhmét—	bir‿şişé‿şaráp‿çók‿déyilʸmì?	Bir şişe şarap çok değilmi?
òsmán—	háyìr. bén‿hér‿ákşàm ikʸí‿şişé‿içèrim!	Hayır. Ben her akşam iki şişe içerim!

3. *Getting cleaned up.*

Record 17B, beginning.

òsmán—	èlʸimí, yüzümü‿yikamák‿istiyòrùm. lʸûtfèn sıcák‿suyú‿ákıtírmisınìz?	Elimi yüzümü yıkamak istiyorum. Lûtfen sıcak suyu akıtırmısınız?
àhmét—	tráşta‿olmák‿istiyórmúsunùz?	Traş da olmak istiyormusunuz?
òsmán—	évèt. sicák‿sù onún‿içinde‿lʸá:zìm.	Evet. Sıcak su onun için de lâzım.
àhmét—	havá‿çók‿sicàk, bányoda‿almák‿istiyórmúsunùz?	Hava çok sıcak, banyo da almak istiyormusunuz?
òsmán—	évèt, fákàt váktìm‿yók.	Evet, fakat vaktim yok.
àhmét—	sàbún vé‿diş‿firçanìz nérédè?	Sabun ve diş fırçanız nerede?
òsmán—	kʸüçûkʸ‿çántamın‿içindelʸér.	Küçük çantamın içindeler.
	ústurámda‿onlarin‿yánındà.	Usturam da onların yanında.
	lʸûtfèn, onúdá‿gʸetìriniz.	Lûtfen, onu da getiriniz.
àhmét—	ìşté. búyrùn!	İşte. Buyrun!
	başká‿bir‿şéy‿istiyórmúsunùz?	Başka bir şey istiyormusunuz?
òsmán—	dişlʸérimí‿óvmàk, saçlarımí‿táramák‿istiyòrúm.	Dişlerimi ovmak, saçlarımı taramak istiyorum.
	lʸûtfèn, taraımi‿gʸetíriǹiz!	Lûtfen tarağımı getiriniz!

àhmét—	taraınız‿nérédè?	Tarağınız nerede?
òsmán—	tàrák sáç vé‿él^{y}bi:sé‿fırçalarının‿yánındà.	Tarak saç ve elbise fırçalarının yanında.
àhmét—	òradá‿yók!	Orada yok!
òsmán—	másanın‿üzérindédir.	Masanın üzerindedir.
	háyır, óradáda‿deyil^{y}.	Hayır, orada da değil.
	gá:l^{y}ibà tràş‿aynasının‿áltındá.	Galiba traş aynasının altında.
àhmét—	búyrùn, işté‿kolónyá‿şişesidé.	Buyrun, işte kolonya şişesi de.
òsmán—	teşék^{y}k^{y}úr‿edèrim.	Teşekkür ederim.
àhmét—	bir‿şèy‿déyil^{y}.	Bir şey değil.

4. *At a party.*

òrhán—	mérhábà, áhmèt!	Merhaba, Ahmet!
àhmét—	mérhábà, órhàn!	Merhaba, Orhan!
	bú àrkadáşím, múzàffér.	Bu arkadaşım, Muzaffer.
òrhán—	müşérréf‿óldùm!	Müşerref oldum!
múzàffér—	kìzlár nérédè?	Kızlar nerede?
àhmét—	g^{y}üzél^{y}‿kizlàr dáima‿g^{y}éç‿g^{y}el^{y}irl^{y}èr.	Güzel kızlar daima geç gelirler.
òrhán—	kızlár‿çókmú‿g^{y}üzèl^{y}?	Kızlar çokmu güzel?
àhmét—	évèt, çók!	Evet, çok!

5. *The girls liven the party.*

l^{y}èyl^{y}á:—	mérhábà, çócúklàr!	Merhaba, çocuklar!
	bú‿ákşàm hávà‿g^{y}üzél^{y}, déyil^{y}mì?	Bu akşam hava güzel, değilmi?
òrhán—	mérhábà, l^{y}éyl^{y}à:!	Merhaba, Leylâ!
	évèt, çók‿g^{y}üzèl^{y}! sizdè!	Evet, çok güzel! Siz de!
	déyil^{y}mì, múzáffèr?	Değilmi, Muzaffer?

múzàffér—	évèt, çók!	Evet, çok!
	bizim‿tóplántımíz‿içìn!	Bizim toplantımız için!
lʸèylʸá:—	teşékʸkʸûr‿edèrim!	Teşekkür ederim!
	fákàt àlʸiyé vé‿şûkʸrüyé gʸélʸiyórlármì?	Fakat Aliye ve Şükrüye geliyorlarmı?
àhmét—	évèt, gʸelʸíyórlàr.	Evet, geliyorlar.
	bir‿şéy‿içmékʸ‿istiyórmúsunùz, lʸéylʸà:?	Bir şey içmek istiyormusunuz, Leylâ?
lʸèylʸá:—	évèt, şaráp‿vármì?	Evet, şarap varmı?
òrhán—	évèt, kìrmizí![1]	Evet, kırmızı!
	üç‿şişé‿vàr!	Üç şişe var!
múzàffér—	háydi‿ìçélʸím!	Haydi içelim!
àhmét—	bén‿gʸétiriríìm!	Ben getiririm!

Section E—Conversation

1. Covering the Turkish in Basic Sentences (Individual Study)

Cover the Turkish of the *Basic Sentences* and practice saying the Turkish equivalents of the English expressions.

2. Vocabulary Check-Up

Give the Turkish expressions for the English equivalents in the *Basic Sentences* as the Leader calls for them.

3. Conversation

As you have done in the *Conversation* in the previous units, begin to converse by following the models outlined below fairly closely; then change the situations somewhat. Invent new combinations of subject matter.

[1] red (wine)

1. Getting ready for dinner.

Tom, reading a book, calls to his friend, Ahmet, asking him to draw the hot water, saying he wants to take a bath. Ahmet, observing that the weather is very hot, says he too wants to bathe. Tom tells him to take his first, saying he wants to shave. They call to each other for various things, and give each other directions as to where to find them.

2. At dinner.

Tom suggests that they go to the hotel restaurant for dinner. There they order, discuss what to drink with the meal, ask for cigarettes, matches, etc. They call for the check and leave. Tom says he wants to go to a movie, asks Ahmet if he wants to come along. Ahmet thanks him, but says he has something else to do.

SECTION F—CONVERSATION (*Cont.*)

1. Conversation (*Cont.*)

Continue the conversations started in Section E, with a review of parts 1 and 2 of the section if necessary.

2. Questions and Answers

First run through the *Listening In* once more. Then answer the following questions when the Guide asks you, or take turns asking them of others and answering them:

1.	1.	bú‿ákşàm osmán‿néreyé‿gʸi̇diyòr?	Bu akşam Osman nereye gidiyor?
	2.	bú‿tóplántì kʸi̇mín‿evi̇ndè?	Bu toplantı kimin evinde?
	3.	saát‿káçtá‿gʸitmesi̇‿lʸá:zìm?	Saat kaçta gitmesi lâzım?
	4.	kʸi̇mín‿ilʸé‿gʸi̇diyòr?	Kimin ile gidiyor?
	5.	dáhá‿évvèlʸ né‿yapmák‿i̇stiyòr?	Daha evvel ne yapmak istiyor?
	6.	nérede‿yemékʸ‿yemékʸ‿i̇stiyòr?	Nerede yemek yemek istiyor?
2.	7.	şi̇mdi‿né‿yapmák‿lʸá:zìm?	Şimdi ne yapmak lâzım?
	8.	yémékʸ‿i̇lʸè osmán‿né‿i̇stiyòr?	Yemek ile Osman ne istiyor?
	9.	çók‿déyílʸmì?	Çok değilmi?
	10.	hér‿ákşàm káç‿şişé‿i̇çèr?	Her akşam kaç şişe içer?

3.	11. òsmán nelʸérinı́‿yıkamák‿i̍stiyòr?	Osman nelerini yıkamak istıyor?
	12. àhmét né‿i̍çi̍n sıcák‿sú‿ákıtíyòr?	Ahmet ne için sıcak su akıtıyor?
	13. bú né‿içi̍nde‿lʸá:zìm?	Bu ne için de lâzım?
	14. hàvá bú‿gʸùn násìl?	Hava bu gün nasıl?
	15. ónún‿i̍çi̍n başká‿né‿yapmákta‿lʸá:zìm?	Onun için başka ne yapmak da lâzım?
	16. osmanin‿vakti̍‿vármì?	Osmanın vakti varmı?
	17. sàbún vé‿dı́ş‿firçasì nérédè?	Sabun ve diş fırçası nerede?
	18. ónlarín‿yánindà né‿vàr?	Onların yanında ne var?
	19. kʸı́m‿onúda‿gʸeti̍riyòr?	Kim onu da getiriyor?
	20. òsmán başká‿né‿i̍stiyòr?	Osman başka ne istiyor?
	21. kʸi̍mı́n‿táraì?	Kimin tarağı?
	22. tárák‿i̍lʸè né‿yapmák‿i̍stiyòr?	Tarak ile ne yapmak istiyor?
	23. àhmét tarai‿búluyórmù?	Ahmet tarağı buluyormu?
	24. tarák‿nérédè?	Tarak nerede?
	25. órada‿yókmù?	Orada yokmu?
	26. gá:lʸi̍bà nérédè?	Galiba nerede?
	27. àhmét neyı́dé‿gʸeti̍riyòr?	Ahmet neyi de getiriyor?
4.	28. àhmét kʸi̍mı́n‿misá:firi̍?	Ahmet kimin misafiri?
	29. áhmét‿i̍lʸè toplantıyá‿kʸı́m‿gʸi̍diyòr?	Ahmet ile toplantıya kim gidiyor?
	30. kızlár‿óradàmi?	Kızlar oradamı?
	31. bú‿kizlàr çókmú‿gʸüzèlʸ?	Bu kızlar çokmu güzel?
5.	32. gʸüzélʸ‿kizlàr dáima‿né‿yapárlàr?	Güzel kızlar daima ne yaparlar?
	33. şi̍mdi‿kʸı́m‿gʸélʸiyòr?	Şimdi kim geliyor?
	34. havá‿násìl?	Hava nasıl?
	35. kʸı́mdè?	Kim de?

36. né‿içìn? — Ne için?
37. kʸimlʸérdé‿gʸélʸiyórlàr? — Kimler de geliyorlar?
38. lʸèylʸá: né‿içmékʸ‿istiyòr? — Leylâ ne içmek istiyor?
39. káç‿şişé‿kırmızi‿şaráp‿vàr? — Kaç şişe kırmızı şarap var?
40. kʸím‿onú‿gʸetìriyòr? — Kim onu getiriyor?

FINDER LIST

We include the conventional spelling in parentheses after each entry.

akıt- . . . (akıt- . . .) (aor. *-ır-*) — draw (lit. make run)
    ȧkítınìz! (akıtınız!) — draw! spend! squander!
    ȧkıtírmisınìz? (akıtırmısınız?) — will you draw [it]?
    pȧrá‿akìtıniz! (para akıtınız!) — squander money!

al- . . . (al- . . .) (aor. *-ır-*) — take
    bányȯ‿ȧlmàk (banyo almak) — to take a bath

**alt-* (*alt-) — under side, bottom
    àltí (altı) — its bottom
    ȧltìndá (altında) — (on the) under (side of) (lit. at its under side)
    hȧvlunún‿ȧltindà (havlunun altında) — under the towel

àyná (ayna) — mirror
    tráş‿ȧynasì (traş aynası) — shaving mirror

bányò (banyo) — bath
    bányȯ‿ȧlmàk (banyo almak) — to take a bath

bul- . . . (bul- . . .) (aor. *-ur-*) — find
    bulámıyòrúm (bulamıyorum) — I can't find [it]

**bu*(*n*) (non-existent base)	this
bùnlár (bunlar)	these
bùnú (bunu)	this
bùnún (bunun)	this one's, of this
çántà (çanta)	bag
dí̦ş (diş)	tooth
dí̦ş‿firçàm (diş fırçam)	my tooth brush
dí̦ş‿firçanìz (diş fırçanız)	your tooth brush
dí̦ş‿firçasì (diş fırçası)	tooth brush
ėlʸbì:sé (elbise)	clothing
ėlʸbi:sé‿firçasì (elbise fırçası)	clothes brush
fìrçá (fırça)	brush
gá:lʸibà (galiba)	perhaps
gʸetir- . . . (getir- . . .) (aor. *-ir-*)	bring
hìzmét (hizmet)	service
hizmètçí (hizmetçi)	servant
hizmètçilʸíkʸ (hizmetçilik)	servant's work
ìçín (için)	for
ónún‿içìn (onun için)	for that
ónún‿içìndė (onun için de)	for that, too
íç (iç)	inside, interior
ìçí (içi)	its inside

içìndé (içinde)	(on the) in(side of) (lit. on its inside)
çántamin‿içìndè (çantamın içinde)	in my bag
içìndél^{y}ér (içindeler)	they [are] inside
ìşté (işte)	here is (are)
kìrmizí (kırmızı)	red
kòlónyà (kolonya)	(eau de) Cologne
kolónyá‿şişesì (kolonya şişesi)	eau de Cologne bottle
k^{y}ùçúk^{y} (küçük)	small, little
l^{y}à:zím (lâzım)	necessary
l^{y}a:zım‿ol- . . . (lâzım ol- . . .) (aor. *-ur-*)	be necessary
másà (masa)	table
néréдè (nerede)	where
néredél^{y}èr? (neredeler?)	where [are] they?
*$o(n)$ (non-existent base)	he, she, it; that
ònlár (onlar)	they; those
ònú (onu)	him, her, it; that
ònún (onun)	his, her, its; that one's
ov- . . . (ov- . . .) (aor. *-ar-*)	brush; rub
sàbún (sabun)	soap
sáç (saç)	hair
sàçlár (saçlar)	hair(s)

sìcák (sıcak)	hot
şìşé (şişe)	bottle
kolónyà‿şíşesì (kolonya şişesi)	eau de Cologne bottle
tara- . . . (tara- . . .)	comb
tàrámá (tarama)	combing
tàrák (tarak)	comb
tàráí (tarağı) (definite objective)	the comb
táràıníz (tarağınız)	your comb
tòplàntí (toplantı)	party
tóplàntıyá (toplantıya)	to [the] party
tráş (traş)	shaving
tráş‿áynanìz (traş aynanız)	your shaving mirror
tráş‿áynasì (traş aynası)	shaving mirror
tráş‿firçasì (traş fırçası)	shaving brush
traş‿ol- . . . (traş ol- . . .) (aor. *-ur-*)	shave
tráş‿ólmà (traş olma)	shaving
ústúrà (ustura)	razor
**üzer-* (*üzer-)	top
ǜzérí (üzeri)	top
üzérìndé (üzerinde)	on (top of) (lit. on its top)
másanin‿üzérìndè (masanın üzerinde)	on (lit. top of) [the] table

vàkìt (vakit)	time
váktìm‿yók (vaktim yok)	I haven't time (lit. my time there isn't)
yán (yan)	side
yànı́ (yanı)	its side
yánìndá (yanında)	beside (lit. at the side of, at its side)
élʸbi:sé‿fırçasının‿yanındà (elbise fırçasının yanında)	beside (lit. at the side of) the clothes brush
yıka- . . . (yıka- . . .)	wash

UNIT 9

LET'S EAT

SECTION A—BASIC SENTENCES

Go once through the *Basic Sentences* in unison, concentrating on the *Aids to Listening*, then do the *Hints on Pronunciation;* go once through the *Basic Sentences* individually, and then read the *Hints on Spelling*. The last time through individually, notice also the *Conventional Spelling*.

1. Basic Sentences

Mr Kaya and Mr. Metin go to dinner.

ENGLISH EQUIVALENTS	AIDS TO LISTENING	CONVENTIONAL TURKISH SPELLING
	Mr. Metin	
Record 18A, beginning.		
It's seven o'clock.	sáàt‿yédí.	Saat yedi.
my stomach	kàrním.	karnım
[it's] hungry	áç.	aç
I'm hungry.	kárním‿àç.	Karnım aç.
	Mr. Kaya	
Here's a good restaurant.	iștè‿iyi‿bir‿l^{y}ókántà.	İşte iyi bir lokanta.
Let's go in!	g^{y}ìrél^{y}ím!	Girelim!

	Mr. Metin	
waiter	gàrsón.	garson
to us	bìzé.	bize
the menu	yémékʸ‿lʸìstesini.	yemek listesini
bring it!	gʸetíriniz!	getiriniz!
Waiter, please bring us the menu!	gársòn, lʸûtfèn bizé‿yeméкʸ‿lʸistesiní‿gʸetìriniz!	Garson, lûtfen bize yemek listesini getiriniz!
	Waiter	
a minute	bír‿daki:kà.	bir dakika
permit [me]!	müsáadé‿èdiniz!	müsaade ediniz!
Excuse me for a moment, please!	lʸûtfèn, bír‿daki:kà müsáadé‿èdiniz!	Lûtfen, bir dakika müsaade ediniz!
	Mr. Metin	
What do you want to eat?	siz‿né‿yemékʸ‿istiyòrsunúz?	Siz ne yemek istiyorsunuz?
	Mr. Kaya	
chicken	tàvúk.	tavuk
they make	yapíyórlàr.	yapıyorlar
They make very good chicken here.	búrádà çók‿iyi‿távúk‿yápıyórlàr.	Burada çok iyi tavuk yapıyorlar.
	Mr. Metin	
I don't happen to like [it]	sévmiyòrúm.	sevmiyorum
I don't happen to like chicken.	bén tavúk‿sévmiyòrúm.	Ben tavuk sevmiyorum.
fish	bàlík.	balık
I want fish.	bálík‿istiyòrúm.	Balık istiyorum.

	Mr. Kaya	
O. K. *The fish is nice here, too.*	pék^y‿iyì. búrada‿ba-líktá‿g^{y}üzèl^{y}dir.	Pek iyi. Burada balık da güzeldir.
	Waiter	
order!	émrèdin!	emredin!
Your orders, gentlemen!	émrèdin, ėféndim!	Emredin, efendim!
	Mr. Kaya	
A chicken!	bir‿távúk!	Bir tavuk!
	Waiter	
your chicken	tavùúnuzú.	tavuğunuzu
How do you want your chicken?	tavuunuzú‿násil‿istiyòrsunúz?	Tavuğunuzu nasıl istiyorsunuz?
Boiled?	hàşlánmíş?	Haşlanmış?
	Mr. Kaya	
fried	kizàrmíş.	kızarmış
No, I want it fried.	háyìr, kızármíş‿istiyòrúm.	Hayır, kızarmış‿istiyorum.
	Waiter	
You?	síz?	Siz?
	Mr. Metin	
I want fish.	bálík‿istiyòrúm.	Balık istiyorum.
	Waiter	
What kind?	né‿cins?	Ne cins?
	Mr. Metin	
Black Sea anchovies.	hàmsí.	Hamsi.

As the waiter goes out:

Record 18B, beginning.

	Waiter	
I put	kòydúm.	koydum
into [the] pan	tàvàyá.	tavaya
[it] began	bàşládí.	başladı
to jump	hóplàmayá.	hoplamaya
I put anchovies into the pan, and they began to jump.	hámsi‿kóydùm távayádà, bàşládí hóplàmayá.	Hamsi koydum tavaya **da** başladı hoplamaya.
	Mr. Kaya	
with [a] song	şárkí‿ilʸè.	şarkı ile
we'll eat	yémékʸ‿yiyecèyiz.	yemek yiyeceğiz
We'll have music with our dinner.	şárkí‿ilʸè yémékʸ‿yiyecèyiz.	Şarkı ile yemek yiyeceğiz.
	Waiter	
What else do you want?	başká‿né‿arzù‿ediyórsunuz?	Başka ne arzu ediyorsunuz?
	Mr. Kaya	
Fried potatoes.	kızarmiş‿pátátès.	Kızarmış patates.
	Mr. Metin	
salad	sálátà.	salata
I *want salad.*	bén salátá‿istiyòrúm.	Ben salata istiyorum.
	Waiter	
(one's going) to drink	içécékʸ.	içecek
Do you want something to drink?	içecékʸ‿bir‿şéy‿istiyórmúsunùz?	İçecek bir şey istiyormusunuz?

	Mr. Kaya	
red	kìrmizí.	kırmızı
Yes, I want red wine.	évèt, kırmızi‿şáráp‿istiyòrúm.	Evet, kırmızı şarap istiyorum.
	Mr. Metin	
and to me	bánádà.	bana da
And bring me beer, please!	bȧnádà, l^{y}ûtfèn, bírá‿g^{y}etìriniz!	Bana da, lûtfen, bira getiriniz!
	Waiter	
(from) the meal	yémèk^{y}tén.	yemekten
after	sónrà.	sonra
fruit	mèyvá.	meyva
After dinner do you want fruit and coffee?	yemék^{y}tén‿sọnrá mèyvá vé‿kahvė‿istiyórmúsunùz?	Yemekten sonra meyva ve kahve istiyormusunuz?
	Mr. Kaya	
orange[s]	pòrtákál.	portakal
apple[s]	èl^{y}má.	elma
Yes. Orange and apples.	évèt. pòrtákál vé‿èl^{y}má.	Evet. Portakal ve elma.
	Mr. Metin	
without sugar	şék^{y}èrsíz.	şekersiz
let [it] be!	òlsún!	olsun!
My coffee without sugar!	bénìm‿káhvèm şek^{y}érsíz‿ólsùn!	Benim kahvem şekersiz olsun!
	Mr. Kaya	
mine	bénìmk^{y}í.	benimki
with sugar	şék^{y}èrl^{y}í.	şekerli
Mine with sugar.	bénìmk^{y}í şék^{y}èrl^{y}í.	Benimki şekerli.

my coffee	kàhvémi.	kahvemi
sweet (lit. tasty)	tàtlí.	tatlı
I like [it]	sévérim.	severim
I like my coffee sweet.	bén kahvemi‿tátlí‿sevèrim.	Ben kahvemi tatlı severim.

Before you go through the *Basic Sentences* a second time, read the following:

2. Hints on Pronunciation

There is one small difference between Turkish *t, d, s, z, n, l^y, l, r* and the corresponding English sounds. When one pronounces them in English, the tip of the tongue (in the case of *t, d, n, l*), or the part just behind the tip (in the case of *s, z, r*), approaches or rests on the gums above the upper teeth. In Turkish, however, the tip of the tongue (*t, d, n, l, r*) or the part just behind the tip (*l^y, s, z*), approaches or rests on the upper teeth themselves. To acquire this pronunciation, we should try to push the tongue a bit forward, until we feel the teeth.

PRACTICE 1 **Record 19A, beginning.**

(ENGLISH)	*(TURKISH)*
potatoes	pá*tát*ès.
potatoes	pá*tát*ès.
potatoes	pá*tát*ès.

Turkish *ç, c, ş* are also pronounced in this way, with the tongue moved forward. Here are examples for practice:

PRACTICE 2 **Record 19A, after 1st spiral.**

*t*àvúk.	tavuk	(*chicken*)
ö*té*.	öte	(*other side*)
ká*t*.	kat	(*floor, storey*)

*d*áimà.	daima	(*always*)
hà*d*èmé.	hademe	(*janitor*)
*s*é*s*.	ses	(*sound*)
*z*á:*t*.	zat	(*gentleman*)
kìz.	kız	(*girl*)
á*nn*è.	anne	(*mother*)
è$l^y l^y$ér.	eller	(*hands*)
à*ll*áh.	Allah	(*God*)
müşè*rr*éf.	müşerref	(*honored*)
*ç*ò*c*úk.	çocuk	(*boy*)
*ş*ì*ş*é.	şişe.	(*bottle*)

We have seen a number of cases of pairs of identical consonants. One must be very careful to "hold" such consonants a little longer than the simple ones, or confusion may result. Compare:

PRACTICE 3 **Record 19A, after 2nd spiral.**

èl^yí.	eli	(*his hand*)
è$l^y l^y$í.	elli	(*fifty*)
èl^yí.	eli	(*his hand*)
è$l^y l^y$í.	elli	(*fifty*)
èl^yí.	eli	(*his hand*)
è$l^y l^y$í.	elli	(*fifty*)

Here are the cases of paired or *double consonants* which we have met thus far:

PRACTICE 4 **Record 19A, after 3rd spiral.**

à*ll*áh.	Allah	(*God*)
teşé$k^y k^y$ür‿edèrim.	teşekkür ederim	(*thank you*)

ìráhmé*tt*.	Ahmettir	([*it*]'*s Ahmet*)
müşè*rr*éf.	müşerref	(*honored*)
hà*kk*í.	Hakkı	(*Hakki*)
á*nn*è.	anne	(*mother*)
múzà*ff*ér.	Muzaffer	(*Muzaffer*)
kárdeşí*mm*ìdìr?	kardeşimmidir?	(*is* [*it*] *my brother?*)
dáhá‿é*vv*èl^y.	daha evvel	(*first*)

In Unit 1, we commented on the pronunciation of groups of vowels, pointing out they were to be pronounced clearly, one after the other and not run together. We gave as an example *sàát* (saat) 'hour'. Words like *saat* (conventional spelling) are sometimes pronounced (by over-careful speakers) with a *catch in the throat* between the two vowels. This catch may also be heard in words such as *sànát* 'art', between the ***n*** and the *a*. If one listens carefully, one may also occasionally hear it before any word which begins with a vowel, especially in groups of words, the first of which ends, and the second of which begins with a vowel. Here are examples of this catch which we have seen thus far. We shall indicate it here with an apostrophe.

PRACTICE 5 **Record 19A, after 4th spiral.**

dá'ímà.	daima	(*always*)
'ísmà'íl^y.	İsmail	(*Ishmael*)
ma'ál^yésèf.	maalesef	(*unfortunately*)
müsà'adé.	müsaade	(*permission*)
sà'át.	saat	(*hour*)
né‿'ò?	ne o	(*what's that*)
dáhá‿'évvèl^y.	daha evvel	(*first*)
sàn'át.	san(')at	(*art*)

Before you go through the *Basic Sentences* a third time, read the following:

3. Hints on Spelling

Note the following differences between the *Aids to Listening* and the *Conventional Spelling.*

AIDS TO LISTENING	CONVENTIONAL SPELLING
(optional) '	: (') optional
Examples:	
sà'át	saat
dá'i̍mà	daima
ma'ál^{y}ėsèf	maalesef
'i̍smȧ'íl^y	İsmail
mü̍sà'adé	müsaade
né‿'ò	ne o
dȧhá‿'ėvvèl^y	daha evvel
sàn'át	san(')at

Since the catch in the throat may or may not be pronounced, we have not bothered to indicate it in the *Aids to Listening* except here and in the previous section of *Hints on Pronunciation*, and we shall not indicate it elsewhere, with one exception. We note here that in the *Conventional Spelling*, in a word like *sàn'át*, the apostrophe is sometimes written. In this case the apostrophe acts just like any other consonant and goes with the following vowel, so that the word is divided *san-at.* We shall follow this custom consistently, and shall always write the apostrophe in such cases, both in our *Aids to Listening* and in the *Conventional Spelling* although the latter may frequently omit it, and it may frequently, in rapid speech, go unpronounced. This is our first note on our *Standardized Conventional Spelling* which we shall outline in Unit 11, and which we shall use for everything from Unit 13 on.

SECTION B—WORD STUDY AND REVIEW OF BASIC SENTENCES

1. Word Study (Individual Study)

1. *Turkish equivalents of English "calling"-words such as, "Oh, John!"*

Here are some of the examples we have seen thus far:

Column I				Column II		
çócùklár	çocuklar	*'children'*	:	çócúklàr!	Çocuklar!	*'Children!'*
múzàffér	Muzaffer	*'Muzaffer'*	:	múzáffèr!	Muzaffer!	*'Muzaffer!'*
çòcúúm	çocuğum	*'my child'*	:	çócúùm!	Çocuğum!	*'My child!'*
àhmét	Ahmet	*'Ahmet'*	:	áhmèt!	Ahmet!	*'Ahmet!'*
gàrsón	garson	*'waiter'*	:	gársòn!	Garson!	*'Waiter!'*
bàylár	baylar	*'gentlemen'*	:	báylàr!	Baylar!	*'Gentlemen!'*
ánnè	anne	*'mother'*	:	ánnè!	Anne!	*'Mother!'*

If we compare Column I with Column II, we see that the calling-forms in Column II are all followed by the exclamation mark (!). This is the basic difference. We also notice, however, that in every case, except the last one, in Column I the strongest vowel is the last one, whereas in Column II, it is the *next to the last.* In the case of *ánnè*, in Column I the strong vowel was already the next to the last, so that all that marks the "call-form" is the exclamation mark (!). In words whose last vowel is strong, therefore, the "call-form" has the next to the last vowel strong. In words where any vowel *not* the last is strong, the "call-form" makes no change, other than to change the tone of voice from statement to exclamation.

We shall name these "call-forms" *vocative* forms.

2. *Turkish equivalents of English forms such as "I'll go"*

a. We have already met the following cases:

ó sónrá‿g^{y}él^{y}ecèk^{y}.	O sonra gelecek.	*'She'll come later.'*
otél^{y}démi‿yemék^{y}‿yiyecèk^{y}siniz?	Oteldemi yemek yiyeceksiniz?	*'Will you eat at the hotel?'*
şárkí‿il^{y}è yémék^{y}‿yiyecèyiz.	Şarkı ile yemek yiyeceğiz.	*'We'll eat with music (lit. a song).'*
içecék^{y}‿bir‿şéy‿istiyórmúsunùz?	İçecek bir şey istiyormusunuz?	*'Do you want something to drink (lit. a "one's-going-to-drink" thing)?'*

Summarizing these forms and rounding them out with a few others, we find:

	Column I				*Column II*		
				Group I			
i	g^{y}it- . . .	git- . . .	*'go'*	:	g^{y}i̍decéyìm	gideceğim	*'I'll go'*
e	g^{y}el^y- . . .	gel- . . .	*'come'*	:	g^{y}él^{y}ecèk^{y}l^{y}ér	gelecekler	*'they'll come'*
ü	g^{y}ül^y . . .	gül- . . .	*'laugh'*	:	g^{y}ǘl^{y}ecéyìz	güleceğiz	*'we'll laugh'*
ö	g^{y}ör- . . .	gör- . . .	*'see'*	:	g^{y}ȍrécék^y	görecek	'[*he*]'*ll see* [*it*]'
				Group II			
ı	akıt- . . .	akıt- . . .	*'draw'*	:	akitacáksinìz	akıtacaksınız	*'you'll draw'*
a	toplan- . . .	toplan- . . .	*'gather'*	:	tóplánacàklár	toplanacaklar	*'they'll gather'*
u	konuş- . . .	konuş- . . .	*'talk'*	:	kónùşacáiz	konuşacağız	*'we'll talk'*
o	ol- . . .	ol- . . .	*'be'*	:	ȍlácák	olacak	'[*it*]'*ll be*'
e	ye- . . .	ye- . . .	*'eat'*	:	yi̍yecéyìz	yiyeceğiz	*'we'll eat'*
a	başla- . .	başla- . . .	*'start'*	:	bàşliyacák	başlıyacak	'[*he*]'*ll start*'

If we compare Group I with Group II, we see that the ending of these "I'll go" forms:

1. follows Vowel Harmony Type I;
2. is *-ecek^y-*, *-acak-* after consonants;
3. is *-yecek^y-*, *-yacak-* after vowels.

Note 1: Verb roots which end in *e* change it to *i*, those in *a* to *ı*, before the initial *-y-* of this ending.

Note 2: The *-k-* final in *-ecek^y-* changes to *-y-*, in *-acak-* disappears, before personal endings beginning with a vowel (*-im*, *-ız*):

g^{y}ìdécék^y	gidecek	:	g^{y}i̍decéyìm	gideceğim
kónùşacák	konuşacak	:	konúşacáìz	konuşacağız

We shall call this ending, which refers to future time, the *future* ending.

b. Here we see these future forms with the *negative* ending:

	Column I				*Column II*	
g^{y}ídecéyìm	gideceğim	*'I'll go'*	:	g^{y}ítmíyecèyím	gitmiyeceğim	*'I'll not go'*
g^{y}él^{y}ecèk^{y}l^{y}ér	gelecekler	*'they'll come'*	:	g^{y}él^{y}miyecék^{y}l^{y}èr	gelmiyecekler	*'they'll not come'*
g^{y}ül^{y}ecéyìz	güleceğiz	*'we'll laugh'*	:	g^{y}úlmíyecèyíz	gülmiyeceğiz	*'we'll not laugh'*
g^{y}òrécék^{y}	görecek	'[*he*]'*ll see* [*it*]'	:	g^{y}órmíyecèk	görmiyecek	'[*he*]'*ll not see* [*it*]'
akìtacáksinìz	akıtacaksınız	*'you'll draw'*	:	akítmıyacàksınìz	akıtmıya-caksınız	*'you'll not draw'*
tóplánacàklár	toplanacaklar	*'they'll gather'*	:	tóplánmıyacáklàr	toplanmıya-caklar	*'they'll not gather'*
konúşacáìz	konuşacağiz	*'we'll talk'*	:	konúşmıyacàiz	konuşmı-yacağız	*'we'll not talk'*
òlácák	olacak	'[*it*]'*ll be*'	:	ólmiyacàk	olmıyacak	'[*it*]'*ll not be*'

From the comparison of the forms in Column I and II, we see:

1. that the negative ending *-me-*, *-ma-* comes immediately after the verb root;
2. is followed by the form of the future ending after a vowel, *-yecek^{y}-*, *-yacak-;*
3. the *e* and *a* of the negative have become *i* and *ı*, before the *y* of the future;
4. the *strongest vowel* comes immediately before the negative ending; it is more important than other strong vowels of the base forms, which weaken to second and third place.

c. Now let us compare the following *interrogative* forms:

	Column I				*Column II*	
g^{y}ídecéyìm	gideceğim	*'I'll go'*	:	g^{y}ídecék^{y}mí-yìm?	gidecekmi-yim?	*'will I go?'*
g^{y}élecèk^{y}l^{y}ér	gelecekler	*'they'll come'*	:	g^{y}él^{y}ecék^{y}-l^{y}érmì?	geleceklermi?	*'will they come?'*

g^{y}ü̇l^{y}ecéyi̇̀z	güleceğiz	*'we'll laugh'*	: g^{y}ü̇l^{y}ecék^{y}mi̇yi̇̀z?	gülecekmiyiz?	*'will we laugh?'*
g^{y}ö̀récék^{y}	görecek	'[*he*]'*ll see* [*it*]'	: g^{y}örecék^{y}mì?	görecekmi?	'*will* [*he*] *see* [*it*]?'
aki̇tacáksi̇nìz	akıtacaksınız	*'you'll draw'*	: aki̇tacákmi̇sınìz?	akıtacakmısınız?	*'will you draw?'*
tóplánacàklár	toplanacaklar	*'they'll gather'*	: tóplánacáklármì?	toplanacaklarmı?	*'will they gather?'*
konúşacáìz	konuşacağiz	*'we'll talk'*	: konúşacákmi̇yìz?	konuşacakmıyız?	*'will we talk?'*
òlácák	olacak	'[*it*]'*ll be*'	: ólacákmì?	olacakmı?	'*will* [*it*] *be?*'

If we compare the forms in Columns I and II, we see:

1. that the interrogative ending comes immediately after the future ending; or after the personal ending *-l^{y}er*, *-lar*, 'they', when the form has that ending;
2. that those personal endings which do not always begin in a consonant, have the form with *-y-* which occurs after a vowel (*-yim*, *-yiz*);
3. and that the *strongest vowel* comes immediately before the interrogative ending and happens in these forms to coincide with the strongest vowel of the base forms.

d. Finally, let us compare the following *interrogative negative* forms:

	Column I			*Column II*	
g^{y}i̇́tmi̇yecèyi̇m	gitmiyeceğim	*'I'll not go'*	: g^{y}i̇́tmi̇yecèk^{y}miyi̇m?	gitmiyecekmiyim?	*'will I not go?'*
g^{y}él^{y}miyecék^{y}l^{y}èr	gelmiyecekler	*'they'll not come'*	: g^{y}él^{y}miyecék^{y}l^{y}èrmi̇?	gelmiyeceklermi?	*'will they not come?'*
konúşmıyacàksıniz	konuşmıyacaksınız	*'you'll not talk'*	: konúşmıyacàkmısıniz?	konuşmıyacakmısınız?	*'will you not talk?'*

gʸúlʸmiyecèyíz	gülmiyeceğiz	*'we'll not laugh'*	: gʸúlʸmiyecèkʸ-miyíz?	gülmiyecek miyiz?	*'will we not laugh?'*
ólmiyacàk	olmıyacak	*'[it]'ll not be'*	: ólmiyacàkmí?	olmıyacakmi?	*'will [it] not be?'*

If we compare Column I with Column II, we see that the *strongest vowel* comes immediately before the negative ending and is thus more important than the strong vowel just before the interrogative ending; this last one is reduced to second place, and all the other strong vowels to third place.

e. In the sentence

içecékʸ‿bir‿şéy‿istiyórmúsunùz? (İçecek bir şey istiyormusunuz?)

'Do you want something to drink (lit. a "one's-going-to-drink" thing)?'

we find a form *ìçècékʸ* (içecek) which looks like *ìçècékʸ* (içecek) 'he (she, it) will drink' used before *bìr‿şéy* (bir şey) but which means rather "one's going to drink" and is used to tell us *what kind of a thing* one wants. The use of a *verb* form *before* a *noun* form in this fashion, is entirely parallel to the use of one noun form before another in *gʸüzèlʸ‿bir‿kíz* (güzel bir kız) so that here *ìçècékʸ* (içecek) is parallel to *gʸüzélʸ* (güzel), and therefore is used as a noun. We shall find many similar cases of verb forms used as nouns, dependently, or as here, to qualify other nouns.

3. *Turkish word equivalents of English "with" and "without" phrases*

In this and previous units we have seen forms like *èvlʸí* (evli) 'married', *şékʸèrlʸí* (şekerli) 'with sugar', *şékʸèrsíz* (şekersiz) 'without sugar'. If we tabulate these with others, we find:

	Column I				*Column II*	
			Group I			
i	díş	diş	*'tooth'*	: dìşlʸí	dişli	*'toothed'*
e	év	ev	*'house'*	: èvlʸí	evli	*'married (lit. housed)'*
a	tráş	traş	*'shaving'*	: tràşlí	traşlı	*'shaven'*
u	çòcúk	çocuk	*'child'*	: çócùklú	çocuklu	*'with child(ren)'*
o	bányò	banyo	*'bath'*	: bányólù	banyolu	*'with bath'*

Group II

i	díş	diş	*'tooth'*	:	dìşsíz	dişsiz	*'toothless'*
e	şèkʸér	şeker	*'sugar'*	:	şékʸèrsíz	şekersiz	*'without sugar'*
a	tráş	traş	*'shaving'*	:	tràşsíz	traşsız	*'unshaven'*
u	çòcúk	çocuk	*'child'*	:	çócùksúz	çocuksuz	*'childless'*
o	bányò	banyo	*'bath'*	:	bányósùz	banyosuz	*'without bath'*

If we compare Column I with Column II and Group I with Group II, we see that the "with" ending in Group I is *-lʸi, -lʸü, -lı, -lu*, and the "without" ending in Group II is *-siz, -süz, -sız, -suz*, that is, they both follow Vowel Harmony Type I. In both cases the ending *vowel* is *strongest* if the last vowel of the base form is strongest. If some other vowel of the base form is strongest, however, as in *bányò* (banyo), the base vowel remains strongest, and the vowel of the ending becomes second strongest.

The ending *-lʸi, -lʸü, -lı, -lu* usually seems to attribute something or other to the word which follows it: *şekʸèrlʸí‿kàhvè* (şekerli kahve) 'coffee with sugar, sugared coffee', so we shall call it the attributive ending, or more specifically, the *-li, -lü, -lı, -lu attributive* ending.

The ending *-siz, -süz, -sız, -suz* usually seems to deprive the word which follows it of something or other: *şekʸèrsíz‿kàhvè* (şekersiz kahve) 'coffee without sugar, sugarless coffee', so we shall call it the *privative* ending.

2. Covering English and Turkish of Word Study (Individual Study)

Check yourself on your knowledge of the *Word Study* by covering, first the English, then the Turkish, and making sure you know everything thoroughly.

3. Review of Basic Sentences

With the Guide or records, review the first half of the *Basic Sentences* as in previous units.

Section C—Review of Basic Sentences (*Cont.*)

1. Review of Basic Sentences (*Cont.*)

Review the second half of the *Basic Sentences*.

2. Covering the English of Basic Sentences (Individual Study)

Go through the *Basic Sentences* covering up the English and reading aloud the Turkish. Check up on anything you do not know, until you are sure of everything.

3. Word Study Review (Individual Study)

Work through the following exercises. Do not write anything down. If you cannot do the work rapidly, review again the *Word Study*. Be prepared to do what is required when the Leader calls on you. Always repeat the entire expression, phrase or sentence as you work.

1. Complete the following sentences by supplying the proper *vocative* form of the noun in parentheses:

1. (lʸèylʸá:)! bú‿ákşàm gʸelʸírmísiniz?
   (Leylâ)! Bu akşam gelirmisiniz?
2. néreyé‿gʸídiyòrsunúz, (òsmán)?
   Nereye gidiyorsunuz, (Osman)?
3. gʸörüyórmúsunùz, (àyşé)?
   Görüyormusunuz, (Ayşe)?
4. "(şùkʸrüyé)!" "né‿dédinìz, (ánnè)?"
   "yémékʸ‿váktì!"
   "(Şükrüye)!" "Ne dediniz, (anne)?"
   "Yemek vakti!"

2. Complete the following sentences by supplying the corresponding *future* forms of the verbs in parentheses:

1. bíz órhán‿ílʸè (konuş- . . .).
   Biz Orhan ile (konuş- . . .).
2. síz toplantıyá‿(gʸelʸ- . . .)?
   Siz toplantıya (gel- . . .)?
3. háyìr, bén (gʸel- . . .).
   Hayır, ben (gel- . . .).
4. fákàt, kárdeşím‿órada‿(ol- . . .).
   Fakat, kardeşim orada (ol- . . .).
5. misà:fírlʸér bú‿odadámı‿(toplan- . . .)?
   Misafirler bu odadamı (toplan- . . .)?

3. Complete the following sentences with the proper *attributive* or *privative* forms of the nouns in parentheses:

1. bú‿sǜt íyì‿déyílʸ. çók‿(sú)dùr.
   Bu süt iyi değil. Çok (su)dur.
2. (gʸǜnéş)‿gʸǘnlérdè gʸǿkʸ‿yüzǜ kárádìr.
   (Güneş) günlerde gök yüzü karadır.
3. (sés)‿çócùk ánnesinin‿hóşuná‿gʸídèr.
   (Ses) çocuk annesinin hoşuna gider.
4. (yà:múr)‿hávalárdà havá‿(bulut)dùr.
   (Yağmur) havalarda hava (bulut)dur.

4. What Would You Say? (Individual Study)

Read aloud each of the following and then pick out the expression you think most suitable:

1. *Mr. Metin says he's hungry:*

a. kárìm‿áç.	Karım aç.
b. kárnìm‿áç.	Karnım aç.

2. *Mr. Kaya points to a restaurant and says:*

a. g^{y}ìrèl^{y}ím!	Girelim!
b. g^{y}írmiyecèyiz.	Girmiyeceğiz.

3. *When they are seated, Mr. Metin calls to the waiter:*

a. áhmèt, l^{y}útfèn yedi‿şişé‿şáráp‿g^{y}etìriniz!	Ahmet, lûtfen yedi şişe şarap getiriniz!
b. gársòn, l^{y}útfèn bizé‿yemék^{y}‿l^{y}istesini‿g^{y}etìriniz!	Garson, lûtfen bize yemek listesini getiriniz!

4. *The waiter replies:*

a. yedi‿şişémi‿içecèk^{y}siniz?	Yedi şişemi içeceksiniz?
b. l^{y}útfèn, bír‿daki:kà müsáadé‿èdiniz!	Lûtfen, bir dakika müsaade ediniz!

5. *Mr. Metin asks his friend:*

a. síz tráş‿ólacákmisınìz?	Siz traş olacakmısınız?
b. síz né‿yemék^{y}‿istiyòrsunúz?	Siz ne yemek istiyorsunuz?

6. *Mr. Kaya explains the restaurant's specialty:*

a. búrádà çók‿iyi‿távúk‿yápıyórlàr.	Burada çok iyi tavuk yapıyorlar.
b. búrádà tavúklár‿hóplárlàr.	Burada tavuklar hoplarlar.

7. *Mr. Metin says he wants fish:*

a. balíktá‿hóplayacàk.	Balık da hoplayacak.
b. bén bálík‿istiyòrúm.	Ben balık istiyorum.

8. *Mr. Kaya orders chicken:*	
a. hòplıyálím!	Hoplıyalım!
b. bìr‿távúk!	Bir tavuk.
9. *The waiter asks Mr. Metin about his fish:*	
a. né‿cìns?	Ne cins?
b. tavuunuzú‿haşlanmíşmi‿yiyecèk^{y}siniz?	Tavuğunuzu haşlanmışmı yiyeceksiniz?
10. *Mr. Metin answers:*	
a. hàmsí. kizàrmíş.	Hamsi. Kızarmış.
b. g^{y}üzél^{y}l^{y}erí‿g^{y}örel^{y}ìm!	Güzelleri görelim!
11. *The waiter begins to sing:*	
a. hámsi‿kóydùm tàváyá, bàşládí hóplàmayá.	Hamsi koydum tavaya, başladı hoplamaya.
b. g^{y}üzél^{y}l^{y}erí‿g^{y}ördùm sinémádà, bàşládılár hóplàmayá.	Güzelleri gördüm sinemada, başladılar hoplamaya.
12. *Mr. Kaya then orders his drink:*	
a. kırmızí‿şaráptá‿istiyòrúm.	Kırmızı şarap da istiyorum.
b. şàráp, kìzlár, ve‿şárkí‿il^{y}é‿éyl^{y}énecèyiz!	Şarap, kızlar, ve şarkı ile eğleneceğiz!
13. *Mr. Metin tells the waiter what he wants:*	
a. éyl^{y}énmiyecèk^{y}miyiz?	Eğlenmiyecekmiyiz?
b. bánádà l^{y}útfèn bírá‿g^{y}etìriniz!	Bana da lûtfen bira getiriniz!
14. *Mr. Kaya orders his coffee:*	
a. bénim‿káhvèm şek^{y}érsiz‿ólsùn!	Benim kahvem şekersiz olsun!
b. şèk^{y}ér! bánádà onú‿g^{y}etírìniz!	Şeker! Bana da onu getiriniz!
15. *Mr. Metin orders his:*	
a. bénìmk^{y}í şék^{y}èrl^{y}í!	Benimki şekerli!
b. bénìmk^{y}í şék^{y}ér‿ólsùn!	Benimki şeker olsun!

1. What Did You Say?

Give your answers in Turkish for each of the exercises in the preceding section, when the Leader calls for them. Then, as the Leader calls for them, give the English equivalents of all the expressions in the exercise.

2. Word Study Check-Up

As you have done in the previous units, go back to the *Word Study* and give the correct Turkish for each English expression, without having to read it from the book. The Leader or one of the members of the group should read the English. As a final check the Leader will call for your answers to the exercises in the *Word Study Review* (Sec. C. 3).

3. Listening In

With your book closed, listen to the following conversations as read by the Guide or phonograph record. Repeat the Turkish immediately after hearing it. After the first repetition of each conversation, check up on the meaning of anything you do not understand, by asking someone else or by going back to the *Basic Sentences* if no one knows. Repeat again if necessary, then take parts and carry on the conversation.

1. *Meeting at a restaurant.*

Record 19A, after 5th spiral.

múzàffér—	háydi‿álʸì! gʸéç‿kálacàiz!	Haydi Ali! Geç kalacağız!
àlʸí—	dahá‿çók‿vákít‿vàr.	Daha çok vakit var.
	fákàt, bù‿kahvé‿tátsíz.	Fakat bu kahve tatsız.
	onú‿íçmiyecèyim.	Onu içmiyeceğim.
múzàffér—	bir‿áz‿dahá‿şékʸér‿koymák‿lʸá:zìm.	Bir az daha şeker koymak lâzım.
àlʸí—	gársòn!	Garson!
	lʸûtfèn, bir‿áz‿dahá‿şekʸér‿gʸétirírmísinìz?	Lûtfen bir az daha şeker getirirmisiniz?
gàrsón—	búyrùn.	Buyrun.
múzàffér—	bunún‿hépsi‿çók‿déyílʸmì?	Bunun hepsi çok değilmi?
àlʸí—	háyìr, dèyílʸ.	Hayır, değil.

múzàffér—	çók‿tátlí‿ólacàk!	Çok tatlı olacak.
àlʸí—	bén kahvemi‿tátlí‿sevèrim.	Ben kahvemi tatlı severim.
	síz bir‿şéy‿içmiyecèkʸmisiniz?	Siz bir şey içmiyecekmisiniz?
múzàffér—	háyìr, içmiyecèyim.	Hayır, içmiyeceğim.
àlʸí—	háydi‿gʸìdélʸím!	Haydi gidelim!

2. *Going to pick up a date.*

múzàffér—	arkadaşınızin‿evi‿nérédè?	Arkadaşınızın evi nerede?
àlʸí—	bir‿áz‿ilʸérdé.	Bir az ilerde.
[múzàffér][1]—	óraya‿né‿için‿gʸidiyòrúz?	Oraya ne için gidiyoruz?
àlʸí—	lʸeylʸa:yi‿gʸörmékʸ‿için‿gʸidiyòrúz.	Leylâyı görmek için gidiyoruz.
múzàffér—	çók‿kálacákmiyìz?	Çok kalacakmıyız?
àlʸí—	háyìr, bír‿àz.	Hayır, bir az.
	sónra‿lʸéylʸá:‿ilʸè sinémayá‿gʸidecèyiz.	Sonra Leylâ ile sinemaya gideceğiz.
múzàffér—	lʸeylʸá:‿benim‿i-çin‿bir‿kiz‿arkadáş‿gʸétirecékʸmì?	Leylâ benim için bir kız arkadaş getirecekmi?
àlʸí—	gʸetìrécékʸ!	Getirecek!
múzàffér—	çók‿iyì! ikʸimizde‿éylʸenecéğiz!	Çok iyi! İkimiz de eğleneceğiz!
àlʸí—	sinémadàmi?	Sinemadamı?
múzàffér—	háyìr, sónrà!	Hayır, sonra!

3. *Ordering a meal.*

Record 19A, beginning.

bày‿métín—	yemékʸ‿yemékʸ‿istiyórmúsunùz?	Yemek yemek istiyormusunuz?
bày‿káyá—	évèt. karnim‿çók‿àç. sáàt‿káç?	Karnım çok aç. Saat kaç?
bày‿métín—	sáàt‿yédí.	Saat yedi.

[1]Not on record.

bày‿káyá—	bú‿otel^{y}in‿l^{y}okàntasi iyi‿bir‿l^{y}okàntá.	Bu otelin lokantası iyi bir lokanta.
	óraya‿g^{y}idel^{y}im!	Oraya gidelim!
bày‿métin—	gársòn!	Garson!
	l^{y}ûtfèn yémék^y‿l^{y}istesini‿g^{y}etiriniz!	Lûtfen yemek listesini getiriniz!
gàrsón—	pék^y‿iyi, éféndim.	Pek iyi, efendim.
	bir‿daki:kà müsáadé‿èdiniz!	Bir dakika müsaade ediniz!
	búyrùn, eféndim. né‿èmrediyórsunuz?	Buyrun, efendim. Ne emrediyorsunuz?
bày‿káyá—	tàvúk vé‿kızarmiş‿patátés‿istiyòrúm.	Tavuk ve kızarmış patates istiyorum.
	siz né‿yiyecék^{y}siniz?	Siz ne yiyeceksiniz?
bày‿métin—	bén bàlík vé‿yanındá‿bir‿áz‿patátés‿istiyòrúm.	Ben balık ve yanında bir az patates istiyorum.
	fákàt, patátes‿háşlánmíş‿ólsùn!	Fakat patates haşlanmış olsun!
gàrsón—	né‿cins‿balik‿istiyòrsunúz?	Ne cins balık istiyorsunuz?
bày‿métin—	hàmsi.	Hamsi.
gàrsón—	başká‿b.r‿şey‿arzú‿édiyórmúsunùz?	Başka bir şey arzu ediyormusunuz?
bày‿métin—	évèt, sálátà vé‿bir‿şişé‿kirmızí‿şáràp.	Evet, salata ve bir şişe kırmızı şarap.
bày‿káyá—	bir‿şişé‿çók‿déyil^{y}mi?	Bir şişe çok değilmi?
	bén birá‿içmék^y‿istiyòrúm.	Ben bira içmek istiyorum.
gàrsón—	yemék^{y}tén‿sònrá içecék^y‿bir‿şéy‿istiyórmúsunùz?	Yemekten sonra içecek bir şey istiyormusunuz?
bày‿káyá—	évèt. şek^{y}érl^{y}i‿bır‿káhvé.	Evet. Şekerli bir kahve.
gàrsón—	sizink^{y}ide‿şek^{y}erl^{y}imi‿ólsùn?	Sizinki de şekerlimi olsun?
bày‿métin—	háyìr. bénimk^{y}i şek^{y}érsiz‿ólsùn.	Hayır. Benimki şekersiz olsun.
gàrsón—	meyvá‿yiyecék^{y}mişiniz?	Meyva yiyecekmisiniz?

bày‿káyá—	évèt. èl^{y}má vé‿pòrtákál.	Evet. Elma ve portakal.
	fákàt, onlari‿dáhá‿sónra‿g^{y}etìriníz!	Fakat, onları daha sonra getiriniz!
gàrsón—	pék^{y}‿íyì, éféndìm.	Pek iyi, efendim.
bày‿métín—	tavúk‿çók‿hóşunuzá‿g^{y}ídecèk^{y}.	Tavuk çok hoşunuza gidecek.
	búrada‿onú‿dáima‿tatli‿şáráp‿il^{y}é‿yapárlàr.	Burada onu daima tatlı şarap ile yaparlar.
bày‿káyá—	şáráp‿íl^{y}è hér‿şéy‿g^{y}üzél^{y}‿ólùr.	Şarap ile her şey güzel olur.
bày‿métín—	işté‿yemek^{y}l^{y}ér‿g^{y}él^{y}íyòr.	İşte yemekler geliyor.
gàrsón—	hámsí‿kóydùm taváyá, bàşládí hóplàmayá.	Hamsi koydum tavaya, başladı hoplamaya.
bày‿káyá—	şarkí‿íl^{y}è yémék^{y}‿yíyecèyíz.	Şarkı ile yemek yiyeceğiz.
bày‿métín—	tavúk‿násìl? g^{y}üzél^{y}mì?	Tavuk nasıl? Güzelmi?
bày‿káyá—	évèt, çók.	Evet, çok!

SECTION E—CONVERSATION

1. Covering the Turkish in Basic Sentences (Individual Study)

Cover the Turkish of the *Basic Sentences* and practice saying the Turkish equivalents of the English expressions.

2. Vocabulary Check-Up

Give the Turkish expressions for the English equivalents in the *Basic Sentences* as the Leader calls for them.

3. Conversation

As you have done in the *Conversation* in the previous units, begin to converse by following the models outlined below fairly closely; then change the situations somewhat. Invent new combinations of subject matter.

1. Eating out.

Tom asks his friend Ali if he wants to eat. Ali says he's very hungry. They talk about the hour, the restaurant, where to find it, etc. They go in, choose a table, and sit down. Ali calls the waiter, and asks for the menu. Tom asks for the wine list. They study them, discuss what they like and dislike, order their meat and side dishes, drinks and dessert. The waiter asks how they want their coffee and they tell him. When they finish they call for the check, pay, and leave.

2. Meeting before a date.

Osman meets Orhan on the street and they exchange greetings. Osman asks Orhan where he's going. Orhan tells him he has a date and invites him to come along. Osman wonders if they can find a date for him, too. Orhan says they can and that he'll enjoy himself. Osman says he thinks the two of them will have fun.

SECTION F—CONVERSATION (*Cont.*)

1. Conversation (*Cont.*)

Continue the conversations started in Section E, with a review of parts 1 and 2 of the section if necessary.

2. Questions and Answers

First run through the *Listening In* once more. Then answer the following questions when the Guide asks you, or take turns asking them of others and answering them:

1.	1. k^{y}i̍ml^{y}ér‿g^{y}èç‿kalacaklȧr?	Kimler geç kalacaklar?
	2. vaki̍t‿vármì?	Vakit varmı?
	3. ȧl^{y}inin‿kȧhvesi̍ násìl?	Alinin kahvesi nasıl?
	4. onú‿i̍çecék^{y}mi̍?	Onu içecekmi?
	5. né‿koymȧk‿l^{y}ȧ:zìm?	Ne koymak lâzım?
	6. gàrsón né‿g^{y}eti̍recèk^y?	Garson ne getirecek?
	7. àl^{y}i̍ çók‿şek^{y}ér‿kóyuyórmù?	Ali çok şeker koyuyormu?

	8.	çók‿tatlı‿ólmıyacàkmı?	Çok tatlı olmıyacakmı?
	9.	àl^{y}i kahvesini‿násil‿sévèr?	Ali kahvesini nasıl sever?
	10.	múzàffér bir‿şéy‿içmiyecèk^{y}mi?	Muzaffer bir şey içmiyecekmi?
2.	11.	al^{y}inin‿árkadáşının‿évì nérédè?	Alinin arkadaşının evi nerede?
	12.	àl^{y}i óraya‿né‿için‿g^{y}itmék^{y}‿istiyòr?	Ali oraya ne için gitmek istiyor?
	13.	órada‿çók‿kálacáklármì?	Orada çok kalacaklarmı?
	14.	sónrà néreyé‿g^{y}idecék^{y}l^{y}èr?	Sonra nereye gidecekler?
	15.	l^{y}èyl^{y}á: kimin‿için bir‿kíz‿arkadáş‿g^{y}etirecèk^{y}?	Leylâ kimin için bir kız arkadaş getirecek?
	16.	k^{y}iml^{y}ér‿eyl^{y}énecék^{y}l^{y}èr?	Kimler eğlenecekler?
	17.	sinémadàmi?	Sinemadamı?
3.	18.	k^{y}imin‿karni‿àç?	Kimin karnı aç?
	19.	şimdi‿sáàt‿káç?	Şimdi saat kaç?
	20.	ótel^{y}in‿l^{y}okàntasi násìl?	Otelin lokantası nasıl?
	21.	gàrsón né‿g^{y}etirecèk^{y}?	Garson ne getirecek?
	22.	fákàt dáhá‿évvèl^{y} né‿diyòr?	Fakat daha evvel ne diyor?
	23.	bày‿káyá né‿istiyòr?	Bay Kaya ne istiyor?
	24.	bày‿métin né‿yiyecèk^{y}?	Bay Metin ne yiyecek?
	25.	patátes‿násil‿ólsùn?	Patates nasıl olsun?
	26.	bày‿métin né‿cins‿balik‿istiyòr?	Bay Metin ne cins balık istiyor?
	27.	bày‿métin başká‿né‿istiyòr?	Bay Metin başka ne istiyor?
	28.	báy‿kayáda‿onú‿içecék^{y}mì?	Bay Kaya da onu içecekmi?
	29.	yemék^{y}tén‿sònrá içecék^{y}‿bir‿şéy‿istiyórlàrmi?	Yemekten sonra içecek bir şey istiyorlarmı?
	30.	kahvelerini‿násil‿istiyórlàr?	Kahvelerini nasıl istiyorlar?

31. né‿cíns‿meyvá‿yiyecék^{y}l^{y}èr?	Ne cins meyva yiyecekler?
32. gàrsón onlari‿né‿vakít‿g^{y}etírsìn?	Garson onları ne vakit getirsin?
33. tàvúk k^{y}ímín‿hoşuná‿g^{y}ídecèk^{y}?	Tavuk kimin hoşuna gidecek?
34. bú‿l^{y}okàntadá onú‿dáima‿né‿il^{y}é‿yapárlàr?	Bu lokantada onu daima ne ile yaparlar?
35. gársonún‿şárkısì násìl?	Garsonun şarkısı nasıl?
36. g^{y}üzél^{y}mì?	Güzelmi?

FINDER LIST

áç (aç)	hungry
kárním‿àç. (Karnım aç.)	I'm hungry.
bàlík (balık)	fish
bàná (bana)	see *ben*
başla- . . . (başla- . . .)	begin
bàşládí (başladı)	(he, she, it) they began
bàşládılár	they began
bén (ben)	I
bàná (bana)	to me
bánádà (bana da)	and to me
bènìm (benim)	my, minc
bénìmk^{y}í (benimki)	mine (my coffee, etc.)
bír (bir)	one; a, an
bír‿àz (bir az)	a little
bíz (biz)	we
bìzé (bize)	to us

cíns (cins)	kind; species
né‿cìns? (ne cins?)	what kind?
dàhá (daha)	more; still (more), yet
bìr‿áz‿dáhá (bir az daha)	a little more
dahá‿çók‿vakit‿vàr (daha çok vakit var)	there's still lots of time
dàkì:ká (dakika)	minute
bír‿daki:kà (bir dakika)	a minute
èlʸlʸí (elli)	fifty
èlʸmá (elma)	apple(s)
emret- . . . (emret- . . .) (aor. *-er-*)	order
gàrsón (garson)	waiter
gársòn (Garson!)	Waiter!
gʸir- . . . (gir- . . .) (aor. *-er-*)	go in, enter
gʸör- . . . (gör- . . .) (aor. *-ür-*)	see
gʸòrdǘm (gördüm)	I saw
gʸǜzélʸ (güzel)	beautiful; (a) beauty
gʸüzèlʸlʸér (güzeller)	[the] beauties
hàmsí (hamsi)	(Black Sea) anchovy (anchovies)
háşlànmíş (haşlanmış)	boiled
hép (hep)	all, everything; everyone; always (see *hepi)

****hepi*** (see *hép*)	
hepisi (hépsì) (hepsi)	all of it (them)
bunún‿hépsì (bunun hepsi)	all of this
hopla- . . . (hopla- . . .)	jump
hóplàmayá (hóplàmaá) (hoplamaya) (hoplamağa)	to jump
iç- . . . (iç- . . .) (aor. *-er-*)	drink
içecèk^{y}‿bir‿şéy (içecek bir şey)	something to drink (lit. a thing which one will drink)
kal- . . . (kal- . . .)	stay, remain; be
g^{y}éç‿kálacàiz! (geç kalacağız!)	we'll be late!
kàrín (karın)	stomach
kàrní (karnı)	his stomach
kàrním (karnım)	my stomach
kìrmizí (kırmızı)	red
kíz (kız)	girl
kíz‿árkadàş (kız arkadaş)	girl friend ("simple" phrase-compound, see Unit 8 B. 1. 2)
kizàrmíş (kızarmış)	fried
kolónyà‿súyù (kolonya suyu)	eau de Cologne
koy- . . . (koy- . . .) (aor. *-ar-*)	put, place
kòydúm (koydum)	I put (placed)

lìstè (liste)	list
yémékʸ‿lʸìstesi (yemek listesi)	menu (lit. food list)
mèyvá (meyva)	fruit
müsaade‿et- . . . (müsaade et- . . .) (aor. *-er-*)	permit, allow; excuse
ol- . . . (ol- . . .) (aor. *-ur-*)	be; become
òlsún! (olsun!)	let it be!
òlácák (olacak)	it will be
òlúr (olur)	is, becomes
ȍté (öte)	(the) other side
pòrtàkál (portakal)	orange(s)
sàlátà (salata)	salad
sàn'át (san'at)	art
sés (ses)	noise; sound; voice
sèslʸí (sesli)	voiced
sèssíz (sessiz)	voiceless; silent
sev- . . . (sev- . . .) (aor. *-er-*)	like
síz (siz)	you
sìzín (sizin)	your, yours
sìzinkʸí (sizinki)	yours (your coffee, etc.)
sónrà (sonra)	after; afterward; later
yeméḱʸtén‿sònrá (yemekten sonra)	after the meal
dáhá‿sònrá (daha sonra)	(still) later

sàrkí (şarkı)	song
şèk^{y}ér (şeker)	sugar; (a) sweet ("gal")
şėk^{y}èrli̍ (şekerli)	with sugar, sugared
şėk^{y}èrsi̍z (şekersiz)	without sugar, sugarless
tát (tat)	taste; (good) taste
tàtlí (tatlı)	tasty; sweet
tàtsíz (tatsız)	tasteless
tàvá (tava)	(frying) pan
tàváyá (tavaya)	(in)to [the] pan
tàvúk (tavuk)	chicken
tavùúnúz (tavuğunuz)	your chicken
yán (yan)	side
yànindá (yanında)	on the side (lit. at their side)
yap- . . . (yap- . . .)	do; make; prepare
çók‿iyi̍‿távúk‿yápıyórlàr (çok iyi tavuk yapıyorlar)	they prepare (lit. make) very good chicken
yèmék^y (yemek)	meal; food
yémèk^{y}l^{y}ér (yemekler)	(the) foods (dishes)
yémék^y‿l^{y}i̍stesi̍ (yemek listesi)	menu (lit. food list)
yémèk^{y}tén (yemekten)	from the meal
yemék^{y}tén‿sònrá (yemekten sonra)	after the meal

SEEING THE SIGHTS

SECTION A—BASIC SENTENCES

Go once through the *Basic Sentences* in unison, concentrating on the *Aids to Listening*, then do the *Hints on Pronunciation;* go once through the *Basic Sentences* individually, and then read the *Hints on Spelling*. The last time through individually, notice also the *Conventional Spelling*.

1. Basic Sentences

Tom goes for a boat-ride on the Bosporus.

ENGLISH EQUIVALENTS	AIDS TO LISTENING	CONVENTIONAL TURKISH SPELLING
Record 20A, beginning.		
	Ahmet	
to you	sìzé.	size
to show	g^{y}òstérmék^{y}.	göstermek
I want to show you the city this morning.	sizė‿bú‿sȧbàh şehrí‿g^{y}östérmék^{y}‿ís-tiyòrúm.	Size bu sabah şehri göstermek istiyorum.
	Tom Carr	
in Istanbul	istánbu̇ldà.	İstanbulda
(going) to be seen	g^{y}örù̇l^{y}ėcék^{y}.	görülecek
what places (of its)?	nérel^{y}ėrì?	nereleri?
What is there to be seen in Istanbul?	istánbuldȧ‿g^{y}örü̇l^{y}ecèk^{y} nérel^{y}erí‿vàr?	İstanbulda görülecek nereleri var?

	Ahmet	
all kinds of	hér‿türlʸǜ.	her türlü
view[*s*]	mánzárà.	manzara
There are all kinds of sights.	hér‿türlʸü‿mánzará‿vàr.	Her türlü manzara var.
mosques	cà:milʸér.	camiler
palaces	sáràylár.	saraylar
museums	mǘzélʸèr.	müzeler
[*the*] *Bosporus*	bóáz‿içì.	Boğaziçi
Mosques, palaces, museums, the Bosporus.	cà:milʸér, sáràylár, mǘzélʸèr, bóáz‿içì.	Camiler, saraylar, müzeler, Boğaziçi.
	Tom Carr	
to palaces	saràylárá.	saraylara
or the like	fìlʸán.	filân
I don't want	ìstémém.	istemem
Today I don't want to go to palaces or to places like that.	bú‿gʸǜn saráylará‿filʸàn gʸitmèkʸ‿istemém.	Bu gün saraylara filân gitmek istemem.
	Ahmet	
if [*it*]'*s that way*	ő́ylʸé‿isè.	öyle ise
to [*the*] *Bosporus*	bóáz‿içinè.	Boğaziçine
Then let's go the Bosporus!	őylʸé‿isè boáz‿içiné‿gʸidelʸìm!	Öyle ise Boğaziçine gidelim!
	Tom Carr	
one goes	gʸìdilʸír.	gidilir.
How do you go there?	óraya‿násil‿gʸidilʸìr?	Oraya nasıl gidilir?

	Ahmet	
from here	búrȧdȧ̀n.	buradan
to [the] pier	ískʸélʸeyè.	iskeleye
as far as	kȧ̀dár.	kadar
by (lit. with) street car	trȧ́mváylȧ̀.	tramvayla
and from there	óradȧ̀ndȧ́,	oradanda
by (lit. with) boat	vȧ́púrlȧ̀.	vapurla

Record 20B, beginning.

From here to the pier by street car and from there by boat.	búrȧdȧ̀n ískʸelʸeyė‿kȧ́dȧ̀r trȧ́mváylȧ̀ óradȧ̀ndȧ́ vȧ́púrlȧ̀.	Buradan iskeleye kadar tramvayla oradan da vapurla.
[it] does not go	gʸi̇̀tméz.	gitmez
This boat doesn't go to the Bosporus.	bú‿vȧ́pù̇r bȯ́ȧ̀z‿içinė́‿gʸi̇tméz.	Bu vapur Boğaziçine gitmez.
the other	ȍbű̇r.	öbür
(on) to [the] boat	vȧ̀pú̇rȧ́.	vapura
let's get on	bi̇̀nélʸi̇́m.	binelim
Let's get on the other boat!	ö̇bű̇r‿vapurȧ́‿bi̇nelʸi̇̀m!	Öbür vapura binelim!
last	són.	son
to [the] landing-place	ískʸélʸeyè.	iskeleye
we'll not get off	i̇nméyi̇̀z.	inmeyiz
We won't get off until the last stop.	són‿ískʸelʸeyė́‿kȧ́dȧ̀r i̇nméyi̇̀z.	Son iskeleye kadar inmeyiz.
	Tom Carr	
the surroundings	ètrȧ́:fí.	etrafı
will we see?	gʸörű̇rmü̇yü̇̀z?	görürmüyüz?
Will we see everything well?	etra:fi‿iyi̇‿gʸörű̇rmü̇yü̇̀z?	Etrafı iyi görürmüyüz?

	Ahmet	
both sides	hér‿ik^{y}i‿tárafídà.	her iki tarafı da
because	çǘnk^{y}ǜ.	çünkü
Asia	ásyà.	Asya
to Europe	ȧvrúpayà.	Avrupaya
near	yàkín.	yakın
Yes, we'll see both sides, because here Asia is very close to Europe.	évèt, hér‿ik^{y}i‿tarafida‿g^{y}örǘrǜz, çǘnk^{y}ǜ búrádà ásyà avrúpaya‿çók‿yȧkìn.	Evet, her iki tarafı da görürüz, çünkü burada Asya Avrupaya çok yakın.
	Tom Carr	
look!	bákìn!	bakın
big	bǜyǘk^{y}.	büyük
beach	pl^{y}áj.	plâj
Look! There's a big beach there.	bákìn! ȯrada‿büyǘk^{y}‿bir‿pl^{y}áj‿vàr.	Bakın! Orada büyük bir plâj var.
will we not swim?	yüzmézmiyìz?	yüzmezmiyiz?
Won't we go swimming there?	ȯrada‿yüzmézmiyìz?	Orada yüzmezmiyiz?
	Ahmet	
(from) noon	ȍyl^{y}édén.	öğleden
after	sónrà.	sonra
Yes, in the afternoon.	évèt, öyl^{y}edén‿sònrá.	Evet, öğleden sonra.
	Tom Carr	
It might rain in the afternoon.	ȍyl^{y}edén‿sònrá gá:l^{y}ibà yá:múr‿yáacàk.	Öğleden sonra galiba yağmur yağacak.
The weather is cloudy.	hávà‿bulútlú.	Hava bulutlu.

Before you go through the *Basic Sentences* a second time, note the following *new sound*:

LETTER	STANDS FOR A SOUND	EXAMPLES
j	like English *s* in *pleasure*	pl^{y}áj (plâj) (*beach*)

Now read the following:

2. Hints on Pronunciation

Turkish *p*, *t*, *ç*, *k*^{y}, *k* are pronounced much like English *p*, *t*, *ch*, *c*, *k* in *pin*, *tin*, *chin*, *cute*, *kick*. If one pronounces these English words while holding a piece of paper in front of the lips, the paper will be blown back by a puff of breath which comes out after the *p*, *t*, *ch*, *c*, *k*. This puff of breath is not present in English, however, when these consonants occur *after* the strong vowel and before another vowel in the middle of the word, as in *apple*, *latter*, *matches*, *racket*, and so on, or several syllables *before* it as in the *ck* in *lackadaisical*.

Here, in Turkish, one must be very careful to pronounce Turkish *p*, *t*, *ç*, *k*^{y}, *k* clearly with a distinct puff of breath after them. Practice the following:

PRACTICE 1 **Record 21A, beginning.**

ávrú*p*à.	Avrupa	(*Europe*)
bá*k*ìn!	bakın!	(*look*)
àl*t*ìndá.	altında	(*under*)
án*k*árà.	Ankara	(*Ankara*)
àr*k*ádáş.	arkadaş	(*friend*)
çán*t*à.	çanta	(*bag*)
çì*k*álím!	çıkalım!	(*let's go up!*)
g^{y}é*t*iríyòr.	getiriyor	([*he*] *is bringing*)
ì*ç*ìndé.	içinde	(*in*)
ì*k*^{y}ìncí.	ikinci	(*second*)
k^{y}à:*t*ibí.	kâtibi	(*his secretary*)
pòr*t*ákál.	portakal	(*orange*)

tǘrk^{y}çè.	türkçe	(*Turkish*)
yìkȧmák.	yıkamak	(*to wash*)

In Unit 4. A. 2, we discussed Turkish long vowels *a:* and *o:*. We have met a number of cases of *a:*, a few of *o:*, and in the last few units we have met cases of *i:*. Practice the following:

PRACTICE 2 **Record 21A, after 1st spiral.**

èl^{y}bi̇́:sé.	elbise	(*clothing*)
dȧkì:ká	dakika	(*minute*)

All the vowels of Turkish *may* occur long, (*i*:, *e*:, *ü*:, *ö*:, *ı*:, *a*:, *u*:, *o*:) but only a few of them are common.

We have described Turkish k^{y} as being like English *c* in *cute*, and g^{y} as like *g* in *argue*. We have meant, of course, that they are like a part of these words, if we spelled them *kyoot*, *argyoo*, that is like *k* and *g* with a brief *y* after them. In English we get these combinations only before *u*. In Turkish, k^{y} may occur before and after and g^{y} before any vowel except *ı* or *o*. Practice the following, making the ^{y} very short and as much a part of the *k* or *g* as possible:

PRACTICE 3 **Record 21A, after 2nd spiral.**

èk^{y}mék^{y}.	ekmek	(*bread*)
tǘrk^{y}çè.	türkçe	(*Turkish*)
g^{y}ǘn.	gün	(*day*)
èrk^{y}én.	erken	(*early*)
g^{y}éç.	geç	(*late*)
g^{y}i̇́di̇̀n!	gidin!	(*go!*)
g^{y}ö́k^{y}.	gök	(*heaven*)
k^{y}à:ti̇́p.	kâtip	(*secretary*)
k^{y}i̇́m.	kim	(*who*)
i̇̀k^{y}i̇́.	iki	(*two*)
k^{y}ö̀şé.	köşe	(*corner*)

k^{y}ûçû*k*^{y}.	küçük	(*small*)
rûzg^{y}ár.	rüzgâr	(*breeze*)
ṣè*k*^{y}ér.	şeker	(*sugar*)
teṣė*k*^{y}*k*^{y}ûrl^{y}ér!	teşekkürler!	(*thanks!*)

Before you go through the *Basic Sentences* a third time, read the following:

3. Hints on Spelling

In Units 7, 8, and 9, we have noted the following correspondences between our *Aids to Listening* and the *Conventional Spelling:*

Table I

AIDS TO LISTENING					CONVENTIONAL SPELLING			
	l^y			:		**l**		
l^{y}i	l^{y}ü		l^{y}u	:	li	lü		lû
l^{y}e		l^{y}a:	l^{y}o	:	le		lâ	lo
il^y	ül^y				il	ül		
el^y					el			

Table II

AIDS TO LISTENING		CONVENTIONAL SPELLING	
k^y		**k**	
k^{y}i	k^{y}ü	ki	kü
	k^{y}ö		kö
ek^y	ök^y	ek	ök
	ük^y		ük
	ürk^y		ürk

Table III

AIDS TO LISTENING				CONVENTIONAL SPELLING		
	g^y		:		**g**	
g^{y}i	g^{y}ü			gi	gü	
g^{y}e	g^{y}ö	g^{y}a		ge	gö	gâ

Table IV

: (length)		:	**ğ**	
a:	o:		ağ	oğ

Table V

: (length)		:	**zero**	
i:			i	
	a:			a

Table VI

(zero)		:	**ğ**	
	uu			uğu
aı	ou		ağı	oğu
aa			ağa	

Table VII

y	:	**ğ**
ey		eğ

Table VIII

iyi	iği
eyi	eği

If we compare the tables for $l^y : l$, $k^y : k$, and $g^y : g$, we note that, although incomplete, there seems to be some connection between the ^{y} of our *Aids to Listening* and the vowel which precedes or follows. If we were to complete the tables they would look something like this:

Table I

	l^yi	l^yü	---	l^yu		li	lü	---	lû
	l^ye	l^yö	l^ya	l^yo		le	lö	lâ	lo
l^y					**l**				
	il^y	ül^y	---	ul^y		il	ül	---	ûl
	el^y	öl^y	al^y	ol^y		el	öl	âl	ol

Table II

	k^yi	k^yü	---	k^yu		ki	kü	---	kû
	k^ye	k^yö	k^ya	---		ke	kö	kâ	---
k^y					**k**				
	ik^y	ük^y	---	uk^y		ik	ük	---	ûk
	ek^y	ök^y	ak^y	---		ek	ök	âk	---

Table III

	g^yi	g^yü	---	g^yu		gi	gü	---	gû
g^y					**g**				
	g^ye	g^yö	g^ya	---		ge	gö	gâ	---

We now see that when l^y (Table I) comes before *i*, *e*, *ü*, or *ö*, the *Conventional Spelling* writes plain *l*. However, when l^y comes before *a* or *u*, the *Conventional Spelling* writes plain *l*, but puts a circumflex (^) over the *a* or *u*, to indicate that the *l* which precedes is to be pronounced l^y and not *l*.

When l^y comes before a consonant or at the end of a word and after *i*, *e*, *ü*, or *ö* the same thing happens. The *Conventional Spelling* writes plain *l*, and after *a* or *u* writes a circumflex (^) over these two vowels to indicate that the plain *l* which follows is l^y and not *l*.

The *Conventional Spelling* is not consistent in the case of *o*. It does not write a circumflex, so one must learn the words with *lo* or *ol*, and those with l^y*o* or *o*l^y. We shall remedy this defect in our *Standardized Conventional Spelling* to be described in Unit 11. The blanks in the table indicate combinations which do not occur.

If we examine Table II, we see that k^y works just like l^y. Before or after *i*, *e*, *ü*, or *ö*, the *Conventional Spelling* writes plain *k*. It likewise writes plain *k* before or after *a* or *u*, but here puts a circumflex (^) over the *a* or *u* to indicate that the *Conventional Spelling k* which precedes or follows is to be pronounced k^y and not *k*. The blanks indicate combinations which do not occur.

In Table III, likewise, g^y works like l^y and k^y. We note that g^y occurs only *before* vowels. The *Conventional Spelling* writes plain *g* before *i*, *e*, *ü*, or *ö*, and plain *g* followed by circumflex (^) before *a* or *u*.

Now if we complete the next two tables on length (long vowels), we get:

Table IV

i:	----	ı:	u:	iğ	----	ığ	uğ
--	----	a:	o:	--	----	ağ	oğ

Table V

i:	ü:	--	u:	i	ü	--	u
e:	ö:	a:	--	e	ö	a	---

We see that the *Conventional Spelling* handles long vowels in two ways:

1. it writes short vowel followed by a *g* with a wedge on top (*ğ*) (Table IV);
2. it writes plain short vowel and doesn't indicate the length at all (Table V).

This means, that in 1, you have to remember that *ğ* after one of the vowels *i*, *ı*, *a*, *u*, or *o* and before a consonant or at the end of a word, is not pronounced, but simply makes the preceding vowel long, and in 2, you have to learn all the words which have long vowels but where the *Conventional Spelling* doesn't mark them. We shall also remedy this defect of the *Conventional Spelling* in our *Standardized Conventional Spelling* to be described in the next unit.

If we complete the next table, we get:

Table VI

	ıı	uu		ığı	uğu
üe	ıa	ua	üğe	ığa	uğa
	aı	ou		ağı	oğu
öe	aa	oa	öğe	ağa	oğa

Here we see that *Conventional Spelling* *ğ* between any two of the four vowels *ı*, *a*, *u*, *o* and between *ü*, or *ö* and *e*, has zero value, that is, is not pronounced at all.

Now, completing the last two tables, we get:

Table VII

---	üy	---	üğ
ey	öy	eğ	öğ

Table VIII

y	iyi	üyü	**ğ**	iği	üğü
	iye	üe		iğe	üğe
	eyi	öyü		eği	öğü
	eye	öe		eğe	öğe

In Table VII we see that after *e*, *ü*, or *ö* and before a consonant, *Conventional Spelling ğ* is pronounced *y*.

In Table VIII we see that between two of the vowels *i*, *e*, *ü*, or *ö* *Conventional Spelling ğ* is pronounced *y*, except that *üğe* and *öğe* are pronounced *üe* and *öe*, with no *y* between the two vowels. In this they are like *ığa* and *ağa*, pronounced *ıa* and *aa*.

We may now summarize our comparisons:

l^{y}	1. *before* i, e, ü, ö, â, û, o 2. *before consonant* (*or final*) *after* i, e, ü, ö, â, û, o	**l**
k^{y}	1. *before* i, e, ü, ö, â, û 2. *before consonant* (*or final*) *after* i, e, ü, ö, â, û	**k**
g^{y}	*before* i, e, ü, ö, â, û	**g**
(length)	1. *in* i:, ı:, a:, u:, o:	**ğ**
	2. *in* i:, e:, ü:, ö:, a:, u:	zero
zero	*between the two vowels of* üe, öe, ıı, ıa, aa, uu, ua, ou, oa	**ğ**
y	1. *before a consonant and after* e, ö, or ü 2. *in* iyi, iye, eyi, eye, üyü, öyü	**ğ**

DEFECTS

l^{y} *and l*, *k*^{y} *and k*, *g*^{y} *and g*

We may now ask: if *Conventional Spelling l* in the above cases is to pronounced *l*^{y}, when is it to be pronounced just as plain *l*?

If *Conventional Spelling k* in the above cases is to be pronounced as *k*^{y}, when is it to be pronounced as plain *k*?

If *g* in the above cases is to be pronounced as *g*^{y}, when is it to be pronounced as plain *g*?

We summarize the answer to these three questions:

l	1. *before* ı, a, u, o 2. *before consonant* (*or final*) *after* ı, a, u, o	**l**
k	1. *before* ı, a, u, o, i, e, â, û 2. *before consonant* (*or final*) *after* ı, a, u, o, i, e, â, û	**k**
g	*before* ı, a, u, o, i, e, â, û	**g**

If we compare the summaries for l^y, k^y, g^y with those for *l*, *k*, *g*, we see certain defects of the *Conventional Spelling* in representing these six sounds:

1. both l^yo and *lo*, ol^y and *ol* (before consonant or final), are written with plain *l*; following the usual spelling, one has to learn arbitrarily which words have l^y and which have *l* before or after *o*, that *kolonya* has *lo* and *lokanta* has l^yo;
2. both k^y and *k* are written with plain k before or after *i*, *e*, *â*, *û;* one must learn the words where *Conventional Spelling ki* is pronounced *ki* instead of k^yi or *Conventional Spelling ke* sounds like *ke* instead of k^ye, or where *ik* or *ek* sounds like *ik* or *ek* rather than ik^y or ek^y, just as one must learn the words in which the circumflex in the conventional *kâ* refers to a following *l* and not to the preceding *k*, or where in *âk* it refers to a preceding *l* or *k* or *g* and not to the following *k*; that *vakit* has *ki* and *iki* has k^yi;
3. both g^y and *g* are written with plain *g* before *i*, *e*, *â*, *û;* here just as with k^y and *k*, one must learn in which words *gi* or *ge* is to be g^yi, g^ye and where it sounds like *gi*, *ge;* and in which the circumflex in *gâ*, *gû* refers not to the *g*, but to a following *l*.

Long Vowels

If we look at the summaries for *length* (:), we see that there is one way of indicating it in the *Aids to Listening* (:), and two ways in the *Conventional Spelling*, 1: before a consonant and after a vowel, with ğ, or 2: no mark at all. The first way is not very common, but in any case one has to learn all the words which have ğ with this value. Most of the words with long vowels do not indicate them in any way. They have to be learned. Occasionally one finds the circumflex (^) used here also, to indicate length, and so one is in doubt as to whether *kâ*, for example, means k^ya or *ka:*, or for that matter, even k^ya:. One must learn that *Leylâ* has l^ya: and *filân* has l^ya. This double use of the circumflex is another defect of the *Conventional Spelling.*

and ğ

If we look at the summary for *zero* between vowels, we see that it sometimes equals *ğ* in the *Conventional Spelling*. But we remember that two vowels may come together in both the *Aids to Listening* and in the *Conventional Spelling*. We also remember that in such cases between the two vowels one may pronounce the catch in the throat which we wrote with ('). So to distinguish, for example, between *Aids to Listening aa* in *sàát* (saat) 'hour' and *aa* in *yàár* (yağar) 'it rains', one listens for a very careful slow pronunciation with ('). One may often hear *sà'át*, but *never *yà'ár*. In ordinary speech, however, one hears *aa* in both cases (sàát, yàár), so one must learn the words with *ğ* between the two vowels of the groups listed in the summary.

ğ and y

Looking at the summary for *y*, we see that *Aids to Listening y* may sometimes be represented by *ğ* (in the cases indicated) in the *Conventional Spelling*. We can reverse the statement and say that *ğ* in these cases always is pronounced like *y*. However, *y* in these and many other cases may also be written *y* in the *Conventional Spelling*, so we have to learn the words which have *ğ* and those which have *y* in the cases listed. For example, we must learn that *ȍyl^{y}é* 'noon', is spelled *öğle*, and *ȍyl^{y}é* 'thus, so', is spelled *öyle.*

In the following unit we shall suggest remedies for some of these defects in our *Standardized Conventional Spelling*.

Section B—Word Study and Review of Basic Sentences

1. **Word Study** (Individual Study)

1. *Turkish equivalents of English "with"*

Since Unit 4, we have seen many instances of words followed by *ȉl^{y}é* (ile) 'with'. In Unit 7 we saw *asànsőrl^{y}è* (asansörle) 'with [the] elevator', and in this unit we have seen *tràmváylà* (tramvayla) 'by (lit. with) street car', and *vàpúrlà* (vapurla) 'by (lit. with) boat'. These last three words have, instead of a separate word *ȉl^{y}é* (ile) (*asànsőr‿ȉl^{y}è* (asansör ile), *tràmváy‿ȉl^{y}è* (tramvay ile), *vàpúr‿ȉl^{y}è* (vapur ile), an ending. Here we give a summary of the forms of this ending:

	Column I				*Column II*		
			Group I				
i	k^{y}ìmín	kimin	*'whose; whom'*	:	k^{y}i̇́minl^{y}è	kiminle	*'with whom'*
e	yèmék^y	yemek	'[*the*] *meal*'	:	yėmék^{y}l^{y}è	yemekle	*'with* [*the*] *meal'*
ü	sǘt	süt	'[*the*] *milk*'	:	sǘtl^{y}è	sütle	*'with* [*the*] *milk'*
ö	ásànsö́r	asansör	'[*the*] *elevator*'	:	asánsö́rl^{y}è	asansörle	*'with* [*the*] *elevator'*
			Group II				
ı	bàlík	balık	'[*the*] *fish*'	:	bȧlíklà	balıkla	*'with* [*the*] *fish'*
a	tàrák	tarak	'[*the*] *comb*'	:	tȧráklà	tarakla	*'with* [*the*] *comb'*
u	tàvúk	tavuk	'[*the*] *chicken*'	:	tȧvúklà	tavukla	*'with* [*the*] *chicken'*
o	ón	on	*'ten'*	:	ónlà	onla	*'with ten'*
			Group III				
ı	àl^{y}í	Ali	*'Ali'*	:	ȧl^{y}i̇́yl^{y}è	Aliyle	*'with Ali'*
e	àyşé	Ayşe	*'Ayesha'*	:	ȧyşéyl^{y}è	Ayşeyle	*'with Ayesha'*
ı	şàrkí	şarkı	*'song'*	:	şȧrkíylà	şarkıyla	*'with* [*a*] *song'*
a	l^{y}èyl^{y}á:	Leylâ	*'Leyla!'*	:	l^{y}ėyl^{y}á:ylà	Leylâyla	*'with Leyla'*
u	sú	su	*'water'*	:	súylà	suyla	*'with water'*

If we compare Column I with Column II, Group I with Group II, Groups I and II with Group III, we find that the ending which means "with":

1. follows Vowel Harmony Type II;
2. is *-l^{y}e, -la* after a consonant;
3. is *-yl^{y}e, -yla* after a vowel;
4. has the *strongest vowel* before the ending, never on it. We also note that in the form *k^{y}i̇́minl^{y}è* (kiminle) 'with whom', the ending is not added directly to the base *k^{y}ím* (kim) 'who', as it is with all the other forms listed, but is added to the form with the genitive ending *-(n)in, -(n)ün, -(n)ın, -(n)un.*

This is also true of the forms *bėni̇́ml^{y}è* (benimle)

'with me', *ònúnlà* (onunla) 'with him, her, it', *sízínlʸè* (sizinle) 'with you'. We have not yet met *bìzím* (bizim) 'our', but from that we also get *bìzímlʸè* (bizimle) 'with us'.

From *ònlár* (onlar) 'they', however, one forms *ònlárlà* (onlarla) 'with them'.

Of the genitive forms, we note that *bènim* (benim) 'my' and *bìzím* (bizim) 'our' are irregular in that they add *-im* intead of *-in*.

We may note that *ìlʸé* (ile) may also mean 'and', as in *lʸèylʸá:‿ìlʸè* (Leylâ ile) or *lʸèylʸá:ylà* (Leylâyla) *bén* (ben) 'Leyla and I'. This "with" ending indicates an accompanying or concomitant element, so we shall call it the *concomitive* ending.

2. *Turkish equivalents of English "to, for"*

Here are some of the examples we have seen thus far:

saát‿yediyė‿béş‿kàlà.	Saat yediye beş kala.	*'It's five to seven.'*
àllahá‿ısmárladìk!	Allaha ısmarladık!	*'Good-bye! (lit. we have commended [you] to God)'*
sizė‿iş‿vermėkʸ‿istiyòrúz.	Size iş vermek istiyoruz.	*'We want to give you work.'*
hoşunuzá‿gʸidiyórmù?	Hoşunuza gidiyormu?	*'Do you like it? (lit. does it go to your pleasure?)'*
bȧy‿ákyüreyin‿hoşuná‿gʸidi-yórmù?	Bay Akyüreğin hoşuna gidiyormu?	*'Does Mr. Akyurek like it? (lit. does it go to his pleasure?)'*
sinémáyà daimá‿berá:bér‿gʸi-dérlʸèr.	Sinemaya daima beraber giderler.	*'They always go to the movies together.'*
yá:múr‿ya:maá‿báşlıyòr.	Yağmur yağnıağa başlıyor.	*'It's beginning to rain.'*
banádá‿bira‿gʸetiriniz!	Bana da bira getiriniz!	*'And bring me beer!'*
bóáz‿içinė‿gʸidelʸìm!	Boğaziçine gidelim!	*'Let's go to the Bosporus!'*
búrádà ásya‿avrúpaya‿çók‿yákìn.	Burada Asya Avrupaya çok yakın.	*'Here Asia is very close to Europe.'*

If we take these examples, and add others, we get:

		Column I				*Column II*	
				Group I			
i	sı́z	siz	'*you*'	:	sı̀zé	size	'*to you*'
e	év	ev	'*house*'	:	èvé	eve	'*to [the] house*'
ü	sǘt	süt	'*milk*'	:	sǜté	süte	'*[in] to [the] milk*'
ö	g^{y}ö́k^{y}	gök	'*heaven*'	:	g^{y}ö̀é	göğe	'*to heaven*'
				Group II			
ı	kíz	kız	'*girl*'	:	kìzá	kıza	'*to [the] girl*'
a	àlláh	Allah	'*God*'	:	àllahá	Allaha	'*to God*'
u	çòcúk	çocuk	'*boy*'	:	çòcúá	çocuğa	'*to [the] boy*'
o	ó(n)	o	'*he, (she, it)*'	:	òná	ona	'*to him (her, it)*'
				Group III			
i	yèdí	yedi	'*seven*'	:	yèdi̍yé	yediye	'*to seven*'
e	ísk^{y}él^{y}è	iskele	'*pier*'	:	ísk^{y}él^{y}eyè	iskeleye	'*to [the] pier*'
ı	tòplántí	toplantı	'*party*'	:	tóplàntıyá	toplantıya	'*to [the] party*'
a	si̍némà	sinema	'*movies*'	:	sinémáyà	sinemaya	'*to [the] movies*'
				Group IV			
i	bóáz‿i̍çì	Boğaziçi	'*Bosporus*'	:	bóáz‿i̍çinè	Boğaziçine	'*to [the] Bosporus*'
ı	hòṣlárí	hoşları	'*their pleasure*'	:	hóṣlàrıná	hoşlarına	'*to their pleasure*'
u	hòṣú	hoşu	'*his pleasure*'	:	hòṣúná	hoşuna	'*to his pleasure*'
i	èví	evi	'*his house*'	:	èvi̍né	evine	'*to his house*'

If we compare Column I with Column II, Group I with Group II, Groups I and II with III, Groups I, II, and III with IV, we see that the ending which means "to (into, onto, in order to, up to, etc.), for":

1. follows Vowel Harmony Type II;
2. after consonants is *-e*, *-a*;
3. after vowels is *-ye*, *-ya*;
4. except that after the possessive ending *-(s)i*, *-(s)ü*, *-(s)ı*, *-(s)u*, it is *-ne*, *-na*;
5. if the *last* vowel of the base is strongest, the vowel of the ending is *strongest*;
6. but if some other vowel of the base is strongest, the vowel of the ending is then *second strongest*.

Note also the form *bànā́* 'to me', with its irregular *a's*, instead of *e*.

We also notice that before some verbs we find forms with this ending. Compare:

yüzmékʸ‿istiyòr	yüzmek istiyor	'[*he*] *wants to swim*'
with		
yüzmeyé‿báşlıyòr	yüzmeğe başlıyor	'[*he*] *begins to swim*'
yüzmeyé‿gʸidiyòr	yüzmeğe gidiyor	'[*he*] *goes swimming* (*lit. for to swim*)'
and		
ónú‿gʸörüyòr	onu görüyor	'[*he*] *sees it*'
with		
óná‿bákıyòr	ona bakıyor	'[*he*] *is looking at it*'

The verbs *başla- . . .* (başla- . . .) 'begin', *gʸit- . . .* (git- . . .) 'go', *bak- . . .* (bak- . . .) 'look at' are preceded by infinitives or nouns, as the case may be, with this ending.

This "to" ending may, among other things, mark the thing to which something is given, so we shall call it the *dative* ending.

3. *Turkish equivalents of English "I do not" forms*

In the *Basic Sentences* of this unit, we have seen the forms *ìstèmém* (istemem) 'I [do] not want', the negative of *ìstérìm* (isterim) 'I want', *gʸìtméz* (gitmez) '[it] does not go', the negative of *gʸìdér* (gider) '[it] goes', *ìnméyìz* (inmeyiz) 'we'll not get off', the negative of *ìnérìz* (ineriz) 'we'll get off', and *yüzmézmiyìz* (yüzmez-miyiz) 'won't we swim?' the negative of *yüzérmìyìz* (yüzermiyiz) 'will we swim?'.

a. Now if we take these negative forms and add others to complete the table, we get:

	Column I				Column II		
			Group I				
i	ìnér	iner	'[*he*] *gets off*'	:	ìnméz	inmez	'[*he*] *doesn't get off*'
e	g^{y}èl^{y}ír	gelir	'[*he*] *comes*'	:	g^{y}èl^{y}méz	gelmez	'[*he*] *doesn't come*'
ü	yǜzér	yüzer	'[*he*] *swims*'	:	yǜzméz	yüzmez	'[*he*] *doesn't swim*'
ö	g^{y}ö̀rǘr	görür	'[*he*] *sees*'	:	g^{y}ö̀rméz	görmez	'[*he*] *doesn't see*'
			Group II				
ı	çìkár	çıkar	'[*he*] *goes up*'	:	çìkmáz	çıkmaz	'[*he*] *doesn't go up*'
a	àrár	arar	'[*he*] *looks for* [*it*]'	:	àrámáz	aramaz	'[*he*] *doesn't look for* [*it*]'
u	ùnútúr	unutur	'[*he*] *forgets*'	:	únùtmáz	unutmaz	'[*he*] *doesn't forget*'
o	òvár	ovar	'[*he*] *brushes*'	:	òvmáz	ovmaz	'[*he*] *doesn't brush*'

If we compare Column I with Column II, and Group I with Group II, we see that in Column I we have the following *aorist* endings: *-er*, *-ir*, *-ür*, *-ar*, *-r*, *-ur*.

In Column II, however, we have only *-ez* and *-az*. That is, the *aorist with the negative* always follows Vowel Harmony Type II. We note also that instead of ending in *-r*, it ends in *-z*.

We see that here the negative suffix has its short form *-m-*, having lost its vowel *-e-*, *-a-* before the *-ez*, *-az* of the aorist ending.

We note, likewise, that in the negative, just as in the positive, it is the vowel of the ending which is *strongest*, in spite of the negative ending *-m(e)-*, *-m(a)-* which comes before it, and which usually requires the last vowel before itself to be strongest.

Now observe the following forms:

Column I				Column II		
g^{y}idérsinìz	gidersiniz	'*you go*'	:	g^{y}itmézsinìz	gitmezsiniz	'*you don't go*'
báşlársınız	başlarsınız	'*you begin*'	:	báşlamázsinìz	başlamazsınız	'*you don't begin*'
içèrl^{y}ér	içerler	'*they drink*'	:	içmèzl^{y}ér	içmezler	'*they don't drink*'
yikàrlár	yıkarlar	'*they wash* [*it*]'	:	yikamàzlár	yıkamazlar	'*they don't wash* [*it*]'

We see from these forms that with the "you" and "they" forms of the negative aorist, also, the aorist ending is *-ez*, *-az*, and the negative ending is *-m-*.

We note in the "they" form, however, that it is the "they" ending which has the *strongest vowel*, and the vowel of the aorist ending has been reduced to second place.

Then note the following:

Column I				*Column II*		
i̇çérìz	içeriz	*'we drink'*	:	i̇çméyiz	içmeyiz	*'we don't drink'*
gʸǘlʸérìz	güleriz	*'we laugh'*	:	gʸǘlʸméyìz	gülmeyiz	*'we don't laugh'*
ẏápárìz	yaparız	*'we do'*	:	ẏápmáyìz	yapmayız	*'we don't do'*
ṫárárìz	tararız	*'we comb'*	:	ṫáramáyìz	taramayız	*'we don't comb'*

Here we see that in the "we" form of the negative aorist:

1. the aorist ending has been reduced to *-e-*, *-a-*, retaining only its strong vowel, and losing the *-z-*;
2. after the aorist vowel, we find the form of the "we" ending with initial *-y-*.

Now compare:

Column I				*Column II*		
i̇stérìm	isterim	*'I want'*	:	ìstémém	istemem	*'I don't want'*
ṡévérìm	severim	*'I like'*	:	sèvmém	sevmem	*'I don't like'*
ȧnlárìm	anlarım	*'I understand'*	:	ànlámám	anlamam	*'I don't understand'*
kónuşū́rùm	konuşurum	*'I talk'*	:	kónùşmám	konuşmam	*'I don't talk'*

Here we see that in the "I" form of the negative aorist, just as in the "we" form,

1. the aorist ending has been reduced to *-e-*, *-a-*, retaining only its strong vowel, and losing the *-z-*;
2. we note, however, that here, instead of the form of the "I" ending with the initial *-y-* after a vowel (*-yim*, *-yım*), we have only *-m*; this final *-m*, meaning "I", is an ending we shall meet again with other verb forms, but it occurs with the aorist forms only here, in the "I" form of the negative aorist.

b. Now observe the following *interrogative* aorist forms:

Column I				*Column II*		
g^{y}ė́l^{y}írim	gelirim	*'I'll come'*	:	g^{y}el^{y}írmi̍yim?	gelirmiyim?	*'will I come?'*
kȧ́lkárìz	kalkarız	*'we'll get up'*	:	kȧ́lkármıyìz?	kalkarmıyız?	*'will we get up?'*
i̍slanírsinìz	ıslanırsınız	*'you'll get wet'*	:	islanírmisınìz?	ıslanırmısınız?	*'will you get wet?'*
kònúṣúr	konuşur	'[*he*] *talks*'	:	kȯ́nuṣúrmù?	konuşurmu?	*'does [he] talk?'*
ȯ́vàrlár	ovarlar	*'they brush'*	:	ovárlármì?	ovarlarmı?	*'do they brush?'*

We note that:

1. the interrogative ending (*-mi*, *-mü*, *-mı*, *-mu*) immediately follows the aorist ending (or the "they" ending, when it is present);
2. in the "I" and "we" forms, one finds the forms of the "I" and "we" endings which have initial *-y-*, after the vowel of the interrogative;
3. the *strongest vowel* of the aorist ending happens also to be the strong vowel immediately before the interrogative ending, except with the "they" ending, where the "they" ending vowel is strongest, the vowel of the interrogative second strongest, and the vowel of the aorist is reduced to third place.

c. Finally, observe these *interrogative negative aorist* forms:

Column I				*Column II*		
g^{y}ìrmém	girmem	*'I don't enter'*	:	g^{y}i̍rmézmiyìm?	girmezmiyim?	*'do I not enter?'*
dèméz	demez	'[*he*] *doesn't say*'	:	dė́mézmì?	demezmi?	'*does* [*he*] *not say?*'
yü̇́zméyìz	yüzmeyiz	*'we don't swim'*	:	yü̇́zmézmiyìz?	yüzmezmiyiz?	*'do we not swim?'*
kóṣmázsınìz	koşmazsınız	*'you don't run'*	:	kóṣmázmi- sınìz?	koşmazmı- sınız?	*'do you not run?'*
tȯ́plánmàzlár	toplanmazlar	*'they don't gather'*	:	tȯ́plánmázlár- mì?	toplanmazlar- mı?	*'do they not gather?'*

We find that:

1. before the interrogative ending one gets the full form of the aorist with the negative (*-ez*, *-az*) in all cases;
2. in all cases except that of the "they" form, the *strong vowel* of the aorist ending happens also to be the strong vowel immediately before the interrogative ending, except with the "they" ending, where the vowel of this ending is strongest, the vowel of the interrogative second strongest, and the vowel of the aorist is reduced to third place.

2. Covering English and Turkish of Word Study (Individual Study)

Check yourself on your knowledge of the *Word Study* by covering, first the English, then the Turkish, and making sure you know everything thoroughly.

3. Review of Basic Sentences

With the Guide or records, review the first half of the *Basic Sentences* as in previous units.

SECTION C—REVIEW OF BASIC SENTENCES (*Cont.*)

1. Review of Basic Sentences (*Cont.*)

Review the second half of the *Basic Sentences*.

2. Covering the English of Basic Sentences (Individual Study)

Go through the *Basic Sentences* covering up the English and reading aloud the Turkish. Check up on anything you do not know, until you are sure of everything.

3. Word Study Review (Individual Study)

Work through the following exercises. Do not write anything down. If you cannot do the work rapidly, review again the *Word Study*. Be prepared to do what is required when the Leader calls on you. Always repeat the entire expression phrase or sentence as you work.

1. Complete the following sentences with the proper *concomitive* forms of the nouns in parentheses:

1. síz (bén)‿g^{y}el^{y}írmisiniz?
   Siz (ben) gelirmisiniz?
2. òrhán (l^{y}èyl^{y}á:)‿berá:bèr sinémayá‿g^{y}idecèk^y.
   Orhan (Leylâ) beraber sinemaya gidecek.
3. ik^{y}ínci‿kátà (ne)‿çikalìm?
   İkinci kata (ne) çıkalım?
4. (tàvúk)‿berá:bèr né‿yemék^y‿istèrsiniz?
   (Tavuk) beraber ne yemek istersiniz?
5. g^{y}üzél^y‿bir‿(kíz) néreyé‿g^{y}itmék^y‿istiyòrsunúz?
   Güzel bir (kız) nereye gitmek istiyorsunuz?

2. Complete the following sentences with the corresponding *dative* forms of the nouns in parentheses:

1. (ánkárà)‿néyl^{y}é‿g^{y}ídil^{y}ìr?
   (Ankara) neyle gidilir?
2. (istásyón‿k^{y}öşesì) trénl^{y}émi‿g^{y}ídil^{y}ìr?
   (İstasyon köşesi) trenlemi gidilir?
3. şímdi‿(bén)‿bakíyórlàr.
   Şimdi (ben) bakıyorlar.
4. saát‿(dòkúz)‿ón‿kálà.
   Saat (dokuz) on kala.
5. tomún‿(èví)‿yákìn bír‿sinémá‿vàr.
   Tomun (evi) yakın bir sinema var.

3. Complete the following sentences with the corresponding *negative aorist* forms of the verbs in parentheses:

1. bíz saát‿áltıyá‿kádàr (g^{y}ir- . . .).
   Biz saat altıya kadar (gir- . . .).
2. türk^{y}çe‿iyi‿kónuşúrmúsunùz? háyìr, maál^{y}ésèf, iyì‿(konuş- . . .).
   Türkçe iyi konuşurmusunuz? Hayır, maalesef, iyi (konuş- . . .).
3. árkadàşlarí l^{y}okántada‿(toplan- . . .)? háyìr (toplan- . . .).
   Arkadaşları lokantada (toplan- . . .)? Hayır (toplan- . . .).
4. ya:murdá‿(ıslan- . . .)? évèt, ıslanírìz.
   Yağmurda (ıslan- . . .)? Evet, ıslanırız.
5. òrhán bír‿şéy‿(unut- . . .).
   Orhan bir şey (unut- . . .).

4. What Would You Say? (Individual Study)

Read aloud each of the following and then pick out the expression you think most suitable:

1. *Ahmet meets Tom Carr early in the morning and says to him:*

a. sìzí bú‿sábàh şehré‿g^{y}östérmék^y‿istiyòrúm. — Sizi bu sabah şehre göstermek istiyorum.
b. sìzé bú‿sábàh şehri‿g^{y}östérmék^y‿istiyòrúm. — Size bu sabah şehri göstermek istiyorum.

2. *Tom wants to know what there is to see:*

a. istánbúldà g^{y}örül^{y}ecék^{y}‿nérel^{y}eri‿vàr?	İstanbulda görülecek nereleri var?
b. pl^{y}àjdá g^{y}örül^{y}ecék^{y}‿k^{y}iml^{y}ér‿vàr?	Plâjda görülecek kimler var?

3. *Ahmet exclaims with great enthusiasm:*

a. órádà hér‿türl^{y}ü‿kíz‿vàr.	Orada her türlü kız var.
b. hér‿türl^{y}ü‿mánzará‿vàr.	Her türlü manzara var.

4. *Ahmet then goes into detail:*

a. g^{y}üzél^{y}‿yüzl^{y}èr, èl^{y}l^{y}ér, sàçlár! başká‿né‿istiyòrsunúz?	Güzel yüzler, eller, saçlar! Başka ne istiyorsunuz?
b. cà:mil^{y}ér, sáràylár, mûzél^{y}èr, bóáz‿içì!	Camiler, saraylar, müzeler, Boğaziçi!

5. *Tom says he isn't interested:*

a. bú‿g^{y}ùn cá:mil^{y}erè‿fil^{y}án‿g^{y}itmék^{y}‿istemém!	Bu gün camilere filân gitmek istemem!
b. bú‿g^{y}ùn yùzl^{y}ér, èl^{y}lér, sáçlár‿fil^{y}àn hoşumá‿g^{y}itmiyòr!	Bu gün yüzler, eller, saçlar filân hoşuma gitmiyor!

6. *Ahmet suggests that they do something else then:*

a. öyl^{y}é‿isè mûzeyé‿g^{y}idel^{y}ìm!	Öyle ise müzeye gidelim!
b. öyl^{y}é‿isè bóáz‿içiné‿g^{y}idel^{y}ìm!	Öyle ise Boğaziçine gidelim!

7. *Tom asks how one gets there:*

a. óraya‿yüzecék^{y}miyìz?	Oraya yüzecekmiyiz?
b. óraya‿násil‿g^{y}idil^{y}ìr?	Oraya nasil gidilir?

8. *Ahmet explains the means of transportation:*

a. búrádàn vápurá‿kádàr kóşárìz. óradàndá yüzérìz.	Buradan vapura kadar koşarız. Oradan da yüzeriz.
b. búrádàn ìsk^{y}el^{y}eyé‿kádàr trámváylà. óradàndá vápúrlà.	Buradan iskeleye kadar tramvayla. Oradan da vapurla.

9. *When they arrive at the pier, Tom asks:*

a. búradàndȧ néylé‿g^{y}idèri̍z? — Buradan da neyle gideriz?

b. bú‿vapùrlȧ g^{y}i̍tmézmiyi̍z? — Bu vapurla gitmezmiyiz?

10. *Ahmet explains:*

a. háyìr, bú‿vȧpùr bȯȧz‿içinė‿g^{y}i̍tméz. ȯbű́r‿vapurȧ‿bi̍nel^{y}i̍m! — Hayır, bu vapur Boğaziçine gitmez. Öbür vapura binelim!

b. búradàndȧ trénl^{y}é‿g^{y}idèri̍z. — Buradan da trenle gideriz.

11. *When they are on the boat, Tom asks:*

a. bú‿kȧttàn etra:fi‿iyi̍‿g^{y}örű́rmü̇yü̂z? — Bu kattan etrafı iyi görürmüyüz?

b. búrȧdàn g^{y}üzél^y‿kızlari‿iyi̍‿g^{y}örű́rmü̇yü̂z? — Buradan güzel kızları iyi görürmüyüz?

12. *Ahmet answers:*

a. háyìr, bú‿tarȧftà yüzmèzl^{y}ér! — Hayır, bu tarafta yüzmezler!

b. évèt, hėr‿ik^{y}i̍‿tȧrafídà g^{y}ȯrű́rü̂z. — Evet, her iki tarafıda görürüz.

13. *Tom, looking over the scenery, sees something and exclaims:*

a. bákìn! bi̍zi̍m‿yȧnımizdà ik^{y}i̍‿ta:nė‿yüzű́yòr! — Bakın! Bizim yanımızda iki tane yüzüyor!

b. bákìn! órȧdà büyü̇k^y‿bi̍r‿pl^{y}áj‿vàr. — Bakın! Orada büyük bir plâj var.

14. *Tom asks if they are going to swim there and Ahmet answers:*

a. évèt, öyl^{y}edén‿sònrȧ. — Evet, öğleden sonra.

b. évèt, akşám‿yemėyi̍ndén‿sònrȧ. — Evet, akşam yemeğinden sonra.

Section D—Listening In

1. What Did You Say?

Give your answers in Turkish for each of the exercises in the preceding section, when the Leader calls for them. Then, as the Leader calls for them, give the English equivalents of all the expressions in the exercise.

2. Word Study Check-Up

As you have done in the previous units, go back to the *Word Study* and give the correct Turkish for each English expression, without having to read it from the book. The Leader or one of the members of the group should read the English. As a final check the Leader will call for your answers to the exercises in the *Word Study Review* (Sec. C. 3).

3. Listening In

With your book closed, listen to the following conversations as read by the Guide or phonograph record. Repeat the Turkish immediately after hearing it. After the first repetition of each conversation, check up on the meaning of anything you do not understand, by asking someone else or by going back to the *Basic Sentences* if no one knows. Repeat again if necessary, then take parts and carry on the conversation.

1. *Seeing the Bosporus.*

Record 21A, after 3rd spiral.

àhmét—	sizė‿bú‿sabáh‿boáz‿içini‿g^{y}östérmék^{y}‿isti-yòrúm.	Size bu sabah Boğaziçini göstermek istiyorum.
	istánbulun‿én‿g^{y}üzél^{y}‿mànzaralari óradàdir.	İstanbulun en güzel manzaraları oradadır.
tòm‿kár—	boáz‿içindė‿g^{y}örül^{y}ecék^{y}‿nérel^{y}eri‿vàr?	Boğaziçinde görülecek nereleri var?
[àhmét][1]—	g^{y}üzél^{y}‿cá:mil^{y}èr, sáràylár, vé‿pl^{y}ájlár‿vàr.	Güzel camiler, saraylar, ve plâjlar var.
tóm—	sáraylará‿fil^{y}àn bú‿g^{y}ùn g^{y}itmèk^{y}‿istemém.	Saraylara filân bu gün gitmek istemem.
	havá‿çók‿g^{y}üzèl^{y}.	Hava çok güzel.
	pl^{y}ajá‿yüzmeyé‿g^{y}idel^{y}im!	Plâja yüzmeğe gidelim!
àhmét—	pék^{y}‿iyi.	Pek iyi.
tóm—	óraya‿násil‿g^{y}idil^{y}ir?	Oraya nasıl gidilir?
àhmét—	búrádàn isk^{y}el^{y}eyé‿kádàr trámváylà, óradàndá vápúrlà.	Buradan iskeleye kadar tramvayla, oradan da vapurla.
tóm—	bú‿vápùr boáz‿içinė‿g^{y}idérmi?	Bu vapur Boğaziçine gidermi?

[1]Not on record.

àhmét—	háyìr. g^{y}ìtméz.	Hayır. Gitmez.
	öbúr‿vapurá‿binmemìz‿l^{y}a:zim.	Öbür vapura binmemiz lâzım.
	vápurún‿kálkmásınà dahá‿çók‿vákít‿vàr.	Vapurun kalkmasına daha çok vakit var.
	bir‿káhvé‿içel^{y}ìm!	Bir kahve içelim.
	sónrá‿binèriz.	Sonra bineriz.
tóm—	néredé‿inecèyiz?	Nerede ineceğiz?
	són‿ísk^{y}él^{y}edèmi?	Son iskeledemi?
àhmét—	háyìr. bìr‿évvél^{y}.	Hayır. Bir evvel.
tóm—	vápurún‿kálkmásınà béş‿daki:ká‿vàr.	Vapurun kalkmasına beş dakika **var.**
àhmét—	öyl^{y}é‿isè bìnél^{y}ím.	Öyle ise binelim.
	ik^{y}incí‿katá‿çikalìm.	İkinci kata çıkalım.
	óradan‿etra:fi‿dáhá‿iyi‿g^{y}örùrüz.	Oradan etrafı daha iyi görürüz.
tóm—	birincí‿káttàn g^{y}órmézmiyìz?	Birinci kattan görmezmiyiz?
àhmét—	ò‿kadár‿iyi‿déyíl^{y}.	O kadar iyi değil.
tóm—	bákìn!	Bakın!
	ó‿büyúk^{y}‿vápùr néreyé‿g^{y}idiyòr?	O büyük vapur nereye gidiyor?
àhmét—	gá:l^{y}ibà rúsyayá‿g^{y}idiyòr.	Galiba Rusyaya gidiyor.
tóm—	búrada‿boazin‿hér‿ik^{y}i‿tarafınádà çók‿yákínìz.	Burada Boğazın her iki tarafına da çok yakınız.
àhmét—	bír‿taráftà ásyà, bír‿taráftà ávrúpà.	Bir tarafta Asya, bir tarafta Avrupa.

2. *On the way to the beach.*

Record 21B, beginning.

tóm—	pl^{y}áj‿çók‿sıcákmi‿ólùr?	Plâj çok sıcakmı olur?
àhmét—	háyìr, çúnk^{y}ù bú‿g^{y}ùn g^{y}ók^{y}‿yüzündè bulútlár‿vàr.	Hayır, çünkü bu gün gök yüzünde bulutlar var.

tóm—	óraya‿né‿vakit‿g^{y}él^{y}ecèyiz?	Oraya ne vakit geleceğiz?
àhmét—	béş‿ón‿daki:ká‿sònrá.	Beş, on dakika sonra.
tóm—	né‿kadár‿kálacàiz?	Ne kadar kalacağız?
àhmét—	öyl^{y}é‿yeméyiné‿kádàr.	Öğle yemeğine kadar.
tóm—	öyl^{y}é‿yeméyinì néredé‿yiyecèyiz?	Öğle yemeğini nerede yiyeceğiz?
àhmét—	pl^{y}ájín‿l^{y}okàntasındá.	Plâjın lokantasında.
tóm—	iyi‿yemek^{y}l^{y}eri‿vármì?	İyi yemekleri varmı?
àhmét—	évèt. çók‿iyi‿bálík‿yemek^{y}l^{y}eri‿vàr.	Evet. Çok iyi balık yemekleri var.
tóm—	pl^{y}ajdá‿g^{y}üzél‿kızlár‿vármì?	Plâjda güzel kızlar varmı?
àhmét—	várdìr!	Vardır!
tóm—	onlárla‿konúşacákmiyìz?	Onlarla konuşacakmıyız?
àhmét—	paraniz‿vármì?	Paranız varmı?
tóm—	pl^{y}ajdá‿pará‿l^{y}á:zìm‿déyil^{y}.	Plâjda para lâzım değil.
àhmét—	háyìr, fákàt sónrà¿	Hayır, fakat sonra?
tóm—	sónrà, állahá‿ısmárladìk!	Sonra, Allaha ısmarladık!

3. *On the boat.*

tóm—	mánzara‿çók‿g^{y}üzèl^{y} déyil^{y}mì?	Manzara çok güzel değilmi?
àhmét—	nérédè? g^{y}őrmüyòrúm!	Nerede? Görmüyorum!
tóm—	il^{y}èrdé. ik^{y}inci‿káttà!	İlerde. İkinci katta!
àhmét—	simdi‿g^{y}örűyórùm!	Şimdi görüyorum!
	sizde‿hér‿şeyi‿g^{y}örűyórsunùz!	Siz de her şeyi görüyorsunuz!
	gá:l^{y}ibà onún‿bir‿kiz‿árkadaşí‿vàr.	Galiba onun bir kız arkadaşı var.
tóm—	il^{y}eriyé‿g^{y}idel^{y}immì?	İleriye gidelimmi?
àhmét—	dáimà!	Daima!

4. *At the last pier.*

àhmét—	şimdi‿són‿ìskʸelʸeyė yȧklaşíyórùz.	Şimdi son iskeleye yaklaşıyoruz.
tóm—	bůrada‿çók‿kȧlacákmiyìz?	Burada çok kalacakmıyız?
àhmét—	háyìr, yȧlnız‿ón‿daki:kà.	Hayır, yalnız on dakika.
tóm—	bú‿ìskʸelʸė plʸajȧ‿yȧkínmì?	Bu iskele plâja yakınmı?
àhmét—	háyìr dèyílʸ.	Hayır değil.
	plʸáj‿istánbula‿dȧhá‿yȧkìn.	Plâj İstanbula daha yakın.
	öylʸedén‿sònrȧ gʸörecékʸsinìz.	Öğleden sonra göreceksiniz.

5. *On the way back.*

àhmét—	istȧnbul‿hoşunuzȧ‿gʸidiyórmù?	İstanbul hoşunuza gidiyormu?
tóm—	évèt, gʸidíyòr.	Evet, gidiyor.
àhmét—	ėn‿çók‿néresi‿gʸidiyòr?	En çok neresi gidiyor?
tóm—	şímdiyė‿kádàr én‿çòk bóáz‿içi‿hóşumà‿gʸidiyór.	Şimdiye kadar en çok Boğaziçi hoşuma gidiyor.
àhmét—	istánbulun‿én‿gʸüzélʸ‿taraflarındán‿birì[1] órasìdir.	İstanbulun en güzel taraflarından biri orasıdır.
	fákàt istánbuldȧ‿gʸörülʸecèkʸ başkȧ‿çók‿mánzarálár‿vàr.	Fakat İstanbulda görülecek başka çok manzaralar var.
	onlari‿yȧváş‿yavȧş‿gʸörecèkʸsiniz.	Onları yavaş yavaş göreceksiniz.
tóm—	évèt, onlari‿gʸörmém‿lʸȧ:zìm, çûnkû istánbulda‿çók‿kálmıyacàim.	Evet, onları görmem lâzım, çünkü İstanbulda çok kalmıyacağım.
àhmét—	sónra‿néreyė‿gʸidecèkʸsiniz?	Sonra nereye gideceksiniz?
tóm—	rúsyȧyà.	Rusyaya.

[1]One of Istanbul's most beautiful parts.

Section E—Conversation

1. Covering the Turkish in Basic Sentences (Individual Study)

Cover the Turkish of the *Basic Sentences* and practice saying the Turkish equivalents of the English expressions

2. Vocabulary Check-Up

Give the Turkish expressions for the English equivalents in the *Basic Sentences* as the Leader calls for them.

3. Conversation

As you have done in the *Conversation* in the previous units, begin to converse by following the models outlined below fairly closely; then change the situations somewhat. Invent new combinations of subject matter.

1. Tom sees the sights.

   Ahmet says good morning to Tom and asks him how he likes the weather. Tom replies. Ahmet offers to show him about town. Tom is not too much interested, wonders what there is to see. Ahmet lists the sights. Tom would rather go to the Bosporus. So they decide to go there. They talk about how to get there. When they are on the boat, they discuss the sights, the water, the other boats, where they're going, etc.

2. Tom combines bathing with sight-seeing.

   Tom, sitting beside Ahmet on the upper deck of the steamer, complains that it's cloudy. Ahmet points out that the beach will not be hot. They talk about how long the trip takes, what they'll see when they get there, whether Tom has any money or not, where they'll eat, etc. Arriving at the beach, Tom takes in the sights, immediately heads for them. Ahmet advises him to take it easy. They say hello to the girls, talk about the weather, buy sodas for them, make dates for the evening, etc.

Section F—Conversation (*Cont.*)

1. Conversation (*Cont.*)

Continue the conversations started in Section E, with a review of parts 1 and 2 of the section if necessary.

2. Questions and Answers

First run through the *Listening In* once more. Then answer the following questions when the Guide asks you, or take turns asking them of others and answering them:

1.

1.	àhmét ó‿sábàh k^{y}i̍mé‿boáz‿içini̍‿g^{y}öster-mék^y‿i̍stiyòr?	Ahmet o sabah kime Boğaziçini göstermek istiyor?
2.	istánbulun‿én‿g^{y}üzél^y‿nél^{y}eri̍‿òradádır?	İstanbulun en güzel neleri oradadır?
3.	óràdà g^{y}örül^{y}ecék^y‿nérel^{y}eri̍‿vàr?	Orada görülecek nereleri var?
4.	si̍zín saráylarí‿fil^{y}án‿g^{y}örmèk^y hoşunuzá‿g^{y}i̍dérmi̍?	Sizin sarayları filân görmek hoşunuza gidermi?
5.	pl^{y}ajá‿né‿yapmaá‿g^{y}i̍del^{y}i̍m?	Plâja ne yapmağa gidelim?
6.	búrádàn órayá‿kádàr násil‿g^{y}i̍dil^{y}i̍r?	Buradan oraya kadar nasıl gidilir?
7.	bú‿vápùr néreyé‿g^{y}i̍dèr?	Bu vapur nereye gider?
8.	néyé‿binmemi̍z‿l^{y}á:zìm?	Neye binmemiz lâzım?
9.	vapurún‿né‿yapmasıná‿dahá‿çók‿vaki̍t‿vàr?	Vapurun ne yapmasına daha çok vakit var?
10.	dáhá‿évvèl^y né‿yápalìm?	Daha evvel ne yapalım?
11.	sónrà né‿yapàriz?	Sonra ne yaparız?
12.	néredé‿i̍necék^{y}l^{y}èr?	Nerede inecekler?
13.	vápurún‿kálkmasınà káç‿daki:ká‿vàr?	Vapurun kalkmasına kaç dakika var?
14.	öyl^{y}é‿isè né‿yápalìm?	Öyle ise ne yapalım?
15.	néreyé‿çikalìm?	Nereye çıkalım?
16.	óráyà né‿içi̍n‿çikalìm?	Oraya ne için çıkalım?
17.	óràdàn néyi̍‿g^{y}örǜrüz?	Oradan neyi görürüz?
18.	biri̍nci̍‿káttàn ó‿kadár‿iyi‿g^{y}örmézmiyi̍z?	Birinci kattan o kadar iyi görmezmiyiz?
19.	néyé bákalìm?	Neye bakalım?
20.	vàpúr néreyé‿g^{y}i̍diyòr?	Vapur nereye gidiyor?
21.	búrádà nérel^{y}eré‿çók‿yakìniz?	Burada nerelere çok yakınız?

	22.	bír‿taráftà néresí‿vàr?	Bir tarafta neresi var?
	23.	öbǘr‿taráftàdá néresiní‿g^{y}örüyòrúz?	Öbür tarafta da neresini görüyoruz?
2.	24.	bú‿g^{y}ǜn pl^{y}áj‿násìl?	Bu gün plâj nasıl?
	25.	g^{y}ők^y‿yüzǘndè né‿vàr?	Gök yüzünde ne var?
	26.	pl^{y}ajá‿né‿vakít‿g^{y}él^{y}ecèyíz?	Plâja ne vakit geleceğiz?
	27.	né‿kadár‿kálacàiz?	Ne kadar kalacağız?
	28.	őyl^{y}é‿yeméyimizì néredé‿yíyecèyíz?	Öyle yemeğimizi nerede yiyeceğiz?
	29.	pl^{y}àjdá başká‿né‿vàr?	Plâjda başka ne var?
	30.	onlárla‿konúşmák‿íçìn pará‿l^{y}á:zímmì?	Onlarla konuşmak için para lâzımmı?
	31.	sónra‿l^{y}a:zim‿ólacákmì?	Sonra lâzım olacakmı?
	32.	őyl^{y}é‿ísè onlará‿sónrà né‿díyecèyíz?	Öyle ise onlara sonra ne diyeceğiz?
3.	33.	mánzara‿násìl?	Manzara nasıl?
	34.	néredél^{y}èr?	Neredeler?
	35.	gá:l^{y}íbà k^{y}ímín‿bir‿kiz‿arkadaşi‿vàr?	Galiba kimin bir kız arkadaşı var?
	36.	néreyé‿g^{y}ídel^{y}ìm?	Nereye gidelim?
4.	37.	şímdi‿néyé‿yákláşıyòrúz?	Şimdi neye yaklaşıyoruz?
	38.	búrada‿né‿kadár‿kálacàiz?	Burada ne kadar kalacağız?
	39.	pl^{y}áj néreyé‿dáhà‿yakin?	Plâj nereye daha yakın?
	40.	né‿vakít‿g^{y}őrecèk^y?	Ne vakit görecek?
5.	41.	ístánbùl tomún‿hoşuná‿g^{y}ídiyórmù?	İstanbul Tomun hoşuna gidiyormu?
	42.	én‿çók‿néresí‿g^{y}ídiyòr?	En çok neresi gidiyor?
	43.	istánbulun‿én‿g^{y}üzél^y‿nérel^{y}erindén‿bírì órasìdir?	İstanbulun en güzel nerelerinden biri orasıdır?
	44.	nél^{y}erí‿yaváş‿yaváş‿g^{y}őrecèk^y?	Neleri yavaş yavaş görecek?
	45.	tóm istánbulda‿çók‿kálmıyacàkmi?	Tom İstanbulda çok kalmıyacakmı?
	46.	sónrà néreyé‿g^{y}ídecèk^y?	Sonra nereye gidecek?

FINDER LIST

ȧkşám‿yėmeyì (akşam yemeği)	dinner (evening meal)
akşȧm‿yemėyi̇ndén‿sònrȧ (akşam yemeğinden sonra)	after dinner
ásyà (Asya)	Asia
ȧvrúpà (Avrupa)	Europe
bak- . . . (bak- . . .) (aor. *-ar-*)	look at
nėyé‿bȧkalìm (neye bakalım?)	what shall we look at?
bànά (bana)	see *ben*
bén (ben)	I
bàná (bana)	to me
bènı́m (benim)	my, mine; me
bénı́mlʸè (benimle)	with me
bénı́m‿i̇çi̇̀n (benim için)	for me
bin- . . . (bin- . . .) (aor. *-er-*)	get on (to)
bı́r (bir)	one; a, an
bi̇rìncı́ (birinci)	first
biri̇ncı́‿kàt (birinci kat)	lower (first) deck
bı́z (biz)	we
bìzé (bize)	to us
bìzı́ (bizi)	(definite objective) us
bìzı́m (bizim)	our, ours; us

bízím‿içìn (bizím için)	for us
bizímlʸè (bizimle)	with us
bòáz (boğaz) (Boğaz)	throat; straits; (the) Bosporus
bóáz‿içì (Boğazici)	Bosporus (lit. the throat interior)
**bura* (non-existent base)	this place
búràdàn (buradan)	from here
búràsì (burası)	this place
búràyà (buraya)	to this place, here (hither)
bǜyǘk^{y} (büyük)	big, large
cà:mí (cami)	mosque
çǘnk^{y}*ǜ* (çünkü)	because
de- . . . (de- . . .)	say
diyecéyìz (diyeceğiz)	we'll say (with change of *e* to *i* before initial *y* of the ending)
ètráf (etraf)	the surroundings
étrà:fí (etrafı)	its surroundings; (definite objective) the surroundings
fìl^{y}*án* (filân)	and (or) the like, and such; such things as
g^{y}*idil*^{y}- . . . (gidil- . . .) (aor. *-ir-*)	go (impersonal)
g^{y}ìdil^{y}ír (gidilir)	one goes
g^{y}*örül*^{y}- . . . (görül- . . .) (aor. *-ür-*)	be seen
g^{y}örǜl^{y}écék^{y} (görülecek)	(going) to be seen
g^{y}*öster-* . . . (göster- . . .) (aor. *-ir-*)	show

hér (her)	each, every; all
hér‿türl^{y}ù (her türlü)	all kinds of
hér‿ik^{y}i- . . . ‘-dè (-dà) (her iki . . . de)(da)	both (lit. and each two)
hér‿ik^{y}i‿tárafídà (her iki tarafı da)	(definite objective) both sides
íç (iç)	inside, interior
ìçí (içi)	its interior
içìndé (içinde)	in its interior, in(side) of
bóáz‿içì (Boğaziçi)	(the) Bosporus (lit. throat interior)
ìl^{y}érí (ileri)	up ahead
il^{y}èriyé (ileriye)	(to) forward
in- . . . (in- . . .) (aor. ***-er-***)	get off (from)
ísk^{y}él^{y}è (iskele)	pier, landing place
istánbùl (İstanbul)	Istanbul (Constantinople)
istánbulda‿g^{y}örül^{y}ecék^y‿nérel^{y}eri‿vàr? (İstanbulda görülecek nereleri var?)	‘what places has Istanbul to be seen (lit. in Istanbul what places of its which will be seen are there?)’
kàdár (kadar)	(preceded by dat.) as far as, up to, to; until
ó‿kádàr (o kadar)	as, so, that much, that far
bú‿kádàr (bu kadar)	as, so, this much, this far
kát (kat)	floor, storey; deck
bú‿káttàn (bu kattan)	from this deck
birinci‿káttàn (birinci kattan)	from the lower (first) deck
k^{y}ím (kim)	who
k^{y}ìmé (kime)	to whom

k^{y}ìmin (kimin)	whose; whom
k^{y}i̍mín‿i̍çìn (kimin için)	for whom
k^{y}i̍mínl^{y}è (kiminle)	with whom
mánzàrà (manzara)	view, sight
mǘzè (müze)	museum
né (ne)	what
né‿için (nc için)	for what
né‿kádàr (ne kadar)	how long (lit. up to what)
nèl^{y}érí (neleri)	what things (of its)
nèyé (neye)	to what, onto what, at what
nèyí (neyi)	(definite objective) what? (lit. the what?)
néylè (neyle)	with what, by what means
*nere (non-existent base)	what place
nérél^{y}erè (nerelere)	to what places
nérel^{y}érì (nereleri)	what places (of its)
nérel^{y}erindén‿bi̍rì (nerelerinden biri)	one of what places (of its)
nérésì (neresi)	what place
néréyè (nereye)	to what place, where (whither)
ó (o)	he, she, it; that
ó‿kádàr (o kadar)	as, so, that (much)
ònún (onun)	his, her, its; that one's;
ónún‿i̍çìn (onun için)	for him (her, it, that);
ónúnlà (onunla)	with him (her, it, that)

**ora* (non-existent base)	that place
óràdàn (oradan)	from there
órȧsì (orası)	that place
óráyà (oraya)	to that place (thither)
ȍbű́r (öbür)	the other
ȍyl^{y}é (öğle)	noon
ö̇yl^{y}edén‿sònrá (öğleden sonra)	(in the) afternoon
ö̇yl^{y}é‿yėmeyı̀ (öğle yemeği)	lunch (noon meal)
ȍyl^{y}é (öyle)	thus, so, that way
ö̇yl^{y}é‿ı̇sè (öyle ise)	if it is (lit. be) that way, then, so
pl^{y}áj (plâj)	beach
rúsyà (Rusya)	Russia
sàráy	palace
sı́z (siz)	you
sı̀zé (size)	to you
sı̀zı́ (sizi)	(definite objective) you
sı̀zı́n (sizin)	you, yours; you
sı̇zı́n‿ı̇çı̀n (sizin için)	for you
sı̇zı́nl^{y}è (sizinle)	with you
són (son)	last; end
sónrà (sonra)	after; later
ón‿daki:ká‿sònrá (on dakika sonra)	in (lit. after) ten minutes

tàráf (taraf)	side
hėr‿ikʸi̇‿tárafídà (her iki tarafı da)	both sides
taràflárindán (taraflarından)	(out) of its parts
taráflárindán‿bi̇rì (taraflarından biri)	one of its parts
tràmváy (tramvay)	street car
trámváylà (tramvayla)	by street car
tụ̀rlʸű (türlü)	kind, sort
hér‿türlʸù (her türlü)	all kinds of
vàkít (vakit)	time
né‿vákìt (ne vakit)	what time, when
vàpúr (vapur)	boat
vápúrlà (vapurla)	by boat
vápurún‿kálkmasì (vapurun kalkması)	[the] boat's departure
yàkín (yakın)	(preceded by dat.) near, close to
ásyà avrúpaya‿çók‿yákìn (Asya Avrupaya çok yakın)	Asia is very close to Europe.
yèmékʸ (yemek)	food; dish (of food)
bálík‿yemėkʸlʸerì (balık yemekleri)	seafood (lit. fish dishes)
yüz- . . . (yüz- . . .) (aor. *-er-*)	swim
yụ̀zmékʸ (yüzmek)	to swim
yụ̀zméyé (yüzmeğe)	(in order) to swim

(before *gʸìtmékʸ*, the infinitive has the dative ending)

UNIT 11

SHOPPING

Section A—Basic Sentences

Go once through the *Basic Sentences* in unison, concentrating on the *Aids to Listening*, then do the *Hints on Pronunciation;* go once through the *Basic Sentences* individually, and then read the *Hints on Spelling*. The last time through individually, notice also the *Conventional Spelling*.

1. Basic Sentences

Mr. Gunduz and his friend go shopping.

ENGLISH EQUIVALENTS	AIDS TO LISTENING	CONVENTIONAL TURKISH SPELLING
	Mr. Gunduz	
Record 22A, beginning.		
(*to*) *shopping*	ȧlı̇̀ş‿vėrişé.	alış verişe
I'm going shopping.	alı̇ş‿vėrişé‿g^{y}idiyòrúm.	Alış verişe gidiyorum.
	His friend	
with you	sėni̇nl^{y}è.	seninle
I want to go with you, too.	bėnde‿seni̇́nl^{y}ė‿g^{y}i̇t- mèk^{y}‿istiyórum.	Bende seninle gitmek istiyorum.
	Mr. Gunduz	
to buy	sȧtín‿ȧlmàk.	satın almak
you want	isti̇́yórsùn.	istiyorsun
What do you want to buy?	né‿satin‿almȧk‿i̇stiyòrsún?	Ne satın almak istiyorsun?

	His friend	
a suit	bìr‿él^{y}bi̍:sé.	bir elbise
a [pair of] shoe[s]	bi̍r‿ayákkȧbì.	bir ayakkabı
A suit and a pair of shoes.	bìr‿ėl^{y}bi:sé vė‿bi̍r‿ayákkȧbì.	Bir elbise ve bir ayakkabı.
	Mr. Gunduz	
a hat	bi̍r‿şápkȧ.	bir şapka
I shall buy [it]	ȧlacáìm.	alacağım
I'm going to buy a hat.	bén bi̍r‿şápkȧ‿ȧlacàim.	Ben bir şapka alacağım.
	His friend	
are you going to buy [it]?	ȧlacákmisìn?	alacakmısın?
Are you going to buy anything else?	başkȧ‿bi̍r‿şéy‿ȧlacákmisìn?	Başka bir şey alacakmısın?
	Mr. Gunduz	
sock[s]	çòráp.	çorap
handkerchief[s]	mèndíl^{y}.	mendil
Yes, socks and handkerchiefs.	évèt, çòráp vė‿mèndíl^{y}.	Evet, çorap ve mendil.
	His friend	
[the] salesman	sàticí.	satıcı
Are you the salesman?	satıcı‿sízmi̍sinìz?	Satıcı sizmisiniz?
	Salesman	
Yes, I am!	évèt, bénìm!	Evet, benim!
	Mr. Gunduz	
How much is this hat?	bú‿şápkȧ káç‿pȧrȧ?	Bu şapka kaç para?

	Salesman	
fourteen	ón‿dòrt.	on dört
Fourteen lira, sir.	ón‿dört‿l^{y}ìrá, éféndìm.	On dört lira, efendim.
	Mr. Gunduz	
expensive	pàhálí.	pahalı
It's very expensive.	çók‿páhalì.	Çok pahalı.
than (lit. from) that	òndán.	ondan
cheaper (than it)	dáhá‿úcuzù.	daha ucuzu
[is]n't there?	yókmù?	yokmu?
Isn't there anything cheaper than that?	ondán‿dahá‿ucuzú‿yókmù?	Ondan daha ucuzu yokmu?
	Salesman	
as this one	búnún‿kádàr.	bunun kadar
Yes, but it's not as good as this one.	évèt, fákàt búnùn‿kadár‿iyi‿déyil^y.	Evet, fakat bunun kadar iyi değil.
	Mr. Gunduz	
its waste	ziyà:ní.	ziyanı
there [is]n't	yók.	yok
It doesn't matter.	ziyá:nì‿yók.	Ziyanı yok.
rainy	yà:múrlú.	yağmurlu
in weather(s)	hàvalárdá.	havalarda
to put on	g^{y}ìymék^y.	giymek
I want to put it on in rainy weather.	ya:murlú‿havalardá‿g^{y}iymék^y‿için‿istiyòrúm.	Yağmurlu havalarda giymek için istiyorum.

Record 22B, beginning.

	Salesman	
cheap	ùcúz.	ucuz
durable	dàyaniklí.	dayanıklı
Then I'll find a cheap hat for you that'll stand up.	öyl^{y}é‿i̍sè si̍zè‿úcúz vé‿dayanıkli‿bi̍r‿şáp-ká‿búlacàim.	Öyle ise size ucuz ve dayanıklı bir şapka bulacağım.
	His friend	
summer (time)	yàzlík.	yazlık
I want a summer suit.	yazlìk‿bi̍r‿él^{y}bi:sé‿i̍stiyòrúm.	Yazlık bir elbise istiyorum.
its front	ònú	önü
let [it] be open	áçík‿ólsùn.	açık olsun
A single-breasted one!	önü‿áçík‿ólsùn!	Önü açık olsun!
	Salesman	
what color	né‿rènk^y?	ne renk?
you prefer	1. tèrci̍h‿édiyòrsunúz 2. terci̍h‿edi̍yórsunùz	tercih ediyorsunuz
What color do you prefer?	né‿rénk^y‿térci̍h‿ediyórsunuz?	Ne renk tercih ediyorsunuz?
	His friend	
Navy blue.	l^{y}à:ci̍vért.	Lâcivert.
	Salesman	
Unfortunately we don't have a single-breasted navy blue suit.	maál^{y}ésèf l^{y}à:ci̍vért önü‿áçìk‿el^{y}bi:semi̍z‿yók.	Maalesef lâcivert önü açık elbisemiz yok.

in that color	ó‿rénkʸtè.	o renkte
double-breasted	kùrvázé.	kurvaze
There's only double-breasted in that color.	ó‿rénkʸtè yálnız‿kúrvazé‿vàr.	O renkte yalnız kurvaze var.
	His friend	
gray	kùrşú:ni:	kurşuni
Then make it a gray (colored) suit.	őylʸé‿isè kurşu:ni:‿renkʸ-tè‿bir‿élʸbi:sé‿ólsùn.	Öyle ise kurşuni renkte bir elbise olsun.
	Salesman	
How is this one?	bú‿násìl?	Bu nasıl?
Do you like it?	beyéniyórmúsunùz?	Beğeniyormusunuz?
	His friend	
bad	fènà:	fena
Yes. It's not bad.	évèt. fénà:‿déyilʸ.	Evet. Fena değil.
its price	fìyàtí.	fiyatı
What's the price of this one?	búnún‿fiyatì né‿kádàr?	Bunun fiyatı ne kadar?
	Salesman	
It's not expensive.	páhalì‿déyilʸ.	Pahalı değil.
twenty	yìrmí.	yirmi
Twenty lira.	yirmi‿lʸìrá.	Yirmi lira.

Before you go through the *Basic Sentences* a second time, read the following:

2. Hints on Pronunciation

We have imitated carefully the various *risings* and *fallings of the voice* as we listened to the Guide or the records. We present here examples of the most frequent patterns we have met thus far:

PRACTICE 1

Note here the short pauses and slight rises or suspensions of the voice between the phrases (marked by *spaces* after a phrase), or the longer pauses and more noticeable rises (marked by *commas*) (,).

Record 23A, beginning.

bénìmk^{y}í şék^{y}èrl^{y}í.	Benimki şekerli.	*'Mine with sugar.'*
háyìr, dèyíl^y.	Hayır, değil.	*'No, [it is]n't.'*
bú‿vápùr bóàz‿içiné‿g^{y}i̍tméz.	Bu vapur Boğaziçine gitmez.	*'This boat doesn't go to the Bosporus.'*
bú‿şàpká káç‿párà?	Bu şapka kaç para?	*'How much is this hat?'*
ón‿dört‿l^{y}ìrá, éféndìm.	On dört lira, efendim.	*'Fourteen lira, sir.'*

PRACTICE 2

Note here (in the first three examples only) the fall of the voice (marked by *periods*) (.). Occasionally a sentence followed by a question mark (?) in the conventional spelling, has the same fall of the voice as you hear in these first three examples. On the records unfortunately the last two examples in this practice are ordinary questions and really belong to *Practice 3*. The last example (áhmèt!) belongs to *Practice 4*. Listen for examples of the (conventional spelling) question with a statement (.) fall of the voice in the *Listening In*'s.

Record 23A, after 1st spiral.

çók‿iyi̍‿bálík‿yemek^{y}l^{y}eri̍‿vàr.	Çok iyi balık yemekleri var.	*'They have very good sea food.'*
aliş‿vérişé‿g^{y}i̍diyòrúm.	Aliş verişe gidiyorum.	*'I'm going shopping.'*
háyìr. i̍çmiyecèyi̍m.	Hayır. İçmiyeceğim.	*'No, I won't drink [it].'*
tavúk‿násìl?	Tavuk nasıl?	*'How's [the] chicken?'*
k^{y}ím‿g^{y}él^{y}iyòr? áhmèt!	Kim geliyor? Ahmet!	*'Who's coming? Ahmet!'*

PRACTICE 3

Note here the unusually high level of the voice on the strongest vowel (ʹ), and the way in which it falls off gradually. This voice contour is indicated with a *question mark* (?) and is characteristic of many questions. We have heard at least two other kinds of voice contour for questions, the one mentioned above (.), which is like that of a statement, and which we have met occasionally, and another we have heard **a** few times and which we marked with (¿). In this last one the voice stays fairly high after the first peak, and then rises again at the end. Listen for this wherever we have marked (¿) for the material on the records.

Record 23A, after 2nd spiral.

yókmù?	Yokmu?	*'[Is]n't there [any]?'*
sénmi̍sìn?	Senmisin?	*'[Is] it you (informal)?'*
síz?	Siz?	*'You?'*
bú‿vápùr boáz‿içiné‿gʸi̍dérmì?	Bu vapur Boğaziçine gidermi?	*'Does this boat go to [the] Bosporus?'*
onlárla‿konúşacákmiyìz?	Onlarla konuşacakmıyız?	*'Will we talk with them?'*

PRACTICE 4

Here we note that the voice rises to a peak on the strongest vowel, and then continues fairly evenly on this high note until the end, where it falls suddenly. We indicate this exclamatory voice contour with the exclamation mark (!).

Record 23A, after 3rd spiral.

áhmèt! gʸélʸìn!	Ahmet! Gelin!	*'Ahmet! Come (here)!'*
bóáz‿içiné‿gʸi̍delʸìm!	Boğaziçine gidelim!	*'Let's go to [the] Bosporus!'*
bákìn!	Bakin!	*'Look!'*
mérhábà!	Merhaba!	*'Hello!'*
évèt, çók!	Evet, çok!	*'Yes, very much!'*

Listen carefully to the records of all these:

1. (space)
2. (,)
3. (.)
4. (?)
5. (!)

and for the others mentioned here. Notice other patterns not mentioned here, or variations in these, and imitate them all carefully. Try to figure out what the various voice contours indicate as to the speaker's attitude toward what he is saying or toward the people with whom he is speaking.

Before you go through the *Basic Sentences* a third time, read the following:

3. Hints on Spelling

In Unit 10 we gave a summary of the correspondences between our *Aids to Listening* and the usual Turkish spelling, the *Conventional Spelling*. We pointed out the few *defects* of the *Conventional Spelling*:

1. the circumflex (ˆ) is not used to distinguish l^yo from *lo*, or ol^y from *ol;*
2. there is no way to distinguish *ki* from k^yi or ke from k^ye, *ik* from ik^y or *ek* from ek^y; kal^y from k^yal^y or lak^y from l^yak^y, kul^y from k^yul^y or luk^y from l^yuk^y, and so on;
3. there is no way to distinguish *gi* from g^yi or *ge* from g^ye, gal^y from g^yal^y or gul^y from g^yul^y, and so on;
4. long vowels are indicated a. by short vowel plus *ğ* before a following consonant or at the end of a word, or b. they aren't marked at all; in either case one has to learn arbitrarily which words write *ğ* and which write nothing at all; or c. the circumflex is also sometimes used to mark long vowels, and here one runs the risk of confusing things like *ka:* and $k^ya{:}$ (both written *kâ*), or l^ya and $l^ya{:}$ (both written *lâ*);
5. two vowels together in the pronunciation may mean, for example, either *ağa* or *a'a* since one never pronounces *ğ* between certain vowels and one usually does not pronounce ('); in either case one has to learn arbitrarily which words write *ğ* and which write nothing at all;
6. after certain vowels before a consonant, as well as between certain vowels either *ğ* or *y* is written for the sound *y*; in either case one has to learn arbitrarily which words write *ğ* and which write *y*.

Here we shall note a few *other defects*:

7. the usual Turkish writing does not mark the varying degrees of strength of its vowels (' ` ´) and many confusions may result as between *benim* '[it's] mine' and *benim* '[it is] I' (*bènim* and *bénim* in our *Aids to Listening*);
8. The usual Turkish writing sometimes writes (?) where the pattern of ups and downs in the voice is no different from where (.) is written.
9. The usual Turkish writing separates the ending *-de, -da, -te, -ta* (usually written only with *de, da*) 'and, too, also', from the base word to which it is attached but does not cut off the locative ending *-de, -da, -te, -ta, -nde, -nda*; here the place of the strongest vowel (*before* the ending with "and, too, also", and in the ending with the locative) distinguishes between *bizdè* (biz de) 'we, too' and *bìzdé* (bizde) 'at our house' and one ending is just

as much a part of the word to which it is attached as the other;

10. The usual Turkish writing sometimes separates other parts of words from the base word to which they are attached, such as the interrogative ending *-mi*, *-mü*, *-mı*, *-mu*, and all that follows it in the particular word, or the 'is, are, am' ending *-dir*, *-dür*, and so on.

We shall now suggest certain *remedies* for these defects, which we shall resort to in our *Standardized Conventional Spelling:*

1. we shall use the circumflex *always* and *only* to mark preceding or following (before a consonant or at the end of a word) l^y, k^y, g^y;
2. we shall italicize[1] *k* and *g* before *i*, *e*, *â*, *û*, so that one will *not* be tempted to pronounce k^y or g^y but will pronounce simple *k* or *g*;
3. we shall mark with (:) all long vowels not indicated by following *ğ* (before a consonant or at the end of a word); we shall *never* use the circumflex (^) to indicate length;
4. we shall always write (') in words like *san'at* to indicate the division into syllables (*san-at*); but we shall not write it elsewhere;
5. we shall continue to mark the varying degrees of strength (' ` ´) throughout;
6. we shall continue to use the linking sign (‿) to join the words in a phrase;
7. we shall write (?) wherever the usual Turkish spelling writes it, but you must be careful to listen for the times when it is no different from (.).
8. we shall never separate any part of a word from the rest of it.

These remedies do nothing, however, about the letter *ğ*, which continues to have three values:

1. (:) after certain short vowels (before a consonant or at the end of a word);
2. *zero* between certain vowels;
3. *y* between certain vowels, and after certain vowels before a following consonant.

Here one must learn:

1. when to write *ğ* and when (:);
2. when to write *ğ* and when nothing;
3. when to write *ğ* and when *y*.

We include the *Turkish alphabet* with two complete check lists in the appendix, one of the *Aids to Listening*, with the *Standardized Conventional* equivalents, and another of the letters of the alphabet plus the additional signs, and their *Aids to Listening* equivalents. When in doubt about any letter in our *Standardized Conventional Spelling*, consult these lists. They are for reference only.

---

[1]Plain type in words printed in italics; cf. vàkít : *vàkít*.

SECTION B—WORD STUDY AND REVIEW OF BASIC SENTENCES

1. Word Study (Individual Study)

1. *Other Turkish equivalents of English "you"*

In the ***Basic Sentences*** of this unit, we met the following:

né‿satin‿almák‿istiyòrsún?	Ne satın almak istiyorsun?	*'What do you want to buy?'*
baṣká‿bir‿ṣéy‿álacákmisìn?	Başka bir şey alacakmısın?	*'Are you going to buy anything else?'*

We see here the forms *istiyórsùn* (istiyorsun) 'you want', and *àlacákmisìn* (alacakmısın?) 'will you buy?', instead of the usual *istiyórsúnùz* (istiyorsunuz), *àlacákmisınìz* (alacakmısınız?). Adding other similar forms, we get the following table:

	Column I				Column II		
				Group I			
i	gʸèlʸír	gelir	'[*he*] *comes*'	:	gʸélʸírsìn	gelirsin	'*you come*'
e	sèvér	sever	'[*he*] *likes*'	:	sévérsìn	seversin	'*you like*'
ü	bůyúkʸ	büyük	'*big*'	:	büyúkʸsùn	büyüksün	'*you* [*are*] *big*'
ö	gʸőkʸ	gök	'*heaven*'	:	gʸőkʸsùn	göksün	'*you* [*are*] *heaven*'
				Group II			
ı	kíz	kız	'*girl*'	:	kízsìn	kızsın	'*you* [*are*] [*the*] *girl*'
a	bàşlár	başlar	'[*he*] *begins*'	:	báşlársìn	başlarsın	'*you begin*'
u	çòcúk	çocuk	'*child*'	:	çócúksùn	çocuksun	'*you* [*are*] [*the*] *boy*'
o	kóşúyòr	koşuyor	'[*he*] *is running*'	:	koşúyórsùn	koşuyorsun	'*you are running*'

If we compare Column I with Column II and Group I with Group II, we see that:

1. this personal ending "you" is *-sin*, *-sün*, *-sın*, *-sun* and follows Vowel Harmony Type I;

2. it never has the *strongest vowel* and does not require any change in the place of the strong vowel before it.

We have given examples of this personal ending used both with verb forms (*gʸèlʸìrsìn, sèvérsìn, bàşlársìn, koşúyórsùn*) and with noun forms with a zero "is, are, am" copula ending (*bǜyǘkʸsǜn, gʸǿkʸsǜn, kízsìn, çòcúksùn*).

This shorter "you" ending is used only when speaking to close friends, or relatives, to small children, and to animals. It refers to only *one* person. We shall call it the *informal* "you" ending. When speaking informally to more than one person, the longer ending (*-siniz, -sünüz, -sınız, -sunuz*) is used, just as when speaking formally to one or more people.

2. *Turkish equivalents of English "from, out of, than"*

In the last few units we have seen the following:

yemèkʸtén‿sònrá meyvá‿vè‿kahvè‿istiyórmúsunùz?	Yemekten sonra meyva ve kahve istiyormusunuz?	*'After* [*the*] *meal do you want fruit and coffee?'*
búrádàn iskʸèlʸeyè‿kádàr trámváylà óradàndá vápúrlà.	Buradan iskeleye kadar tramvayla oradan da vapurla.	*'From here to* [*the*] *pier by street car and from there by boat.'*
ǿylʸedén‿sònrá.	Öğleden sonra.	*'In* [*the*] *afternoon.'*
akşàm‿yeméyindén‿sònrá.	Akşam yemeğinden sonra.	*'After dinner.'*
bú‿káttàn etra:fi‿iyi‿gʸörǘrmüyǜz?	Bu kattan etrafı iyi görürmüyüz?	*'Will we see the surroundings well from this deck?'*
birinci‿kattán‿gʸörmézmiyìz?	Birinci kattan görmezmiyiz?	*'Won't we see from* [*the*] *lower deck?'*
ondán‿dahá‿ucuzú‿yókmù?	Ondan daha ucuzu yokmu?	*'Isn't there anything cheaper than that?'*

Summarizing these forms, we get:

	Column I				Column II		
				Group I			
i	sèhi̋r	şehir	*'city'*	: ṣėhi̇rdén	şehirden	*'from [the] city'*
e	ȍyl^{y}é	öğle	*'noon'*	: ȍyl^{y}ėdén	öğleden	*'from (than) noon'*
ü	ó‿g^{y}ȕn	o gün	*'that day'*	: ó‿g^{y}ündèn	o günden	*'from that day'*
				Group II			
ı	kíz	kız	*'girl'*	: kìzdán	kızdan	*'from [the] girl'*
a	*bura		*'this place'*	: búrȧdàn	buradan	*'from here'*
u	*bun	bu	*'this'*	: bùndán	bundan	*'from (than) this'*
o	*on	o	*'that'*	: òndán	ondan	*'from (than) that'*
				Group III			
e	yèmék^{y}	yemek	*'meal'*	: yémèk^{y}tén	yemekten	*'from (than) [the] meal'*
ö	g^{y}ő k^{y}	gök	*'heaven'*	: g^{y}ȍk^{y}tén	gökten	*'from heaven'*
a	kát	kat	*'deck'*	: kàttán	kattan	*'from [the] deck'*
a	sı̀ınák	sığınak	*'shelter'*	: sıınàktán	sığınaktan	*'from [the] shelter'*
				Group IV			
	yȕzű	yüzü	*'his face'*	: yüzȕndén	yüzünden	*'from his face'*
	ȧkṣám‿yémeyȉ	akşam yemeği	*'dinner'*	: ȧkṣám‿yemė-yi̇ndèn	akşam yemeğinden	*'from (than) dinner'*
	àrásí	arası	'*(space) between*'	: àrasindán	arasından	*'from between (them)'*

By comparing Column I with Column II, Group I with Group II, Groups I and II with III, and with IV, we see that:

1. the "from" ending follows Vowel Harmony Type II;
2. is *-den*, *-dan* after humming sounds, such as *r*, *e*, *n*, *z*, *a*;
3. is *-ten*, *-tan* after non-humming sounds, such as k^y, *t*, *k*;
4. is *-nden*, *-ndan* after forms of the possessive ending -(*s*)*i*, -(*s*)*ü*, -(*s*)*ı*, -(*s*)*u*;
5. has the *strongest vowel*, whenever it is the last vowel of the base form which is strongest, otherwise the ending has the second strongest vowel.

We note that before *sonra* 'after, later (than)', we find a noun with this ending.

We note also that this ending may mean "than" in a comparison:

ondán‿dáhá‿úcuzù yókmù?	Ondan daha ucuzu yokmu?	*'Isn't there anything cheaper than that* (*lit. than that a cheaper one of them isn't there*)*?'*

We shall call this *-den*, *-dan*, *-ten*, *-tan*, *-nden*, *-ndan* ending, which means "from, out of, than, because of, etc.", the *ablative* ending.

3. *Turkish equivalents of English "I, you, he", etc.*

We have met the form *sėnínl*^{y}*è* (seninle) 'with you' in this unit and we note that here, too, as in the case of *síz* (siz) 'you', and so on, one uses the form with the genitive ending before the word *ìl*^{y}*é* (ile), or its form as an ending, *-l*^{y}*e*, *-la*.

From *sènín* 'your, yours; you', we abstract *sén* 'you (informal),' corresponding to verb forms with the informal "you" ending, *-sin*, *-sün*, *-sın*, *-sun*, just as *síz* 'you (informal)' corresponds to forms with the formal "you" ending *-siniz*, *-sünüz*, *-sınız*, *-sunuz*.

We have now completed our list of these short words, used in place of nouns, and we shall call them *pronouns*. We summarize the pronouns here:

bén	ben	*'I'*
sén	sen	*'you* (*informal*) (*to one person*)'.
ó	o	*'he, she, it; that'*
bíz	biz	*'we'*
síz	siz	*'you* (*formal*) (*to one or more persons*); (*informal*) (*to two or more persons*)'
ɔ́nlár	onlar	*'they'*

The *genitive* forms of these pronouns are:

bènim	benim	*'my, mine; me'*
sènin	senin	*'your, yours; you (informal)'*
ònún	onun	*'his, her, its'*
bìzím	bizim	*'our, ours; us'*
sìzín	sizin	*'you, yours; you (formal) (to one or more persons); (informal) (to two or more persons)'*
ònlárín	onların	*'their, theirs; them'*

We have already noted that *bènim* (benim) and *bìzím* (bizim) are irregular in that they have the ending *-im* instead of *-in*.

Returning now to the form *sènìnlʸè* (seninle) 'with you (informal)', we note that not only before *ìlʸé* (ile) 'with', but also before *ìçín* (için) 'for' (and certain other words which we shall meet later), one uses the genitive form of all these pronouns except *ònlár* (onlar). Besides *ònún* (onun), one also finds *bùnún* (bunun) 'of this' and *kʸìmin* (kimin) 'of whom' which fall in this same class. We shall meet other words (besides *ìlʸé* and *ìçín*) before which the genitive form of these pronouns is used.

We have already seen the following:

bénim‿için	benim için	*'for me'*
ónún‿için	onun için	*'for that'*

Summarizing:

bénim‿için	benim için	*'for me'*
sénin‿için	senin için	*'for you (informal)'*
ónún‿için	onun için	*'for him, her, it; that; therefore'*
bizim‿için	bizim için	*'for us'*
sizin‿için	sizin için	*'for you (formal)'*

We may now note an irregular dative form *sànā́* (sana) 'to you', parallel to *bànā́* (bana) 'to me', which we have already met.

The *dative* forms of the pronouns are:

bàná	bana	*'to, for me'*
sàná	sana	*'to, for you (informal)'*
òná	ona	*'to, for, him (her, it; that)'*
bìzé	bize	*'to, for us'*
sìzé	size	*'to, for you (formal)'*
ònlárá	onlara	*'to, for them'*

The locative, definite objective, and ablative forms are all completely regular:

bèndé	bende	sèndé	sende,	*etc.*
bènı́	beni	sènı́	seni	*etc.*
bèndén	benden	sèndén	senden	*etc.*

4. *Turkish general personal endings* (*summary*)

With the personal ending 'you (informal)', presented in this unit, we have now completed the list of *general personal endings*. We call these endings "general" to distinguish them from the "limited" personal endings, one of which we have already met (*-m* in the "I" form of the negative aorist) (see Unit 10 B. 1. 3), and others of which we shall meet later.

GENERAL PERSONAL ENDINGS

-(y)im, -(y)üm, -(y)ım, -(y)um	*'I'*
-sin, -sün, -sın, -sun	*'you (informal)'*
-0	*'he, she, it'*
-(y)iz, -(y)üz, -(y)ız, -(y)uz	*'we'*
-siniz, -sünüz, -sınız, -sunuz	*'you (formal)'*
-l^{y}er, -lar	*'they'*

Note: *-yim* after a vowel, *-im* after a consonant, etc.

These general personal endings have thus far been used:

a. with the *aorist copula:*

Examples:

-im	bénìm	benim	*'it [is] I'*
-sun	çócúksùn	çocuksun	*'you [are] [a] child'*
-0	ódùr	odur	*'[it] is he'*
-0	iyil^{y}érdìr	iyilerdir	*'[it]'s the good ones'*
-yiz	iyíyìz	iyiyiz	*'we [are] well'*
-sünüz	k^{y}üçǘk^{y}sünǜz	küçüksünüz	*'you [are] small'*
-l^{y}er	iyídirl^{y}èr	iyidirler	*'they are well'*

b. with the *aorist*:

Examples:

-yim	yapármiyìm?	yaparmıyım?	*'[do] I do?'*
-sın	ìslanírsìn	ıslanırsın	*'you get wet'*
-0	ìstér	ister	*'[he] wants'*
-yiz	g^{y}ö́rméyiz	görmeyiz	*'we'll not see'*
-sunuz	únutúrsúnùz	unutursunuz	*'you forget'*
-lar	táràrlár	tararlar	*'they comb'*

c. with the *momentary*:

Examples:

-yum	giriyórmúyùm?	giriyormuyum?	*'am I going in?'*
-sun	aríyórsùn	arıyorsun	*'you are looking for [it]'*
-0	bákmiyòr	bakmıyor	*'he's not looking at [it]'*
-uz	éyl^{y}eniyórùz	eğleniyoruz	*'we're having fun'*
-sunuz	g^{y}etiriyórsúnùz	getiriyorsunuz	*'you're bringing [it]'*
-lar	tóplaníyórlàr	toplanıyorlar	*'they are gathering'*

d. with the *future*:

Examples:

-im	óvacáìm	ovacağım	*'I'll brush'*
-sin	yiyecék^{y}misìn?	yiyecekmisin?	*'will you eat?'*
-0	yáklášmiyacàk	yaklaşmıyacak	*'[it] won't approach'*
-yız	ánlámıyacàkmıyiz?	anlamıyacakmıyız?	*'won't we understand [it]?'*
-siniz	g^{y}ül^{y}ecék^{y}sinìz	güleceksiniz	*'we'll laugh'*
-lar	çíkmıyacáklàr	çıkmıyacaklar	*'we won't go up'*

5. *Turkish aorist copula* (*summary*)

We call the copula ('is, are, am') forms we have seen thus far "aorist" forms because they usually refer to a general fact and because there are no other simple copula forms which are clearly aorist. Only *òlúr* (olur) from the verb root *ol-* . . . (ol- . . .) 'be; become' approaches at times the value of the "aorist" copula, since it is an aorist form, but it more often means 'becomes', rather than 'is'.

AORIST COPULA ENDINGS

-dir, -dür, -dır, -dur
-tir, -tür, -tır, -tur
-0

Note 1: *-dir* after humming sounds, *-tir* after non-humming sounds.

Note 2: the aorist with these endings is "zero", so that we have *çocúk-0-úm-dùr : *çocúùmdùr* (çocuğumdur) 'I am [a] boy'. We shall see later such forms as *çocúktúmdùr* (çocuktumdur) 'I was [a] boy', with *-tu-* indicating past time.

Examples:

-0	bénìm	benim	*'it ['s] I, I [am]'*
-0	sénmisìn?	senmisin?	*'[is] it you?'*
-dir	èvdédìr	evdedir	*'[he]'s at home'*
-dir	èvl^{y}iyizdìr	evliyizdir	*'we're married'*

-0	ánnésinìz	annesiniz	*'you['re] [a] mother'*
-dir	iyídirí^{y}èr	iyidirler	*'they are well'*
-0	ìyil^{y}ér	iyiler	*'they [are] well'*

6. *Turkish aorist endings* (*summary*).

We have seen a number of endings for the aorist, some with the positive, some with the negative, one with the copula.

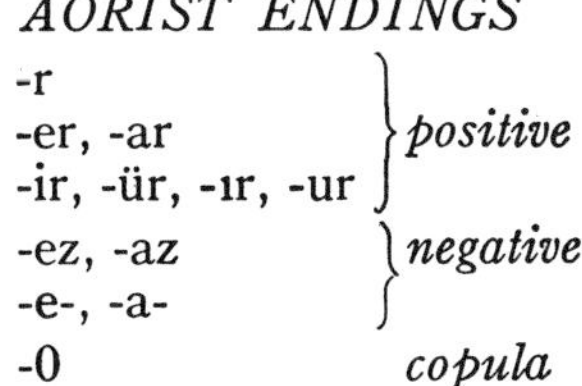

AORIST ENDINGS

-r -er, -ar -ir, -ür, -ır, -ur	*positive*
-ez, -az -e-, -a-	*negative*
-0	*copula*

Note 1: *-r* after all verb roots ending in a vowel.
Note 2: *-er*, *-ar* after some verb roots ending in a consonant.
Note 3: *-ir*, *-ür*, *-ır*, *-ur* after other verb roots ending in a consonant.
Note 4: *-e-*, *-a-* with the "I" and "we" forms of the negative aorist; *-ez*, *-az*, with the other forms.

Examples:

başla- . . .	başla- . . .	*'begin'*	*-r* :	bàşlár	başlar	'*[he] begins*'
yüz- . . .	yüz- . . .	*'swim'*	*-er* :	yǜzér	yüzer	'*[he] swims*'
yap- . . .	yap- . . .	*'do'*	*-ar* :	yàpár	yapar	'*[he] does*'
g^{y}el^{y}- . . .	gel- . . .	*'come'*	*-ir* :	g^{y}èl^{y}ír	gelir	'*[he] comes*'
g^{y}ör- . . .	gör- . . .	*'see'*	*-ür* :	g^{y}ö̀rǘr	görür	'*[he] sees*'

yıkan- . . .	yıkan- . . .	*'wash'*	*-ır* :	yìkánír	yıkanır	'[*he*] *washes*'
unut- . . .	unut- . . .	*'forget'*	*-ur* :	ùnútúr	unutur	'[*he*] *forgets*'
g^y^it- . . .	git- . . .	*'go'*	*-ez* :	g^y^ìtméz	gitmez	'[*he*] *doesn't go*'
çık- . . .	çık- . . .	*'go up'*	*-az* :	çìkmáz	çıkmaz	'[*he*] *doesn't go up*'
sev- . . .	sev- . . .	*'find'*	*-e* :	sèvmém	sevmem	*'I don't like'*
başla- . . .	başla- . . .	*'start'*	*-a* :	báşlamáyìz	başlam yız	*'we don't start'*
iyi- . . .	iyi- . . .	*'well'*	*-0* :	iyíyìm	iyiyim	'*I*['*m*] *well*'

7. *Turkish negative endings* (*summary*)

NEGATIVE ENDINGS

-me-, -ma-
-mi-, -mı-
-m-

Note 1: *-me-*, *-ma-*, in the "don't do [it]" forms.
Note 2: *-mi-*, *-mı-* in the "let's not do [it]" forms, and in the future forms.
Note 3: *-m-* in the momentary forms, and in the aorist forms.

Examples:

-me, -ma	íçméyinìz!	içmeyiniz!	*'don't drink!'*
-mi, -mı	báşlámıyálìm!	başlamıyalım!	*'let's not begin!'*
	g^y^ő́rmiyecèk^y^	görmiyecek	'[*he*]'*ll not see* [*it*]

-m-	istémiyòr	istemíyor	'[he] *does not want*'
	gʸìtméz	gitmez	'[*it*] *doesn't go*'

2. Covering English and Turkish of Word Study (Individual Study)

Check yourself on your knowledge of the *Word Study* by covering, first the English, then the Turkish, and making sure you know everything thoroughly.

3. Review of Basic Sentences

With the Guide or records, review the first half of the *Basic Sentences* as in previous units.

SECTION C—REVIEW OF BASIC SENTENCES (*Cont.*)

1. Review of Basic Sentences (*Cont.*)

Review the second half of the *Basic Sentences*.

2. Covering the English of Basic Sentences (Individual Study)

Go through the *Basic Sentences* covering up the English and reading aloud the Turkish. Check up on anything you do not know, until you are sure of everything.

3. Word Study Review (Individual Study)

Work through the following exercises. Do not write anything down. If you cannot do the work rapidly, review again the *Word Study*. Be prepared to do what is required when the Leader calls on you. Always repeat the entire expression, phrase or sentence as you work.

1. Complete the following sentences by supplying the corresponding *informal* "you" forms of the verbs and pronouns in parentheses:

   1. òsmán (sén)‿né‿dìyòr?
      Osman (sen) ne diyor?
   2. sén bú‿àkşàm né‿(yap- . . .)?
      Sen bu akşam ne (yap- . . .)?

3. évèt, (sén)‿berá: bèr sinémayá‿gʸitmèkʸ hóşuná‿gʸidiyòr.
   Evet, (sen) beraber sinemaya gitmek hoşuna gidiyor.
4. órhàn! benimlʸe‿(gʸelʸ- . . .)?
   Orhan! Benimle (gel- . . .)?
5. (sén)‿için bir‿şéy‿álacàim.
   (Sen) için bir şey alacağım.

2. Complete the following sentences by supplying the corresponding *ablative* forms of the nouns in parentheses:

1. bú‿(şápkà) dahá‿pahalısi‿vármì?
   Bu (şapka) daha pahalısı varmı?
2. (ó)‿sònrá konúşacáiz.
   (O) sonra konuşacağız.
3. (*nere)‿gʸélʸiyòrsún?
   (*Nere) geliyorsun?
4. (sàticí)‿né‿álacàksin?
   (Satıcı) ne alacaksın?
5. (yèmékʸ)‿sònrá evimizé‿gʸelʸirmisin?
   (Yemek) sonra evimize gelirmisin?

3. Complete the following sentences with the corresponding forms of the *pronouns* in parentheses:

1. (biz)‿hóşumuzà şáráp‿gʸidèr.
   (Biz) hoşumuza şarap gider.
2. (sén)‿bir‿şéy‿vérmiyòr.
   (Sen) bir şey vermiyor.
3. (ònlár)‿evindè toplánacáklármì?
   (Onlar) evinde toplanacaklarmı?
4. (sén)‿bákıyórlàr. (ònlár)‿né‿diyecèkʸsin?
   (Sen) bakıyorlar. (Onlar) ne diyeceksin?
5. (sén)‿bir‿şéy‿istémiyòrúm.
   (Sen) bir şey istemiyorum.

4. What Would You Say? (Individual Study)

Read aloud each of the following and then pick out the expression you think most suitable:

1. *Mr. Gunduz tells his friend he is going shopping:*

a. tráş‿olmaá‿gʸidiyòrúm. — Traş olmağa gidiyorum.
b. aliş‿vérişé‿gʸidiyòrúm. — Alış verişe gidiyorum.

2. *His friend is interested:*

a. seninlʸe‿gʸitmékʸ‿istiyòrúm. — Seninle gitmek istiyorum.

b. bénimdè trấṣ‿olmám‿lʸá:zìm. — Benim de traş olmam lâzım.

3. *Mr. Gunduz wonders why:*

a. sinémaya‿gʸitmékʸ‿istiyórmúsùn? — Sinemaya gitmek istiyormusun?

b. né‿satin‿almák‿istiyòrsún? — Ne satın almak istiyorsun?

4. *His friend explains why:*

a. ét vé‿patátés‿almám‿lʸá:zìm. — Et ve patates almam lâzım.

b. bìr‿élʸbi:sé vé‿bir‿ayákkabi‿almám‿lʸá:zìm. — Bir elbise ve bir ayakkabı almam lâzım.

5. *Mr. Gunduz explains his motives:*

a. kárnìm‿áç. — Karnım aç.

b. bén bir‿ṣápká‿álacàim. — Ben bir şapka alacağim.

6. *On arriving at the clothing store, Mr. Gunduz asks the salesman:*

a. bú‿ṣàpká káç‿pàrà? — Bu şapka kaç para?

b. kirmızí‿ṣáràp úcúzmù? — Kırmızı şarap ucuzmu?

7. *The salesman answers:*

a. bú‿ṣàpká çók‿páhalì! — Bu şapka çok pahalı!

b. yálnız‿ón‿dört‿lʸìrá, éféndìm. — Yalnız on dört lira, efendim.

8. *Mr. Gunduz bargains:*

a. évèt. çók‿úcùz! déyilʸmì? — Evet. Çok ucuz. Değilmi?

b. ondán‿dahá‿ucuzú‿yókmù? — Ondan daha ucuzu yokmu?

9. *The salesman has something more in Mr. Gunduz's line, but he talks it down:*

a. háyìr, yálnız‿dahá‿pahálısí‿vàr. — Hayır, yalnız daha pahalısı var.

b. vár, fákàt búnún‿kadár‿iyì dèyilʸ. — Var, fakat bunun kadar iyi değil.

10. *Mr. Gunduz, unperturbed, explains what he wants it for:*

a. ziyá:nì‿yók. benim‿çók‿parám‿vàr. — Ziyanı yok. Benim çok param var.

b. ziyá:nì‿yók. yá:múrlú‿havalar-dá‿g^{y}iymék^y‿için‿istiyòrúm. — Ziyanı yok. Yağmurlu havalarda giymek için istiyorum.

11. *The salesman proposes something suited to Mr. Gunduz's purpose:*

a. öyl^{y}é‿isè, sizè‿úcúz vé‿dáyaniklí‿bir‿şápka‿búlacàim. — Öyle ise, size ucuz ve dayanıklı bir şapka bulacağım.

b. öyl^{y}é‿isè, sizè‿páhalí vé‿g^{y}ünéşl^{y}í‿havalardá‿g^{y}iymék^y‿için bir‿şápkà‿búlacàim. — Öyle ise, size pahalı ve güneşli havalarda giymek için bir şapka bulacağım.

12. *Mr. Gunduz's friend then asks about a suit:*

a. kişlík‿bir‿el^{y}bi:sé‿istiyòrúm. — Kışlık bir elbise istiyorum.

b. yázlík‿bir‿el^{y}bi:sé‿istiyòrúm. — Yazlık bir elbise istiyorum.

13. *The salesman asks for particulars:*

a. né‿rénk^y‿tércih‿ediyórsunuz? — Ne renk tercih ediyorsunuz?

b. bir‿ayákkabidámi‿istiyòrsunúz? — Bir ayakkabıdamı istiyorsunuz?

14. *Mr. Gunduz's friend specifies:*

a. kìrmizí. — Kırmızı.

b. l^{y}à: civért. — Lâcivert.

15. *When the salesman has brought it out, he asks:*

a. bú násìl. beyéniyórmúsunùz? — Bu nasıl? Beğeniyormusunuz?

b. bú‿şápkanın‿réng^{y}ì hoşunuzá‿g^{y}idiyórmù? — Bu şapkanın rengi hoşunuza gidiyormu?

16. *Mr. Gunduz's friend answers:*

a. şápka‿istémiyòrúm. — Şapka istemiyorum.

b. évèt. fénà:‿déyil^y. búnún‿fiyatì né‿kádàr? — Evet. Fena değil.Bunun fiyatı ne kadar?

17. *The salesman replies:*

a. páhalì‿déyilʸ. yirmí‿lʸìrá. — Pahalı değil. Yirmi lira.

b. çók‿úcùz! élʸlʸí‿lʸìrá. — Çok ucuz. Elli lira.

Section D—Listening In

1. What Did You Say?

Give your answers in Turkish for each of the exercises in the preceding section, when the Leader calls for them. Then, as the Leader calls for them, give the English equivalents of all the expressions in the exercise.

2. Word Study Check-Up

As you have done in the previous units, go back to the *Word Study* and give the correct Turkish for each English expression, without having to read it from the book. The Leader or one of the members of the group should read the English. As a final check the Leader will call for your answers to the exercises in the *Word Study Review* (Sec. C. 3).

3. Listening In

With your book closed, listen to the following conversations as read by the Guide or phonograph record. Repeat the Turkish immediately after hearing it. After the first repetition of each conversation, check up on the meaning of anything you do not understand, by asking someone else or by going back to the *Basic Sentences* if no one knows. Repeat again if necessary, then take parts and carry on the conversation.

1. *Ali invites Ahmet to go shopping.*

Record 23A, after 4th spiral.

àhmét—	álʸì, sénmisìn?	Ali senmisin?
	bú‿kádár‿erkʸén‿búrada‿né‿yápıyòrsún?	Bu kadar erken burada ne yapıyorsun?
àlʸí—	aliş‿vérişé‿gʸidiyòrúm.	Alış verişe gidiyorum.
àhmét—	né‿aliş‿veriş‿yápacàksin?	Ne alış veriş yapacaksın?
àlʸí—	èlʸbi:sé, şápkà vé‿ayákkabi‿álacàim.	Elbise, şapka ve ayakkabı alacağım.
	benimlʸe‿gʸelʸírmisìn?	Benimle gelirmisin?

àhmét—	évèt. gʸélʸirìm.	Evet. Gelirim.
	dáhá‿évvèlʸ néreyé‿gʸidecèkʸsin?	Daha evvel nereye gideceksin?
àlʸi—	dáhá‿évvèlʸ élʸbi:sé‿álacàim.	Daha evvel elbise alacağım.

2. *Buying a suit.*

àhmét—	gʸün‿áydín. satıci‿sizmisinìz?	Gün aydın. Satıcı sizmisiniz?
sàticí—	gʸün‿áydín, éféndìm.	Gün aydın, efendim.
	évèt, bénìm.	Evet, benim.
	né‿árzù‿ediyórsunuz?	Ne arzu ediyorsunuz?
àhmét—	àrkadáşím bir‿élʸbi:sé‿istiyòr.	Arkadaşım bir elbise istiyor.
sàticí—	búrayá‿bùyrún, éféndìm.	Buraya buyrun, efendim.
	elʸbi:sé‿násil‿ólsùn?	Elbise nasıl olsun?
àlʸí—	yazlik‿bir‿élʸbi:sé‿istiyòrúm.	Yazlık bir elbise istiyorum.
sàticí—	né‿rénkʸ‿tércìh‿ediyórsunuz?	Ne renk tercih ediyorsunuz?
àlʸí—	lʸá:civért‿rénkʸtè vé‿önü‿áçík.	Lâcivert renkte ve önü açık.
sàticí—	maálʸésèf, lʸà:civért önü‿açik‿élʸbi:semìz‿yók.	Maalesef, lâcivert önü açık elbisemiz yok.
	ó‿rénkʸtè yálnız‿kúrvazé‿vàr.	O renkte yalnız kurvaze var.
àlʸí—	başká‿né‿rénkʸ‿élʸbi:selʸériniz‿vár?	Başka ne renk elbiseleriniz var?
sàticí—	çók‿gʸüzélʸ‿kurşu:ni:‿bir‿élʸbi:semiz‿vàr.	Çok güzel kurşuni bir elbisemiz var.
àlʸí—	lʸútfèn, gʸöstérinìz!	Lûtfen gösteriniz!
àhmét—	násìl, álʸì? beyéniyórmúsùn?	Nasıl, Ali? Beğeniyormusun?
àlʸí—	fénà:‿déyílʸ. fiyati‿né‿kádàr?	Fena değil. Fiyatı ne kadar?
sàticí—	yirmi‿dókúz‿lʸìrá, ón‿yedi‿kúrùş.	Yirmi dokuz lira, on yedi kuruş.
àlʸí—	bú‿çók‿páhalì.	Bu çok pahalı.
sàticí—	háyìr, éféndìm, dèyilʸ.	Hayır, efendim, değil.

àlʸí—	pékʸ‿iyì, àlacáìm. işté‿pàrá.	Pek iyi, alacağım. İşte para.
sàticí—	teşékʸkʸűr‿edèrim, éféndim!	Teşekkür ederim, efendim!

3. *Looking for a hat.*

Record 23B, beginning.

àhmét—	şimdi‿né‿àlacàksin?	Şimdi ne alacaksın?
àlʸí—	bir‿şápkà‿almák‿istiyòrúm.	Bir şapka almak istiyorum.
	benimlʸe‿gʸélʸecékʸsin, déyílʸmì?	Benimle geleceksin, değilmi?
àhmét—	évèt, seninlʸe‿gʸélʸecéyim.	Evet, seninle geleceğim.
àlʸí—	satıci‿nérédè?	Satıcı nerede?
	bú‿kurşu:ni:‿şàpkaya‿bákmák‿istiyòrúm.	Bu kurşuni şapkaya bakmak istiyorum.
sàticí—	búyrùn, éféndim.	Buyrun, edendim.
àlʸí—	bú bir‿áz‿büyűkʸ, fákàt, ziyá:nì‿yók.	Bu bir az büyük, fakat, ziyanı yok.
	búnún‿fiyatì né‿kádàr?	Bunun fiyatı ne kadar?
sàticí—	ón‿alti‿lʸìrá, éféndim.	On altı lira, efendim.
àlʸí—	bir‿áz‿páhalí, déyílʸmì?	Bir az pahalı, değilmi?
	ondán‿dahá‿ucuzú‿yókmù?	Ondan daha ucuzu yokmu?
sàticí—	évèt fákàt bunún‿kadár‿iyì‿bir‿şàpka‿dé-yílʸ.	Evet, fakat bunun kadar iyi bir şapka değil.
àlʸí—	ziyá:nì‿yók.	Ziyanı yok.
	ya:murlú‿havalardá‿gʸiymékʸ‿içìn dàyaniklí vé‿ucúz‿bir‿şéy‿istiyòrúm.	Yağmurlu havalarda giymek için dayanıklı ve ucuz bir şey istiyorum.
sàticí—	búrádà öylʸè‿bir‿şàpka‿yók.	Burada öyle bir şapka yok.
àlʸí—	pékʸ‿iyì. teşékʸkʸűr‿edèriz.	Pek iyi. Teşekkür ederiz.
	állahá‿ısmárladìk.	Allaha ısmarladık.

4. *Planning the evening.*

àl^{y}í—	şìmdi‿çóráp, mèndíl^y, vé‿ayákkabı‿almám‿l^{y}a:zìm.	Şimdi çorap, mendil, ve ayakkabı almam lâzım.
	şápkayı‿başká‿bir‿g^{y}ǘn‿árıyacàim.	Şapkayı başka bir gün arıyacağım.
	sén né‿yápacàksin?	Sen ne yapacaksın?
àhmét—	bír‿áz‿sònrá kárím‿g^{y}él^{y}ecèk^y.	Bir az sonra karım gelecek.
	benimde‿onúnla‿aliş‿verişé‿g^{y}itmém‿l^{y}á:zìm.	Benim de onunla alış verişe gitmem lâzım.
	bú‿ákşàm sén vé‿bayàn‿g^{y}ündǘz né‿yápacàksıniz?	Bu akşam sen ve bayan Gündüz ne yapacaksınız?
àl^{y}í—	biz‿sinémayá‿g^{y}idecèyiz.	Biz sinemaya gideceğiz.
àhmét—	bizíml^{y}è hakki‿il^{y}é‿şük^{y}rüyenin‿eviné‿g^{y}idérmisiniz?	Bizimle Hakkı ile Şükrüyenin evine gidermisiniz?
àl^{y}í—	teşék^{y}k^{y}ǘr‿edèriz.	Teşekkür ederiz.
	g^{y}idérìz.	Gideriz.
	órada‿dáhá‿iyi‿éyl^{y}enìriz.	Orada daha iyi eğleniriz.

5. *At the party.*

àl^{y}í—	mérhábà, hákkì!	Merhaba, Hakkı!
şǜk^{y}rüyé—	mérhábà, fátmà!	Merhaba, Fatma!
àhmét—	erk^{y}énmi‿g^{y}éldìk^y?	Erkenmi geldik?
hàkkí—	háyìr, háyìr! búyrùn!	Hayır, hayır! Buyrun!
àl^{y}í—	çocuklár‿nérédè?	Çocuklar nerede?
şǜk^{y}rüyé—	ódalàrindalár.	Odalarındalar.
fàtmá—	k^{y}üçük^y‿kızınızi‿çók‿g^{y}örmék^y‿istiyòrúm.	Küçük kızınızı çok görmek istiyorum.
şǜk^{y}rüyé—	g^{y}él^{y}ìn! öbür‿ódayá‿g^{y}idel^{y}ìm, g^{y}örǘrsünǜz.	Gelin! Öbür odaya gidelim, görürsünüz.
fàtmá—	çók‿g^{y}üzél^y‿bir‿kíz‿ólacàk!	Çok güzel bir kız olacak!
	onú‿benim‿ó:lumá‿álalìm!	Onu benim oğluma alalım!

Section E—Conversation

1. Covering the Turkish in Basic Sentences (Individual Study)

Cover the Turkish of the *Basic Sentences* and practice saying the Turkish equivalents of the English expressions.

2. Vocabulary Check-Up

Give the Turkish expressions for the English equivalents in the *Basic Sentences* as the Leader calls for them.

3. Conversation

As you have done in the *Conversation* in the previous units, begin to converse by following the models outlined below fairly closely; then change the situations somewhat. Invent new combinations of subject matter.

1. Mr. Gunduz goes shopping.

   Mr. Gunduz meets his friend Ahmet, and they exchange greetings. Ahmet asks where he's going. Mr. Gunduz says he's going shopping and invites Ahmet to come along. Ahmet accepts and they go on talking about what they want to buy. At the store they find the salesman, explain what they want. The salesman shows them the merchandise (shoes, socks, handkerchiefs, a suit, etc.). They ask about the price, color, size, etc. They buy what they want and leave.

2. Planning the evening.

   Mr. Gunduz invites Ahmet and his wife for dinner. Ahmet accepts, talks about the time, compliments Mr. Gunduz on his wife's cooking, etc. They take their leave.

Section F—Conversation (*Cont.*)

1. Conversation (*Cont.*)

Continue the conversations started in Section E, with a review of parts 1 and 2 of the section if necessary.

2. Questions and Answers

First run through the *Listening In* once more. Then answer the following questions when the Guide asks you, or take turns asking them of others and answering them:

1.	1.	àl^{y}í áhmét‿il^{y}è iyi‿árkadáşmidìr?	Ali Ahmet ile iyi arkadaşmıdır?
	2.	àl^{y}í bú‿sábàh néreyé‿g^{y}idiyòr?	Ali bu sabah nereye gidiyor?
	3.	né‿álacàk?	Ne alacak?
	4.	k^{y}ím‿onúnla‿g^{y}itmék^{y}‿istiyòr?	Kim onunla gitmek istiyor?
	5.	àl^{y}í dáhá‿évvèl^{y} né‿satin‿almák‿istiyòr?	Ali daha evvel ne satın almak istiyor?
2.	6.	ál^{y}inin‿él^{y}bi:sesì násil‿ólsùn?	Alinin elbisesi nasıl olsun?
	7.	né‿rénk^{y}‿tércìh‿ediyór?	Ne renk tercih ediyor?
	8.	sàtıcinín ó‿rénk^{y}tè el^{y}bi:sesi‿vármì?	Satıcının o renkte elbisesi varmı?
	9.	öyl^{y}é‿isè né‿renk^{y}té‿ólsùn?	Öyle ise ne renkte olsun?
	10.	àl^{y}í bú‿el^{y}bi:seyi‿beyéniyórmù?	Ali bu elbiseyi beğeniyormu?
	11.	búnún‿fiyatì né‿kádàr?	Bunun fiyatı ne kadar?
3.	12.	óndán‿sònrá né‿álacàk?	Ondan sonra ne alacak?
	13.	àhmét onúnla‿g^{y}él^{y}ecék^{y}mì?	Ahmet onunla gelecekmi?
	14.	néyé‿bakmák‿istiyòr?	Neye bakmak istiyor?
	15.	bú‿şàpká násìl?	Bu şapka nasıl?
	16.	úcúzmù?	Ucuzmu?
	17.	ondán‿dahá‿ucuzú‿yókmù?	Ondan daha ucuzu yokmu?
	18.	úcúz‿şàpká iyimì?	Ucuz şapka iyimi?
	19.	né‿için bú‿şápkayi‿istiyòr?	Ne için bu şapkayı istiyor?
	20.	órádà öyl^{y}é‿bir‿şápka‿vármì?	Orada öyle bir şapka varmı?
4.	21.	né‿vákìt şápkayi‿árıyacàk?	Ne vakit şapkayı arıyacak?
	22.	bír‿áz‿sònrá k^{y}ím‿g^{y}él^{y}ecèk?	Bir az sonra kim gelecek?

23. ónúnlà àhmédín néreyé‿gʸitmesí‿lʸá:zìm?	Onunla Ahmedin nereye gitmesi lâzım?
24. ó‿ákşàm báy vé‿báyàn‿gʸündúz né‿yápacáklàr?	O akşam bay ve bayan Gündüz ne yapacaklar?
25. nérédè dáhá‿iyí‿éylʸenírlʸèr?	Nerede daha iyi eğlenirler?
5. 26. misà:fírlʸér erkʸénmí‿gʸéldilʸèr?	Misafirler erkenmi geldiler?
27. çocuklár‿nérédè?	Çocuklar nerede?
28. fàtmá kʸimí‿gʸörmékʸ‿ístiyòr?	Fatma kimi görmek istiyor?
29. onú‿gʸörmékʸ‿íçin néreyé‿gʸídiyórlàr?	Onu görmek için nereye gidiyorlar?
30. násil‿bír‿kiz‿ólacàk?	Nasıl bir kız olacak?
31. onú‿kʸimé‿almák‿ístiyórlàr?	Onu kime almak istiyorlar?

FINDER LIST

àçík (açık)	open
al- . . . (al- . . .) (aor. *-ır-*)	get; buy; engage, betroth
álìş‿vèríş (alış veriş)	shopping (lit. take and give)
ara- . . . (ara- . . .)	look for
árıyacáìm (arıyacağım)	I'll look for it (with *ı* for *a* before future *-y-*)
ayákkàbì (ayakkabı)	shoe
beyen- . . . (beğen- . . .) (aor. *-ir-*)	like
bul- . . . (bul- . . .) (aor. *-ur-*)	find
**bun* (bu)	this
bú‿kádàr (bu kadar)	this much, this, so
bùnún (bunun)	of this, (to) this
búnún‿kádàr (bunun kadar)	as this one (lit. up to this)

çòráp (çorap)	sock(s); stockings
dàyanìklí (dayanıklı)	durable
èlʸbì:sé (elbise)	clothing, clothes; (a) suit
fènà: (fena)	bad
fìyát (fiyat)	price
gʸit- . . . (git- . . .) (aor. *-er-*)	(preceded by dative) go (to)
alìş‿vérişé‿gʸidiyòrúm. (Alış verişe gidiyorum.)	I'm going shopping.
gʸiy- . . . (giy- . . .) (aor. *-er-*)	put on; wear
hàvá (hava)	air; weather
hàválár (havalar)	airs; weather
yà:múrlú‿hávalárdà (yağmurlu havalarda)	in rainy weather
kíş (kış)	winter
kìşlík (kışlık)	winter (time)
kişlík‿bir‿élʸbi:sè (kışlık bir elbise)	a winter (time) suit
kùrşù:ní: (kurşuni)	gray (lit. leaden)
kùrvàzé (kurvaze)	double-breasted (suit)
lʸà:civért (lâcivert)	navy-blue
mèndílʸ (mendil)	handkerchief(s)
ol- . . . (ol- . . .) (aor. *-ur-*)	be; become
òlsún! (olsun!)	let it be!

*on (o) — he, she, it; that
    òndán (ondan) — (from) than that

ón‿àltì (on altı) — sixteen

ón‿dȍrt (on dört) — fourteen

ón‿yėdȉ (on yedi) — seventeen

ő̇n (ön) — front
    ő̇nů‿áçík (önü açık) — single-breasted (lit. its front open)
    önű‿áçík‿bi̍r‿él^{y}bi̍:sè (önü açık bir elbise) — a single-breasted suit

ȍyl^{y}é (öyle) — thus, so
    ő̇yl^{y}é‿bȉr (öyle bir) — such a

**pàhá* (paha) — cost; price
    pàhálí (pahalı) — expensive, costly
    dȧhá‿pahȧlısì (daha pahalısı) — a more expensive one (of them)

rénk^y (renk) — color
    né‿rènk^y (ne renk) — what color
    ó‿rėnk^{y}tè (o renkte) — in that color

sànȧ́ (sana) — (to) you (inf.) (see *sen*)

sat- . . . (sat- . . .) (aor. *-ar-*) — sell
    sàticí (satıcı) — salesman

satın‿al- . . . (satın al- . . .) (aor. *-ır-*) — buy

sén (sen) — you (informal to one person)

sènin (senin) — your, yours; you

séninl^{y}è (seninle) — with you

sénmisin (senmisin?) — [is] it you?

şápkà (şapka) — hat

tercih‿et- . . . (tercih et- . . .) (aor. *-er-*) — prefer

traş‿ol- . . . (traş ol- . . .) (aor. *-ur-*) — be (get) shaved, shave

tráş‿ólmàk (traş olmak) — to be (get) shaved

tráş‿ólmaà (traş olmağa) — (for) to be (get) shaved

tráş‿olmaá‿g^{y}idiyòrúm (traş olmağa gidiyorum) — I'm going to get shaved

ùcúz (ucuz) — cheap

dáhá‿úcùz (daha ucuz) — cheaper

dáhá‿úcuzù (daha ucuzu) — a cheaper one (of them)

yáz (yaz) — summer

yàzlík (yazlık) — summer (time)

yázlík‿bir‿él^{y}bi:sè (yazlık bir elbise) — a summer (time) suit

yìrmi (yirmi) — twenty

yirmì‿dókúz (yirmi dokuz) — twenty-nine

zìyá:n (ziyan) — waste; expense; deficit, loss

ziyà:ní (ziyanı) — its waste, its loss

ziyá:nì‿yók (ziyanı yok) — it doesn't matter (lit. there is no loss)

REVIEW

SECTION A—WORD STUDY REVIEW

This section is just like Section A of Unit 6. Work through the exercises individually following the instructions carefully, reading aloud the completed or altered forms or sentences. Do not write anything down. Be prepared to do on sight any one of the exercises, when your Leader calls on you.

I. Fill in the blanks with the correct form of the *locative* ending:

1. nére – –‿yeméky‿yiyecèyiz?	Nere – – yemek yiyeceğiz?
2. gyöky – –‿kará‿bulútlár‿vàr.	Gök – – kara bulutlar var.
3. ótelyín‿ódaları – – – hávlulár‿vàr.	Otelin odaları – – – havlular var.
4. áhmedín‿elyi – – – ikyi‿élymá‿vàr.	Ahmedin eli – – – iki elma var.
5. oda – –midìr?	Oda – –mıdır?

II. Make questions out of these statements, adding the *interrogative* ending to the italicized *nouns:*

1. *otèlydé*‿yémèky‿yiyecéyiz.	*Otelde* yemek yiyeceğiz.
2. *şàráp*‿istiyòrsunúz.	*Şarap* istiyorsunuz.
3. *bàlík*‿yapárlàr.	*Balık* yaparlar.
4. *bírà*‿içérlyèr.	*Bira* içerler.
5. *sinémayá*‿gyidérlyèr.	*Sinemaya* giderler.

III. With the following roots make "*let's do it*" forms:

(Example: yüz- . . . 'swim' : yùzélyím! 'let's swim!')

1. eylyen- . . .	eğlen- . . .
2. iç- . . .	iç- . . .

3. ara- . . .	ara- . . .
4. unut- . . .	unut- . . .
5. yıka- . . .	yıka- . . .
6. traş‿ol- . . .	traş ol- . . .
7. de- . . .	de- . . .
8. akıt- . . .	akıt- . . .
9. kalk- . . .	kalk- . . .
10. ov- . . .	ov- . . .

IV. Fill in the blanks with the correct form of the "*do it*" ending:

1. baná‿bú‿şápkayı‿g^{y}ö́stér----, l^{y}útfèn.	Bana bu şapkayı göster----, lûtfen.
2. çócúklàr! saçlarınızi‿tárá-(--)--!	Çocuklar! Saçlarınızı tara-(--)--!
3. pék^y‿iyì, báyàn‿kár! bizé‿tarai‿vér----, l^{y}útfèn.	Pek iyi, bayan Kar! Bize tarağı ver----, lûtfen.
4. yüzl^{y}érinizídé‿yıkà-(--)--!	Yüzlerinizi de yıka-(--)--!
5. báylàr, báşlá-----!	Baylar, başla-----!
6. l^{y}útfèn, yávâş‿yaváş‿konùş----!	Lûtfen, yavaş yavaş konuş----!
7. sáàt‿üçté bú‿ódadà tóplán----!	Saat üçte bu odada toplan----!
8. çócúklàr! bizíml^{y}e‿berá:bér‿g^{y}èl^y(--)--!	Çocuklar! Bizimle beraber gel(--)--!
9. báylàr! trámvayá‿bín----!	Baylar! Tramvaya bin----!
10. çócúklàr! tóplántıyá‿g^{y}ìd(--)--!	Çocuklar! Toplantıya gid(--)--!

V. Change the following sentences to *negative* by using the correct forms of the negative ending:

1. búraya‿g^{y}él^{y}íniz!	Buraya geliniz!
2. óradan‿ínìn!	Oradan inin!
3. bú‿şarabi‿içel^{y}ìm!	Bu şarabı içelim!

4. ìș‿árıyálìm! | İş arıyalım!
5. yüzüyóruz. | Yüzüyoruz.
6. ėylyeniyórlàr. | Eğleniyorlar.

VI. Make *phrase-compounds* with the following pairs of words:

(Example: ėlybi:sé 'clothing', fìrçá 'brush' : ėlybi:sé‿firçasì 'clothes-brush')

1. şàráp, şìşé | şarap, şişe
2. yüzmé, vàkit (vakt-) | yüzme, vakit (vakt-)
3. bàlík, yèmékʸ (yemey-) | balık, yemek (yemeğ-)
4. èlymá, àáç (aaç-) | elma, ağaç (ağac-)
5. şàráp, lyistè | şarap, liste

Add the "my", "your", "our" possessive endings to the resulting phrase compounds.

VII. Fill in the blanks with the correct forms of the *definite objective* endings;

1. saçlarımız–‿táramamíz‿lyá:zìm. | Saçlarımız– taramamız lâzım.
2. lyútfèn, şáráp‿şişesi––‿gyetiriniz! | Lûtfen, şarap şişesi–– getiriniz!
3. yüzü––‿yıkamák‿istiyòr. | Yüzü–– yıkamak istiyor.
4. bú‿şárab– né‿vakit‿içecèkysiniz? | Bu şarab– ne vakit içeceksiniz?
5. süt–‿kyim‿içecèky? | Süt– kim içecek?
6. şükyrüye––‿kyim‿sévèr? | Şükrüye–– kim sever?
7. lyeylya:––‿bén‿sevèrim. | Leylâ–– ben severim.

VIII. Fill in the blanks with the correct forms of the *-me, -ma* action noun ending, and of the possessive endings "my", "our", "his", "your":

1. saçlar–(n)i‿tára–––‿lyá:zìm. | Saçlar–(n)ı tara––– lâzım.
2. ev–(n)ė‿gyir–––‿lyá:zìm. | Ev–(n)e gir––– lâzım.

IX. Fill in the blanks with the correct forms of the *infinitive* endings:

1. ó dáima‿sú‿iç–·–‿istèr.	O daima su iç---- ister.
2. dáhà‿érkʸén, fákàt bírá‿iç---·‿báşlıyalìm!	Daha erken, fakat bira iç---- başlıyalım!
3. hér‿gʸǜn plʸajá‿yüz---·‿gʸidèriz.	Her gün plâja yüz---- gideriz.
4. sáàt‿áltıdá konúş--·‿báşlıyacàk.	Saat altıda konuş---- başlıyacak.
5. ikʸinci‿katá‿çik-·-‿istiyòrúm.	İkinci kata çık--- istiyorum.

X. Turn these forms into "call-forms" by making the *vocative* change:

1. şǜkʸrüyé.	Şükrüye.
2. òsmán.	Osman.
3. kàrí.	Karı.
4. ò:lúm.	Oğlum.

XI. Fill in the blanks with the proper forms of the *future* endings:

1. yemékʸtén‿sònrá içmeyé‿báşl(a)----·-làr.	Yemekten sonra içmeğe başl(a)-----lar
2. saát‿áltí‿buçúktà yémékʸ‿y(é)----·-iz.	Saat altı buçukta yemek y(e)-----iz.
3. óraya‿gʸid--·-im.	Oraya gid----im.
4. bú‿ákşàm bày‿kár konǜş·--·-.	Bu akşam bay Kar konuş----.
5. gʸör--·-siniz.	Gör----siniz.

Make questions out of these statements.
Change the statements from positive to negative.
Now change the negative statements into questions.

XII. Fill in the blanks with the correct forms of the *attributive* ending:

1. bú‿ótelʸin bányo--‿odalari‿vármì?	Bu otelin banyo-- odaları varmı?
2. bú‿filʸimin‿ismì çocúk-·‿kìz.	Bu filimin ismi "Çocuk-- Kız."

3. bú‿gʸûn havá‿gʸünéṣ−−́dìr.	Bu gün hava güneş−−dir.
4. ónún‿yüzû dàimá‿tráṣ−−́.	Onun yüzü daima traş−−.
5. bén‿hák−−́yìm.	Ben hak−−yım.

XIII. Fill in the blanks with the correct forms of the *privative* ending:

1. bú‿ótèlʸ, maálʸésèf, ṣímdi‿sú−−́−dùr.	Bu otel, maalesef, şimdi su−−−dur.
2. onún‿évì‿yók. év−−́−dìr.	Onun evi yok. Ev−−−dir.
3. sízín‿káhveníz ṣekʸér−−́−‿ólsùn!	Sizin kahveniz şeker−−− olsun!
4. kʸüçûkʸ‿kárdeṣìm dìṣ−−́−. yálnız‿sût‿íçèr.	Küçük kardeşim diş−−−. Yalnız süt içer.
5. bú‿hávà çók‿sicàk vé‿yá:mùr−−́−.	Bu hava çok sıcak ve yağmur−−−.

XIV. Change the following phrases with independent word *ìlʸé* (ile) 'with' to single words with the *concomitive* ending:

1. díz‿ílʸè	diz ile
2. élʸbí:sé‿ílʸè	elbise ile
3. ayákkabi‿ílʸè	ayakkabı ile
4. kíz‿ílʸè	kız ile
5. méyvá‿ílʸè	meyva ile
6. bányó‿ílʸè	banyo ile
7. ṣáráp‿ílʸè	şarap ile
8. hávlú‿ílʸè	havlu ile
9. kárdéṣ‿ílʸè	kardeş ile
10. kúṣ‿ílʸè	kuş ile

Give the Turkish equivalents of "with whom, with me, with you (informal), with you (formal), with us, with him, with them."

XV. Fill in the blanks with the correct form of the *dative* ending:

1. saát‿sek^{y}iz–‿yédí‿kálà. — Saat sekiz– yedi kala.
2. onlar–‿bakíyórlàr. — Onlar– bakıyorlar.
3. bú‿ákşàm toplantı––‿g^{y}idérmísinìz? — Bu akşam toplantı–– gidermisiniz?
4. èvímíz k^{y}öşe––‿çók‿yákìn. — Evimiz köşe–– çok yakın.
5. k^{y}üçûk^y‿çócu– bíra‿vérméyinìz! — Küçük çocuğ– bira vermeyiniz!
6. g^{y}ö–‿çikacákmíyìz? — Göğ– çıkacakmıyız?
7. tavúk‿sú‿íçèr vé‿állah–‿bákàr. — Tavuk su içer ve Allah– bakar.
8. yüzmey–‿g^{y}ídecék^{y}míyìz? — Yüzmeğ– gidecekmiyiz?
9. şímdi‿konúşma–‿bâşlıyòr. — Şimdi konuşmağ– başlıyor.
10. b(e)n–‿bír‿k^{y}ibrít‿verírmísinìz? — B(e)n– bir kibrit verirmisiniz?

XVI. Change the aorist forms in the following sentences to ***negative***:

1. şáráp‿içmék^y‿ístèr. — Şarap içmek ister.
2. hér‿sábàh bú‿g^{y}üzél^y‿mánzarayá‿bákàr. — Her sabah bu güzel manzaraya bakar.
3. bén kirmızí‿el^{y}bi:sé‿g^{y}iyèrím. — Ben kırmızı elbise giyerim.
4. g^{y}él^{y}írìz! — Geliriz!
5. hér‿g^{y}ûn g^{y}üzél^{y}lerí‿g^{y}örûrsünüz. — Her gün güzelleri görürsünüz.
6. arkadaşlará‿istánbulú‿g^{y}österírl^{y}èr. — Arkadaşlara İstanbulu gösterirler.
7. dáima‿öyl^{y}é‿báşlàrsin. — Daima öyle başlarsın.

Change the above sentences to questions.
After changing them to negative, then make the negative forms interrogative.

XVII. Fill in the blanks in the following sentences, with the "*informal*" *you*-ending:

1. sén hér‿g^{y}ûn g^{y}ül^{y}ér–––. — Sen her gün güler–––.
2. sén íyí‿bír‿çocùk–––. — Sen iyi bir çocuk–––.

3. néreyė‿kóṣuyȍr –·–?	Nereye koşuyor---?
4. órȧdȁn néyi‿gʸörecȅkʸ –·–?	Oradan neyi görecek---?
5. sén öylė‿bir‿ṣėy‿déméz –·–.	Sen öyle bir şey demez---.
6. búrȧdȁn néyė‿bakȁr –·–?	Buradan neye bakar---?

XVIII. Fill in the blanks with the correct forms of the *ablative* ending:

1. ískʸélʸe –·– néyė‿binecȅkʸsin?	İskele--- neye bineceksin?
2. sabah –·–‿ȧkṣamá‿kȧdȁr bírȧ‿içȅrsin.	Sabah--- akşama kadar bira içersin.
3. bun –·–‿dahȧ‿ucuzú‿yókmȕ?	Bun--- daha ucuzu yokmu?
4. öylʸé‿yemeyi ––·–‿sȍnrá né‿yȧpacȁiz?	Öğle yemeği---- sonra ne yapacağız?
5. ben –·–‿né‿istiyȍrsún?	Ben--- ne istiyorsun?

Section B—Conversation

Take parts and work through the following outlined conversations. When you can do them easily, branch out, and include anything discussed in the previous units.

1. Ahmet meets Tom and Mrs. Carr at the train.

   Ahmet welcomes Tom and Mrs. Carr. They return the greeting. Tom introduces his wife and Ahmet acknowledges the introduction. They talk about how to get to the hotel, how far it is, etc. They make plans for the day.

2. They go to the hotel.

   Mrs. Carr says she's hungry. Tom suggests that they go first to the hotel, then to eat, and then to the movies. Ahmet agrees. They take a street car, after waiting a while, and letting several cars pass. As they go by Ahmet explains where each one goes. Tom wonders where they'll eat. Ahmet tells them about the hotel-restaurant, the food and drink there, meal hours and so on.

3. At the hotel.

   As they arrive at the hotel, Tom checks on the time. They find the manager, who shows them a room. They look it over, comment on the view of the Bosporus, the ships going by, etc. Mrs. Carr reminds the manager to send towels. The manager excuses the oversight. Ahmet says good-bye, and they agree to meet in the restaurant.

4. Cleaning up.

Mrs. Carr comments on the heat, and asks Tom if he wants to bathe. Tom says he does and asks where various things are. Mrs. Carr finds the things, reminds him he ought to shave. Tom makes a remark about clean-shaven faces. They call back and forth for various things, locate them, finally finish cleaning up. Tom goes to look at the view, while waiting for Mrs. Carr. They exchange remarks about the weather.

5. Eating.

Tom and Mrs. Carr go down to eat, ask their way to the restaurant. The manager directs them. They find Ahmet there, ask for a table for three. They take their places and ask for a menu. Ahmet asks for the wine list. They order the main dish, side dishes, drinks, coffee and dessert. They tell the waiter how they want their coffee. They smoke. The waiter returns with the food. They finish, call for the check, and leave.

SECTION C—LISTENING IN (QUESTIONS)

Listen to the Guide or the phonograph record as each one of the conversations is read. The second time listen carefully for points you may have missed the first time. Then answer the questions, which are listed below, on the particular conversation.

Record 24A, beginning.

1. *Ali Gunduz helps Mr. Carr find a hotel.*

1. bày‿kár néreyė‿g^{y}itmėk^y‿i̍stiyòr?	Bay Kar nereye gitmek istiyor?
2. néredė‿úcùz vė‿iyi̍‿bi̍r‿ótél^y‿vàr?	Nerede ucuz ve iyi bir otel var?
3. bányolu‿odalari‿vármì?	Banyolu odaları varmı?
4. g^{y}ündel^{y}iyi̍‿káç‿párà?	Gündeliği kaç para?
5. ótel^{y}é‿yákìn bi̍r‿l^{y}okánta‿vármì?	Otele yakın bir lokanta varmı?
6. bày‿kár yemek^{y}l^{y}erini̍‿néredė‿yi̍yecèk^y?	Bay Kar yemeklerini nerede yiyecek?

2. *Two days later.*

1. òdá báy‿karin‿hoşuná‿g^{y}i̍diyórmù?	Oda bay Karın hoşuna gidiyormu?
2. odanin‿nėsí‿çók‿g^{y}üzèl^y?	Odanın nesi çok güzel?

3. bày‿kár l^{y}okántanın‿yemek^{y}l^{y}erini‿beyéniyórmù? — Bay Kar lokantanın yemeklerini beğeniyormu?
4. şèhír báy‿karín‿hoşuná‿g^{y}idiyórmù? — Şehir bay Karın hoşuna gidiyormu?
5. àl^{y}í báy‿kará‿néyí‿g^{y}österecèk^{y}? — Ali bay Kara neyi gösterecek?

3. *Ali is going to show Mr. Carr the town.*
   1. báy‿kárín‿árkadaşì dáimà né‿yapmák‿istiyòr? — Bay Karın arkadaşı daima ne yapmak istiyor?
   2. hér‿g^{y}ǜn néreyé‿g^{y}idèr? — Her gün nereye gider?
   3. bày‿kár né‿yapmák‿istiyòr? — Bay Kar ne yapmak istiyor?
   4. öyl^{y}é‿isè né‿yápacáklàr? — Öyle ise ne yapacaklar?
   5. k^{y}ímin‿yemék^{y}l^{y}erì báy‿karín‿hóşuná‿g^{y}idiyòr? — Kimin yemekleri bay Karın hoşuna gidiyor?
   6. k^{y}ímin‿kárısì iyi‿yémék^{y}‿yápàr? — Kimin karısı iyi yemek yapar?
   7. karısının‿nésí‿vàr? — Karısının nesi var?

Record 24B, beginning.

4. *Mr. and Mrs. Carr prepare for guests.*
   1. bú‿ákşàm báy‿karín‿nél^{y}erí‿g^{y}él^{y}ecèk^{y}? — Bu akşam bay Karın neleri gelecek?
   2. evdé‿içecék^{y}‿bír‿şéy‿vármì? — Evde içecek bir şey varmı?
   3. öyl^{y}é‿isè né‿almák‿l^{y}á:zìm? — Öyle ise ne almak lâzım?
   4. başká‿né‿l^{y}á:zìm? — Başka ne lâzım?
   5. nédé‿yòk? — Ne de yok?
   6. báyàn‿kár né‿istiyòr? — Bayan Kar ne istiyor?
   7. bày‿kár başká‿bír‿şéy‿istiyórmù? — Bay Kar başka bir şey istiyormu?
5. *Mr. Day looks for a job.*
   1. bày‿g^{y}ündǘz né‿árıyòr? — Bay Gündüz ne arıyor?
   2. néredé‿árıyòr? — Nerede arıyor?
   3. ó né‿iş‿yápàr? — O ne iş yapar?

4. fákàt, né‿yápacàk?	Fakat, ne yapacak?
5. oná‿káç‿pará‿vérecék^{y}l^{y}èr?	Ona kaç para verecekler?
6. bày‿g^{y}ündúz èvl^{y}ímì?	Bay Gündüz evlimi?
7. ònún káç‿ta:né‿çocuú‿vàr?	Onun kaç tane çocuğu var?

6. *Getting in out of the rain.*

1. né‿yapmaá‿báşlıyòr?	Ne yapmağa başlıyor?
2. né‿yápalìm?	Ne yapalım?
3. ó‿sinèmadá né‿g^{y}östériyórlàr?	O sinemada ne gösteriyorlar?
4. bú‿fil^{y}ìm násìl?	Bu filim nasıl?
5. fil^{y}imín‿ismì‿né?	Filimin ismi ne?
6. sinéma‿násìl?	Sinema nasıl?
7. àl^{y}í né‿istiyòr?	Ali ne istiyor?
8. öyl^{y}é‿isè né‿yápalìm?	Öyle ise ne yapalım?
9. yà:múr şimdi‿né‿yápacàk?	Yağmur şimdi ne yapacak?
10. g^{y}ünéş né‿yapmaá‿báşlıyòr?	Güneş ne yapmağa başlıyor?
11. yá:múrdán‿sònrá havá‿násil‿ólacàk?	Yağmurdan sonra hava nasıl olacak?
12. fená:mi‿ólùr?	Fenamı olur?

SECTION D—TRUE-FALSE

Records 25A and 25B.

This section is a true-false quiz exactly like the one in Unit 6, except that the first item is not a practice item. Prepare a piece of paper with numbers from 1 to 40 and mark the statements that you will hear from your Guide or the phonograph record either *T* or *F*. After you finish the quiz, the Leader will give the correct answers for each statement. Check your paper and give your score to your Leader. He will figure out the average for your group. If your score is less than the average number of correct answers or less than 80% correct, you need more review of the previous units.

Spend the rest of the time going over the items on which you had difficulty.

KEY TO EXERCISES AND TESTS

The following pages give in condensed form a Key to the exercises contained in the *Word Study Review*, *What Would You Say*, and *Conversation* Sections of each regular Unit, and to the tests and exercises contained in the Review Units. You will also find here the tests themselves, so that you can read them even if you have no guide.

Each part of the Key is identified by a heading giving the Unit and the Section in which the exercise occurs.

Unit 1. What Would You Say? (Pages 20–21)

1. b	7. a	13. a	19. a
2. a	8. b	14. b	20. b
3. b	9. c	15. a	21. b
4. a	10. a	16. a	22. b
5. c	11. b	17. a	
6. a	12. b	18. a	

Unit 2. Word Study Review (Page 57)

1. áh-mét-tìr	bú-dùr	ná-sil-dìr
ál-láh-tìr	dé-yil^y-dìr	ṣá-ráp-tìr
ál-tí-dìr	k^{y}íb-rít-tìr	yók-tùr

2.	**3.**	**4.**	**5.**
àl-là-hím	àl-là-hín	àl-là-hí	àl-là-hín
bà-yím	bà-yín	bà-yí	bà-yín
bí-ràm	bí-ràn	bí-rà-sì	bí-rà-nìn
è-tím	è-tín	è-tí	è-tín
kàh-vém	kàh-vén	kàh-vé-sí	kàh-vé-nín
k^{y}ìb-rí-tím	k^{y}ìb-rí-tín	k^{y}ìb-rí-tí	k^{y}ìb-rí-tín
pà-rám	pà-rán	pà-rà-sí	pà-rà-nín

6. kár-dé-ṣi-ni-zín‿ká-rı-sì
tó-mún‿si-gà-ra-si
báy‿ká-ya-nín‿pá-ra-sì
á-l^{y}i-nín‿bí-ra-si
ki-zín‿kár-de-ṣì
fát-ma-nín‿káh-ve-sì
ba-yán‿ká-ya-ní-n‿é-tì

ár-ka-da-şín‿kìz‿kár-de-şi
ká-rı-nı-zín‿kár-déş-lʸe-rì
bú‿lʸo-kán-ta-nin‿bì-ra-si

Unit 2. What Would You Say? (Pages 58–59)

1. b	6. b	11. c	16. c
2. b	7. c	12. a	17. c
3. b	8. a	13. b	18. b
4. b	9. b	14. b	19. b
5. b	10. c	15. b	

Unit 2. Answers (Page 67)

1. bé-ní-m‿is-mìm ——dìr.
2. bú‿zá:-tí-n‿is-mì ——dìr.
3. bé-n‿ev-lʸi‿dé-yi-lʸìm. *or* bé-n‿év-lʸí-yìm.
4. be-nim‿kár-déş-lʸe-rìm‿yók. *or* be-nim‿(——)‿kár-de-şim‿vár.
5. bé-ním‿ká-rı-mì-n‿is-mi ——dìr.
6. bé-ním‿kar-de-şi-mi-n‿is-mì ——dìr.
7. be-nim‿kíz‿kar-de-şim‿yòk. *or* be-nim‿(——)‿kiz‿kar-de-şim‿ vàr.
8. kíz‿kar-de-şi-mi-n‿is-mì ——dìr.
9. é-vèt bú be-ni-m‿ár-ka-da-şím-dìr. *or* há-yìr bú be-ni-m‿ár-ka-da-şìm‿dé-yilʸ.
10. ár-ka-dáş-lá-rı-mı-zí-n‿is-mì —— vé‿——dìr.
11. é-vèt bi-zím‿kár-déş-lʸé-ri-mìz.
12. bú‿bay-la-ri-n‿i-sim-lʸe-rì —— vé‿——dìr.
13. é-vèt bú‿báy-làr ár-ka-dáş-lá-rı-míz-dìr.
14. báy ——in‿kár-de-şi-ní-n‿is-mì ——dìr.
15. ba-yán ——in‿kár-dé-şi-ní-n‿is-mì ——dìr.
16. báy ——ìn‿kar-deş-lʸe-ri‿vár.
17. ba-yán ——ìn‿kiz‿kar-deş-lʸe-ri‿yók. *or* bá-yàn‿——ín (——) kìz‿kar-deş-lʸe-ri‿vár.

Unit 3. Word Study Review (Page 91)

1.
1. -uyòr
2. -iyór-
3. -íyor-
4. -ıyòr-
5. -iyòr

2.
1. -r-
2. -r-, -ér-
3. -úr-
4. -àr
5. -ir-

Unit 3. What Would You Say? (Pages 92–93)

1. b	7. b	13. a	19. a
2. b	8. b	14. b	20. b
3. a	9. a	15. b	21. a
4. b	10. a	16. b	22. b
5. b	11. a	17. c	23. b
6. c	12. b	18. b	

Unit 3. Answers (Pages 99–100)

1. 1. bá-y‿ák-yü-rèk^y í-ṣ‿á-rı-yòr.
2. bá-y‿ák-yü-rèk^y k^{y}á-tip-l^{y}ík^y‿yá-pàr.
3. bày‿kúrt véz-ne-dár-lík‿yá-pàr.
4. báy‿ká-rìn‿vez-ne-da-ri‿yók.
5. o-nún‿ha-dé-me-sí-dé‿yòk.

2. 6. há-yìr o-nún‿bék^y-çi-sì‿yók.
7. é-vèt o-fís-tè‿iṣ‿vár.

3. 8. é-vèt báy‿ká-rín‿tóp-lán-tı-la-rì báy‿ka-ya-nin‿hó-ṣu-nà‿g^{y}i-dér.
9. bú‿tóp-lán-tì sa-át‿sé-k^{y}íz‿bu-çúk-tà.

4. 10. há-yìr fàt-má-nín bú‿ák-ṣàm bír‿ṣé-yì‿yók.
11. há-yìr bi-r‿i-ṣìm‿yók.
12. á-l^{y}i-nín‿tóp-lán-tı-sì sa-á-t‿ón‿bu-çúk-tà.
13. é-vèt, g^{y}e-l^{y}í-yó-rùm.

5. 14. é-vèt, is-ma-i-l^{y}i-n‿ár-ka-da-ṣí-dá‿ò-ra-dá.
15. é-vèt tòp-lán-tí hak-kı-nin‿hó-ṣu-ná‿g^{y}i-di-yòr.
16. kiz-lár-dà hó-ṣu-ná‿g^{y}i-di-yòr.
17. bé-ním-dè.
18. é-vèt, türk^y-çe‿kó-nu-ṣú-yór-làr.

Unit 4. Word Study Review (Page 125)

1. 1. how are [they]? They are well.
2. is [he] married?
3. where are [they]?
4. is married
5. how are you? I am well.
6. are friends

7. [he is] his son
8. how is [she]? [She] is well.

2. a. -yìm
-ìm
-yìm
-ìm
-ìm
-ìm
-ìm
-ìm

b. g^{y}i-dé-rìm
bȧş-lá-rìm
kȯ-nu-ṣú-rùm
yȧ-pí-yo-rùm
ȧn-lá-mı-yò-rúm

3. bėk^{y}-çí-si-nìz
de-yíl^{y}-si-nìz
ha-de-mé-si-nìz
k^{y}ȧ:-típ-si-nìz
k^{y}ím-si-nìz
mi-sȧ:-fír-si-nìz
vėz-ne-dár-sı-nìz
yȧ-váṣ-sı-nìz
g^{y}i-dér-si-nìz
bȧş-lár-sı-nìz
kȯ-nu-ṣúr-sú-nùz
yȧ-pí-yòr-su-núz
ȧn-lá-mı-yòr-su-núz

4. bėk^{y}-çí-yìz
dė-yí-l^{y}ìz
hȧ-de-mé-yìz
k^{y}ȧ:-tí-bìz
k^{y}í-mìz
mi-sa:-fí-rìz
vėz-ne-dá-rìz
yȧ-vá-ṣìz
g^{y}i-dé-rìz
bȧş-lá-rìz
kȯ-nu-ṣú-rùz
yȧ-pí-yo-rùz
ȧn-lá-mı-yò-rúz

Unit 4. What Would You Say? (Pages 125–127)

1. b	6. b	11. b	16. b
2. a	7. c	12. b	17. b
3. c	8. b	13. b	18. b
4. b	9. b	14. a	19. b
5. a	10. b	15. a	

Unit 4. Answers (Page 132)

1. 1. bày_kár bú_g^{y}ǘn ì-yi.
2. é-vèt báy vė_bá-yàn_kár top-lan-tı-yȧ_g^{y}ė-l^{y}í-yȯr-làr.
3. é-vèt. te-şėk^{y}-k^{y}ǘ-r_e-dè-riz.

2. 4. bá-yàn_mė-tín çó-k_i-yì.
5. bú_g^{y}ǜn çó-k_i-yí-dir-l^{y}èr.
6. bá-yàn_kȧ-rín i-k^{y}í_kı-zi_vàr.

7. i-sìm-l^{y}é-rí à-l^{y}i-yé vé‿şûk^y-rü-yé.
8. bày-lár ko-nùş-má-k‿is-ti-yór-làr.
9. mú-zàf-fér şük^y-rü-yé‿i-l^{y}è çó-k‿i-yi‿ár-ka-dáş-tìr.
10. òn-lár si-né-má-yà dá-i-ma‿be-rá:-bér‿g^{y}i-dér-l^{y}èr.

3. 11. kà-yá-lár hér‿sá-bàh ér-k^{y}én‿kál-kár-làr.

4. 12. há-yìr hák-kí‿i-l^{y}é‿év-l^{y}ì.
13. há-yìr ço-cúk-la-rì‿yók.
14. á-l^{y}i-yé‿si-nè-ma-dá.
15. ór-ha-nín‿kiz‿kar-de-şi‿i-l^{y}é‿be-rá:-bèr.
16. é-vèt a-l^{y}i‿şim-di‿ye-mék^y‿ye-mé-k^y‿is-tí-yòr.
17. l^{y}o-kán-ta-nı-n‿é-tí‿çò-k‿i-yi.

5. 18. is-ma-i-l^{y}ín‿hó-şu-nà şá-ráp‿g^{y}i-di-yòr.
19. ó-nún-dà şà-ráp.
20. fát-má‿i-l^{y}è ìs-má-íl^y bú‿ák-şàm si-né-ma-yá‿g^{y}i-di-yór-làr.
21. é-vèt l^{y}éy-l^{y}á:‿i-l^{y}è mú-zàf-fér ón-lá-r‿i-l^{y}é‿be-rá:-bèr g^{y}it-mé-k^y‿is-tí-yór-làr.
22. sá-àt‿se-k^{y}iz-dé.

Unit 5. Word Study Review (Pages 153–154)

1. àl-ti-míz
bí-rá-mìz
çó-cùk-lá-rı-míz
è-vi-míz
hé-pi-mìz
is-tàs-yó-nu-múz
ì-şi-míz
kàh-vé-míz
kù-şú-múz
l^{y}ó-kán-ta-mìz
mi-sá:-fír-l^{y}è-ri-míz
sù-tü-múz
trè-ni-míz

2. ák-şàm-lár
àr-ka-dáş-lár
i-sìm-l^{y}ér
is-tàs-yón-lár
kár-dèş-l^{y}ér
kùrt-lár
l^{y}ó-kán-ta-làr
ó-tèl^y-l^{y}ér
ó-ùl-lár
şèy-l^{y}ér

3. 1. hér‿kìz g^{y}ü-zél^y-mì?
2. türk^y-çe‿kó-nu-şúr-mú-su-nùz?
3. şa-ráp‿ho-şu-ná‿g^{y}i-dér-mì?
4. i-yí-mi-yìz?
5. g^{y}ö-rúr-mü-sü-nüz?
6. bek^y-çi-lik^y‿ya-pár-lár-mì?

7. bi̇r‿şė-y‿ȧn-lá-mı-yòr-mu-yúm?
8. de-yíl^{y}-l^{y}ér-mi̇?
9. o-nún‿ço-cuk-la-ri‿vár-mì?
10. i-l^{y}ėr-dé-mi̇-di̇r?

4.

1.	bi̇́z-dè	6.	i̇s-ma-í-l^{y}‿i̇-l^{y}è-dė
2.	bú-ra-dà-dȧ	7.	ó-dà
3.	bú‿sa-bàh-tȧ	8.	ȯn-lár-dà
4.	bú‿zà:t-tȧ	9.	pa-tá-tės-tè
5.	çó-cúk-tà	10.	to-mún‿kȧ-rı-sí-dà

Unit 5. What Would You Say? (Pages 154–156)

1. b	6. b	12. b	18. b
2. a	7. b	13. b	19. b
3. c	8. a	14. b	20. b
4. b	9. a	15. b	21. c
5. a	10. b	16. b	22. a
	11. a	17. a	

Unit 5. Answers (Page 162)

1.

1. bú‿g^{y}ùn ha-vȧ‿çók‿g^{y}ü̇-zèl^{y}.
2. é-vèt, bȧy‿ka-ya-nin‿ho-şu-nȧ‿g^{y}i̇-dí-yȯr.
3. g^{y}ùnés çók‿g^{y}ü-zél^{y}‿pȧr-lı-yòr.
4. rü̇z-g^{y}ár-dà çòk‿sė-ri̇́n.
5. a-ȧç-làr-dȧ kùş-lár ö-tű-yór-làr.
6. bu-lùt-lár u-fúk-tá‿tóp-lȧ-nı-yòr.
7. şi̇m-şék^{y}‿pa-rıl-tı-la-ri‿g^{y}ö-zü̇-k^{y}ü-yòr.
8. há-yìr g^{y}ő̇k^{y}‿yü-zü̇ şím-di̇ g^{y}ü̇-zèl^{y}‿dé-yíl^{y}.
9. é-vèt ya:-mur-dȧ‿ıs-la-ní-yór-làr.
10. si̇-ı-na-á‿kȯ-şu-yór-làr.
11. ȯ-ra-da‿çó-k‿i-yí-di̇r-l^{y}èr.
12. şi̇m-di‿ya:-múr‿di̇-ní-yòr.
13. bú-lùt-lár rüz-g^{y}á-**r**‿i-l^{y}ė‿g^{y}é-çi-yòr.
14. havȧ‿tèk^{y}-rȧr‿g^{y}üzél^{y}.

2.

15. u-fuk-tȧ‿şi̇m-şék^{y}‿pa-ril-tı-la-rì g^{y}ü̇-zél^{y}‿pȧr-lı-yòr.
16. ya:-múr-dȧ‿hó-şu-nà‿g^{y}i-di-yór.
17. ȧ-l^{y}i-yé‿g^{y}ė-l^{y}i-yòr.
18. ya:-múr‿ya-váş‿ya-vȧş‿di̇-ní-yòr dì-yór.
19. şi̇m-di‿l^{y}éy-l^{y}á:-dȧ‿g^{y}ė-l^{y}i-yòr.

20. g^{y}ü-zél^{y}‿g^{y}ö-zü-k^{y}ü-yòr.
21. k^{y}ö-şe-dė‿bi̇r‿si-né-má‿vàr.
22. é-vèt ì-yí.
23. şi̇m-di‿ó-ra-da‿g^{y}ü-zél^{y}‿bi̇r‿fi̇-l^{y}ím‿vàr.
24. é-vèt is-tí-yór-làr.

3. 25. sa-à-t‿o-nú‿dó-kúz‿g^{y}e-çė‿kál-kı-yòr.

4. 26. ço-cúk-lár‿si-nė-ma-ya‿g^{y}it-mė-k^{y}‿i̇s-ti-yór-làr.
27. há-yìr is-té-mi̇-yòr.
28. o-nú-n‿ev-dė‿i̇-şí‿vàr.
29. án-ne-si-ni̇-n‿ar-ka-daş-la-ri‿g^{y}é-l^{y}i-yòr.
30. há-yìr g^{y}ü-zél^{y}‿de-yíl^{y}-di̇r-l^{y}èr.
31. há-yír i̇s-té-mi-yòr.

5. 32. á-l^{y}í‿dá-i-ma‿g^{y}èç‿g^{y}e-l^{y}i̇r.
33. a-l^{y}i̇‿şim-di‿l^{y}o-kán-tá-dà.
34. ó-ra-da‿bí-rá‿i̇-çi-yòr.
35. bí-rà o-nún‿çók‿hó-şu-ná‿g^{y}i̇-dèr.
36. hak-kí-dá‿çò-k‿i-çėr.
37. o-nún‿ho-şu-ná‿şá-ráp‿g^{y}i̇-dèr.
38. kız-lá-r‿év-dé‿ká-lı-yór-làr.

SECTION A. Unit 6. **Word Study Review** (Pages 169–172)

I. 1. bi̇-r‿i̇-k^{y}í‿dá-hà ű-çė-dèr.
2. i-k^{y}i̇‿űç‿dá-hà bé-şė-dèr.
3. üç‿dőrt‿dá-hà yė-dí-ė-dèr.
4. dört‿béş‿dá-hà dó-kú-zė-dèr.
5. bė-ş‿űc‿dá-hà sė-k^{y}i̇-zė-dèr.
6. al-ti‿bír‿dá-hà yė-di̇-ė-dèr.
7. se-k^{y}i̇z‿bír‿dá-hà dó-kú-zė-dèr.
8. do-kúz‿bír‿dá-hà ó-nė-dèr.
9. i-k^{y}i̇‿dőrt‿dá-hà ál-tí-ė-dèr.
10. üç‿béş‿dá-hà sė-k^{y}í-zė-dèr.

II. 1. -dir.
2. -dır.
3. -dur.
4. -dür.
5. -dir.
6. -tır.
7. -tur.
8. -tir.
9. -dır.
10. -tur.
11. -tir.
12. -tür.

III. 1. -ım
2. -ı-nız
3. -u-m-
4. -ı-mız
5. -i-niz
6. -ı-nız
7. -im

IV.
1. -nın . . .-sı
2. -un . . . . . .-i
3. -in- . . . .
4. -in . . . -si- . . . ? . . . -nun
   . . . -u- . . . .
5. -ın . . . -sı . . . ? . . . -u . . . .
6. -ın . . . -ı-nın . . . -i
7. -in . . . -sı-nın . . . -i
8. -in . . . ? -in- . . . .
9. -ın . . . -ı
10. -nun . . . -ı

V.
1. -ız!
2. -0.
3. -lar.
4. -ler.
5. -sı-nız? -iz, **-iz.**
6. -su-nuz?
7. -im!

VI.
1. báş-làr
2. ko-nu-şùr-su-núz
3. g^{y}i-dè-riz
4. yá-pı-yòr-su-núz
5. ȍ-tǘ-yòr
6. kál-kár-làr
7. g^{y}i-dér-l^{y}èr
8. tóp-la-ní-yór-làr
9. é-si-yòr
10. g^{y}i-di-yór-mù

VII.
1. -mi-
2. -mu
3. -mı-
4. -mü

VIII.
1. bén-dè
2. ó-dà
3. bú-ra-dà-dȁ
4. ár-ka-dáş-tà
5. k^{y}ib-rit-tè
6. kúrt-tà

Unit 6. Answers (Pages 173–176)

1.
1. bày‿ká-yá ì-yi.
2. báy‿ká-ya-nín‿ká-rı-şì vé‿ço-cùk-lá-rí i-yi-dir-l^{y}èr.
3. bày‿mé-tin yé-mék^{y}‿ye-mé-k^{y}‿is-ti-yòr.
4. i-l^{y}er-dé‿iyi‿bir‿l^{y}o-kán-tá‿vàr.
5. ó-ra-yá‿g^{y}i-de-l^{y}ìm.
6. yá-váş‿ya-váş‿g^{y}i-de-l^{y}ìm.
7. bày‿ká-yá vé‿bày‿mé-tin ét vé‿pa-tá-te-s‿is-ti-yór-làr.
8. bày‿mé-tin káh-vé‿iç-mé-k^{y}‿is-ti-yòr.
9. bày‿ká-yá bi-rá‿iç-mé-k^{y}‿is-ti-yòr.

2.
1. o-tel^{y}-dé‿hák-kı-ní-n‿ar-ka-da-şi‿vàr.
2. hak-kı-ni-n‿ár-ka-dá-şı-ní-n‿is-mì ák-yǘ-rèk^{y}.
3. bá-y‿ák-yü-rèk^{y} k^{y}á:-tip-l^{y}ik^{y}‿yá-pàr.
4. é-vèt, hák-kı-ní-n‿ó-fi-sin-dè.
5. há-yìr.

3. 1. bú‿ák-şàm si-né-ma-yá‿g^{y}i-di-yór-làr.
2. bá-y‿ák-yü-re-yin‿kíz‿kár-de-şì‿i-l^{y}é.
3. bá-y‿ák-yü-re-yin‿kiz‿kar-de-şi-ni-n‿is-mì l^{y}éy-l^{y}á:-dìr.
4. há-yìr, l^{y}ey-l^{y}á:‿g^{y}ü-zèl^y‿dé-yil^y.
5. l^{y}èy-l^{y}á: i-yí-dìr.

4. 1. bú‿ák-şàm bir‿tóp-lán-tí‿vàr.
2. hák-kí‿g^{y}é-l^{y}i-yòr.
3. sé-k^{y}ìz-dé.

5. 1. mi-sá:-fir-l^{y}ér‿g^{y}é-l^{y}i-yòr.
2. şím-di‿g^{y}é-l^{y}i-yór-làr.
3. bày‿ká-yá ì-yí.
4. báy‿ká-ya-ní-n‿ár-ka-da-şì şím-di‿g^{y}é-l^{y}i-yòr.
5. bày‿ká-yá şá-rá-p‿iç-mé-k^y‿is-ti-yòr.

6. 1. à-l^{y}í ó‿sá-bàh ér-k^{y}én‿kalk-má-k‿is-ti-yòr.
2. áh-me-dín‿ka-rı-si‿g^{y}é-l^{y}i-yòr.
3. sá-àt‿se-k^{y}íz-dé.
4. şím-di‿sa-át‿yé-dí‿bú-çùk.
5. kò-şá-lím.
6. vá-kit‿vàr.
7. yá:-múr‿yá:-ı-yòr.
8. şím-di‿di-nér.
9. is-tás-yó-n‿i-l^{y}ér-dè.
10. trén‿g^{y}é-l^{y}i-yòr.
11. há-yìr, áh-me-dín‿ká-rı-sì ò-ra-dá‿dé-yil^y.

7. 1. çó-cùk-lár bú‿ak-şám‿g^{y}i-di-yór-làr.
2. hak-kí-dá‿g^{y}i-di-yòr.
3. há-yìr.
4. o-nú-n‿i-şi‿vàr.
5. òn-lár tré-n‿i-l^{y}é‿g^{y}i-di-yór-làr.

8. 1 hàk-kí i-ş‿á-rı-yòr.
2. ó-nú-n‿is-mì hak-ki‿ák-çày.
3 véz-ne-dár-lík‿yá-pàr.
4. há-yìr, báy‿mé-ti-nìn‿vez-ne-da-ri‿yók.
5. é-vèt, hak-ki‿şim-di‿báş-la-mà-k‿is-tér.

6. é-vèt, ó_o-fis-tè hér_g^{y}ùn i-ş_ér-k^{y}én_báşlàr.
7. sé-k^{y}iz-dé.

9. 1. é-vèt, tóm türk^{y}-çe_án-lí-yòr.
2. ah-mét_şim-di_yá-váş_ya-vàş_ko-nú-şu-yòr.
3. is-tás-yò-n_i-l^{y}ér-dé.
4. sa-át_dör-dü_sé-k^{y}iz_g^{y}e-çé_trèn_vár.
5. é-vèt, tóm şim-di_án-lí-yòr.

10. 1. şim-di_sa-á-t_úç_bú-çùk.
2. is-tás-yón-dá_bir_l^{y}o-kàn-tá_vár.
3. l^{y}o-kán-tá-dà tóm bir_káh-vé_is-ti-yòr.
4. há-yìr.
5. sa-át_ál-tı-dá_báş-lı-yór-làr.

Unit 6. English Equivalents of True-False Statements
(Pages 176–177)

F 1. These gentlemen are Mrs. Metin and Mrs. Kaya.
F 2. Three and two are six.
T 3. Four and five are nine.
F 4. Three o'clock is meal-time.
T 5. The good guest goes early.
F 6. Children are always good.
F 7. Every day there are black clouds on the horizon.
F 8. Every child always runs slowly.
F 9. Every wife has a beautiful sister.
F 10. Every girl talks beautifully
F 11. Mr. Roosevelt is a night-watchman.
F 12. It's very nice to drink wine with milk.
T 13. Every voice is not sweet.
F 14. Girls always run a lot.
F 15. It rains every day.
F 16. The sun appears every day.
T 17. Every child has the right to enjoy himself.
F 18. Trains always come late.
F 19. Every railway station is on the right.
F 20. Every train leaves at half past nine.
F 21. Every house has a night-watchman.
F 22. Every night-watchman has a wife.
F 23. Every woman's name is Ayesha.

T 24. Every house has corners.
F 25. Every girl likes thunder.
T 26. It's very nice to drink wine with meat.
F 27. Every girl is beautiful.
F 28. There's a restaurant in every house.
F 29. Every girl is married.
T 30. It's good to drink water.
F 31. Every friend's name is Ali.
F 32. Every breeze always blows cool.
F 33. Black clouds shine.
T 34. Milk is good.
F 35. The train has a good movie.
F 36. The train is in the restaurant.
F 37. We eat meat and potatoes in the movie.
T 38. We eat bread.
F 39. Orhan is Mrs. Kaya's daughter.
F 40. Every boy's name is Ali Dag.

Unit 7. Word Study Review (Page 192)

1. áacìndá
bìrdé
dà:dá
dókùzdá
fil^{y}ìmdé
kàyalárdá
sìnaindá
ùçté

2. béndémì
évimizdémì
g^{y}üzéllérmì
il^{y}érdémì
báy‿káyanínmì
órayàmi
saát‿dokúzdámì

3. àrıyálím
dìyél^{y}ím
èyl^{y}énel^{y}ím
g^{y}èçél^{y}ím
g^{y}èl^{y}él^{y}ím
ìçél^{y}ím
kàlálím
kàlkálím
òlálím
unùtálím
yìkánalím

4. áráyìn (aráyinìz)
déyìn (déyinìz)
éyl^{y}énìn (éyl^{y}éniniz)
g^{y}éçìn (g^{y}éçinìz)
g^{y}él^{y}ìn (g^{y}él^{y}inìz)
íçìn (íçinìz)
kálìn (kálinìz)
kálkìn (kálkinìz)
ólùn (ólúnùz)
únútùn (unútúnùz)
yikánìn (yıkáninìz)

Unit 7. What Would You Say? (Pages 193–195)

1. b	5. a	9. b	13. b
2. a	6. b	10. b	14. b
3. b	7. a	11. b	15. b
4. b	8. b	12. a	16. a

Unit 7. Answers (Pages 200–201)

1. 1. ál^{y}inín‿ṣéhrindè iyi‿bir‿ótél^y‿vàr.
2. bú‿ótèl^y çók‿g^{y}úzèl^y.
3. àz‿il^{y}érdé.
4. óraya‿g^{y}idel^{y}ìm.

2. 5. ótèl^{y}cí hóṣ‿g^{y}él^{y}diníz dìyór.
6. òsmán bir‿ódá‿istiyòr.
7. bú‿ódà ósmán‿içìn.

3. 8. asánsőrl^{y}é‿çikalìm
9. g^{y}ündel^{y}iyi‿ik^{y}í‿l^{y}ìrá.
10. évèt çók‿hóṣuná‿g^{y}idiyòr
11. òsmán otél^{y}dé‿yemék^y‿yemék^y‿istiyòr.

4. 12. ákṣám‿yémeyì saát‿alti‿il^{y}é‿dókúz‿árasindà.
13. òsmán dáhá‿évvèl^y yikànmák tráṣ‿olmák‿istiyòr.
14. ósmanín‿ódasindà hávlú‿yòk.
15. ánkará‿tréni saát‿dókúz‿buçuktá‿g^{y}él^{y}ecèk^y.

5. 16. ṣímdì l^{y}okántayá‿g^{y}idiyórlàr.
17. àl^{y}í ósmán‿il^{y}è yémék^y‿yemék^y‿istiyòr.
18. évèt l^{y}okánta‿hoṣlarıná‿g^{y}idíyòr.
19. yemeyi‿çók‿g^{y}üzèl^y.

6. 20. ṣimdi‿yá:múr‿diniyòr.
21. ṣimdi‿sáàt‿yédí.
22. háyìr g^{y}èç‿déyíl^y.
23. ónún‿kárısì saát‿dókúz‿buçúk‿treni‿il^{y}é‿g^{y}él^{y}ecèk^y.
24. istásyón‿k^{y}öṣesindè bir‿sinémá‿vàr.
25. àl^{y}í g^{y}itmék‿istiyòr.
26. osmándá‿g^{y}él^{y}iyòr.

7. 27. háyìr.
28. ósmaníndà.
29. évèt osmanin‿sigàrasi‿vár.

8\. 30. şimdi_havá_dáhá_sérìn.
31\. trén_érk^{y}én_g^{y}él^{y}iyòr.

Unit 8. **Word Study Review** (Pages 223–224)

1\. 1. áràmıyalim
2\. démeyiniz
3\. éyl^{y}énmiyórlàr
4\. kàlkmıyalim
5\. yıkámayinìz

2\. bányó_firçasì
yúz_hávlusù
şáráp_şişesì
sáç_firçasì
ótél^{y}_ódasì
çócúk_yüzû
kíz_sésì
kúş_étì
kíş_g^{y}ünû
kíz_ismì
ákşám_él^{y}bi:sesi

3\. bányó_firçàm
bányó_firçàn
bányó_firçasì
bányó_firçamìz
bányó_firçanìz
bányó_firçalarì

ákşám_él^{y}bi:sèm
ákşám_él^{y}bi:sèn
ákşám_él^{y}bi:sesì
ákşám_él^{y}bi:semìz
ákşám_él^{y}bi:senìz
ákşám_él^{y}bi:selerì

4\. 1. g^{y}ók^{y}_yüzünû
2\. diş_fırçami
3\. bunlari
4\. sütü
5\. beşi

5\. 1. konuşmám
2\. kalkmasi
3\. yıkámamíz
4\. yemeniz

6\. 1. başlamák
2\. akıtmák
3\. g^{y}itmék^{y}
4\. yikamàk . . . tráştá_olmák

Unit 8. **What Would You Say?** (Pages 225–226)

1. a	5. a	9. b	12. a
2. b	6. b	10. b	13. b
3. a	7. b	11. a	14. b
4. a	8. b		

Unit 8. **Answers** (Pages 231–233)

1\. 1. bú_ákşàm òsmán bir_tóplántıyá_g^{y}idiyòr.
2\. bú_tóplántì báy_kayanín_evindè.
3\. saát_sek^{y}izdé_g^{y}itmesì_l^{y}a:zim.

4. bir_árkadaşí_ilʸé_gʸidiyòr.
5. dáhá_évvèlʸ yémékʸ_yemékʸ_istiyòr.
6. otelʸin_lʸokántasındá_yemékʸ_yemékʸ_istiyòr.

2. 7. şimdi_yémékʸ_yemékʸ_lʸá-zìm.
8. yémékʸ_ilʸè òsmán bir_şişé_şáráp_istiyòr.
9. háyìr, çòk_déyilʸ.
10. hér_ákşàm ikʸi_şişé_içèr.

3. 11. èlʸlʸérini, yüzünü_yıkamák_istiyòr.
12. àhmét osmanin_tráş_olmasi_içìn sıcák_suyú_ákıtíyòr.
13. bú tráş_olmák_içìndé lʸà:zím.
14. hàvá bú_gʸùn çók_sicàk.
15. bányó_almàktá lʸà:zím.
16. háyìr osmanin_vákti_yók.
17. sàbún vé_diş_firçasì çántanin_içìndè.
18. ónlarín_yanindà ústurá_vàr.
19. àhmét onúdá_gʸetiriyòr.
20. taráınídá_istiyòr.
21. ósmanín_táraì.
22. saçlarıni_táramák_istiyòr.
23. háyìr. bulámiyòr.
24. tarák_másanin_üzérindè.
25. háyìr, yók.
26. gá:lʸibà tráş_aynasının_áltindà.
27. kolónyá_şişesinide_gʸetiriyòr.

4. 28. àhmét órhanín_misá:firì.
29. áhmét_ilʸè tóplàntıyá órhán_gʸidiyòr.
30. háyìr kìzlár òradá_déyilʸ.
31. évèt bú_kizlàr çók_gʸüzèlʸ.

5. 32. gʸüzél_kizlàr dáima_gʸéç_gʸelʸirlʸèr.
33. şimdi_lʸéylʸá:_gʸélʸiyòr.
34. havá_çók_gʸüzèlʸ.
35. lʸéylʸá:dà.
36. tóplántí_içìn.
37. àlʸiyé vé_şükʸrüyédè gʸelʸiyórlàr.
38. lʸèylʸá: şáráp_içmékʸ_istiyòr.
39. úç_şişé_kırmızi_şaráp_vàr.
40. áhmét_onú_gʸetiriyòr.

Unit 9. Word Study Review (Page 253)

1. 1. l^{y}éyl^{y}à:!
2. ósmàn!
3. áyşè!
4. şük^{y}rűyè! ánnè!

2. 1. konúşacáìz
2. g^{y}el^{y}écék^{y}mísinìz
3. g^{y}él^{y}miyecèyím
4. ólacàk
5. tóplánıyórlàr

3. 1. súlú
2. g^{y}ünéşsíz
3. séssíz
4. yá:múrlú . . . bulútlú

Unit 9. What Would You Say? (Pages 254–255)

1. b	5. b	9. a	13. b
2. a	6. a	10. a	14. a
3. b	7. b	11. a	15. a
4. b	8. b	12. a	

Unit 9. Answers (Pages 260–262)

1. 1. àl^{y}í vé_múzàffér g^{y}éç_kalacáklàr.
2. évèt dahá_çók_vakít_vàr.
3. ál^{y}inín_káhvesì tàtsíz.
4. háyìr onú_íçmiyecèk^{y}.
5. bir_áz_dahá_şék^{y}ér_koymák_l^{y}á:zìm.
6. gàrsón bír_áz_dahá_şék^{y}ér_g^{y}etirecèk^{y}.
7. évèt al^{y}í_çók_şek^{y}ér_kóyuyòr.
8. évèt çók_tatlí_ólacàk.
9. àl^{y}í kahvesiní_tátlí_sévèr.
10. háyìr, múzàffér bir_şéy_íçmiyecèk.

2. 11. al^{y}inín_árkadaşınín_évì bìr_áz_il^{y}érdé.
12. àlí óráyà l^{y}eyl^{y}a:yi_g^{y}örmék_íçìn g^{y}ítmék_ístiyòr.
13. háyìr bír_áz_kálacàk.
14. sónra_sinémayá_g^{y}idecék^{y}l^{y}èr.
15. l^{y}èyl^{y}á: muzáffér_íçìn bír_kíz_arkadáş_g^{y}etírecèk.
16. àl^{y}í vé_múzàffér èyl^{y}énecék.
17. háyìr sinèmadá_déyíl sónrà.

3. 18. báy_káyanín_karni_àç.
19. şímdi_sáàt_yédí.

20. ótel^{y}ín_l^{y}okàntasi ìyí.
21. gàrsón yėmék^y_l^{y}istesini_g^{y}etírecèk.
22. bír_daki:ká_müsáadé_èdiníz dìyór.
23. bày_káyá tàvúk vė_kızarmiş_patátės_ístiyòr.
24. bày_métín bàlík vė_patátės_yíyecèk^y.
25. pȧtátès háşlánmíş_ólsùn.
26. bày_métín hámsí_ístiyòr.
27. bày_métín sálátȧ vė_bir_şişė_kirmızí_şaráp_ístiyòr.
28. háyìr íçmíyecèk. ó bírá_ístiyòr.
29. évèt yemėk^{y}tén_sònrȧ kȧhvé_ístiyórlàr.
30. bìr_şek^{y}érl^{y}í vė_bìr_şek^{y}érsíz.
31. èl^{y}má vė_pórtakál_yíyecėk^{y}l^{y}èr.
32. gàrsón ònlárí dȧhá_sónra_g^{y}etírsìn.
33. tàvúk báy_káyanín_hoşuná_g^{y}ídecėk.
34. bú_l^{y}okàntáda onú_dái(:)má_şáráp_il^{y}ė_yapárlàr.
35. hámsí_kóydùm tàváyá bàşládí hóplàmayá.
36. háyìr g^{y}üzèl^y_dėyíl^y.

Unit 10. Word Study Review (Page 288)

1. 1. beníml^{y}e
2. l^{y}eyl^{y}á:ylá
3. néyl^{y}ė
4. tavúklá
5. kízlà

2. 1. ánkaraya
2. k^{y}öşesinè
3. baná
4. dokuzá
5. ėviné

3. 1. g^{y}írméyìz
2. konúşmám
3. tóplánmázlármì . . . tóplánmàzlár
4. íslanmázmisınìz
5. unútmàz

Unit 10. What Would You Say? (Pages 288–290)

1. b	5. a	9. b	12. b
2. a	6. b	10. a	13. b
3. b	7. b	11. a	14. a
4. b	8. b		

Unit 10. Answers (Pages 296–297)

1. 1. àhmét ó_sábàh tómá_boáz_içíni_g^{y}östérmèk^y_istiyór.
2. istánbulun_én_g^{y}üzél^y_mánzaralari_òradádır.

3. gʸüzélʸ_cá:milʸèr, sáràylár, vé_plʸájlár_vàr.
4. háyìr gitméz. *or* é-vèt gʸidér.
5. plʸajá_yüzmeyé_gʸidelʸim.
6. búrádàn iskʸelʸeyé_kádàr trámváylà, óradàndá vápúrlà.
7. bilmiyòrúz.
8. öbúr_vapurá_binmemiz_lʸá:zìm.
9. vapurún_kálkmasıná_dahá_çók_vákit_vár.
10. dáhá_évvèlʸ bir_káhvé_içelʸim.
11. sónra_vápurá_binèriz.
12. són_iskʸélʸedèn bir_evvélʸ_inecékʸlʸèr.
13. vápurún_kálkmasınà béş_daki:ká_vàr.
14. öylʸé_isè binélʸím.
15. ikʸinci_katá_çikalìm.
16. dahá_iyi_gʸörmékʸ_için_çikalìm.
17. órádàn étrá:fí_görürüz.
18. háyìr ò_kadár_iyi_déʸílʸ.
19. vápurá_bákalìm.
20. vàpúr gá:lʸibà rúsyayá_gʸidiyòr.
21. búrádà boazin_hér_ikʸi_tarafınádá_çók_yakìniz.
22. bir_taráftà ásyá_vàr.
23. öbür_taráftádà avrúpayi_görüyòrüz.

2. 24. bú_gʸün plʸáj çók_sicàk_déyílʸ.
25. gʸőkʸ_yüzündè bulútlár_vàr.
26. plʸàjá béş_ón_daki:ká_sónra_gʸélʸecèyiz.
27. öylʸé_yemeyiné_kadár_kálacàız.
28. öylʸé_yeméyimizi plʸajin_lʸokántasındá_yiyecèyiz.
29. plʸajdá_gʸüzélʸ_kizlár_vàr.
30. háyìr onlárla_konúşmák_için pará_lʸá:zìm_déyílʸ.
31. sónrádà lʸá:zìm_déyílʸ.
32. onlará_sónrà "állahá_ısmárladìk" diyecéyiz.

3. 33. mánzárà çók_gʸüzèlʸ!
34. ilʸèrdé ikʸinci_kàttà.
35. gá:lʸibà ónún_bir_kiz_árkadaşì_vár.
36. ilʸériyé_gʸidelʸim.

4. 37. şimdi_són_iskʸelʸeye_yáklaşíyórüz.
38. búrádà gá:lʸibà ón_daki:ká_kálacàiz.
39. plʸáj_istánbulá_dáhà_yakin.
40. öylʸedén_sónra_gʸörecèkʸ.

5. 41. évèt istánbùl tomún_hoşuná_gʸidíyòr.
42. én_çòk bóáz_içi_gʸidiyòr.
43. istánbulun_én_gʸüzélʸ_taráflárindán_biri órasìdir.
44. báşká_mànzaralari yávás_yavás_gʸörecèkʸ.
45. háyìr kálmiyacàk.
46. sónra_rúsyayá_gʸidecèk.

Unit 11. Word Study Review (Pages 323–324)

1. 1. saná
2. yapacàksin
3. senínlʸé
4. gʸelʸírmisin
5. sénín

2. 1. şàpkadán
2. óndán
3. néredén
4. satıcıdán
5. yemékʸtén

3. 1. bizím
2. saná
3. ónlarín
4. sáná . . . onlará
5. sendén

Unit 11. What Would You Say? (Pages 324–327)

1. b	6. a	10. b	14. b
2. a	7. b	11. a	15. a
3. b	8. b	12. b	16. b
4. b	9. b	13. a	17. a
5. b			

Unit 11. Answers (Pages 332–333)

1. 1. évèt àlʸí áhmét_ilʸè iyi_árkadàştir.
2. àlʸí bú_sábàh aliş_vérişé_gʸidiyòr.
3. élbʸì:sé şápkà vé_ayákkabi_álacàk.
4. àhmét onúnla_gʸitmékʸ_istiyòr.
5. àlʸí dáhá_évvèlʸ élʸbi:sé_satin_almák_istiyòr.

2. 6. yázlík_bir_elʸbi:sé_ólsùn.
7. lʸá:civért_tércih_ediyór.
8. háyìr ò_renkʸté_elʸbi:sesi_yók.
9. öylʸé_isè kúrşu:ní:_ólsùn.
10. évèt àlʸí bú_elʸbi:seyi_béyeníyòr.
11. búnún_fiyatì yirmi_dókúz_lʸìrá.

3. 12. óndán‿sònrá bir‿şápká‿álacàk.
13. évèt àhmét onùnlá‿gʸélʸecékʸ.
14. bir‿kurşu:ni:‿şápkayá‿bákmàk‿istiyór.
15. bú‿şàpká bìr‿áz‿büyűkʸ.
16. háyìr úcùz‿déyilʸ.
17. évèt dahá‿úcuzù‿vár.
18. úcúz‿şàpká búnùn‿kadár‿iyi‿déyilʸ.
19. ya:murlú‿havalardá‿gʸiymékʸ‿için‿istiyòr.
20. háyìr órada‿öylʸè‿bir‿şápka‿yók.

4. 21. şápkáyì báşká‿bir‿gʸün‿árıyacàk.
22. bir‿áz‿sònrá ahmedin‿kárısí‿gʸélʸecèkʸ.
23. ónúnlà àhmédin aliş‿vérişé‿gʸitmesi‿lʸá:zìm.
24. sinémayá‿gʸidecékʸlʸèr.
25. hàkkí vé‿şükʸrüyenin‿evindè dáhá‿iyi‿éylʸenirlʸèr.

5. 26. háyìr.
27. çócùklár ódalàrindá.
28. fàtmá şükʸrüyenin‿kʸüçükʸ‿kizıní‿gʸörmèkʸ‿istiyór.
29. onú‿gʸörmékʸ‿için öbűr‿odayá‿gʸidiyórlàr.
30. gʸüzélʸ‿bir‿kiz‿ólacàk.
31. onú‿ó:luná‿álmàk‿istiyór.

Unit 12. Word Study Review (Pages 337–343)

I.
1. néredè
2. gʸökʸté
3. ódalárindà
4. elʸindè
5. ódadá

II.
1. otélʸdémi
2. şarápmi
3. balíkmi
4. bírami
5. sinémayámi

III.
1. éylʸènelʸím
2. ìçélʸím
3. àrıyálím
4. unùtàlím
5. yìkıyálím
6. tráş‿ólalìm
7. dìyélʸím
8. akìtálím
9. kàlkálím
10. òválím

IV.
1. gʸöstériniz
2. taráyinìz
3. vérinìz
4. yıkàyıniz
5. başláyinìz
6. konùşunúz
7. topláninìz
8. gʸèlʸiniz
9. bìniniz
10. gʸìdiniz

V. 1. g^{y}él^{y}méyiniz
2. ínméyin
3. içmiyel^{y}im
4. aràmıyalim
5. yűzmüyòrúz
6. eyl^{y}ẹ́nmiyórlàr

VI. 1. ṣáráp_ṣiṣesi
2. yüzmé_vákti
3. bálík_yémeyi
4. ėl^{y}má_áacì
5. ṣáráp_l^{y}istesi

VII. 1. saçlarımızi
2. ṣiṣesini
3. yüzünű
4. ṣárabì
5. sütü
6. ṣük^{y}rüyeyi
7. l^{y}eyl^{y}a:yi

VIII. 1. saçlarımi_táramám_l^{y}á:zìm.
2. saçlarımızi_táramamíz_l^{y}á:zìm.
3. saçlarıni_táramasí_l^{y}á:zìm.
4. saçlarınızi_táramaníz_l^{y}á:zìm.
5. evimė_g^{y}irmém_l^{y}á:zìm.
6. evimizė_g^{y}irmemíz_l^{y}á:zìm.
7. evinė_g^{y}irmesí_l^{y}a:zìm.
8. evinizė_g^{y}irmeníz_l^{y}á:zìm.

IX. 1. içmėk^y
2. içmeyė
3. yüzmeyé
4. konúṣmaá
5. çikmák

X. 1. ṣük^{y}rűyè!
2. ósmàn!
3. kárì!
4. ó:lùm!

XI. 1. báṣlıyacáklàr.
2. yiyecèyiz
3. g^{y}idecèyim
4. konùṣácák
5. g^{y}örecéksiniz.

questions

1. . . . içmeyė_báṣlıyacáklármì?
2. . . . yemėk^y_yiyecék^{y}miyiz?
3. óraya_g^{y}idecékmiyim?
4. . . . konúṣacákmì?
5. g^{y}örecékmisiniz?

positive to negative

1. . . . içmeyė_baṣlámıyacáklàr.
2. . . . yemėk^y_yémiyecèyiz.
3. óraya_g^{y}itmiyecèyim.
4. . . . konúṣmiyacàk.
5. g^{y}őrmiyecèksiniz.

negative statements into questions

1. içmeyė_báṣlámıyacáklàrmi?
2. . . . yemėk^y_yémiyecèk^{y}miyiz?
3. óraya_g^{y}itmiyecèkmiyim?

4. . . . konúşmıyacàkmi?
5. g^{y}órmiyecèkmisiniz?

XII. 1. bányolu
2. çocúklú
3. g^{y}ünćşlí
4. tráşlí
5. háklíyìm

XIII. 1. súsúz
2. ėvsíz
3. şek^{y}érsíz
4. dìşsíz
5. yà:mùrsúz

XIV. 1. dízl^{y}è
2. él^{y}bi:séyl^{y}è
3. ayákkabìylá
4. kízlà
5. méyváylà
kimínl^{y}è
bénímml^{y}è
sénínl^{y}è
sizínl^{y}è
6. bányòylá
7. şáráplà
8. hávlúylà
9. kárdéşl^{y}è
10. kúşlà
bizíml^{y}è
ónúnlà
ónlárlà

XV. 1. sek^{y}izė
2. onlará
3. toplantıyà
4. k^{y}öşeyè
5. çócuà
6. g^{y}öė
7. állahá
8. yüzmeyė
9. konúşmaá
10. baná

XVI. *negative*

1. şáràp_içmék^{y}_isteméz.
2. . . . bú_g^{y}üzél^{y}_mànzarayá_bákmáz.
3. . . . kirmızì_el^{y}bi:sé_g^{y}iymém.
4. g^{y}élméyìz
5. . . . g^{y}üzél^{y}l^{y}erí_g^{y}örmèzsiniz
6. arkadaşlará_istànbulú_g^{y}östérmézl^{y}ér.
7. dáima_öyl^{y}é_báşlamàzsin.

questions

1. şaráp_içmék^{y}_istérmì?
2. . . . bú_g^{y}üzél^{y}_mánzaraya_bákármì?
3. . . . kırmızi_el^{y}bi:sé_g^{y}iyérmiyìm?
4. g^{y}el^{y}írmiyiz?
5. . . . g^{y}üzel^{y}l^{y}eri_g^{y}örúrmüsünùz?

6. arkadaşlará‿istánbulu‿gʸöstérírlʸérmì?
7. dáima‿öylʸé‿báşlármısìn?

negative interrogative

1. şaráp‿içmékʸ‿istemézmì?
2. . . . bú‿gʸüzélʸ‿mánzaraya‿bákmázmì?
3. . . . kırmızi‿elʸbi:sé‿gʸiymézmiyìm?
4. gʸélʸmézmiyìz?
5. . . . gʸüzelʸlʸeri‿gʸörmézmisinìz?
6. arkadaşlará‿istánbulu‿gʸöstérmézlérmì?
7. dáima‿öylʸé‿báşlamázmısìn?

XVII. 1. gʸülʸérsìn
2. çocùksún
3. kóşuyòrsún
4. gʸörecèkʸsìn
5. démézsìn
6. bakàrsin

XVIII. 1. ískʸélʸedèn
2. sabahtán
3. bundán
4. yemeyindén
5. bendén

Unit 12. Answers (Pages 344–346)

1. 1. bày‿kár bir‿ótelʸé‿gʸitmèkʸ‿istiyór.
2. áz‿ilʸérdè çók‿úcùz vé‿iyí‿bir‿ótèlʸ‿vár.
3. évèt bànyolú‿odalari‿vár.
4. gá:lʸibà ikʸí‿lʸìrá.
5. ótelʸé‿yákìn bir‿lʸokàntá‿vár.
6. bày‿kár yemekʸlʸerini‿óradá‿yiyecèkʸ.

2. 1. évèt òdá báy‿karin‿hóşuná‿gʸidiyòr.
2. odanin‿mánzarasi‿çòk‿gʸüzélʸ.
3. évèt béyeníyòr.
4. évèt şehir‿báy‿karin‿hoşuná‿gʸidíyòr.
5. àlʸí bày‿kárá şehrí‿gʸösterecèkʸ.

3. 1. báy‿karín‿árkadaşì dáima‿éylʸénmékʸ‿istiyòr.
2. hér‿gʸùn plʸájá‿gʸidèr.
3. bày‿kár müzélʸerì vé‿saràylárí gʸörmékʸ‿istiyòr.
4. bir‿sábàh plʸàjá öylʸedén‿sònradá müzelʸeré‿gʸidecéklʸér.
5. álʸinín‿karısının‿yemékʸlʸerì báy‿karin‿hóşuná‿gʸidiyòr.
6. álʸinín‿kárısì iyi‿yémékʸ‿yápàr.
7. karısınin‿kíz‿kardeşi‿vàr.

4. 1. bú‿ákşàm báy‿karin‿árkadáşlarí‿gʸélʸecèkʸ.
2. háyìr evdé‿içecékʸ‿bìr‿şéy‿yók.

3. öyl^{y}é‿isè ik^{y}i‿üç‿şişé‿şáráp‿almák‿l^{y}á:zìm.
4. méyvádá‿l^{y}á:zìm.
5. sigáradà‿yòk.
6. báyàn‿kár pára‿istiyòr.
7. bày‿kár başká‿bir‿kárí‿istiyòr.

5. 1. bày‿g^{y}ündűz íş‿árıyòr.
2. báy‿káyanín‿ófisindè.
3. bày‿g^{y}ündűz békʸçil^{y}ík^y‿yápàr.
4. hadémel^{y}ík^y‿yápacàk.
5. oná‿él^{y}l^{y}í‿l^{y}ira‿vérecék^{y}l^{y}èr.
6. évèt bày‿g^{y}ündűz èvl^{y}í.
7. onun‿ik^{y}í‿ta:né‿çócuù‿vár.

6. 1. yá:múr‿va:maá‿báşlıyòr.
2. kòşálím.
3. ó‿sinèmadá bir‿fil^{y}ím‿g^{y}östériyórlàr.
4. bú‿fil^{y}ìm iyì‿déyíl^y.
5. fil^{y}imín‿işmì "ótél^y‿ódalarì."
6. sinéma‿çók‿sicàk.
7. àl^{y}í bir‿sigárá‿istiyòr.
8. öyl^{y}é‿isè g^{y}ìdél^{y}ím.
9. yá:mùr‿şimdi‿dinecék^y.
10. g^{y}ünéş g^{y}özük^{y}meyé‿báşlıyòr.
11. yá:múrdán‿sònrá havá‿dáhá‿serín‿ólacàk.
12. féná:‿ólmáz.

Unit 12. English Equivalents of True-False Statements

(Page 346)

F 1. Every girl drinks coffee with milk.
F 2. Every cashier has lots of beer.
F 3. Birds sing only in the trees.
F 4. Clouds appear only on the horizon.
T 5. Every tree does not have fruit.
T 6. We wash our hands with soap and water.
T 7. An orange is a fruit.
F 8. Every boat has four decks.
F 9. Tom Carr is a girl's name.
F 10. Every girl has a nice voice.
F 11. There's money in the sky.
T 12. Rain clouds are black.

F 13. We run with our knees.
T 14. Anchovy is a kind of fish.
T 15. A secretary is not necessary to every home.
T 16. We get wet in the rain.
T 17. Coffee is for drinking.
F 18. Water is only for washing.
F 19. Potatoes are a kind of fruit.
T 20. Navy blue is a kind of color.
F 21. Beautiful girls are always good.
F 22. We wear shoes on our hands.
F 23. We get on a street car in an elevator.
F 24. A girl looks at a mirror and becomes more beautiful.
T 25. We go into a bath and we get wet.
F 26. We get on a boat and we always go to Russia.
T 27. We eat bread and we drink wine.
F 28. Oranges and apples are things to drink.
F 29. We go to heaven by train.
T 30. The sun is very hot.
F 31. Maids are always beautiful.
T 32. Anchovies jump in a hot pan.
F 33. There's eau de Cologne in every bottle.
T 34. From the pier we get onto a boat.
F 35. We go from station to station by boat.
T 36. Every evening the sky darkens.
F 37. Winter is very hot.
F 38. Eau de Cologne is a thing to drink.
F 39. Gray skies are very sunny.
F 40. Red stockings are always small.